THE NEW ORDER
AND THE
FRENCH ECONOMY

THE NEW ORDER
AND THE
FRENCH ECONOMY

BY

ALAN S. MILWARD

OXFORD
AT THE CLARENDON PRESS
1970

Oxford University Press, Ely House, London W. 1

GLASGOW   NEW YORK   TORONTO   MELBOURNE   WELLINGTON
CAPE TOWN   SALISBURY   IBADAN   NAIROBI   DAR ES SALAAM   LUSAKA   ADDIS ABABA
BOMBAY   CALCUTTA   MADRAS   KARACHI   LAHORE   DACCA
KUALA LUMPUR   SINGAPORE   HONG KONG   TOKYO

PRINTED IN GREAT BRITAIN
AT THE UNIVERSITY PRESS, OXFORD
BY VIVIAN RIDLER
PRINTER TO THE UNIVERSITY

PREFACE

I HOPE that this book, as a contribution to the history of the New Order, will widen the debate on the nature of fascism. It is written from the standpoint that fascism was no cancer in the body politic but a normal stage in the historical and economic development of Europe, and that it cannot be ultimately comprehended on a merely political level. Its form of economic expression and its form of political expression cannot be meaningfully separated, the final end of both was the New Order.

The National Socialist revolution was the product of the long history of social tensions in Germany in her transition from a rural society to an industrial economy, and as such it was unique to one country. But as the history of German economic and social development was not without its parallels in other countries so was the National Socialist revolution not without echoes and reverberations elsewhere, and it was itself conscious of being but the second fascist revolution. The impact of fascism on other European states was certainly as important as that of jacobinism in 1792 or bolshevism in 1917. Ultimate safety for the National Socialist revolution lay in a reorganization of Europe, the New Order.

Of the formulation of the New Order we still know little. Economists have heaped contempt on it, most historians have been more cautious. This book is an attempt to examine, as far as it may at present be possible, the place of France in that New Order, and by doing so to throw some light on what the fascist European economy would have been like. To set Europe in a new economic and social mould imposed so dire a military necessity on the economy of Germany, and later on the economies of the occupied states, that the book must also be a study in the economics of conquest, a subject about which the world has recently been remarkably reticent considering the history of our own times. The strategic instrument by which the New Order was to be created was the Blitzkrieg. When that failed the 'New Economic Order' began its modulation into the 'European war economy'. This transmutation called into question the basic tenets of the National Socialist revolution itself. Neither in its birth nor in its death was National Socialism a merely national event.

When so much is still left to be known about the revolution in Germany, almost all indeed, it might be thought extravagant to protest that that revolution must ultimately be comprehended on a European scale. If this book raises its critics to that extravagant level I shall be pleased. For, in the present circumstances, it can be no more than an ignorant, patchwork history of one part of the New Order. I can only begin what I hope others, particularly in

France, will take up, as more evidence becomes available. If my book is utterly superseded I shall be justified, and the sooner it is so the more justified I shall be. Nevertheless, the reader may well object that to comprehend the New Order requires far more than a study of the economic relationships between France and Germany. I can but sustain that objection and say that it is my intention to write a further volume following from this one examining the New Order elsewhere in Europe. For that reason I have begun this book with a general essay on the liberal and fascist ideas of conquest, for fascism was a rejection of a whole system of economic and political thought. The reader who wishes to avoid these generalities and begin with that part of the book which is based on historical research might start at the second chapter.

Those French documents relating to the occupation and preserved in the Archives Nationales are covered by the fifty-year rule. When they become available for consultation a volume far more interesting than this one can be written. But the Archives Nationales does not have control over many papers relating to the 'comités d'organisation' which are in some cases being safe-guarded by less scrupulous institutions. Because of this there must be some doubt as to what will be made public when those fifty years have run their course. If for no other reason than this, it would have been worth while to study Franco-German economic relations during the war from the unpublished German materials. Outside France, perhaps in Brussels or in Moscow, there may yet be other documentary collections dealing with these events but not yet open to historians. In the Deutsches Zentralarchiv in Potsdam there are documents which I would very much have liked to consult, and which might well have modified or amplified many of the conclusions drawn here, but the German Democratic Republic refused me permission to use that archive. I am well aware that from one political standpoint at least the book must be the worse for this omission. No doubt the archives administration of the DDR. had more serious reasons for its decisions than the Goldsmiths Library of London University, which refused me access to the books therein on the grounds that I was not a responsible person. I do not think that the inter-pretation of National Socialism which has emerged from East German historical writing is any more biased than that which has emerged in the west, and therefore I continue in the hope that I may one day see the inside of the Deutsches Zentralarchiv.

This book had perforce to be written from the documents that were avail-able. These were mainly in the Foreign Documents Centre of the Imperial War Museum in London, the Bundesarchiv in Koblenz, and the National Archives of the United States in Washington. The catalogues of the General Services Administration of the National Archives of the United States and the *Findbücher* of the Bundesarchiv are now well known to historians; the resources of the Foreign Documents Centre for no very good reason remain neglected. They are described more fully in the 'Note on Sources'. In addition, I was able to use documents in the Hoover Institution on War, Revolution and Peace at Stanford University, some private papers of Hans Hemmen, head of the Special Commission for Economic Affairs of the German Armistice Delegation, and some papers of I. G. Farben in the care of the National Technological Lending Library, Boston Spa, Yorkshire. Of the published collections I should single out two officially published by the French government, *La Délégation Française auprès de la Commission Allemande d'Armistice* and the nine volumes of the *Commission Consultative des Dommages et des Réparations*.

The greater part of this book was written in an atmosphere of considerable intellectual discouragement. In such circumstances I was the more dependent on the help of many people in several countries and often at great distance. Their friendly response showed me that generosity is not always lacking amongst scholars. The prodigality both with his time and with his knowledge, of M. Étienne Dejonghe of the University of Lille exceeded all bounds. His thesis on the northern French coal-field during the occupation has begun that process by which my own work will become out of date. Professor François Crouzet and Monsieur F. Boudot helped me in the early stages of my work. The unflagging energies of Dr. Ing. W. Rohland opened many avenues which might otherwise have remained closed to me. Would we were all so interested in the history of our own times! Dipl. Ing. Albert Speer allowed me access to much information which a less scrupulous man would have kept for himself; he was most kind to a person of no importance when he was engaged on matters of much greater importance to himself. Dr. J.-J. Jäger willingly provided help in a field where he is more expert than I. Professor E. Jäckel and Dr. H.-J. Nordkämper helped me to gain access to Hemmen's papers. For permission to use those papers and for her kindness while I did so I would like to thank Frau Ingeborg Ganse-Hemmen. Mrs Agnes Peterson of the Hoover Institution and Dr. A. Wagner, formerly of the Bundesarchiv, provided a ready welcome and that same practical help they have given to many others in the same field. Professor E. Malinvaud and Professor I. Berend both provided me with information which I could not otherwise have obtained. In addition I would like to thank Dr. M. de Cecco and Professor Gordon Wright, as well as those many anonymous employees of the National Archives of the United States who dispatch their blue boxes to such remote corners of the world. They might well take the motto of the United States Post Office as their own.

Professor W. N. Medlicott and Professor S. B. Saul both read parts of the manuscript for me and their criticism saved me from many of my indiscretions. To Professor Medlicott's warm and consistent encouragement from the beginning I owe more than can be said here. Over a long period of research I came to rely implicitly on the help of Dr. Leo Kahn and Miss Angela Raspin of the Imperial War Museum. They have made the Foreign Documents Centre there into a true centre of research; and in what other centre of research can there be such humane company? Mrs. Norma Alderson, although always busy with other tasks, typed her way remorselessly and perfectly through the manuscript and greatly helped with the design of the statistical tables. And why should I not mention my wife? She has read every word of this book, several times, and even written some of them.

One person above all I would like to thank, Professor M. W. Flinn, whose huge enthusiasm for life and scholarship and whose very practical aid sustained me when I wavered. There is no way to repay such debts, but I would like this book to go some way towards it.

CONTENTS

LIST OF ILLUSTRATIONS

LIST OF ABBREVIATIONS

AA.	Auswärtiges Amt.
BA.	Bundesarchiv, Koblenz.
CCDR.	Commission Consultative des Dommages et des Réparations, *Dommages subis par la France et l'Union Française du fait de la guerre et de l'occupation ennemie (1939–1945), Part imputable à l'Allemagne.*
DFCAA.	*La Délégation Française auprès de la Commission Allemande d'Armistice*; Recueil de documents publié par le gouvernement français.
DGFP.	*Documents on German Foreign Policy 1918–1945.*
FD.	Foreign Document.
GbA.	Generalbevollmächtigter für den Arbeitseinsatz.
IMT.	*Trial of the Major War Criminals before the International Military Tribunal.*
INSEE.	Institut National de la Statistique et des Études Économiques.
Mbh. in B. und Nf.	Militärbefehlshaber in Belgien und Nordfrankreich.
Mbh. in F.	Militärbefehlshaber in Frankreich.
NA.	National Archives of the United States.
NCA.	Nazi Conspiracy and Aggression.
NTLL.	National Technological Lending Library.
OKH.	Oberkommando des Heeres.
OKW.	Oberkommando der Wehrmacht.
Rm.f.B.u.M.	Reichsministerium für Bewaffnung und Munition.
Rm.f.R.u.Kp.	Reichsministerium für Rüstungs- und Kriegsproduktion.
Rwm.	Reichswirtschaftsministerium.
USSBS.	United States Strategic Bombing Survey.
Wi.Abt.	Wirtschafts Abteilung.
Wi.Rü.Amt.	Wirtschafts- und Rüstungsamt.
Wi.Rü.Stab.	Wehrwirtschafts- und Rüstungsstab Frankreichs.

The word ton is used throughout to mean metric tons.

I

THE IDEA OF CONQUEST IN LIBERAL
AND FASCIST THOUGHT

Is the conquest of territory worth while? During the eighteenth century political economists came increasingly to agree that it was not. The growing conviction that economic progress depended on the unity of interests of mankind implied that war, the ultimate demonstration of the opposition of human interests, and economic progress were incompatible. Even after a successful conquest the resistance of the conquered eliminated any possibility of real economic benefit for either party. The National Socialist Party, however, saw conquest as a possible, even a necessary instrument for improving the future of certain sections of mankind. The opposition of interests, 'the general struggle for life' as Hitler called it in *Mein Kampf*, was such that without conquest neither Germany nor Europe could be saved. Liberal economists did not reject conquest for mere reasons of accountancy, but on philosophical grounds also. It followed from their assumptions about the needs and nature of the individual that conquest was a positive impediment to the improvement of humanity. The struggle of the oppressed against the oppressor was a struggle to reassert humanity's hopes and the laws of economic progress. Hence the tone of moral outrage which has greeted acts of conquest in the last century and a half. Conquest was always cruel and nasty, but in our modern history it has come to be seen as a denial of the fine future of mankind. That we still think in the shadow of the eighteenth century may be understood from public comment on the more recent of conquests.

The attack on the liberal concept of economic progress by the National Socialist Party drew its strength from an old-established opposition to liberal economic thought in Germany. But it was given invincible might by the economic events of the inter-war period. When theoreticians declared the Smithian epoch of expanding overseas trade to be finished and demanded a new explanation of the framework of economic development they found a ready response from those who provided an explanation with a relevance peculiar to Germany's own history. The link between the geopolitical school of Haushofer and the *völkisch* school of Daitz was all too readily provided from traditional views of Germany's historical role in Europe. Thus the economic theory of German fascism was able to incorporate a foreign policy predicated on an assumption of German economic and racial dominance in Europe, and even to make such a foreign policy an essential part of that economic theory.

B

Once that link between economic policy and foreign policy had been forged the National Socialist Party was able to present a programme of action representing the absolute rejection of all liberal thought. Liberalism was held to represent an alien code of philosophical and economic thought derived from the economic development of other societies, inappropriate to Germany. To that extent the anti-capitalist strain in the National Socialist Party was the same as that in other fascist parties, the expression of a resentment present since the early nineteenth century. But it was the integral nature of domestic and foreign economic policies which distinguished German fascism from others. The expression of this integral nature was the New Order, involving nothing less than a total economic and political reconstruction of Europe.

That New Order could be created only by military force. The different paths of economic development in European states were such that fascism was unlikely in most to achieve the successful internal revolution that it had in Germany. The plans to create the New Order challenged directly the fundamental liberal assumption about the value of conquest. For it was no more than an assumption, based on philosophical grounds rather than on the empirical exploration of historical fact. In their rejection of liberal economics the National Socialists therefore struck at its very foundations, the most vulnerable part of the whole edifice.

As the view that conquest was not valuable came increasingly to be accepted in the eighteenth century the more firmly did economic writers believe that in previous centuries the opposite view had been held. False though this interpretation of earlier writers was, to the early liberal economists it was very useful, for it made it easier for them to believe their own views to be one step further along a progress that led nearer to truth. The concept of economic progress was equally useful in that it enabled them to defend their theories against arguments culled from the fields of observed historical reality.

In fact, before the eighteenth century, writers on economic affairs had held very divided opinions about the economic value of conquest to the state, where they had discussed this issue at all. Their neglect of what seemed to liberals to be a central problem was the result of their fairly general belief that war was inherent in man's nature. For this reason war seemed an unavoidable part of economic policy. Its usefulness partly depended on the way in which it was deployed by the ruler. But the idea that capital accumulation by means of conquest is a primary advantage of war is uncommon among pre-liberal economists.

Bodin, it is true, replies to the question 'whether it is good to arm and to train subjects for war, to fortify towns, and to conduct war?', that 'conquests made over enemies and which increase the finances, also disburden and relieve subjects'.[1] But the tenor both of his work and that of Montchrétien is

[1] J. Bodin, *Les Six Livres de la république*, 3rd edn. (Paris, 1578), book 5, chapter 5.

that the primary advantage of a war of conquest is one of 'statecraft'.[1] Foreign wars are the most effective preventive of civil wars. It is precisely for this reason that Botero placed such emphasis on conquest as an objective of policy.[2] Since war is a psychological necessity for man it is better from the point of view of statecraft to fight external wars. Botero does not even consider the economic advantages of the ensuing conquests. Serious considerations of what those economic advantages might be had to wait for a different view of man's nature.

The evolution of the liberal idea of conquest can be traced back into the seventeenth century. Sir William Petty, for instance, in his *Treatise of Taxes and Contributions*, published in 1662, emphasized so strongly the cheapness of policies of internal development compared to those of territorial aggrandizement, as to imply that a genuine choice existed for the policy maker.[3] But it was the year 1734 which gave a really strong impulse to the development of economic thought along these lines. In that year both Melon and Vanderlint published the pamphlets by which they are now best known.

Melon assumed a profound opposition between 'the spirit of conquest' and 'the spirit of commerce'. The origin of all economic strength is capital accumulation. The true source of capital accumulation is commerce. War is a direct threat to economic development, even war which leads to the state's territorial aggrandizement. Had the Carthaginians retired behind a defensive wall and actively sought foreign trade they would easily have repulsed the Romans.[4] States founded on conquest have no stability; once the process of conquest stops the state begins to disintegrate. Even while conquest lasts there is no real accretion of capital to the conqueror, only a greatly increased burden of debt. The size of the national territory has no relationship to the strength of the state; Russia only became a significant power when Peter the Great began to pursue policies of internal development.

To encourage marriages, to grant assistance to fathers burdened with large families, to take charge of the education of orphans and foundlings is to strengthen the State much more than conquests would. In so far as what the capture of a town ordinarily costs in men and money, compared to its value, there is always a loss for the conqueror, who is certain to meet with subsequent resistance.[5]

Such internal development is very much a matter of internal colonization. In most circumstances conquests abroad merely prevent conquests at home.

[1] A. de Montchrétien, *Traicté de l'œconomie politique* (Paris, 1615), ed. T. Funck-Brentano (Paris, 1889).

[2] G. Botero, *Della Ragion di Stato* (Venice, ed. 1601); (trans. P. J. and D. P. Waley, *The Reason of the State* (London, 1956)).

[3] Sir W. Petty, *A Treatise of Taxes and Contributions* (London, 1662), ed. H. Hull (Cambridge, 1899).

[4] J.-F. Melon, *Essai politique sur le commerce* (Paris, 1734); in E. Daire (ed.) *Économistes-financiers du XVIIIᵉ siècle* (Paris, 1843), p. 735.

[5] Ibid., p. 718.

The refusal to allow the Moors expelled from Spain to settle in and cultivate the Landes should be compared to the attempts to get German settlers to people Louisiana.

To take new lands into cultivation is to conquer new countries without making anyone unhappy. The heaths of Bordeaux and Bayonne have a diameter of twenty leagues; the legislator who peopled them would do the State a greater service than he who might capture the same amount of land in a murderous war, but, in the eyes of the common man he would not have so brilliant a glory, for it would have been won without military danger, without losing a single citizen, and without incurring the jealousy of his neighbours.[1]

Vanderlint considered the net result of almost all wars to be an over-all capital loss. There was, he argued, no way of accurately costing any intended war; there was therefore no way of establishing whether or not war was worth while as a reply to an encroachment by a foreign power on British trade. The likelihood was that it would not be found so. If the 'Point of Trade' be conceded the other nation will merely accumulate bullion, the main result of a trading gain. In such a case its internal price level would be increased to the point where its trade would be disadvantaged. In almost all circumstances therefore it is 'absurd and wicked' to go to war.[2]

But the Folly of making War, to extend Dominion, appears, in that War lays waste and depopulates countries, and thereby puts such Nations to great and extraordinary Charges and Difficulties, to preserve and defend such unpeopled Territories from the easy Inroads and Invasions of their Neighbours, who have as many more Opportunities of Entrance, as the extended unpeopled Territory of any Potentate doth necessarily afford.[3]

But could there exist a war which is actually favourable to commerce and internal development? The population of the earth's surface is very unevenly distributed, and the eighteenth century had the clearest evidence that redistributing it seemed to increase the volume of trade. Domestic economic development would produce over-population. If such a state of affairs coincided with such under-population in another state as severely to reduce its commercial potentialities the colonization of the latter by the former would benefit the world. Population growth was essentially a function of economic development. If, therefore, neighbouring states attained unequal levels of development the more prosperous country would benefit mankind by transplanting that part of its population which could be considered to be surplus. 'Yet I think there is one Case, in which making War on other Nations may be justifiable, viz. Fighting for Territory when we are over-peopled, and want Land

[1] J.-F. Melon, op. cit., p. 723.
[2] J. Vanderlint, *Money answers all Things* (London, 1734), ed. J. H. Hollander (Baltimore, 1910).
[3] Ibid., p. 121.

for them, which our Neighbours have, but will not part with on amicable and reasonable Terms.'[1]

Thus Melon considered that the eighty thousand men which Holland required to man her East Indian garrisons were better employed there than at home. Providing only a small number of the 'superfluous' go, territory is a valuable acquisition. For this reason Melon believed the Portuguese acquisition of Brazil to have benefited the conquering economy whereas the Spanish conquests had had the opposite effect.[2]

There were certain logical problems involved in this appraisal of the usefulness of conquest. By what yardstick could the superfluousness of the population be measured? Was it a matter of where a unit of labour could be most effectively employed, or were there other considerations which argued in favour of retaining labour in the domestic economy? Verri drew the distinction between conquests not contiguous to the state, and which should therefore be considered economically as colonies, and conquests which were a direct physical extension of the frontiers. In the second case these troublesome questions were partly avoided. But this, in itself, was no argument for territorial conquest. The value of territory acquired in this way depended entirely on the balance between labour and land in that territory. Conquest usually entailed some measure of depopulation and the population of the extended state thus diminished in relation to the supply of land. The consequence might be an ultimate diminution of annual production. In addition there was the further danger that if the newly acquired territory was used to accommodate superfluous population the population of the conquering economy would be sparser, trade would decrease, and so would the rate of human reproduction.[3]

Few conquests approached sufficiently near to these considerations for their profitability to be long discussed. Both Melon and Vanderlint emphasized that the most likely eventuality was always a much lower return to capital than could be obtained by any policy of domestic capital investment. The worst aspect of conquest was the financial loss it entailed. 'One hundred thousand men killed', Melon wrote, 'is really a very small part of twenty million.'[4] His work, indeed, reveals that lack of concern for human existence except as an intellectual problem which marks him a genuine forerunner of the liberal economists.[5]

Given the right circumstances, conquest in Verri's works, is (at least theoretically) advantageous. Von Justi argued that it was in reality quite likely that conquest would represent a substantial capital gain; and yet, in

---

[1] Ibid.   [2] J.-F. Melon, op. cit., p. 722.
[3] P. Verri, *Meditazioni sulla economia politica* (Genoa, 1771); (trans.) *Méditations sur l'économie politique* (Paris, 1823), p. 137.
[4] J.-F. Melon, op. cit., p. 751.
[5] It was on these grounds that he was so splendidly attacked by Voltaire, *Politique et législation*, Lettre à M. T. sur l'ouvrage de M. Melon et sur celui de M. Dutot (Paris, 1738).

spite of this, victorious war was always an economic disaster.[1] If all the social and moral repercussions could be costed the conquering state suffered an enormous loss. The moral loss was self-evident. The perfection of the state did indeed depend on its domestic policies and not the size of its territories. Therefore, although conquest brought substantial material advantages, much more substantial than Melon would have admitted, these were heavily out-weighed by the disadvantages which inevitably ensued.[2] Von Justi's sweeping rejection of conquest was the result of not confining himself to the more narrowly economic arguments. Those who did so confine themselves tended to maintain the theoretical possibility that conquest could be advantageous. Although Herrenschwand drew a particular distinction between territorial acquisition and the acquisition of economic strength, and although the first seldom took place except at the expense of the second, a coincidence of interest was not logically impossible.[3]

The physiocrats regarded these hesitations as unjustified. Peace, in their view, was a logical deduction from the material law of the universe rather than a deliberate political construction. It was therefore not merely true that conquest was of no value, but also that there never had been a time when it had been of value.

In his article on Grains in *The Encyclopaedia* Quesnay argued that any domestic colonization must be more valuable than conquest.[4] But it was left to Baudeau to state the liberal view in its purest form. 'Never to usurp any property, never to violate any liberty, that is the universal commandment which binds all men in every instance, sovereigns and nations as much and in the same way as each individual.'[5] The foundation of such a principle had necessarily to be that conquest could in no circumstances be profitable.

But, is one ever enriched by usurpations? Reckon what you have spent in goods, in time, in skill to lay waste and invade a few of the earth's cantons: had you employed but a third in sovereign advances in your own territory you would there have multi-plied production, men, and arts, and you would have made for yourself a revenue ten times as substantial as any resulting from usurpations, a revenue which, being the just and legitimate fruit of beneficence and not having caused any human blood to be shed, could not have caused, nor, indeed, even be held responsible for, tears other than those of joy.[6]

---

[1] See E. Silberner, *La Guerre dans la pensée économique du XVIe au XVIIIe siècle* (Paris, 1939), p. 154.

[2] G. Von Justi, *Der Grundriss einer guten Regierung* (Frankfurt, 1759), p. 257.

[3] J. Herrenschwand, *De l'économie politique et morale de l'espèce humaine* (London, 1796).

[4] F. Quesnay, 'Grains, article publié dans l'Encyclopédie, 1756', in *Œuvres économiques et philosophiques de Quesnay*, ed. Oncken (Frankfurt am Main, 1888).

[5] N. Baudeau, *Première Introduction à la philosophie économique ou analyse des états policés* (Paris, 1767) in A. Dubois (ed.), *Collection des économistes et des réformateurs sociaux de la France* (Paris, 1910), ii. 174.

[6] Ibid., p. 180.

In essence the rulers of the earth are nothing more than great landed proprietors. Their task is to develop their estates. In such development there is
no place for destructive aggression.

Because, finally, suppose the policy of destruction to have the greatest success for
which it could hope. A conquest, that is an imposing word indicating a fine thing;
but what does one find of use in a natural province? Cultivated and built-on lands,
men, and wealth. Well then . . . how many conquests are there to be made very
peacefully at home at much less expense, without danger and without devastation,
and above all, without any human power being able to prevent them.[1]

The insistence on agriculture as the source of economic development, combined with a very atomistic view of the state, made the physiocrats regard
territorial conquest with abhorrence.

What men, what operations, whose effects on the earth, on its produce, on the improvements and the labour which make it fruitful, on the men who cover its surface,
on their multiplication, are precisely the same, without any kind of difference, as if
thousands of untamable carnivorous animals, a violent epidemic disease, a deluge of
water or of fire had been sent by Heaven to the same countries. If those monsters in
human form who are called conquerors must have statues and altars, as the base
adulation of scholars has frequently suggested, it is in the same way that fever,
famine and plague had temples in pagan antiquity.[2]

The shift in emphasis from considerations of agriculture to considerations
of foreign trade as the mainspring of economic progress led to no modification
of the liberal position as established by the physiocrats. Inasmuch as the
classical economists accepted Say's Law of Markets they were bound to come
to conclusions very similar to those of their immediate precursors. Goods, Say
argued, were obtained only by other goods. Capital accumulation not only
increases the ability to produce but also the ability to consume, to such a
degree that the demand for commodities will be almost entirely in proportion
to their supply. Once this proposition was accepted capital accumulation
appeared as a self-regulating process, and equilibrium as a feature even of a
stationary economy. Conquest seemed therefore to have the same general
utility as colonization.[3] In addition conquest had serious institutional disadvantages besides the disruption of exchange which it caused. Wars of conquest were declared to be 'crimes against the people' by Say.[4] At the same
time the concept of a profound opposition between war and commerce survived with even greater force. 'This (war) is the pestilential wind which blasts
the prosperity of nations. This is the devouring fiend which eats the precious
treasure of national economy.'[5]

[1] N. Baudeau, *Principes économiques de Louis XII, de Henri IV et du duc de Sully* (Paris,
1785), p. 115.   [2] N. Baudeau, *Première Introduction*, op. cit., p. 181.
[3] See the discussions by M. Blaug, *Economic Theory in Retrospect* (New York, 1962), and
D. Winch, *Classical Political Economy and Colonies* (London, 1965).
[4] J.-B. Say, *Cours d'économie politique pratique* (Paris, 1829), p. 176.
[5] J. Mill, *Commerce Defended* (London, 1808), p. 119.

Annexation may have been the result merely of the foolish ignorance of diplomats and statesmen. But Say had no faith that this could be prevented by any international peace-keeping agency. Such an agency would be a more complicated expression of self-interest than the rivalry of independent states. The disappearance of conquest must therefore wait on public enlightenment. In this respect Say's intellectual arrogance was tempered by his unwarranted optimism. He regarded the increasing tendency of warring nations to justify their conquests by public proclamations as a stage in the ultimate victory of enlightenment over prejudice. Similarly, Napoleon Bonaparte, a man by nature callous and cruel, had been obliged by the force of public opinion to behave in a more lenient way than the tyrant Mithridates.[1]

It was not only the optimism of the classical economists about war which had an unreal air but also the extreme logical position they had taken up. To argue that conquest had never been economically valuable was to confront serious historical problems in explaining the economic growth of nation states in the immediate past. The weight of historical evidence accumulating in the nineteenth century suggested that whatever the current economics of conquest it may well have provided in the past in certain favourable circumstances a higher return on capital than other investment choices.[2] Napoleon's campaigns themselves indicated that there were advantages, even if only temporary, in a policy of conquest, and even that such advantages may not be wholly limited to the conquering economy.[3]

Consideration of historical examples led to a more cautious attitude amongst German economists in the nineteenth century. List never accepted the proposition that war was necessarily an impediment to economic development. Britain could be shown to have benefited from the French Wars even in a narrowly commercial sense. More strikingly the United States could be shown to have benefited from a war actually fought on its own soil.[4] In spite

---

[1] J.-B. Say, op. cit., p. 180.

[2] For evidence that this was very likely so see F. Redlich, *De praeda militari* (Beiheft zur Vierteljahrschrift für Sozial- und Wirtschaftsgeschichte, vol. xxxix, Wiesbaden, 1956), and id., *The German Military Enterpriser and his Work Force* (Beiheft zur Vierteljahrschrift für Sozial- und Wirtschaftsgeschichte, vols. xlvii, xlviii, Wiesbaden, 1964–5).

[3] See, for example, G. Thuillier, 'Pour une histoire de l'économie rhénane de 1800 à 1830: les houillères de la Ruhr', in *Annales*, xv (1960); G. Thuillier, 'La métallurgie rhénane de 1800 à 1830', in *Annales*, xvi (1961); H. Kisch, 'Growth deterrents of a medieval heritage; the Aachen area woollen trades before 1790', in *Journal of Economic History*, xxiv (1964); P. Lebrun, *L'Industrie de la laine à Verviers pendant le dix-huitième siècle et le début du dix-neuvième* (Liège, 1948).

For a more comprehensive view see E. Hecksher, *The Continental System* (Oxford, 1922); and F. Crouzet, 'Wars, Blockade and Economic Change in Europe, 1792–1815', *Journal of Economic History*, xxiv (1964); id., *L'Économie britannique et le blocus continental 1806–1813*, 2 vols. (Paris, 1958).

[4] F. List, *Das nationale System der politischen Ökonomie* (Stuttgart, 1841), trans. *National System of Political Economy* (Philadelphia, 1856), p. 167: '. . . reduced, consequently, to their own resources for the supply of their wants, the States of North America, found, during the war of independence, that manufactures of every kind had received a remarkable

of these examples, and others even more persuasive drawn from antiquity, most nineteenth-century German economists accepted that conquest was very seldom profitable and many believed its profitability to have been only a feature of the past. Knies claimed that the gains from conquest were in most cases illusory. It was certainly possible to exact indemnities, as Napoleon had done, or otherwise to increase the stock of capital. But such gains covered only the expenses of the victorious government; they were not usually equal to the total loss to the national economy caused by war.[1] Roscher in later editions of his work estimated that Germany did gain economically in 1871, but only to the extent of one-sixth of the French loss. In fact, if the harmful consequences of the German stock-market boom induced by the French indemnity are taken into account, Germany may not have gained at all.[2] Although the 'historical school' of economists would have agreed that in modern circumstances conquest represented a poor investment decision they would not accept the view of the British and French liberals that it always had been so.

The existence of another school of economists at grips with the historical paradox implicit in the liberal standpoint had little influence in modifying this standpoint. Rather the modifications came from inside the body of liberal economic thought itself. The early advocates in Britain of a planned policy of colonization argued their case in the language of classical economic theory. In so doing they mounted a rather clumsy attack on Say's law. Wakefield argued that the demand for capital was not in effect in proportion to the supply. Capital accumulation could take place without good domestic investment opportunities occurring and could therefore lead to economic disequilibrium.[3] Such an argument was directed to demonstrating that colonies were not as useless as Ricardian theory supposed, but in as much as it involved the rejection of Say's Law it also modified the position on the economics of conquest which the classical economists had inherited from the physiocrats.

It is, therefore, not surprising that not only was Bentham converted into an advocate of colonization by Wakefield but that it was also he who began the liberal retreat to a more tenable position. Bentham had displayed a rather ambivalent attitude towards colonies even before his complete change of heart. As for his views on conquest they may well have been influenced by Hobbes. Both Bentham and Hobbes took the view that the conquests made by

---

impulse, and that agriculture was deriving from them such benefits, that the value of the soil, as well as the wages of labor, were largely increased, in spite of public taxes and the ravages of war'.

[1] K. Knies, *Die politische Ökonomie, vom Standpunkte der geschichtlichen Methode* (Braunschweig, 1853), pp. 54 ff.

[2] W. Roscher, *Betrachtungen über die Währungsfrage der deutschen Münzreform* (Berlin, 1872).

[3] D. Winch, op. cit., p. 79.

the Greek and Roman empires had been profitable. Hobbes, however, considered that the return to capital had ceased to be worth while by his own day.[1] Bentham, stern critic of war though he was, was not so certain.

Conquests made by New Zealanders have some sense in them; while the conquered fry, the conquerors fatten. Conquests made by the polished nations of antiquity— conquests made by Greeks and Romans, had some sense in them. Lands, moveables, inhabitants, everything went into the pocket. The invasions of France in the days of the Edwards and the Henrys, had a rational object. Prisoners were taken and the country was stripped to pay their ransom. The ransom of a single prisoner, a Duke of Orleans, exceeded one-third of the national revenue of England.[2]

War, in fact, argued Bentham, had on several occasions been justifiable on these grounds. The causes of war were not entirely the same as the causes of human criminality and anti-social behaviour; there were differences of scale. The hope of gain and the hope of plunder were both rational motives for war. Because of this, wars of conquest could benefit individual despots where they did not benefit the whole of the conquering nation. The annexation of Silesia by Frederick II in 1740 or the later partitions of Poland all benefited certain individuals or groups in positions of power within the State. Whereas it was unthinkable that an aggressive war could economically benefit Britain, one of the reasons for the historical survival of conquest was that it advantaged the ruling groups in less happy countries.

For Britain or France annexation of territory was the very depth of folly. There was a connection between the degree of economic advancement and the sophistication of the political system. The more economically advanced the country the less it stood to gain by conquest. The more people shared the government the less likely was gain from conquest to be worth distributing. Similarly, the more economically advanced the country the more it would lose from any aggressive war.[3] 'The greatest acquisitions that could be conceived would not be to be wished for,—could they be attained with the greatest certainty, and without the least expense.'[4] But in the case of a less advanced country conquest might still occur from quite rational motives. Bentham offered the beginnings of an explanation of the continued existence of conquest even in the nineteenth century, an explanation which was a considerable improvement on merely attributing it to human ignorance.

It was along these lines that Gustave de Molinari was able finally to re-establish the liberal idea of conquest in a defensive position not far from where it had been before the physiocrats. In so doing he perpetrated a curious blend of Ricardian economics and evolutionary thought.

[1] T. Hobbes, *Leviathan* (London, 1651), p. 250.
[2] J. Bentham, *Principles of International Law*, in J. Bowring (ed.), *The Works of J. Bentham* (Edinburgh, 1843), p. 557.
[3] A view very strongly proposed later by Fawcett. H. Fawcett, *Manual of Political Economy*, 7th edn. (London, 1888), pp. 30 ff.
[4] J. Bentham, op. cit., p. 551.

In the earliest period of history aggressive war, he argued, had been not merely profitable but a necessary condition of man's survival. The origins of war are man's extension of the territorial area which provides his sustenance. Conquest for economic gain is therefore the economic origin of most human communities. Had the conquerors, however, merely pillaged the territories they captured, civilization would have collapsed at the outset. Some form of rational exploitation of the captured area had to be organized.

Civilization would certainly have perished in its early days if a further progress had not intervened to save it: instead of slaughtering the vanquished and plundering the wealth which they had accumulated the more intelligent societies of hunters and plunderers understood that it would be more profitable to occupy permanently the territories on which they were conducting forays and to force the vanquished to share with them the products of their industry.[1]

The foundation of a 'state' in this way was an enterprise subject to the same laws of competition as any other economic enterprise. It was riskier than other enterprises, but potentially more profitable, bringing a greater return than participation in industrial activity. War became a capital investment on which the return was 'booty, tributes, the acquisition and exploitation of a supplement of "subjects" '.[2] But for it to survive it must retain a higher rate of return on capital than peace-time activities. 'The conquest of a territorial domain and the foundation of a political state do not differ in any way from any other enterprise. They are effected, like industrial and commercial enterprises, by co-operation of labour and capital, and their objective is profit.'[3]

Every war which sees an increase in the cost of means of conquest sees a potential inprovement in the future security of civilization. This is mitigated by the fact that security starts to diminish competition. Competition is essential to the conservation of the human race. The danger therefore arises that a diminution of war will impede human progress. But the consolidation of security leads to a new form of competition, competion for markets. Conquest becomes no longer the most profitable, and thus the most rational capital investment. And yet war continues. The explanation for this is the same as the explanation provided by Bentham.

The direction of the enterprises called states becomes an object of competition amongst all those who may hope to attain it. The consequence is a rise of sectional group interests some of whom wish to pursue a policy of conquest which will benefit their section of the state, although the state as a whole would be more advantaged by investing its capital in peaceful activities. These sectional interests are called 'parties'. When the Bonapartist 'party' captured the French state it was able to revive in its own narrow economic interests all the glories of previous wars of economic conquest. The Franco-Prussian war

---

[1] G. de Molinari, *Grandeur et décadence de la guerre* (Paris, 1898), p. 13.
[2] G. de Molinari, *Esquisse de l'organisation politique et économique de la société future* (Paris, 1899), p. 26.   [3] Ibid., p. 29.

was an unsuccessful attempt to repeat the same experiment. In fact such policies have less chance of success because the outlay of war increases all the time. Nevertheless,

in all these states, whatever the form of their government, absolute monarchy, constitutional, or a republic, the conduct of public affairs remains in the hands of a class interested in the persistence of the state of war and of the enormous and costly apparatus of destruction which it necessitates; the reason is that the many who are interested in the advent of a system ensuring permanent peace do not yet possess the necessary influence to compel governments to institute it.[1]

That the loss to those out of power is greater than the gain to those in power can be seen by inspecting the defence budgets of all European states. But with the growth of enlightened public opinion the situation will finally change.

This explanation for the delay in the arrival of permanent peace was a highly convenient one. It offered one reason why countries should be more bellicose the less open their governments were to public opinion. Schumpeter, following de Molinari, argued that the urge to war in modern society was merely atavism, a reversion to the days when conquest had been an evolutionary necessity. Conquest could still benefit narrow groups within the state and such groups were much more likely to seize control of a totalitarian state than a democratic one.[2] This is the view taken up by Robbins. In the historical past conquest had been a matter of profit. 'There can be no doubt that William of Normandy had much to gain in this way by the conquest of England. There is no need to multiply examples; the history of such times is one continuous demonstration of the importance of this kind of thing.'[3] By the twentieth century, however, conquest survived only because it might still be in the interests of a narrow group in control of a totalitarian state.[4]

Like all liberal thought de Molinari's interpretations aim at an ideal in the future. The ideal is none the less Utopian for the way in which he attempts to deduce it from historical reality, for his view of historical reality is not very convincing. But, by refusing to consider the historical past as an aberration, de Molinari was able to grasp a nettle which other liberal economists regarded only very distantly. He was able to construct a system which explained the past and present existence of war and also the certainty of its disappearance in the future. Unfortunately, like many liberals he revealed his essential

[1] G. de Molinari, *Grandeur et décadence*, p. 171.
[2] J. A. Schumpeter, 'Zur Soziologie des Imperialismen', in *Archiv für Sozialwissenschaft und Politik*, xlvii (1918/19).
[3] L. Robbins, *The Economic Causes of War* (London, 1939), p. 68.
[4] The attentive reader of this particular school of liberal writing will note that the existence of a state of war often produces a kind of atavism in the writer himself. Even Mr. Robbins can justify the British neglect of German neo-mercantilist theory by 'our natural aversion from the pretentious and our ingrained unwillingness to read the less elegant of the foreign tongues' (op. cit., p. 73, n. 1).

distaste for his fellow men by blaming them for the delay in the arrival of his particular Utopia.

De Molinari's views were not fully formulated until the last decade of the nineteenth century. By that time the basic liberal refusal to look the awkward fact of war in the face had had profound repercussions on the international law relating to conquest. While superficially international law appeared to be modifying the harshness of military occupation it was moving towards a position of greater and greater unreality, the consequences of which were the Hague Convention of 1899, and the Fourth Hague Convention of 1907.

During the second half of the eighteenth century the legal distinction was first made between acquisition and mere occupation. It did not, however, become a universally accepted distinction until the nineteenth century. The judgement of Sir William Scott in 1814 in the case of *The Foltina* did not admit it, for instance.[1] It was the events of the Napoleonic Wars which accelerated the evolution of legal doctrine on what was coming to be called 'temporary militray occupation'. In 1828 Chief Justice Marshall called such a distinction 'the usage of The World'.[2] The whole force of liberal ideas was to restrict the traditional powers of conquerors by subjecting them to rules preventing the assumption of full sovereignty on their part. Conventional international law came to recognize only one form of military occupation which it called 'belligerent occupation'. Such an occupation, although giving the right to exercise control, involved no actual exchange of sovereignty. In respect of 'belligerent' purposes the occupied territory was part of the domain of the conqueror.[3] But in spite of this there existed a legitimate sovereign power, which might legislate for the territory provided its laws did not clash with the powers accorded by international law to the conqueror.

These powers, in their turn, were also eroded by liberal influence. The belligerent occupier, although the conquered territory was his for belligerent purposes, found his powers theoretically restricted in respect of interference with property interests. War came to be thought of as directed against other sovereign powers and their armed forces and not against civilian subjects. This view was incorporated in the *Instructions for the Government of the Armies of the United States in the Field* issued in 1863. This manual, in turn, served as the forerunner to a whole series of similar manuals issued by the great powers before the First World War. It was embodied in the *Projet de Déclaration* drawn up after the Brussels conference of 1874. Both the Hague Convention with Respect to the Laws and Customs of War on Land (1899), and the Fourth Convention on the same subject (1907), rely heavily on that Brussels conference.

[1] G. von Glahn, *The Occupation of Enemy Territory* (Minneapolis, 1957), p. 3.
[2] 'The American Insurance Co. *v*. 356 Bales of Cotton', *United States Supreme Court Reports*, vol. xxvi (1828) (Rochester, 1926).
[3] As in the case of 'Thirty Hogsheads of Sugar *v*. Boyle and others', ibid., vol. ix (1815).

The Hague Conventions consequently were concerned with protecting the civilian and his private property from exploitation by the conqueror. In this respect they reflected the individualist view of economic existence of the liberal economists.[1] Because of this they provided no real protection for the national economy of an occupied territory. It is not unfair to say that their result was to bequeath one body of conventional international law for civilian rights, in which the civilian was protected against the depredations of occupiers, and another body of law for public interests, in which the ancient right of booty was retained.[2]

The Hague Conventions therefore provided scarcely any economic protection for an occupied country with a developed economy. Indeed, had the great powers ever tried to behave within the terms of those Conventions from 1914 to 1918 they would have found it very difficult to do so. The determined liberal assumption that war and conquest were disappearing left international law quite unprepared to cope with a war which would be decided by the total exploitation of the economies of the combatants to the point where the distinction between civilians and non-civilians was merely arbitrary. In addition, total involvement of society in war was furthered by the deployment of armaments, such as the aeroplane, with which it was almost impossible to discriminate between civilian and public property. Should civilians working in munitions factories be exempt from air attack? The work, and even the private wealth, of every citizen became of much greater military relevance. How much of the fixed capital of an occupied territory was private and, from a belligerent point of view, innocent property?

Such slight protection as did exist under the Conventions was couched, like much liberal thought, in terms of 'rights of individuals'. The basic raw-material resources, so vital to the occupier, and, it could be argued, so vital also to mankind, were not protected. Nor indeed were basic human resources. Women and children were protected only in so far as they were civilians. In 1914–18 when the German occupiers clearly broke the spirit, although perhaps not the letter, of the Hague Regulations in Belgium they did not justify themselves by claiming the rules to be inadequate. Like the Allies when they practised the seizure of contraband goods which were clearly civilian property in terms of international law, they blamed breaches of the law by the other side. In the Versailles Treaties the Allies held Germany responsible for every breach of the law.

That such a state of affairs should have been reached testifies to the illusions of liberal thought on conquest during the preceding one and a half centuries. During the Napoleonic Wars the French government had succeeded in sus-

[1] Y. Guyot, a disciple of de Molinari, believed that one of the reasons why conquest had become unprofitable was that conquerors were now obliged to respect private property. Y. Guyot, *La Jalousie commerciale et les relations internationales* (Paris, 1911).

[2] See E. H. Feilchenfeld, *The International Economic Law of Belligerent Occupation* (Washington, 1942).

taining the war and mitigating the domestic tax burden by the exploitation of occupied territory.[1] In some belligerent occupations, as in the Prussian occupation of France in 1870/1, large sums of money had been demanded from the conquered. Not only had France to pay a war indemnity on the conclusion of peace but in the course of the war itself separate tributes were levied on the cities of Paris and Rouen and the department of Lower Seine. The occupation of French Lorraine which lasted from March 1871 to September 1873 and was the guarantee for the payment of the war indemnity was in fact carried out in an extremely lenient way.[2] This was not uncommon in the case of legally recognized belligerent occupations. Robin, however, lists twenty-three instances of military occupations by foreign powers which were not considered as belligerent occupations.[3] In the Boer War, which, since it was a civil war, does not appear in Robin's list, large numbers of indisputable civilians were interned. In the light of developments during the nineteenth century the revulsion of liberal feeling over German conduct in Belgium in the First World War was really the result of too much utopianism taken with a rather parochial view of the World.

Between 10 December 1914 and May 1918 Germany levied a series of mounting contributions on occupied Belgium which by 21 May 1917 had reached a level of 60,000,000 Belgian francs a month.[4] Such sums were clearly far greater than the sums necessary to sustain German armies in Belgium, to which international law conceded to Germany a 'right'. In the last desperate few months of the war Germany also collected 10,000,000 francs from occupied towns in northern France. Stocks of cash in branch banks in Belgium and France were seized at the outset. Stocks of raw materials discovered in France were likewise transferred to Germany. But it took until 1916 for the German armies to institute any organic connection between themselves and the French economy as a supplement to tributes and booty. In February of that year they organized a census of all fixed capital in French factories.[5] On 14 October 1916 a general law systematized the rather haphazard practice of compulsory labour.[6] Because of the extent to which adult males had been mobilized in the French army such forced labour had often to be female labour. It was under this law also that Russian and Romanian prisoners of war were brought to work in the French economy.

Compulsory labour was of course much more rigorously applied in Belgium. There the policies of Germany had created a large pool of unemployed labour

---

[1] F. Baudhuin, *Le Financement des guerres* (Louvain, 1944).

[2] E. Chantriot, *La Lorraine sous l'occupation allemande* (Nancy, 1922).

[3] R. Robin, *Des occupations militaires en dehors des occupations de guerre* (Paris, 1913).

[4] *La Banque nationale de Belgique sous l'occupation allemande 1914/18, Rapport au Roi* (Brussels, Imprimerie Nationale, 1918).

[5] G. Gromaire, *L'Occupation allemande en France, 1914/18* (Paris, 1925), p. 47.

[6] Ibid., p. 210.

and from 1915 onwards industrialists and generals brought pressure to bear on the German government to use this labour in the German economy. On 23 October 1916 forced deportations of labour from Belgium to Germany began.[1] By 20 January 1917, 58,432 men had been deported to supplement the German labour force. These deportations, besides revealing the inadequacy of the Hague Conventions, since many Germans were convinced they were not actually an infringement of those conventions, were the really decisive blow to all those whose opinion was that occupation was becoming more lenient and thus, perhaps, less profitable. In an interesting volume published in 1916, Prato compared the German actions in Belgium to the French occupations of Piedmont and Catalonia during the War of the Spanish Succession.[2] The depth of his horror at the regression in human behaviour which he believed to see there can only be gauged by reading his book; a scholarly investigation of the eighteenth century turns into a diatribe against the twentieth.

The German attempts to exploit Belgian labour in the interests of the German war economy were the precursor of attempts to implement a much more drastic management of the German economy itself. Their origin was not in any peculiar wickedness of the Germans but in the unforeseen cost, in all factors of production, of the First World War. Ludendorff saw economic exploitation of occupied territory as a necessity if Germany was to survive. The mounting cost of war made such policies a necessity.

From the mid nineteenth century the increasing cost of armaments had also been a theme of most writing on war. The conclusion which liberals generally drew from their observations, however, was that war would eventually price itself out of the market. Say had attempted to make a relative costing of offensive and defensive armaments and had demonstrated to his own satisfaction that defensive warfare was much the cheaper.[3] But it was the mounting armies and navies of the great powers between 1880 and 1914 that led to a widespread conviction that no kind of war could be profitable. Certainly the increasing strain of armaments programmes on budgets played its part in formulating de Molinari's opinions. The mechanism by which conquest ceased to be an evolutionary imperative for the human race was its increasing cost.

Can the profits of war still cover its cost? The history of all wars which have occurred between civilized peoples for a number of centuries attests that these costs have progressively grown, and, finally that any war between members of the civilized community today costs the victorious nation more than it can possibly yield it.[4]

[1] R. B. Armeson, *Total Warfare and Compulsory Labour* (The Hague, 1964), pp. 28–42. See also L. von Köhler, *Die Staatsverwaltung der besetzten Gebiete, I. Belgien* (Stuttgart, 1927); H. Pirenne, *La Belgique et la guerre mondiale* (Paris, 1928).
[2] G. Prato, *L'Occupation militaire dans le passé et dans le présent* (Paris, 1916).
[3] J. B. Say, op. cit., pp. 182–5.
[4] G. de Molinari, *Comment se résoudra la question sociale?* (Paris, 1896), p. 126.

Schäffle and Boccardo, similarly, held that victory in war had become less and less profitable in the course of history because the cost of war had continued to rise.[1]

The most massive exposition of this view is in the books and pamphlets of Jean de Bloch where it is supported by an exhaustive and shrewd analysis of developments in armaments.[2] This analysis led him to an all-too-accurate comprehension of the static and murderous tactics that would ensue in a future war. He was also able to demonstrate that a total war of the kind he forecast would be socially impossible for a government such as that of Imperial Russia. But in the last resort his work still purveys the illusion that war had become too costly to continue and that this would be soon realized.

Whether war had in fact become progressively more costly when measured against the increasing gross national products of western nations is a question which de Bloch and de Molinari avoided. The costing of war in their work, as in that of their predecessors, was largely a matter of adding up annual expenditure above the normal peace-time level. But if war leads to an increase in the national product, as Malthus had argued, in the nineteenth century these sums would have represented little encroachment on that national product, providing correct financial policies had been pursued.

Yet even if war had actually become relatively less costly during the nineteenth century the First World War reversed this trend. The decisions taken by the German administration in Belgium were an acknowledgement that Germany's territorial ambitions could not be fulfilled without striking off the legal shackles imposed by the development of liberal thought. But the persistence of those shackles was demonstrated when the labour transports from Belgium to Germany were stopped on 10 February 1917 in response to pressure of opinion. Nevertheless the events in Belgium cast a long shadow forward. After 1933 Germany was to attempt a total reconstruction of the European economy. That reconstruction was based on a view of economic existence wholly opposed to that which the liberal economists had propounded.

Although the idea of a *Mitteleuropa* created and controlled by German power was an idea derived peculiarly from the historical experience of Germany, the *Mitteleuropa* which Hitler wanted to create was a fascist *Mitteleuropa*. As such it would have been based on an ideological rejection of western liberal capitalism which was not peculiar to Germany but had, indeed, already found expression in the government of Italy for ten years. Under the aegis of German occupation it was also to find expression in Hungary after October 1944. Elsewhere the fascist rejection of liberal capitalism

---

[1] A. Schäffle, *Abriss der Soziologie* (Berlin, 1906), pp. 169 f. G. Boccardo, *Dizionario della economia politica*, 3rd edition (Milan, 1881), p. 197.

[2] J. de. Bloch, *Der Krieg*, 6 vols. (Berlin, 1899), The German and the French translations of Bloch's work are much more complete than W. T. Stead's feeble version, *Is War now Impossible?* (London, 1899).

was embodied in political parties and movements of varying strength. Since one aspect of fascism was an intense concentration on the potentialities of national development, as opposed to that international co-operation which was to liberals the guarantee both of peace and economic growth, these movements frequently came into conflict with German political aspirations, or, indeed, in the case of the Croatian *Ustaša* movement, with Italian ones. That their territorial conceptions of Europe differed diminishes in no way the identity of their ideological conceptions of that continent.

There was a similarity of fascist ideas in all European countries in so far as they affected the nature of fascist economic thought. Fascist economic thought was derived from a different conception of the individual, his needs and his motives, from that which informed liberal economists; and to fascist thinkers liberal economists included, by definition, Marxists, for Marxist economics was adjudged the ultimate liberal heresy. The philosophical pedestal of liberal economics having been overturned the shattering of the liberal idea of conquest was but a small part of the total debris of other and more important parts of liberal economic theory. But whereas the idea of conquest had remained peripheral to liberal economics it became central to fascist economics. The question must be permitted whether a system such as fascism, making such different assumptions about man's role in the economic world, could have survived without conquest in a Europe where most governments were almost unanimously opposed to its economic principles. For the opposition between fascist economics and liberal economics was nothing less than total.

The Italian fascist theorists laid their axe not merely to the branches of eighteenth-century enlightenment from which the science of economics was created but to the very root of the tree, to what they called the 'Greek idea'. This idea they identified as the belief that the struggle to maturity of the human individual, his triumph over his fears and weaknesses until he stood at last emancipated, free and alone, was the noblest aspect of human existence. In place of such an ideal they proposed an ideal of the submission of the will to the interests of the community. This ideal they believed to be Roman. The emancipated individual is disruptive to the community. The individual will is selfish, never more so than when engaged in abstract thought. Of the tyranny of abstract thought democracy was the product. In place of the democratic state, liberal and particularist, the plaything of avaricious groups of vested interests, fascism proposed an ethical state in which the harmony of interest of the whole community should prevail. Although their theorizing was sometimes less historical than this, the conception of the ethical state was common to all fascist parties. It may be found in the writings of Oswald Mosley as in *Mein Kampf*. It gave the National Socialist party a link with nineteenth-century German political thinkers which was much explored by anti-German tracts in Britain in the years immediately following the Second World War.

However much the fascist concept of the ethical state was derived from historical examples, it was revolutionary in so far as it was based on a revolution in the thought of the individual. His selfishness suppressed, his desire for emancipation seen for what it was, a temptation in the wilderness, he emerged with new desires and new needs. But they were no longer the desires and needs of the capitalist entrepreneur and consumer. Renunciation by the individual brought the birth of a new man and thus of a new élite and ultimately of a new state. Transformation by renunciation was the spiritual core of all the fascist movements.[1] For Drieu la Rochelle the failure of France to accept the *Parti Populaire Français* of Doriot was the refusal of the nation to accept that necessary death from which alone rebirth and spiritual regeneration could come. 'I was amongst the "happy few",' he wrote in his ' Récit secret', 'amongst the few people who were in the collaboration movement, not to collaborate but so as not to be elsewhere, in the herd sweating with fear and hatred.'[2] The implications of this renunciation are seen most awfully in Codreanu's writings and in the last years of the Romanian 'All for the Fatherland' party. It was not simply the propaganda of terror that caused Bucharest radio to broadcast the slogan 'Long Live Death' for four days in January 1941.

In Germany renunciation took the form of 'moral armament' which Hitler held as necessary as physical armament.

Anyone who believes that the People's National Socialist State should distinguish itself from the other States only mechanically, as it were, through the better construction of its economic life—thanks to a better equilibrium between poverty and riches, or to the extension to broader masses of the power to determine the economic process, or to a fairer wage, or to the elimination of vast differences in the scale of salaries—anyone who thinks this understands only the superficial features of our movement and has not the least idea of what we mean when we speak of our *Weltanschauung*. All these features just mentioned could not in the least guarantee us a lasting existence and certainly would be no warranty of greatness. A nation that could content itself with external reforms would not have the slightest chance of success in the general struggle for life among the nations of the world. A movement that would confine its mission to such adjustments, which are certainly right and equitable, would effect no far-reaching or profound reform in the existing order. The whole effect of such measures would be limited to externals. They would not furnish the nation with that moral armament which alone will enable it effectively to overcome the weaknesses from which we are suffering today.[3]

---

[1] 'This Movement has been created by simple people in face of money power, party power, and press power, without any aid from the great names of the present system, and in face of every weapon of boycott, and misrepresentation, that the money power could mobilize. Thus ever have been born the great determinist forces of history, in face of all material things, by the force of the spirit alone.

'So has been accomplished the first stage in the mission of regeneration, which is the creation from the people themselves, and from the people alone, of a Movement capable of leading the mass of the people to freedom.' O. Mosley, *Tomorrow We Live* (London, 1939), pp. 10-11.

[2] J. Plumyène and R. Lasierra, *Les fascismes français 1923-1963* (Paris, 1963), p. 167.

[3] A. Hitler, *Mein Kampf*, book 2, chapter iv.

The needs and qualities of the new individual were those conducive to a social system without disruptive striving for profit. At first that system could only be brought into existence by an élite. Life is an art and so is politics. Neither can be entirely reduced to the ratiocination of Smith nor the dialectic of Marx. As artist the politician rediscovers the older principles of human existence. These principles turn out to be more or less incompatible with the pursuit of maximum aggregate national wealth, for such a pursuit makes the social system 'unhealthy'. Fascist writers did not blink the fact that the exercise of their principles of government would curb the development of capitalism. And why should they have done, since that is exactly what their supporters wished? But very few fascist theorists could honestly face up to the question whether any form of economic growth would have been possible in a fascist Europe, because, much as they disliked the process of economic growth they had also to meet the objection that *to some extent* it may be necessary for national survival. Most evaded the issue. Szalasi's comments in 1936 might stand for all:

We must not fear that the Hungarian national socialist economy will harm the talent, the diligence, and the know-how of the nation, because it will only limit that extremely unjust process of getting rich which in its present form lends to an orgy of the degeneration of millions. The Hungarian national socialist economy is inseparable from the Hungarian national socialist moral and spiritual life; its aim being the material welfare of the community of the people. Thus our national economy and its every part is a means and not an end. . . .[1]

When the materialistic and individualistic outlook of the Greeks rediscovered in Renaissance Europe, and enshrined in economic science by the liberal economists, had been entirely replaced by fascism what virtues would then have been seen? In place of greed, the fascist answered, self-sacrifice; in place of international exploitation, patriotism; in place of cowardly peace, heroism. But when it was asked in which part of the community these virtues still existed nearest to their pristine state fascist parties all replied, in the peasantry. Hence those agricultural policies which preserved and strengthened the small, and in the liberal eye inefficient, food producer. When other social groups menaced by economic change cast their votes with the small farmers how could fascist parties both retain their supporters and pursue the paths of economic development?[2] Such problems were acute in Germany and Italy between the wars and would no doubt have been common elsewhere had fascist parties come to power.

In the thirties the majority of European governments outside Russia were feeling their way back to a system of sufficient international co-operation to

[1] F. Szalasi, *Ut es Cel* (Budapest, 1936), quoted in E. Weber, *Varieties of Fascism* (Princeton, 1964), p. 159.

[2] The ease with which the peasant could be persuaded in Germany to cast his vote for fascism is well illustrated in H. Gies, 'NSDAP. und Agrarverbände vor 1933', *Vierteljahrshefte für Zeitgeschichte*, xv (1967).

attempt to guarantee, to a greater or lesser extent, according to their political persuasions, the economic growth of their countries. In Germany and Italy these arrangements were regarded as anachronisms, for economic development was no longer thought to be dependent on the mechanisms of international exchange. But the fascist rejection of the economic policy of other European states went much deeper than this, for the assumptions on which it was founded called into question the very meaning of economic development.

For in every country where it existed the fascist movement drew its strength from those groups who were protesting against the deterioration of the quality of their own existence as a result of the process of economic development. In the Marxist sense it is true that fascism was but a form of capitalism, for the ownership of capital was scarcely affected by the advent of fascist goverments to power. But it is not true that fascism was the last stage or even a more advanced stage of capitalism. To the fascist economist all modern economies were capitalist because they needed capital; the important question to him was not its ownership but the effects on the total community of its deployment. All capitalism as it had previously existed was considered to have had a divisive, disruptive, and vicious effect on the community because of the way capital had been deployed. Economic growth, in the sense in which the liberal economist now understands the term, implies rapid social and economic change, 'growth stresses' as they are inelegantly called. Fascism rejected all development which involved such stresses. In the eyes of the Liberal economist it therefore rejected all possibility of growth since there cannot be growth without stresses. And since the political arrangements of fascism for securing economic development without social stress proved so unacceptable to so large a part of the populations of fascist states it cannot be argued that, economically speaking, fascism had a convincing alternative to the pains of capitalist, or communist, development. Indeed, there is a good case for arguing that at the heart of the fascist movement lay no desire for development but a search for a state of economic stability. In place of growth the fascist dreamed of a state of social and economic equilibrium. In that state the growing material disadvantages would find compensation in spiritual consolation.

At the best this equilibrium would be achieved by an increasingly nationalistic and autarchic economy withdrawing by stages from the international economy. At worst, as in the case of Germany, it implied the extension by conquest of that autarchic system to large areas of Europe. But the fascist *Mitteleuropa* which Hitler wished to create could only be created by conquest. That conquest was advantageous could not be doubted. For the economic disadvantages on which liberals laid so much stress were irrelevant to an economy not interested in international co-operation and seeking in the long run only an elusive and perhaps undiscoverable point of equilibrium. In the pursuit of autarchy more territory could easily be construed as an advantage. And as for the immorality of conquest, because of its effects on the individual, that could not hold in a fascist society. For in the conquest of other territories what opportunities must exist for the exercise, even for the creation, of those fascist virtues of heroism and self-sacrifice, and how many opportunities to exalt the primacy of action as a release from suffering.

Hitler must be numbered among the less intellectual theorists of fascism. There is more than a hint of robust demagoguery in his prose style. But he was no more of an opportunist than political circumstances forced him to be. In the last resort he remained deeply faithful to the fascist ideology. When he became effective champion of that ideology in Europe Mussolini was already sullied with years of political compromise, often of a kind which Hitler would scorn.[1] Over time it becomes increasingly apparent that neither Chamberlain nor Daladier nor those whom they represented had any realization of the depth of the revolutionary with whom they were dealing.

Yet it is also true, as historians writing only with the diplomatic events of the thirties in mind have emphasized, that in foreign policy Hitler was a traditionalist. The rejection of liberal ideas of conquest by the fascist philosophy and the substitution for them of a philosophy in which conquest was advantageous can not by itself explain the growth of the New Order. That New Order was designed to solve specifically German problems. It was to create a new Europe but one which would be in Germany's interests. To those particular problems it is now necessary to turn.

---

[1] 'There is a difference as between day and night between the genuine fascists and the others. Those society people with whom we are compelled to associate, that cosmopolitan world, they're more or less the same there [Italy] and here. . . . The fascists and the others, they're really two worlds in watertight compartments. . . . I was greeted at the station by the Duke of Pistoia, a real degenerate. Beside him was another duke, no less degenerate. Then there was an admiral there who looked like a court toad, a bogus coin, a liar. Happily there was also a group of fascists. All of them, even Ciano, spoke with the deepest contempt of this ridiculous masquerade.' *Hitler's Secret Conversations*, 31 January 1942.

II

FRANCE AND THE NEW ORDER

NATIONAL SOCIALIST economists based their thought on an initial rejection of liberal economic ideas. They believed that a variety of observable international economic phenomena demonstrated the end of an epoch in the history of national economies. One of these was that a declining proportion of the world's goods was now being exchanged through the mechanism of international trade. The profound international economic difficulties of the period between the two world wars could therefore only be cured by the destruction of the international economic system as it had evolved since the eighteenth century, and its replacement by a system more appropriate to the current epoch. Both at home and abroad the National Socialist New Order can only properly be understood as an attempt to achieve an anti-liberal solution to the economic problems of the inter-war period.

The solution achieved in Germany itself was a most uneasy compromise. The long resistance of German society to capitalism reached its last stage in the National Socialist period, and that government had to meet, if not always satisfy, the anti-capitalist aspirations of many social groups. The attempt to depict German fascism as the last stage of monopoly capitalism has always broken down against the clear evidence that the government's economic policy included important restrictions on the activities of private capital and in many respects, as in its dealings with the agricultural community, was most conservative.[1] Of late more attention has been paid to the anti-capitalist aspects of National Socialism, although there is little agreement on their importance or their significance.[2] To say that National Socialism was an uneasy compromise between capitalism and anti-capitalism is to say that it was a distinctive response to Germany's own economic and political development. Neither capitalist nor socialist, Germany found a different solution and one appropriate to her own history, fascism. The creation of the New Order was

[1] F. L. Neumann, *Behemoth: The Structure and Practice of National Socialism* (2nd edn., New York, 1944).

[2] A. Schweitzer, *Big Business in the Third Reich* (Bloomington, 1964); W. S. Allen, *The Nazi Seizure of Power: The Experience of a Single German Town, 1930–1935* (Chicago, 1965); R. Heberle, *Landbevölkerung und Nationalsozialismus: Eine soziologische Untersuchung der politischen Willensbildung in Schleswig-Holstein 1918 bis 1932* (Stuttgart, 1963); D. Schoenbaum, *Hitler's Social Revolution: Class and Status in Nazi Germany 1933–39* (New York, 1966); W. Sauer, 'National Socialism: Totalitarianism or Fascism?', *American Historical Review*, lxxiii, 2 (1967). The link between anti-capitalism and anti-semitism in Germany has not received enough attention.

the result of the fascist revolution, and German economic policy in France
was an integral part of the development of an anti-liberal European economy.
Although there were many things on which National Socialist economists
disagreed, of one thing they were certain; it was essential to construct an
economic system based on new and more valid principles of organisation.

These principles were variously construed from the ideas of *Grosslebens-
raum* or *Grossraumwirtschaft*, the economics of large areas, and were based
on the assumption that the Europe of the future would be dominated economically, socially, and racially by Germany. Karl Haushofer, the President
of the Society for Geopolitics, proclaimed the close of the Smithian epoch of
overseas expansion and free trade and its supersession by an epoch dominated
by land-based power blocs. The economies of these new powers would be
geared to the domestic demand of a large market. Autarchy, rather than sensitivity to international opportunities, would be their distinguishing feature. If
Germany were to survive, her economic base must become larger. For survival Germany must impose her leadership and industrial supremacy on all
the economies of central Europe. Haushofer regarded the Monroe Doctrine
as the first example of these 'geopolitical' developments which he saw as the
inner logic of historical and economic evolution.[1] Thus Haushofer and his
followers adduced a vaguely scholarly set of 'laws' of economic development
from economic geography.[2] They carried out a veritable propaganda barrage
in three different periodicals.

Haushofer never aligned himself with those who based their arguments for
the creation of a large German-dominated economic area in central Europe on
the concept of 'Volk'. He left this aspect of human geography to others who
came, however, to what were ultimately very similar conclusions. The most
prominent of the 'biological' exponents of such an idea was Werner Daitz.
Daitz held that the only true basis for the new economic order of the future
was blood; thus the geopolitical groupings of the future would have to be based
on racial similarities.[3]

Economic ideas of this kind, although in Daitz's case having a very distinctive National Socialist hue, harked back to the much older concepts of a
Mitteleuropa and to the whole problem of the politico-economic relations
between Austria and the other German states over the course of modern
German history. They had therefore a direct link with Hitler's own ideas of

---

[1] For the use made by National Socialist theorists of the Monroe Doctrine see L.
Gruchmann, *Nationalsozialistische Grossraumordnung* (Stuttgart, 1962).

[2] K. Haushofer, *Grenzen in ihrer geographischen und politischen Bedeutung* (Berlin, 1927);
Geopolitik der Pan-Ideen (Berlin, 1931); *Wehr-Geopolitik: geographische Grundlagen einer
Wehrkunde* (Berlin, 1932); *Weltpolitik von heute* (Berlin, 1934); 'Die geopolitische Betrach-
tung grenzdeutscher Probleme', in K. C. von Loesch and A. H. Ziegfeld (eds.), *Volk und
Völker* (Breslau, 1925).

[3] W. Daitz, *Der Weg zur völkischen Wirtschaft und zur europäischen Grossraumwirtschaft* (Dresden, 1938), re-issued as *Der Weg zur Volkswirtschaft, Grossraumwirtschaft
und Grossraumpolitik* (Dresden, 1943).

an expansionist foreign policy. At least in respect to Russia and to France, Hitler pursued a consistent policy from his seizure of power. German plans for expansion lay in the East. To realize them France must first be weakened to the point where she could no longer thwart German wishes. Hitler's ideas on foreign policy naturally gave hope to the more theoretically inclined of his supporters. The very existence of Hitler himself in power offered a real hope for the creation of a new economic order.[1]

At the time when the first campaign against Russia was at its most successful Hitler seems to have felt freer to identify his aims with the *Grossraumwirtschaft* of the future. Von Etzdorf, the Representative of the German Foreign Ministry with the High Command of the Army, records him as having told Otto Abetz, the Ambassador to France:

Once the Asiatics had been driven out, Europe would no longer be dependent on any outside power; America, too, could 'get lost' as far as we were concerned. Europe would itself provide all the raw materials it needed and have its own markets in the Russian area, so that we would no longer have any need of other world trade. The new Russia, as far as the Urals, would become 'our India', but one more favourably situated than that of the British. The new Greater German Reich would comprise 135 million people and rule over an additional 15 million.[2]

Ten days later Hitler expatiated on the same theme to Seyss-Inquart, Reichs Commissar for the Netherlands:

In the past it had really been an absurdity that a great empire should have existed in the east of the European continent with almost inexhaustible mineral resources and raw materials, which furthermore was only sparsely settled, whereas in the thickly-settled central and western European countries there existed a scarcity of raw materials and their need had to be filled in far-distant overseas areas. For this reason the areas in the European east, rich in raw materials, to be entirely opened up for the thickly-populated areas of the west. If this was done successfully one could also in the main do without the overseas transports which were time-consuming, complicated, and dangerous at times of warlike complications.[3]

Evidence of this kind can not be said to be definite proof of Hitler's intentions. For him this was the high point of the war. It is clear that the fairly precise ideas of a New Economic Order which appear in the economic literature of the epoch filtered through to Hitler's mind in rather less precise fashion. Nevertheless, his foreign policy was based on a military strategy which showed how clearly he was aware of Germany's economic limitations.

---

[1] It may have been Konrad Heiden's book *Der Führer* (London, 1945) that first gave the impression that Hitler was an unscrupulous opportunist who had turned the National Socialist movement into a platform for supporting his own views. Before that the view that Hitler was the tool of other groups was more common. But *Mein Kampf* was no merely personal expression of opinion, it was a work on National Socialism. It is curious that those who use it to help unravel the threads of Hitler's foreign policy do not draw the further conclusions about the origins of that foreign policy.

[2] DGFP., xiii, no. 327.   [3] Ibid., no. 377.

TABLE I

The Production and Consumption of Foodstuffs and Raw Materials in Continental Europe and European Russia

Area	Commodity	Measure	Production	Consumption	Surplus	Shortage
Continental Europe*	Wheat	1,000 tons	40,461	43,625	..	3,164
European Russia†		average of	21,471	20,891	580	..
N. Africa		1935–7	3,515	3,184	279	..
Continental Europe*	Rye	,, ,,	20,840	21,154	..	314
European Russia†			18,593	18,380	213	..
N. Africa			2	1	1	..
Continental Europe*	Barley	,, ,,	14,515	15,022	..	507
European Russia†			7,336	7,025	311	..
N. Africa			2,610	2,421	178	..
Continental Europe*	Oats	,, ,,	21,386	21,801	..	415
European Russia†			11,760	11,680	80	..
N. Africa			257	229	28	..
Continental Europe*	Maize	,, ,,	18,432	22,293	..	3,861
European Russia†			3,500	3,476	24	..
N. Africa			1,782	1,747	30	..
Continental Europe*	Potatoes	1,000 tons	144,500	144,148	352	..
European Russia†		average of	51,722	51,692	30	..
N. Africa		1936–8	191	199	..	8
Continental Europe*	Sugar	1,000 tons	5,938	6,550	..	612
European Russia†		raw value	1,822	1,753	69	..
N. Africa		average of 1936–7	138	510	..	372
Continental Europe*	Meat	1,000 tons	11,975	11,840	135	..
European Russia†		1937	2,644	2,602	42	..
Continental Europe*	Butter	1,000 tons	1,703	1,536	167	..
European Russia†		1937	341	282	59	..
Continental Europe*	Eggs	millions	38,260	36,923	1,337	..
European Russia†		1937	9,250	9,124	126	..
N. Africa			..	..	244	..
Continental Europe*	Cotton	1,000 tons	35	1,424	..	1,389
European Russia†		1937	287	327	..	40
N. Africa			594	243	346	..
Continental Europe*	Wool	1,000 tons	88	320	..	232
European Russia†		1937	38	73	..	35
N. Africa			17	5	8	..
Continental Europe*	Natural	,, ,,	..	268	..	268
European Russia†	rubber		..	26	..	26
Continental Europe*	Mineral	1,000,000	7·5	25	..	17·5
European Russia†	oil	tons	27	23	4	..
N. Africa		1938	0·2	1·5	..	1·3
Continental Europe*	Iron	1,000,000	30·9	30·7	0·2	..
European Russia†	ore	tons fe	14·3	12·7	1·6	..
N. Africa		content 1937	2·6		2·6	..
Continental Europe*	Manganese ore	1,000 tons	336	926	..	590
European Russia†		manganese	1,210	1,000	210	..
N. Africa		content 1938	87	..	87	..

TABLE I (cont.)

Area	Com-modity	Measure	Produc-tion	Consump-tion	Surplus	Short-age
Continental Europe†	Copper	1,000 tons	153	790	..	637
European Russia*	ore	Cu con-	83	145	..	62
N. Africa		tent 1938	..	2	..	2
Continental Europe†	Nickel	1,000 tons	3·5	27·6	..	24·1
European Russia*	ore	Nz con-	2·5	15·2	..	12·7
N. Africa		tent 1938	0·2	0·1	0·1	..
Continental Europe†	Zinc	1,000 tons	514	615	..	101
European Russia*	ore	Z content	25	62	..	37
N. Africa		1938	10	2	8	..

* Not including Turkey, Lithuania, Latvia, and Estonia.
† Including Lithuania, Latvia, Estonia, and Transcaucasia.

He was also aware that they could be removed by the creation of a German *Mitteleuropa*.

Thus, for example, it had turned out that even at this time large quantities of rubber of good quality were being produced in the Kharkov area. The Führer had said in this connection that the samples presented to him made an excellent impression, and that by intensifying the cultivation of rubber there one could hope to make Greater Germany and if possible all of Europe independent of rubber deliveries from overseas in the future. With regard to the production of petroleum the case was similar.[1]

Hitler's views on the possibilities of a reconstructed European economy were no vaguer than those of many German industrialists who subscribed to the same idea. In fact those who attended the monthly meetings of the 'Europe Circle' at the Hotel Esplanade to consider European planning questions showed a rather less realistic grasp of these affairs than Hitler. Even in June 1944 Hugo Stinnes was advocating a customs union to embrace all the states between Sweden and the Balkans except Russia and Italy. Germany would be the central manufacturing core of this common market within which freedom of study or employment in Germany would be offered to all inhabitants of the associated states.[2]

In 1941 the *Institut für Konjunkturforschung* brought out a study on the extent to which 'continental Europe' and 'European Russia' could be regarded as comparable powers from the standpoint of raw material and foodstuff surpluses.[3] The general conclusion, after some statistical manipulation of doubtful validity, was that Russia's surpluses would only balance those of the rest of Europe provided Europe could also draw on North African surpluses. The other possibility of course was drastically to reduce consumption in

[1] DGFP., xiii, no. 377.
[2] FD 3045/49, Section IV, Sc. 146, Folder 1, Planungsamt, 'Handakten Kehrl'.
[3] Ibid., Sc. 146, Folder 2, Institut für Konjunkturforschung, 'Rohstoffbilanz Kontinentaleuropas'.

Russia by reducing the flow of food and raw materials from 'European Russia' to Siberia. The largeness of this conception testifies to the cosmic juggling that was involved in National Socialist thinking, particularly at the height of the Blitzkrieg's success (see Table I).

The concept of a reconstructed European economy within which Germany would play a central and dominating role was widespread in the National Socialist administration. Although Daitz was ordered to confine himself to research and to refrain from public propaganda in 1940 this had only tactical importance.[1] His ideas and those of Karl Haushofer and his son Albrecht, professor of geopolitics at the University of Berlin, were not direct influences on the German administration but symptons of widely held views in German society. Albert Speer, who in 1942 became Minister of Armaments and Munitions, had plans for a peaceful solution to the war which envisaged a Europe reconstructed on lines not unlike the present Common Market.

It would have been the supposition that the tariff was lifted from this large economic area and through this a mutual production was really achieved. For any deeply-thinking individual it is clear that the tariffs which we have in Western Europe are unbearable. So the possibility for producing on a large scale only exists through this scheme.[2]

It would, however, have been a customs union founded on military victory and heavily in the German interest.

The plans of the *Grossraumwirtschaft* theorists seemed to be nearing fulfilment in the years between 1933 and 1939 with the development of a central-European trading bloc. The development of German economic policy towards her eastern neighbours over those years showed how genuine was the coincidence of interest between Hitler's foreign policy and the economic aims of the National Socialist Party. The growth of bilateral trade within this trading bloc was on the one hand a rational and successful economic response to the conclusions which the Party's economic theorists had drawn from the economic history of the previous period, and on the other hand a mere device to facilitate Hitler's military plans.

It was clear whatever strategy Hitler chose to adopt one of Germany's greatest weaknesses in the event of a future war would be shortages of raw materials, especially certain raw materials of peculiar strategic value. Since the Treaty of Versailles Germany had been left heavily dependent on foreign supplies of iron ore. The German steel industry itself has responded by consuming increasing quantities of high-grade Swedish iron ores.[3] In addition

---

[1] DGFP., x, no. 320.

[2] Speer Report no. 30, Intelligence Report EF/AM/6, Interrogation of Albert Speer.

[3] It has even been argued that as late as 1940 the German war effort was wholly dependent on this supply. R. Karlbom, 'Sweden's Iron Ore Exports to Germany, 1933–44', in *Scandinavian Economic History Review*, xiii, 1 (1965). But see also J. J. Jäger, 'Sweden's Iron Ore Exports to Germany, 1933–1944', ibid. xv, 1 and 2 (1967), and A. S. Milward, 'Could Sweden have stopped the Second World War?', ibid.

many of the rarer metal ores necessary in the manufacture of armaments and of armour-plating were also lacking. Germany produced no chrome, nickel, or wolfram ore, all of which were indispensable to a war economy. Imports of molybdenum, manganese, zinc, and lead could easily be cut off by enemy action. The output of bauxite was quite inadequate to maintain the level of aluminium production. Even more serious was the potential oil shortage. Germany produced only small quantities of crude mineral oil; nor of course did she produce natural rubber. The British Ministry of Economic Warfare even based their hopes of winning the war on these weaknesses in the German economy.

By a carefully managed trading policy with her neighbours Germany could to some extent remedy these critical deficiencies. Romania was one of the world's greatest oil producers. Hungary was an important bauxite producer. Manganese was produced in Russia, chrome in Turkey, and copper in Yugoslavia. To all these economies Germany could offer a dynamic and expanding market in return for a guaranteed continuity of supply. In this respect much of the criticism of the 'selfishness' of Germany's economic policy in south-eastern Europe has been wide of the mark. The Balkan countries were indeed being forced to buy in dearer markets, but they were also selling dearer and at a guaranteed scale. In the state of the international conjuncture of the 1930s these were important advantages. The 'selfishness' of German policy lay rather in the way in which the Balkan powers were forced into producing exactly to meet the demands of the German market. It is clear that in many cases it was not the best bargain that interested the German negotiators but the possibility of continuity of supply. This insistence on continuity was dictated by strategic consideration, the securing of a strategic raw material base from which to launch German plans for expansion.

The new *Mitteleuropa* would also depend on the creation of a central manufacturing area in the European economy, an area whose boundaries would be nearly coincidental with those of the Reich. Hitler's plans to remedy the raw material shortages in the German economy meant a deliberate policy of autarchic development of certain industries of great strategic importance in Germany. For this reason Germany created an enormous synthetic oil industry and a synthetic rubber industry. At the same time political pressure was brought on the German steel industry to use a greater proportion of domestic iron ores. The rapid growth in the German aluminium industry was a function of the expansion of German aircraft production. These domestic policies, which began in a tentative way in 1933, were given absolute priority over other economic objectives in the Second Four Year Plan of September 1936.[1] A considerable part of the growth in industrial production

---

[1] For full details of the operation of the Four Year Plan, D. Petzina, *Autarkiepolitik im Dritten Reich. Der nationalsozialistische Vierjahresplan* (Stuttgart, 1968). On the production of synthetic oil, W. Birkenfeld, *Der synthetische Treibstoff 1933–1945* (Göttingen, 1964).

from 1936 onwards was accounted for by industries which were important to the fulfilment of Hitler's foreign policy.

The striking production increases in so many industrial sectors of the economy were not intended as a permanent solution of Germany's balance of payments problem. They had a specific military purpose. At least from September 1936 onwards economic policy was subordinated to achieving a state of rearmament which would enable Germany to solve her long-run economic

TABLE 2

German Production Increases in the Area of the Four Year Plan*
(Thousand tons)

Commodity	1936 output	1938 output	1942 output
Mineral oil	1,790	2,340	6,260
Aluminium	98	166	260
Buna rubber	0·7	5	96
Nitrogen	770	914	930
Explosive	18	45	300
Powder	20	26	150
Steel	19,216	22,656	20,480
Iron ore	2,255	3,360	4,137
Brown coal	161,382	194,985	245,918
Hard coal	158,400	186,186	166,059

* D. Petzina, op. cit., p. 182.

problems by conquest. In this respect it should be noted that the great increases in synthetic production and in the output of certain metals were still based on a raw material base which was far from satisfactory by the canons of Germany's own economic policy. One example will suffice. Aluminium production had been merely 19,000 tons in 1932. By 1939 it had been raised to 194,000 tons.[1] The raw material from which it was produced, bauxite, existed in only very limited quantities in Germany. The output of bauxite in 1929 was 7,000 tons, in 1939 it was 104,000 tons.[2] Germany therefore remained heavily dependent on Hungary and Yugoslavia for supply.

Although the nature of Germany's domestic economic policies changed the pattern of European trade, the progress towards autarchy within the frontiers of the Reich was essentially temporary. Once the German frontiers had been advanced the situation would change. Indeed, complete strategic security from the economic standpoint could never come purely within the existing frontiers. From this viewpoint the Führer's opinion, which General Thomas, Head of the War Economy and Armaments Office received from Todt, the Minister of Munitions, on 20 June 1941, is particularly interesting.

[1] Deutsches Institut für Wirtschaftsforschung, *Die deutsche industrie im Kriege 1939–45* (Berlin, 1954), p. 18.
[2] B. H. Klein, *Germany's Economic Preparations for War* (Cambridge, Mass., 1959), p. 46.

The course of the war shows [it ran] that we have gone too far in our striving for autarchy. It is impossible to produce everything that is lacking by synthetic processes or other methods. For example, it is impossible for us to develop our benzine position to a point where we can rely on it alone. All these efforts to attain autarchy demand a great supply of labour which cannot easily be provided. We must take another way and must seize all the necessary things that we do not have. The labour force necessary to do that will not be so great as that currently necessary for the construction of the alternative synthetic works. The aim must be to secure through conquest all the territories that are of special economic interest for us.[1]

But this unity of interest between the long-run policies of the National Socialist economic theorists and the economic policies pursued by Hitler to improve his strategic position was in reality very frail. On the surface the developments of the 1930s seemed to be moving towards a realization of Haushofer's theories. But underneath there was a fundamental contradiction between the ends of the *Grossraumwirtschaft* he envisaged in central Europe and the means by which Hitler intended to enlarge the boundaries of Germany. The tool by means of which Hitler hoped to implement his foreign policy was the Blitzkrieg. And this concept of the Blitzkrieg in itself militated against any long-term economic reorganization until it had achieved its end. The Blitzkrieg was merely the strategic device by which Hitler chose to achieve his New Order in Europe, a device which he imposed on a distrustful Army. But its economic and social implications were so powerful that the means, once adopted, came to dominate the ends to which the policy was ultimately directed.

The Blitzkrieg was a method of waging war without the total commitment of the economy and society to war. In a long war between mass-productive economies, a war such as the First World War had become, the economic, social, and political weaknesses of Germany would have become apparent. If Hitler were to achieve success he must avoid being drawn into a long struggle with more powerful opponents. The Blitzkrieg both on the merely military and also on the economic and social level was a way of avoiding such a struggle.[2]

The Blitzkrieg was administratively, politically, diplomatically, and economically suited to Germany's position. It required a higher quantity of ready armaments than any single possible opponent, but it did not require much basic investment in armaments manufacturing capacity. A temporary superiority in armaments allied to a speedy mobilization and a plan of campaign aimed at delivering a quick knock-out blow to the enemy meant a series of short wars involving little economic effort beyond what had come to be considered as peace-time normality. Only a limited part of the economy was organized for war-production. Within that limited sector great flexibility

[1] G. Thomas, *Grundlagen für eine Geschichte der deutschen Wehr- und Rüstungswirtschaft (1918–1943/45)* ed. W. Birkenfeld, Schriften des Bundesarchivs 14 (Boppard am Rhein, 1966).
[2] For a fuller discussion of the Blitzkrieg see A. S. Milward, *The German Economy at War* (London, 1965).

of response was needed. But outside that sector the civilian economy could function as though there were no war.

A war economy of this type made very few administrative demands beyond those of the normal management of the economy. Since the National Socialist administration was to a certain extent built on competing administrative bodies, since the very competition between these bodies led to constant disputes over spheres of control, and since the way in which the National Socialist administration had been superimposed on the preceding administration exaggerated these disputes, the Blitzkrieg was administratively a very convenient method of waging war. Indeed in such a war the German administration had a considerable advantage. The power and position of Hitler enabled all questions of priorities to be decided with dramatic simplicity. All 'Führer Commands' became top priority without further possibility of blurring the issue. Since the success of the Blitzkrieg depended so greatly on flexibility this was of great use.

The maintenance of levels of consumption at or around the pre-war levels meant that the regime did not have to depend on the common will and support of its citizens in the same way that, for example, the British government had to after the retreat from Dunkirk. At the same time the relatively low level of basic investment in armaments manufacturing capacity meant that Germany was not committed to any particular plan of military or diplomatic action. A war to be waged against Russia would, for example, require a very different plan of investment in armaments than one against Britain. Since there were limitations to the volume of basic investment necessary to the German plans Hitler's policy could be more flexible. Since Germany was ringed by a collection of economies all militarily weaker than her own, flexibility of decision was all the more important. The Blitzkrieg was thus an ideal instrument for Hitler's foreign policy.

Economically, the Blitzkrieg seemed to mask the fundamental weaknesses of Germany's economy until such time as by acquisition of territory she could again emerge as a great power. In a series of short wars delivered against relatively weaker enemies from positions of strength Germany could achieve success without the basic weaknesses of her raw material supply becoming too apparent. In spite of the direction of investment since 1933 and the economic penetration into the Balkans Germany was obliged to accumulate very large stockpiles of strategic materials. Of those raw materials essential in a war economy Germany was self-sufficient only in one, coal. On short-run calculations the German economy was very favourably endowed for war, on long-run calculations the picture was very different. In the economic sphere too, therefore, Hitler's choice of the Blitzkrieg was a rational calculation rather than an act of ignorant daring.

The consciousness of such a plan was never very deep or widespread among those who managed the German economy. Indeed little more management of the economy than in peace-time was required. Yet it was Hitler's most important contribution to modern strategy; it offered the best possibility of his achieving his war aims, and it led to one of the most astonishing periods of conquest in the history of the world. Until it failed in Russia in the winter of 1941/2 Hitler pursued the Blitzkrieg with the same logical tenacity that he showed in pursuing his diplomatic aims. For each separate campaign armaments production was violently readjusted from one set of needs to another, so violently that had there been a greater level of armaments production such a readjustment would have been impossible within the required time. After the defeat of France armaments production for the needs of the army was reduced in favour of more bombers, mines, and torpedoes.[1] Within ten weeks these priorities had been reversed in favour of more military equipment for the projected attack on Russia. On the eve of the invasion of Russia the ultimate logical decision, in the context of the Blitzkrieg economy, was taken to cut down the level of munitions production. Three weeks after the invasion this decision was further confirmed and a decision made to increase submarine production.[2]

The Blitzkrieg was designed to eliminate western opposition to Hitler's plans in the East. In the case of France it did so with startling success. But the consequence of this was that economic policy in conquered France was conceived solely in terms of the Blitzkrieg economy. No peace-treaty was possible until the war in the West was over. All long-run economic considerations of the French economy were subordinated to the Blitzkrieg against Britain and then to the Blitzkrieg against Russia. German economic policy towards France from the signing of the armistice was determined wholly within this framework. It was not merely that the New European Order, with whatever role France was destined to play in it, had to wait until the decision in the East before it could be revealed, but that the economic and strategic mechanism by which Hitler had chosen to reach that decision was fundamentally opposed to any long-term planning concerning a New Order.

If economic exploitation of occupied territory be possible up to certain limits, the acquisition of France should have greatly changed Germany's fundamental strategic position. In terms of the Blitzkrieg war economy such an acquisition was indeed thought of as an accretion of strength. Because the margin between success and failure in such a policy was so small, because the risks were so fearful, to opt for the Blitzkrieg had been to opt also for the economic exploitation of the defeated. But at the same time as the Blitzkrieg economy drove Germany towards a policy of exploitation in France, so did it

---

[1] FD 5447/45, OKW./Wi.Rü.Amt., 'An alle Wirtschaftsorganisationen', 14 July 1940.
[2] FD 5452/45, OKW./Wi.Rü.Amt., 'Richtlinien des Führers vom 14.7.41. für die künftige Kriegführung usw.', H. R. Trevor-Roper (ed.), *Hitler's War Directives 1939–1945* (London, 1964), p. 78.

impose strict limits on that policy. The French economy was not thought of as a whole but as a miscellaneous collection of industries and factors of production only certain of which were actually useful to the German economy. Germany's economic needs were all immediate, even the campaign against Russia was to last only five months. In this context certain weaknesses of supply in the German economy could be remedied by the exploitation of France, but the organization of France's total economic strength for German purposes seemed irrelevant.

Blitzkrieg economics therefore had a dual effect on the economics of occupied European territories. In the first place the very existence of the Blitzkrieg was an acknowledgement that Germany was not economically a strong enough power to launch a long war against Russia entirely from her own resources; exploitation of the conquered was a part of the Blitzkrieg strategy. In the second place the methods of economic thinking appropriate to the Blitzkrieg meant that the conflict between the liberal and fascist ideas of conquest did not fully develop before 1942.

The piecemeal view of the French economy implicit in Blitzkrieg economics comes out clearly in a study prepared by the Reichs Office for War-Economic Planning in May 1940.[1] The only attempts made at assessing the value of French production were in cases where Germany's own supply seemed precarious. The economic strength of France was measured by the same yardstick as that of Germany.

To look at the French economy in this narrow way was quite arbitrarily to limit its potential value to Germany, for many of the supply weaknesses of the German economy were also present in France. Of the three major raw materials covered by the Second Four Year Plan, oil, rubber, and iron ore, France was endowed with only one, iron ore. She was as deficient in crude oil and natural rubber as Germany. The rich reserves of iron ore to be found in France were counter-balanced by the fact that France was more dependent on coal imports than any other major economy in Europe. As for the rarer metal ores France was as dependent on overseas supply as Germany.

In 1939 France had only one very small natural crude-oil field, at Pechelbronn in Alsace. Its output was a mere 70,000 tons a year and it was nearing exhaustion. Diligent exploration carried out by the government since 1923 had discovered no further source of supply. A small additional quantity of oil was extracted from the shale beds of Autun and Saint-Hilaire, but the French shale oil industry resembled its European fellows in the poor quality of its equipment and the costliness of its processes. There were three very small experimental synthetic oil works on the northern coalfield. Most of the annual internal consumption, which averaged around 6,900,000 tons, was

---

[1] FD 1808/44, Reichsamt für wehrwirtschaftliche Planung, 'Beiträge zur Wehrwirtschaftsstruktur Frankreichs', May 1940.

therefore provided for by imports of crude oil refined in France. On average 45 per cent of the imports came from Iraq.

Nor could the acquisition of France cure German deficiencies in non-ferrous metals. Since 1936 France had imported about 20,000 tons of raw and refined copper a year, mainly from Chile. She was almost totally dependent on external sources of supply. No nickel ore was mined in France, and pure nickel was imported from New Caledonia. Zinc ore was imported from Mexico Spain, Yugoslavia, and Turkey. There was one very small wolfram mine still in operation at Leucamp in Cantal. If, therefore, there were any interruption

TABLE 3

Percentage of Raw Material Consumption in France covered by Domestic Production 1938–1939*

Coal	67	Leather	100
Mineral oils	1	Rubber	..
Pig Iron	100 (108)	Cocoa	..
Copper	..	Vegetable oils	4
Lead	5	Cotton	..
Zinc	1	Wool	8
Tin	..	Silk	12
Aluminium	100 (200)	Jute	..
Phosphates	6	Linseed	3

*M. Mitzakis, Principaux Aspects de l'évolution financière de la France 1936–44 (Paris 1944), p. 123.

of supply to France the output of those industries which particularly interested the German war effort would be endangered. Nor, in any of these instances, could Germany compensate for these shortages from her own supply. On 31 July 1940 Britain declared France to be enemy territory and from that moment, at the latest, acute problems of supply were inevitable.

Nevertheless, in spite of these difficulties, and within the narrow framework of the Blitzkrieg, there were three sectors of the French economy which seemed capable of providing a useful immediate supplement to the German war effort. These were the mining of iron ore and bauxite and the manufacture of aeroplanes. Here France seemed capable of immediately increasing the output of munitions and armaments available to Germany without any further burden falling on the German civilian population.

France was the world's second greatest producer of iron ore. In 1938 French output was 33,176,000 tons compared to an output within the frontiers of Greater Germany of 15,021,000 tons.[1] The output within the frontiers of the Old Reich was 12,351,000 tons.[2] There can be no doubt that the control of French iron-ore resources was regarded as an important benefit by Hitler. While discussion was beginning on the form of German policy in France, Hermann Rœchling, the Saar steel manufacturer, between 26 June and 1 July,

---

[1] CCDR., v., M.P. 1.   [2] J.-J. Jäger, op. cit., p. 140.

took under his control the iron works in the department of Meurthe-et-Moselle, the only area of Lorraine not actually annexed by Germany.[1]

France was equally favourably placed with regard to bauxite, the basic raw material of aluminium and, therefore, of aeroplane manufacture. A total output of 683,400 tons of bauxite in 1938 made France one of the world's most important sources of supply. The annual exports surplus was usually about 300,000 tons. Since 1934 French bauxite exports had been increasingly diverted away from Germany towards Britain, but even in 1938 84,100 tons of bauxite were exported from France to Germany.[2] Domestic bauxite ores provided only 10 per cent of total German consumption in 1939, in spite of a fifteenfold increase in production between 1929 and 1939.[3] German capital

TABLE 4

*Production of Aluminium in Selected Countries**

(thousand tons)

	1913	1929	1937	1938
Germany	1·0	33·3	127·5	165·0
U.S.A.	20·9	102·3	132·8	150·0
Canada	5·9	38·6	42·6	65·0
France	13·5	29·1	34·5	45·3
Russia	··	··	45·0	40·0
United Kingdom	10·0	8·1	19·4	23·2

*Statistisches Jahrbuch 1941/1942, p. 79.

penetration into Hungary and Yugoslavia gave some control over bauxite production in those countries, and, given the fairly restricted level of aeroplane output in Germany, the economy was in no sense dependent on French bauxite supply. But bauxite was one of the few raw materials consumed in large quantities by the armaments industry, where not only was Germany's endowment utterly inadequate, but France's endowment very rich.

Partly in consequence of her rich raw material resources France had early developed a large aluminium-making industry. In 1929 the French and German industries had been of comparable size. The output of aluminium in the inter-war period had been closely related to the expansion of the only really large market, the aeroplane industry. Because of this in the National Socialist period the aluminium industry grew powerfully to the point where it exceeded in output that of the United States. Although being outdistanced by her neighbour, France remained an important aluminium producer.

Although French aircraft production was fairly small in the inter-war period the standard of design remained high and the industry, the largest in

[1] E. Jäckel, *Frankreich in Hitlers Europa* (Stuttgart, 1967), p. 77. R. Aron, *Histoire de Vichy 1940–1944* (Paris, 1954), p. 256.
[2] FD 1808/44, op. cit.   [3] *Statistisches Jahrbuch 1941/1942*, p. 79.

the world at the close of the First World War, had considerable unutilized capacity. The rearmament programme begun on 1 April 1938 succeeded in expanding very rapidly. Total employment in the industry expanded from 35,000 in 1938 to 230,000 in May 1940.[1] The expansion was partly based on imports of machine-tools from the United States, certain of which Germany was precluded from purchasing by foreign exchange shortages and others by political pressures. The French aircraft industry therefore in spite of the vicissitudes of its recent history had a particular value as an adjunct to Germany's own war economy.

TABLE 5

Deliveries of War Planes in France*

1937	418
1938	425
1939	2,304

* M. J. Roos, *Quinze Ans d'aéronautique française, 1932–1947* (Paris, 1949). There was much political argument about the timing and success of rearmament in France and there are several figures for war-plane output. The *delivery* figures given here are less for 1937 and 1938 and greater for 1939 than the *output* figures given in A. Sauvy, *Histoire économique de la France entre les deux guerres* (Paris, 1965), ii. 438. The miscellaneous output figures given in CCDR., iv, A. 1. 44 are: 1938—425; 1 January to September 1939—1,253.

Even Göring, in general an advocate of restricting manufacturing activity in all occupied territories, was interested in using the French aircraft industry for German purposes. Before the invasion of France the Czech aircraft industry had been promised full order books by Göring in his capacity as Commander-in-Chief of the Air Force in return for its loyal co-operation. Between 130,000 and 150,000 workers were already employed in aircraft production in Bohemia and Moravia in March 1939, and the German Armed Forces were trying to bring pressure to bear to moderate the harsh treatment of civilians.[2] On 22 July 1940 Germany demanded permission for a party of industrialists to inspect French aluminium and aircraft factories even in the unoccupied zone.[3] This was the beginning of an attempt to impose a programme of aircraft manufacture which would be common to both occupied and unoccupied France.[4]

Had German exploitation been confined to these few areas of the French economy it might be thought at least to have been possible without any general economic controls or over-all plans. But even in these areas the total disruption of established lines of trade meant that bottlenecks in supply would soon appear. The French machine-tool industry, for example, had already proved insufficient to sustain the rearmament programme. The value of

[1] CCDR., iv., A. 1. 44.
[2] FD 5590/45, Der Generalluftzeugmeister, 'Auswirkung der politischen Verhältnisse im Protektorat auf die Rüstungsindustrie', December 1939.
[3] DFCAA., i. 75.   [4] Ibid. ii. 462.

French holdings of machine tools was estimated at only one-ninth of German or American holdings.[1] But the tightest of all bottlenecks would be that of industrial power. Certain to be cut off from most of her oil supply France would be dependent on hydroelectric power and coal. Since 1935 more electric current had been produced in France by hydroelectric power-stations than by coal-fired ones. But the distribution of hydroelectric power remained very local, largely confined to the hilly areas of south and central France. Of the consumption of 2,650,000,000 kilowatt hours in Paris in 1936 about 40 per cent was hydroelectric power. In the other main industrial centres the current consumed was mainly obtained from coal.

Looked at simply from the point of view of the economic exploitation of the conquered territory, nothing better illustrates the limitations placed on German policy by the concept of the Blitzkrieg than the question of French coal supply. On the eve of the war France was the greatest coal importer in the world. French coal imports accounted for about 20 per cent of the total world imports of coal, and 30 per cent of French annual domestic coal consumption. All the four countries which consumed greater quantities of coal than France supplied their own needs in entirety.[2] Two of them, Britain and Germany, were the greatest competitors on the French market. What could be supplied neither from Britain nor Germany came in much smaller quantities from Belgium, Poland, and Luxembourg. If France were to be denied British coal 40 per cent of her coal imports would be cut off unless a reconstructed European economy could make up the deficiency. If industrial production for German purposes were really to be effective in France, even in the extremely narrow sense implied by the Blitzkrieg economy, Germany had either to supply coal to France herself, or forcibly reconstruct the whole pattern of the European coal trade, or commit herself to a sufficient degree of over-all planning of the French economy to permit a basic re-allocation of coal supply within that economy. The Blitzkrieg meant that such comprehensive solutions could not be attempted. So long as it remained Hitler's instrument for achieving the New Order, no picture of the new Europe could emerge, and occupation policy was economic exploitation of a very limited kind.

But what would happen once the Blitzkrieg had achieved its ultimate aims? What place was reserved for France in the New Order when that order was finally created? There are few clues in this search. Immediately after the armistice Hitler seems to have considered a peace treaty with France as a not-too-distant event. After the British attack on the French fleet at Mers-el-Kébir, however, he came to the conclusion that a peace treaty which did not include Britain was worthless.[3] In this interval of time it is possible to find

---

[1] FD 1808/44, op. cit.

[2] International Labour Office, Studies and Reports, Series B, no. 31, *The World Coal-Mining Industry* (Geneva, 1938), i. 69.

[3] See the discussion by E. Jäckel, op. cit., pp. 46 ff.

certain indications as to the France of the future. The indications are nebulous and puzzling, but there is some circumstantial evidence as to what the peace treaty would have been like. That Alsace-Lorraine would have reverted to Germany is very obvious. Although there are no suggestions before the war that this was one of Hitler's war aims, as early as the first half of July 1940 Josef Bürckel, Gauleiter of Saarland-Palatinate, and Robert Wagner, Gauleiter of Baden, had already been chosen for their task of integrating the three French departments of Bas-Rhin, Haut-Rhin, and Moselle, into the Reich. On 15 July the customs barrier between France and Germany was readjusted to the frontier of 1871. Not until 2 August did Hitler issue a decree on the administration of this area, and even then the decree was not published.[1] Nor was the decree of 18 October published, although by that time Germany had weathered the storm of French protest at the Armistice Commission.

This public hesitancy was in sharp contrast to the measures actually used in Alsace. The intention was to Germanize the population within ten years.[2] The Reichsbank, whose custom it was to publish a regular series of reports on other European economies, published as early as 16 August 1940 a special report on the economy of Alsace-Lorraine.[3] Since the acquisition of Alsace-Lorraine from France was no small part of the total gain which Germany had from the French economy during the war, and since from August 1940 onwards all economic information about that area becomes inextricably tangled with German national statistics, it is interesting to consider exactly what Germany did annex.

The total population of the area was 1,900,000, of whom 22 per cent were employed in agriculture. Although the general level of yields was lower than in Germany the 1937 harvest was 167,000 tons of wheat, 154,000 tons of oats, 66,000 tons of barley, 41,000 tons of rye and 1,100,000 tons of potatoes. In addition, of course, the wine harvest was also very important. But of much greater value to Germany were the supplies of iron ore, coal, and phosphates, and the steel and textile industries. The development of the minette iron ore field from the 1880s onwards had seen a steady increase in iron-ore production until the First World War. After that the output had remained stagnant and then fallen. The sluggishness of domestic demand in the inter-war years in France meant that France had never utilized to its full capacity the modern steel industry which she had acquired from Germany in the Versailles Treaty. Nevertheless, the iron ore output in 1928 in the three departments annexed by Germany was 13,100,000 tons. In the Lorraine coalfield the story was different. The coalfield was the most modern, the most efficient, and the most productive in France, responsible for 14·5 per cent of total French output. In 1938 6,700,000 tons of coal were mined there and the trend of production was upwards. The Alsace phosphates were the only large source of French

[1] Ibid., p. 79.   [2] L. Gruchman, op. cit., p. 76.
[3] FD 232/45, Deutsche Reichsbank, Volkswirtschaftliche Abteilung, 16 August 1940.

supply in Europe. Their return to France in 1919 broke what had been a German natural monopoly. After a bitter commercial struggle the Alsatian producers had entered into a cartel with their German competitors in 1926. Their re-entry into the German Reich was to disrupt this long-standing agreement.

Hitler intended to leave no scope for doubt as to the ethnic qualifications of the inhabitants of Alsace-Lorraine. The expulsions from that territory into France began on 12 November. 'Mistakes are not always avoidable', said Hitler in 1941, 'but what difference does it make if it can be reported to me in ten years, "Danzig, Alsace and Lorraine are German . . ." '.[1] There were even projects mooted for the re-peopling of Alsace-Lorraine with a more satisfactory population.

. . . but we still have to get rid of a further quarter of a million of 'frenchified' Alsatians. Should we send them to France, or should we send them to colonize the Eastern territories? From the point of view of principle, this is of no great importance. It is just a question of opportunity. And to fill the void left by their departure presents no problem at all. Baden alone can provide innumerable peasant sons willing to settle in Alsace and Lorraine, particularly as there is little room for them to remain in their own homeland.[2]

As for the remainder of France, Hitler's intentions are much more doubtful. At the end of June 1940 Stuckart, State-Secretary in the Ministry of the Interior, was instructed to prepare a memorandum on the historical frontiers between France and Germany. The frontier which Hitler was considering was akin to the late medieval frontier including Flanders, the Ardennes, and the Argonne in Germany.[3] Ribbentrop, the Foreign Minister, appears to have received no copy of this memorandum. There is further evidence that Hitler thought in terms of a frontier 'from about the mouth of the Somme eastwards to the northern edge of the Paris region and along Champagne to the Argonne swinging thence southwards and going through Burgundy and westwards through Franche Comté to the Lake of Geneva'.[4] Hitler spoke later of Burgundy as historically German soil,[5] a fact not to be forgotten when the peace treaty was drawn up. Goebbels reported in his Diary after the same conversation: 'However the war may end, France will have to pay dearly, for she caused and started it. She is now being thrown back to her borders of A.D. 1500. This means that Burgundy will again become part of the Reich.'[6]

Against these dramatic claims must be set Hitler's statements when in more euphoric mood. 'The French were a decent people', he told Abetz in September

[1] H. Picker (ed.), *Hitlers Tischgespräche im Führerhauptquartier 1941–1942* (Stuttgart, 1963), 1 August 1941.
[2] Ibid., 12 May 1942; *Hitler's Secret Conversations*, p. 444. See also, IMT., xxvii. 31, 115–PS.   [3] E. Jäckel, op. cit., p. 47.
[4] IMT., vi. 472, RF–602, L. Gruchmann, op. cit., p. 77.
[5] *Hitlers Tischgespräche*, 25 April 1942.
[6] L. Lochner (ed.), *The Goebbels Diaries* (London, 1948), 26 April 1942.

1941, 'and consequently they were also to have a part in the "new Europe" and would undoubtedly experience great prosperity.'[1] At that time, filled with expectations of an empire in the East, Hitler spoke as though he envisaged taking only Alsace-Lorraine and retaining a military force in Pas-de-Calais.

Whatever Hitler's intentions he was National Socialist enough to hope for little from the French 'collaborators'. In so far as the fascist revolution affected France it produced the rival parties of Déat and Doriot, the *Rassemblement National Populaire* and the *Parti Populaire Français*. Hitler knew them for the unimportant groups they were and realized well enough that if France were incorporated in the New Order it would be by force and not by any internal change in that country. The existence of politicians of a more conservative frame of mind wishing to pursue a policy of Franco-German alignment to form a European bloc saved him from having to force Déat or Doriot on the French as he had had to do with Quisling in Norway. But about Laval, also, Hitler had no illusions. 'It is unfortunate', he said, 'that among Pétain's colleagues there is no one capable of taking the necessary clear decisions. Laval, for example, has nothing but a parliamentary past behind him.'[2] His historical sense told him that spiritually France could contribute nothing to the New Order, the fascist revolution was not indigenous there.

We must not place too great hopes on developments in France [Goebbels wrote]; I consider the French people sick and worm-eaten. No notable contributions towards the reconstruction of Europe can be expected from them. . . . Once again it has been proved that the Führer's policy towards France has been absolutely right.[3]

That policy was to force the best bargain out of French attempts to improve their position. For this reason it was wiser not to let them know what was in store for them.

Accordingly, once the war with Britain was seen to be continuing Hitler did not seek a long-term political settlement with France. After the failure of the Blitzkrieg on Russia, questions relating to any political settlement with France became even more remote. However, questions relating to an economic settlement became more pressing. The existence of the Blitzkrieg precluded any European solution until it was successful. The failure of the Blitzkrieg meant that the only solution possible was a European one. It is therefore the changes in German economic policy in France which are most revealing. In January 1942 Hitler was forced to abandon the military strategy by which he had hoped to win the war. From then onwards the German economy began to be directed towards full-scale war production. Between February 1942 and July 1944 German armaments production increased more than threefold. After January 1942 there could no longer be a sacrosanct civilian sector; German society was faced with the strain of total war. In this massive conversion of the

[1] DGFP., Series D, vol. xiii, no. 327.   [2] *Hitlers Tischgespräche*, 13 May 1942.
[3] *The Goebbels Diaries*, 2 April 1942.

economy it was inevitable that Germany should review her whole policy towards the economic exploitation of the conquered territories. The end of the Blitzkrieg meant the end of the self-imposed limitations on German economic policy abroad.

In fact the changes which subsequently took place in German economic policy have been almost entirely ignored. German economic policy in occupied Europe has been usually presented as a monolithic whole, generally to be criticized, occasionally to be defended, but, whether good or bad, essentially unchanging.

During the Second World War itself there was a spate of glib and nastily patriotic writing by Allied scholars attacking the German concept of the 'New Order'. It was easy to demonstrate, even from the limited information available at the time, that the 'New Order' was merely the old device of economic exploitation in more pretentious dress. The thought behind this exploitation was not understood, and there was a widespread acceptance of the unspoken assumption in German propaganda that the economic exploitation of the occupied territories was based on carefully worked out plans. Writers gave their time to showing that these were wicked plans. Thus their discussion of the New Order was no better as an explanation of what that Order was than the theoretical bombast put out by National Socialist hacks.[1]

War-time writers at least had one point in their favour. They persisted in seeing Hitler's occupation policies on a European rather than a national scale. Since 1945, where historians have considered the economic aspects of occupation at all they have considered them only in relation to single countries. The consequence of this has been a much more exact approach to historical truth. But at the same time the over-all concept of a 'New Order' has been left unexamined. Each single occupation must be seen in the light of Germany's ultimate political and economic plans for Europe.

From the small amount of research that has appeared it has become clear that whatever the principles of German occupation policy, and whatever the ultimate political intentions of the conquerors, they were not the same for all occupied countries. These differences of policy between one occupied area and another seem to have reflected three things. Firstly they reflected Hitler's ultimate intentions for Europe, secondly they reflected differences in the economic strength of the conquered economies, and thirdly they reflected the racial illogicalities of the conquerors. At the outset of the occupations a much harsher regime was devised for the eastern occupied territories. In the case of Poland this had a grim internal consistency.[2] In the case of Russia there was

[1] P. Einzig, *Hitler's New Order in Europe* (London, 1941); P. Einzig, 'Hitler's "New Order" in Theory and Practice', *Economic Journal*, li (1941); C. W. Guillebaud, 'Hitler's New Economic Order for Europe', ibid. l (1940); J. Kuczynski and M. Witt, *The Economics of Barbarism, Hitler's New Economic Order in Europe* (London, 1942); R. de Roussy de Sales (ed.), *My New Order* (New York, 1941).

[2] M. Broszat, *Nationalsozialistische Polenpolitik 1939–1945* (Stuttgart, 1961).

no consistency. The historical problems, the racial prejudices involved, and the extremely important economic issues in question were too complicated to be solved by the National Socialist Party and for that Party still to remain one. It was the economic plans for Russia that were surely the crux of the New Order and the key to economic policy elsewhere. Since Dallin's pioneer study, primarily concerned with political issues, these plans have remained unexplored.[1]

Looked at in this light German economic policy in western occupied Europe may appear of less importance. But it has appeared so only because the changes which took place there after spring 1942 have been ignored. The small number of studies appearing immediately at the end of the war could not, for obvious reasons, be based on extensive research and tended to give an over-all view of certain basic principles seeming to emerge from German policy.[2] The publications of the former *Institut für Besatzungsfragen* at Tübingen considered certain legal or economic aspects of the occupation of various states with the intention of examining the basic principles of policy involved. Unfortunately these principles were often considered in a very legalistic way and some of the volumes were designed partly for the purpose of attacking the international legal principles underlying the post-war Allied occupation of Germany.[3]

German economic policy in occupied France can only be understood as a part of the feverish search for a solution to the problem of future European organization. The National Socialist Party was a revolutionary Party, and its revolution was to extend to a reconstruction of the whole European economy. The European economy would have to be created anew on anti-liberal principles. One part of this reconstruction was the total rejection of the liberal idea of conquest. Since that idea, in the event, proved to have some elements of truth in it, the demonstration that it was false proved more difficult than the National Socialists had at first imagined. On one level, therefore, since the liberal idea of conquest had to be wrong for the new anti-liberal Europe to be created, German policy in France was a search for a solution to this very old economic problem.

On another level German policy was an attempt to carry the National Socialist economic revolution beyond the mere refutation of earlier ideas. To ignore the changes in German economic policies in France is to ignore the nature of the National Socialist government itself, and thus to avoid the whole problem. For it is only in comprehending the failure of the National Socialists to create a satisfactory alternative economic programme to liberal capitalism

[1] A. Dallin, *German Rule in Russia, 1941–45* (London and New York, 1957).
[2] See, for example, F. Baudhuin, *L'Économie belge sous l'occupation, 1940–44* (Brussels, 1945); L. Baudin, *Esquisse de l'économie française sous l'occupation allemande* (Paris, 1945).
[3] G. Moritz, *Die deutsche Besatzungsgerichtsbarkeit während des zweiten Weltkrieges* (Tübingen, 1954); id., *Die Gerichtsbarkeit in den besetzten Gebieten. Historische Entwicklung und völkerrechtliche Würdigung* (Tübingen, 1959).

that it is possible to understand why their policies of economic exploitation met with so much less success than they had hoped for.

Germany derived sufficient economic advantage from the occupation of France to demonstrate the superficiality of the liberal view of exploitation, but not sufficient to justify the National Socialist alternative. Even in Germany National Socialist economic policy was a compromise between barely reconcilable economic principles. The impact of the fascist revolution on other countries apart from Italy was less than in Germany. The New Economic Order could therefore only be imposed by force, and its principles scarcely formed a coherent enough body of doctrine to solve so intractable a problem as the exploitation of an industrialized economy. Consequently the failure of German economic policy in France reveals much about the failure of the fascist revolution in Germany and in Europe. But this becomes clear only when it is accepted that German policies of economic exploitation did change, and when those changes are examined.

III

THE MACHINERY OF EXPLOITATION

ALL Germany's economic plans for France depended on the evolution of German strategy during the war. Since that strategy moved through a time of uncertainty after it had become clear that the invasion of France was a complete success, there was a long delay before German intentions were revealed to the French government. The invasion of France began on 10 May. On 7 June Hitler ordered war production to proceed on the assumption that France was completely defeated.[1] Not until 8 August did Germany present the French government with a definite proposal about the future economic relations of the two countries. This proposal was accepted by the French government on 14 November when the Franco-German clearing agreements were signed.

The interval of time before the German proposals is too great to be explained only in terms of strategic considerations, important though these considerations were. Stuckart had been instructed to prepare his memorandum on a new Franco-German frontier at the end of June. The frontier would resemble the late medieval frontier, both Flanders and eastern Burgundy being included in Germany. On 20 June the General Staff of the Army began to prepare on Hitler's orders a barrier along the general lines of this frontier beyond which refugees would not be allowed to return, the *Nordostlinie*.[2] They had no doubts as to the ultimate implications of this barrier. Pas-de-Calais and Nord were to remain under German military control to further the prosecution of the war against Britain and consequently were controlled by the High Command in Brussels and not from Paris.[3] Those landholdings on the German side of the *Nordostlinie* which had been deserted began to pass into the hands of a German holding company, Ostland G.m.b.H., which had undertaken similar activities in Poland. But these apparent preparations for a peace treaty were soon abandoned, although a map of a frontier designed on these lines found its way into the records of the German Armistice Commission.[4]

The reasons for their abandonment were Hitler's conviction that no peace treaty with France made sense so long as the war with Britain continued. The British attack on the French fleet at Mers-el-Kébir on 3 July, however limited its success as a naval operation, had a direct strategic impact on the war. It

---

[1] FD 5447/45, Wi.Rü.Amt., 'Führerbefehle'.
[2] H. Böhme, *Der deutsch-französische Waffenstillstand im Zweiten Weltkrieg, Entstehung und Grundlagen des Waffenstillstandes von 1940* (Stuttgart, 1966), pp. 260–1.
[3] E. Jäckel, op. cit., p. 46; E. Kordt, *Nicht aus den Akten* (Stuttgart, 1950), p. 393.
[4] E. Jäckel, op. cit., p. 47.

induced Hitler to content himself with the military armistice in France. The possibility of a Franco-German alliance against Britain was extremely remote and did not long occupy Hitler. Convinced by the mildness of the French reaction to the British attack he had decided as early as 5 July that any softening of the terms to France would be an error. This possibility eliminated, however, there remained other strategic doubts. During June and July Hitler had still not rejected the possibility of an invasion of Russia in the autumn. Not until the middle of August did he decide that a large-scale amphibious operation against Britain was out of the question. Only on 17 September was the idea of any invasion of Britain postponed indefinitely.[1]

In spite of these uncertainties the delay in formalizing the economic relations between France and Germany beyond the stipulations of the Armistice Agreement was mainly attributable to disputes within the German government itself as to the best economic policy to adopt in France. The published Foreign Office documents have revealed a dispute between the Foreign Office and the Four Year Plan Office, leading to an acrimonious exchange between Göring, the Head of the Four Year Plan Office, and Ribbentrop as to the precise responsibility for economic affairs in the peace treaty. The dispute was, however, a much wider one than a quarrel about spheres of authority. It was a dispute as to France's role in the New Order and the very nature of that New Order.

The attitude of Göring himself was that France was a conquered country, the main advantages to be derived from it booty and loot. The Reichs Ministry of Economics thought in terms of the creation of an agricultural state with some luxury industries.[2] Both ministries agreed that France should be stripped of her industrial capacity. The Foreign Office, however, took the line that such actions would permanently alienate France from Germany. If France were to be incorporated in the New Order and that New Order to be a lasting affair some less crude policy had to be adopted. The most supple was to incorporate France into the German economic system by a clearing treaty in the same way that the Balkan countries had been incorporated in the previous decade. The military victory gave Germany the opportunity to force through a much more favourable treaty than any previously concluded. This view was supported in the Ministry of Economics. The policy of guaranteeing supply from France to Germany offered a new range of possibilities in the reconstruction of Europe; it might be possible to incorporate a 'European Clause' in a future peace treaty and drive American influence out of French industry.[3] It was this policy which was established by the agreement of 14 November.

The initial period of occupation, during which Germany freely seized booty, was not an interval until better control had been established by the administration. Until the beginning of August the brutal and anachronistic policies

---

[1] R. Wheatley, *Operation Sea-Lion* (Oxford, 1958), pp. 33 ff.
[2] H. Böhme, op. cit., p. 276.   [3] Ibid., p. 277.

favoured by Göring had not been ousted in favour of the Foreign Office's own policy. And it is to these policy disputes in the German government that the delay in presenting the clearing proposals to the French government must primarily be attributed.

The adoption of the Franco-German clearing treaty, although extremely unwilling on the part of the French government, set the seal on Germany's success in the west and on the 'National Revolution' in France, and determined France's role in the New Order. Since 1933 the French and German economies had moved further apart. The German victory and the National Revolution in France reversed this trend. The defeat of France and the survival of Britain meant that economically France had to become a European power, within the German orbit. The Vichy governments were not wholly out of sympathy with the economic outlook of their conquerors, and they saw France's incorporation into the New Order as an acceptance of 'reality'. The way in which Germany chose to undertake the economic exploitation of France completed this reversal of the trend of the 1930s; France was drawn wholly into the *Grossraumwirtschaft*. The doubts which delayed the institution of German policy in France were about the ultimate shape and scope of the *Grossraumwirtschaft*.

The memorandum of 30 May by Carl Clodius, deputy-director of the Economic Policy Department, shows how the Foreign Office intended to maintain the continuity of pre-war policy.[1] The Netherlands, Belgium, and Luxembourg would fall into the greater German economic sphere irrespective of whether they remained as independent states, and a customs and currency union might be forced on them. The treatment of France depended on how far Hitler intended to annex territories in northern France. If these annexations were very extensive Franco-German trade might become quite unimportant. In any case outside the frontiers of France it was essential that Germany brook no commercial rival. The defeat of France also provided Germany with an opportunity to continue the reconstruction of Europe by taking over French capital holdings in south-eastern Europe. French capital was especially important in Yugoslavian copper mines, in the Romanian oil industry, and among the raw materials of peculiar strategic interest to Germany. The policy of replacement of French by German capital in these spheres laid down in Clodius's memorandum was rigorously followed. In only one other case did the Foreign Office show any desire for capital penetration. Before the invasion, German news agencies had been very dependent on Britain and France and the opportunity now presented itself of breaking this dependence. This line of policy also was to be diligently pursued in the future.

One reason for the particular line of policy chosen by the Four Year Plan Office was that its chief, Göring, had a double interest, since he was also Commander-in-Chief of the Air Force. On 20 June he told the Foreign Office

[1] DGFP., ix, no. 354.

that he alone would be responsible for the economic aspects of the peace.[1] Two days later he conferred upon Funk, the Minister of Economics, powers to organize the Greater European economic area.[2] The Foreign Office riposted on 26 June, claiming they already had the preparation of the peace treaty well in hand.[3] But Göring was not intending to abandon the struggle. On 2 July he expressly reserved to himself the preparation of the economic aspects of any peace treaty.[4]

On 27 June General Carl-Heinrich von Stülpnagel, the head of the German Armistice Delegation, found out from the Foreign Office that there would also be an Armistice Delegation for economic affairs, which would be not only separate but independent.[5] The head of this separate body, Hans Hemmen, was chosen in early July. Hemmen was one of the most experienced of the Foreign Office's commercial negotiators. He had been moved to the commercial policy department of the Foreign Office because of his unpopularity with the Party while serving in Buenos Aires and had, indeed, between 1933 and 1934, been in such disfavour as to have no responsibility of any kind. Since then he had played a prominent part in several important commercial negotiations.[6] A man of infinite patience, he was to become extremely unpopular with the French delegates because of the narrowness with which he approached every question. The strength of the position from which he was negotiating tempted him too often into threats, but for the most part his demeanour was that of the faithful civil servant. He negotiated strictly within the terms of his brief.

As to the man's wider aspirations and personal views they remain unclear. He had always been a fervent opponent of 'bolshevism' and his fears for the danger of revolution in France in 1943 were probably quite genuine. On 27 August in his interview with Bouthillier, the French Finance Minister, the negotiator's mask may have slipped. 'He said that Europe can only be organized around important countries. These countries are three in number. He set aside Russia, of which, he said, neither France nor Germany knew anything. These three countries are: Germany, Italy, and France, who will pursue a continental policy.'[7]

The form of the Economic Delegation was decided on 4 July in a conference between the Foreign Office and the Four Year Plan Office. The conference discussed the general problem of the economic exploitation of France. No record of its discussions has yet come to light and their result can only be deduced from the terms of reference of the Economic Delegation.

[1] DGFP., x, no. 82.

[2] Ibid., no. 142, no. 103.

[3] DGFP., Series D, x, no. 23.

[4] Ibid., no. 82.

[5] H. Böhme, op. cit., p. 192.

[6] In October 1913 he had been a King Edward scholar at University College, London, and the London School of Economics, and subsequently had been interned in Britain for three and a half years.

[7] DFCAA., i. 185.

The Foreign Office view seems to have been substantially accepted, although Hemmen's appointment had to be by joint decree of the two ministries. It is clear from subsequent events that Göring did not regard this decision as being a final decision on economic policy towards France. Hemmen himself wrote in 1944 that 'the starting point of the activity of the Economic Delegation to the Armistice Commission was . . . the fact that the conduct of the war against Britain, and later against the United States and the Soviet Union, imposed on the Reich the imperious necessity of utilizing as far as possible the economic potential of France for the final victory of Germany'.[1] Asked by the Foreign Office in February 1942 if his Delegation were still useful, Hemmen concluded a long list of its activities by stating 'all these tasks far exceed the bounds of regulation of the armistice and are a part, beyond all possibility of argument, of the responsibility for commercial policy of the Foreign Ministry. Their objective is the total economic and financial integration of France into the European area.'[2]

When Hemmen was summoned from Switzerland by Ribbentrop to be briefed he was cautioned against all future attempts by Göring to influence the policy of the Delegation. The Delegation was only to receive orders from the Foreign Office and Hemmen was to be held personally responsible for ensuring that none of its members would report directly to their own ministries.[3] The circumstances in which the Delegation had been composed had led to the virtual certainty that Göring would try to influence or even control its members. Indeed, on the very day on which he was briefed Hemmen was summoned to the Four Year Plan Office to receive personally his signed appointment from Göring.[3] He was advised to reply that he had already received his commission from the Foreign Office.

Where the weak situation of the Vichy government could be used to apply greater pressure on France Hemmen would do so. The concessions to be obtained should go well beyond those envisaged in the Armistice Agreement.

Besides discussing the implementation of the economic agreements of the Armistice Agreement, the Economic Delegation will also conduct free negotiations with the French government on economic matters. Its aim in so doing must be so far as possible to place the economic potential of the unoccupied territory in the service of the German war economy.[4]

Since the conference of 4 July had been the first step in rejecting a policy of looting, these aims could only be achieved over time and by free negotiation. It had been decided

that industry should be only indirectly mobilized for the conduct of the war; therefore not directly for the production of war material, but solely for the production of

[1] P. Arnoult, *Les Finances de la France et l'occupation allemande 1940/44* (Paris, 1951), p. 6.
[2] Hemmen Papers, Waffenstillstandsdelegation, Telegram, 7 February 1942.
[3] Hemmen Papers, 'Meine Ernennung zum Vorsitzenden der Waffenstillstands-Delegation für Wirtschaft'.　　　　[4] DGFP., Series D, x, no. 116.

articles that are urgently needed in Germany. . . . Raw materials and economic goods in unoccupied territory which are important for the German war economy can, therefore, be utilized only through the channels of free exchange.[1]

Not only did the armistice impose constraints on the degree to which Germany could exploit France but it implied also that the form of exploitation would be production for limited German purposes in France. The terms under which such production would take place would obviously always be brought back to the terms of the armistice itself, unless every last scrap of sovereignty was to be torn from the French government.

Göring was thinking in terms of production for German purposes only where it was pre-eminently important; the greater value he supposed would be in pillage and capital penetration of French industry by German interests. His letter of 2 August to the Commander-in-Chief in Belgium and the Reich Commissars for Norway and the Netherlands proclaimed that, 'one goal of German economic policy is the increase of German influence in foreign enterprise'.[2] It was necessary while the war was still in progress to achieve this by every means. On 17 August Göring indicated to Funk that German policy should be one of capital control over all key firms in the occupied areas.[3] Even when he had been brought to sanction the policy of production for German purposes in France he still insisted that it must not impede the taking of booty except where absolutely necessary. Where machine tools would not be needed for German purposes in France they should be transported to Germany.[4]

This dispute about the form of the German economic exploitation of France was played out against a highly conventional back-drop. The armistice itself was based closely on that of 1918. Its terms, although vague, were like those of previous agreements of this kind. The earliest measures of the German administration in France could fairly be described in the same way. It took some time for the Foreign Office to assert its own policy in practice. Into the conventional framework of a military occupation, a 'belligerent occupation' in the language of nineteenth-century international lawyers, was gradually inserted a different kind of policy, one which was aimed quite openly at using the Armistice settlement as a deliberate threat to obtain satisfaction for German economic needs. This policy had to jostle for possession of the stage with the more sweeping and more primitive measures put forward by the Head of the Four Year Plan.

On the eve of the invasion of Belgium General von Brauchitsch had been ordered to construct a military administration for the invaded territories.[5]

---

[1] DGFP., Series D, x, no. 106.   [2] DGFP., x, no. 278.
[3] O. Ulshöfer, *Einflussnahme auf Wirtschaftsunternehmungen in den besetzten nord-, west- und südosteuropäischen Ländern während des zweiten Weltkrieges insbesondere der Erwerb von Beteiligungen (Verflechtung)* (Tübingen, 1958), p. 41.
[4] BA., R. 7 VIII 207, 'Auszugsweise Abschrift aus einem Wirtschaftsbericht über die Lage im Bereich des Chefs der Militärverwaltung in Frankreich', September 1940.
[5] DGFP., Series D, ix, no. 213.

Hitler struck out of the decree of 9 May a clause restraining the invading forces from plundering the country.[1] The administration was to depend entirely on the Army. Nothing in these orders foreshadowed the ultimate arrangements for the occupation of France, except, perhaps, the heavy emphasis on economic affairs in the construction of the administration. Hans Posse, a State-Secretary in the Ministry of Economics, filled the post of Commissar-General to the Quartermaster-General.[2] Underneath Posse was a plethora of specialists for almost every aspect of economic existence.[3] On 9 June Posse became head of the Administrative Branch when General Blaskowitz became for a brief period head of the military administration in France.[4] The purpose of the economic administration, however, remained more or less confined to sustaining the vital apparatus of the conquered territory and to supplying the German armies there.

General Halder, Chief of the Army General Staff, was not satisfied that arrangements of this kind would be entirely satisfactory once the fighting was over. Furthermore, he wanted the civil administration of the country, for strategic reasons concerning the war with Britain, to be subordinated entirely to the Commander-in-Chief in France.[5] Nor was he satisfied with the personality of Posse. On 26 June Jonathan Schmid, a Minister of State, an elderly man no longer in the best of health, arrived in France to take over the post of Head of the Civil Administration.[6] He was to occupy that position until June 1942.

The Armistice itself was a military act and embodied strategic considerations above all else. The military administration was based on this military act and the text of the Armistice took on the nature of a written constitution within the terms of which the Army governed the area which they had militarily occupied at the moment when the Armistice was signed on 21 June.[7] The speed with which events took place after Pétain sought armistice terms left the Germans quite unprepared. The Armistice was sought and signed in four days. In the circumstances there was little to do but dig out previous armistice treaties and see how well they could be adapted to the present situation. The night before the meeting in the specially prepared clearing of Rethondes, German interpreters, visited by Hitler and Keitel, worked by candlelight in a church to prepare the French translation of the terms.[8]

---

[1] Böhme, op. cit., p. 156.
[2] Wirtschaftsbevollmächtigter beim Generalquartiermeister.
[3] E. Jäckel, op. cit., p. 59. See also W. Herdeg, *Grundzüge der deutschen Besatzungsverwaltung in den west- und nordeuropäischen Ländern während des zweiten Weltkrieges* (Tübingen, 1953), pp. 3 ff.
[4] E. Jäckel, op. cit., p. 61.
[5] F. Halder, *Kriegstagebuch. Tägliche Aufzeichnungen des Chefs des Generalstabes des Heeres 1939/42* (Stuttgart, 1962–4), i. 369.
[6] E. Jäckel, op. cit., p. 63.
[7] The text of the Armistice is in DFCAA., i. 1–8.
[8] P. Schmidt, *Statist auf diplomatischer Bühne 1923–45* (Bonn, 1949), pp. 484–91.

There were twenty-four clauses in the agreement covering the usual matter of armistice treaties, terms of the cease-fire, of the surrender of French troops and armaments, of the level of armament to be subsequently permitted in France and so on. The wider economic aspects were not covered other than in the most general terms. The Foreign Ministry chose to use the Armistice Commission meetings as a way of bringing pressure to bear on the Vichy government.

Hemmen's arrival at Wiesbaden was therefore the start of a long battle by the German negotiators to break down the defences which the French had been allowed to retain. Every advantage was on the side of the Germans. Not merely was their initial position so much the stronger but the meetings were on their ground. Relentless espionage meant that French moves in the negotiations were often known in advance. On some occasions the German delegates had actually to feign surprise.[1] Although therefore the existence of the Armistice Agreement prevented any total exploitation of the French economy from the outset, its imprecise wording, and, above all, what it left unsaid, meant that in so far as it was a defensive position behind which the French could shelter it was in the long run an untenable one. The imprecise nature of the clause on occupation costs might stand as an example. In the event it proved not too difficult for Germany to secure swingeing costs, far above the real costs of the occupation.

The demarcation line between the occupied and unoccupied zones of France took little or no account of the economic divisions of the country. Its only deference to such matters was that it was adjusted to include Le Creusot in the occupied zone, to comply with Hitler's orders that Le Creusot must be taken before the Armistice. Otherwise its original purpose was to mark clearly that area of France within which the German army operated. It was an almost impenetrable frontier at the outset of the occupation. All official correspondence had to be presented unsealed at Moulins on the frontier. The censors were unable to deal with more than three hundred letters in one day. French Ministers were allowed barely any telephone communication with the occupied zone.[2] Beyond this impassable frontier there were other divisions. The two most northerly departments, after Paris itself, the most industrialized areas of the country and the main source of French coal production, Nord and Pas-de-Calais, were administered by the Commander-in-Chief in Brussels. This division had a clear military basis in view of Hitler's concern with an immediate invasion of Britain. It had also very threatening political undertones. Three departments, Bas-Rhin, Haut-Rhin, and Moselle were discreetly incorporated into the Reich itself. Italy took for herself a small zone embracing Mentone. Finally, Germany imposed the *Nordostlinie* separating the departments of Doubs, Haute-Saône, Meurthe-et-Moselle, Vosges, Ardennes, Meuse, and substantial parts of Jura, Haute-Marne, Aisne, and Somme from

---

[1] H. Böhme, op. cit., pp. 233–5.   [2] R. Aron, op. cit., p. 258.

the rest of the occupied zone. Initially the movement of persons across that line was almost totally prohibited, but economically these restrictions were to prove unworkable. From spring 1941 certain categories of refugees necessary to revive the economic life of the area were allowed back. The burden of guarding so long a barrier line meant that it was less and less effectively policed, and

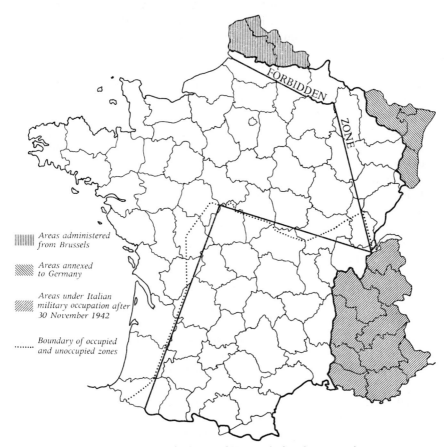

MAP I. Administrative areas of France during the occupation.

many more refugees returned to their homes illegally. In December 1941, when the need for more troops in Russia was acute, policing of the barrier stopped almost entirely.[1]

The strategic element in these frontiers emphasized the degree to which France was controlled by the German armed forces. As soon as hostilities in the Netherlands were over, the control of that country was transferred to a civil administration controlled by a Reichs Commissar. Belgium and France

[1] H. Böhme, op. cit., p. 261.

remained as a fief of the German army, although in July 1944 Belgium was finally subordinated to a Gauleiter. For the duration of the war, however, the German civil administration in France was constitutionally dependent on the Commander-in-Chief of the German army of occupation.

Directly under the Commander-in-Chief stood General Alfred Streccius, Head of the Military Administration. He himself was a taoist, the result of a long residence in China. Below Streccius the administration was sharply divided into its military and civil sections, the *Kommandostab* and the *Verwaltungsstab*, Jonathan Schmid being the head of the latter. The civil branch of the administration had three divisions, the central branch, the administrative branch, and the economic branch. The administrative branch was responsible for roads, transport, and postal services, but otherwise all economic affairs were the province of the third of these branches. That in its turn had ten sections for the various aspects of economic administration.[1] The head of the administrative branch was Werner Best, later to become Reichs Commissar in Denmark. When young he had been imprisoned by the French during the occupation of the Rhineland.[2] The head of the economic branch was Elmar Michel, an official of the Reichs Ministry of Economics. When Schmid eventually retired pleading ill-health Michel succeeded him in office. The administration based on the Hotel Majestic in Paris had about 1,100 officials, of whom the majority had previously been in administrative positions in Germany, although a significant minority, especially in the economic branch of the *Verwaltungsstab*, came from business firms in Germany and maintained their links with those firms.

Between the invasion and the armistice the task of introducing a German administration proceeded spasmodically. The invading forces were supplied with occupation currency, the *Reichskreditkassenschein*, the same currency that had been used in the earlier invasions of Belgium and Holland. The careful anti-inflationary policies pursued in Germany meant that extreme precautions were necessary to prevent German economic policy from being ruined by the use of Reichsmarks in occupied countries. The initial circumstances of any military occupation will tend to be inflationary. Small businessmen have the opportunity to operate in monopoly markets of great scarcity; supply and demand are both inelastic. Therefore the flow of currencies between the Reich and occupied France had to be carefully checked; there had to be no competition between the occupation currency and Reichsmarks for goods in Germany. If the issuing of the *Reichskreditkassenschein* was to be inflationary the burden of that inflation had to fall on the occupied territory alone. Therefore the occupation currency could neither be spent in Germany, nor exchanged against the Reichsmark. The Bank of France had to accept

---

[1] W. Herdeg, op. cit., *passim*, gives an account of the various small changes that took place.

[2] E. Jäckel, op. cit., p. 64.

the occupation notes, redeem them in francs, and charge them as costs of occupation to the French government.

The central *Reichskreditkassen* was founded on 3 May to manage the occupation currencies.[1] In principle the occupation notes were to enable the German armed forces to sustain themselves off the land until some formal agreement had been reached on the costs of the occupation. Once this agreement had been obtained the notes were used for special purposes.[2] Nevertheless the occupation notes continued to circulate after this in too great a volume for German peace of mind. They were extensively used in German black-market purchases, and, although they were gradually withdrawn from circulation after 1 December 1943, they still continued to circulate.

The responsibility for this must be placed firmly on the extremely arbitrary exchange rates established between the occupation currencies and the national currencies of the occupied territories. No genuine equilibrium exchange rates existed before the war between Germany and other countries. The rates used in trade were those specified in the relevant clearing agreements. In general such rates were about 25 per cent below the official exchange quotations. The Foreign Office intention was to pursue both its long-run economic aims and to satisfy Germany's immediate demands for strategic materials by continuing to impose special clearing-treaty exchange rates on the conquered territories. The opportunity to overvalue the Reichsmark in terms of the currency of the occupied territory was overwhelmingly present. In the case of France the exchange rate of the occupation currency against the franc was proclaimed at 20 francs to the *Reichskreditkassenschein* on 20 May. This was the exchange rate fixed later between the franc and the mark when the agreement on occupation costs had been signed. This represented an overvaluation of the German currency by over 50 per cent assuming the previous official rate to have been the dollar exchange rate of both currencies in June 1940. Using the exchange rate of both currencies against the pound sterling in 1939 as a basis, the overvaluation appears as high as 63 per cent. That is to say that as near as can be established the previous equilibrium exchange rate of the franc against the Reichsmark had been between 12·30 and 12·95 to 1.

But the extent of the overvaluation of German currency was not at all constant in the various occupied territories. In Croatia the mark was over-valued by 24 per cent, in the General Government of Poland by 33 per cent, in the Netherlands by 42 per cent, in Belgium by 50 per cent.[3] Only in Greece was the overvaluation greater than in France, and there, eventually, organized trade on the basis of the official rate became more or less impossible. The over-supply of occupation currency in the other Balkan countries

[1] H. Kasten, *Die Neuordnung der Währung in den besetzten Gebieten und die Tätigkeit der RKK während des Krieges 1939/40* (Berlin, 1941), pp. 129–37.

[2] A. Munz, *Die Auswirkung der deutschen Besetzung auf Währung und Finanzen Frankreichs* (Tübingen, 1957), p. 20.

[3] 'The Value of the Reichsmark', *Statist*, 10 May 1941.

meant that there was a drain of notes from there to France where their purchasing power was noticeably higher.[1]

Apart from establishing an occupation currency the military administration forced the French local administration to submit to its decrees according to the widely established conventions. The behaviour of the army suggested that nothing was involved other than a formal 'belligerent occupation', the measures taken were quite correct by military standards.[2] For the local commanders one of the principal economic tasks was to get in the harvest.[3] Even the price and wage freeze decreed on 20 June had its precedents. The French government had decreed a price stop to last for three months after 9 April.[4] It was in any case, although bolstered later by a big administrative effort, an optimistic decree from the outset. In a military occupation market conditions can scarcely be sufficiently stable or sufficiently known to permit permanent stabilization of prices. The price control introduced in France was based on that introduced in Germany in 1936; prices were not to rise above those existing during a previous base period.

Before the arrival of the German Economic Delegation at Wiesbaden, a number of measures in respect of French economic life had thus already been taken. The creation of the Economic Delegation meant that the control of French economic affairs no longer rested solely with the German administration in France. But the likelihood of any serious disagreement was not very high. The High Command in France favoured the Foreign Office attitude to the French economy and joined with them in their resistance to Göring's more brutal attitude. Whatever kept the civil population quiet and made them easier to govern while giving the armed forces a certain limited access to French industry was best. Göring's policy was certain to alienate the population completely. This basic agreement on policy was sufficient, for the Economic Delegation's work only touched on the occupied zone very indirectly, while the High Command in France had no power outside the occupied zone. On 7 July Ribbentrop told General Otto von Stülpnagel, the Commander-in-Chief in Paris, that Hemmen would be directly responsible to the Foreign Office.[5]

At his first meeting with the French, Hemmen made it clear that the Economic Delegation was independent of the military delegates to the Armistice Commission.[6] The corresponding French delegation did not have the same independence. The French delegates drew the impression from the first meeting that Germany was as much concerned with supply from the unoccupied as from the occupied zone. They drew the lesson that 'the German government

---

[1] A. Munz, op. cit., p. 21.
[2] M. Baudot, *L'opinion publique sous l'Occupation, l'exemple d'un département français (1939–1945)* (Paris, 1960), pp. 14 ff.
[3] Hoover Institute, Militärverwaltung B, Angers, 'Entbringung der Ernte', 17 July 1940.
[4] Y. Bouthillier, *Le Drame de Vichy* (Paris, 1950), ii. 445.
[5] H. Böhme, op. cit., p. 193.   [6] DFCAA., i. 47.

in drawing the demarcation line had not the slightest intention to cut in two French economic life'.[1] The aim of the German government was to restore economic activity in both parts of France. If the French government would agree to the establishment of certain controlling bodies in the non-occupied area the harshness with which the demarcation line was operated could soon be reduced.[1] The initial purpose of the Foreign Office was to extend the control over the French economy beyond what had been conceded in the armistice by using the demarcation line as a lever in the negotiations at Wiesbaden. Such a policy was useful whatever the immediate strategic intention, but the pressure on the French negotiators was not urgent.

On 9 July Ribbentrop personally defended the Foreign Office attitude in a letter to Göring. The Foreign Office could not help but be concerned in economic planning affecting foreign countries, especially countries which 'while retaining their own sovereignty, belong to the greater German economic area'.[2] If the future European economy were to serve the general aims of Germany's foreign policy its construction must be left in the hands of the Commercial Policy Department, wherein the Four Year Plan, as all other interested departments, was represented:

This is the only way in which in the interest of the economic negotiations themselves the possibilities of foreign policy to exert influence and pressure can be employed at the proper time and in the proper way—in the negotiations with Rumania of late, for example, this always played a decisive role. And, conversely, this is the only way to guarantee that the capacity of the future greater German economic sphere can be made to serve our general foreign policy aims.[2]

On 11 July the Four Year Plan Office reaffirmed its position that Hemmen's appointment was conditional on his receiving their instructions also. The Foreign Office reply admitted Göring's right to give orders about economic policy in the occupied zone to the administration there. But the Economic Delegation was no part of the machinery for administering the occupied territory, it was a further step in German policy towards a foreign country. The Delegation had 'in matters of substance nothing to do with the armistice negotiations proper, but has as its task the adjustment of purely economic questions by means of German–French negotiations'.[3]

It does not appear that Hemmen was particularly in favour of the policy of using the existence of the demarcation line to put pressure on the French during the negotiations. He could see that the existence of the two parts of France in a completely independent manner was economically impossible. In addition, if France were to be properly exploited raw materials would have to travel across this line in large quantities.[4] Thus the response to the French protests of 15 July was much more sensitive than it seemed to the French.[5]

[1] DFCAA., i. 53.
[2] DGFP., x, no. 142.
[3] DGFP., Series D, x, no. 168.
[4] Ibid., no. 184.
[5] DFCAA., i. 56.

Hemmen travelled to Fontainebleau to discuss the question of the relaxation of the demarcation line with von Brauchitsch. There he was told that Hitler himself had said that he wished to preserve the line for the present, and that in any case the decision to relax it had to be Hitler's.[1]

It was in fact the last day of July, almost six weeks after the signing of the Armistice, before the constant French demands for knowledge of German intentions were met by detailed decisions on the German side. On that day Hemmen attended a meeting in the Economic Policy Department and a plan was marked out within which German economic interests in France, which had already begun to show themselves, could be satisfied.[2] The German government would demand payment of occupation costs amounting to at least twenty million Reichsmarks a day. This sum was not intended in the least to represent the actual costs of the occupation; these would be worked out later by the High Command of the Armed Forces. The French government was to be given no indication of the actual accounting involved.

It was from this moment that a consistent German policy emerged. On 22 July Hemmen had told General Huntziger that German intentions were still as he had described them on 8 July.[3] But he added a more specific statement of interest: the aircraft and aluminium industries in the unoccupied zone must be made available for German orders. The French economy would not be neglected by Germany, indeed Germany had several precise interests in it, but these were partly conditional on France permitting certain general controls over her economy which would enable Germany safely to relax the demarcation line. 'France was going to be made to lower her standard of living and to bring it to a level analogous to that of Germany. Germany wished to reconstruct Europe; she had no interest in France's dying of starvation or undergoing revolutionary dangers.'[4]

At a meeting of the finance sub-commission at Wiesbaden on 25 July the German negotiators had dropped their first hint that France would be required to sign a clearing treaty. On 3 August Hemmen informed the French that a major 'plan of organization' was intended. The Germans would extend their customs posts to the external frontiers of the France of 1914, would unify the country economically, and integrate it in the continental economy by the side of Germany. He said the plan 'would have to be adopted in its entirety by the French government, that it could in no circumstances be a subject for discussion, and that it would be there to take or leave'.[5] The French government were also informed of the official exchange rate of twenty francs to the mark. This blow must have made the note of 8 August conveying the German demands for occupation costs and for a clearing treaty seem even more menacing.[6]

---

[1] DGFP., Series D, x, no. 192.   [2] DGFP., x, no. 267.   [3] DFCAA., i. 75.
[4] Ibid., p. 77.   [5] Ibid., p. 97.
[6] Ibid., p. 158; DGFP., Series D, x, no. 309; Arnoult, op. cit., p. 148.

The huge occupation costs of twenty million Reichsmarks a day measured in severely undervalued francs would be combined with a bilateral trading agreement by which each country would pay its own exporters while clearing the trade debts on a national level. Germany would therefore be provided with an immense purchasing power suspended, like the sword of Damocles, over the French economy. Franco-German trade would inevitably be a largely one-way affair, the clearing accounts grotesquely out of balance.

The arrangements made on 7 August for the purchase of strategically important raw materials in occupied France do not reveal these plans, however. The trade was to be handled by firms that were already established in Franco-German trade and payment was to be made on the *Wifo* accounts which had been used to finance part of the pre-war rearmament programme.[1] Orders had already been both sought by French entrepreneurs and canvassed by German entrepreneurs on a private basis. When pressed as to how far these would be covered in the 'plan of organization' Hemmen dodged the issue. The French delegation threatened to set up a central office to control and supervise these orders themselves in order to protect themselves from the danger of excess German purchasing power.[2]

French protests about the size of the occupation costs were swept aside. General Huntziger, Head of the French Delegation to the Armistice Commission suggested that on the basis of the costs of the French army the German demands were sufficient to maintain an army of eighteen million men in France.[3] The German response was merely to provide another ultimatum, but no more was said about the remainder of the 'plan of organization', which for the French in the circumstances was crucial to any occupation payments. In fact the plans had been delayed by Italian attempts to get greater participation in the French economy.[4] But the concessions made to them by Hitler were purely nominal ones. Unless the German government was prepared to occupy the whole of France it was by no means absolutely certain to obtain all the concessions it desired, even though the sanctions which could be brought against the French for refusal to pay the occupation costs were very strong.[5] On 19 August General Carl-Heinrich von Stülpnagel was still apologizing for the delay in submitting the total plan.[6] The next day, still in an imperfect form, it was resubmitted to the French.[7] The value of the franc to the Reichsmark was definitely to be established in a 20:1 ratio.

The worst fears of the French government were for their currency. Social stability was their ideal above all else, but the German plans seemed to impose an inescapably inflationary situation on the French economy. It became the main aim of the French government to forestall a socially disruptive inflation

---

[1] BA., R 7 VIII 207, Reichswirtschaftsministerium, 'Anweisung über den Ankauf von kriegswichtigen Rohstoffen im besetzten französischen Gebiet', 7 August 1940.
[2] DFCAA., i. 119. [3] Ibid. 159.
[4] DGFP., Series D, x, no. 337. [5] Ibid., no. 378.
[6] DFCAA., i. 149. [7] P. Arnoult, op. cit., p. 19.

at whatever cost. The refusal of the German delegation to modify its demands therefore clarified the plans of the French government. For the first time they had a precise idea of what their own economic policy should be, and it was, naturally, to be an extremely conservative one.

Pétain's supporters were able to believe themselves to be accepting political reality only by subscribing to a wildly over-simplified view of the previous history of their country. The instability of French policies in the years before the invasion was attributed to mistaken ideological commitments and to social disruption. The anachronistic view of French economic society held by Pétain himself was not forcibly imposed on his ministers, many of whom, although not of course Laval, subscribed completely to it. Of no one was this more true than of Bouthillier, the Secretary of State for Finance. The reader of Bouthillier's memoirs will soon become aware of the constant fear of 'uprootedness'. Pétain, in contrast, he thought, had 'his feet planted in the thickness of the earth'.[1] The search for abstractions which would explain the disastrous recent course of French history led Bouthillier, with many of his colleagues, into espousing what they believed to be a 'Realpolitik'. But their 'Realpolitik' was founded on equally dangerous abstractions of their own.

Laval had been faithful to such abstractions throughout the 1930s. The American ambassador to Paris in 1931 wrote in his memoirs that Laval 'envisioned a future where Europe would be more or less united, Russia would be thrust back into Asia, and the Anglo-Saxon world would lead an autonomous existence with the United States and France serving as the point of contact between the European and Anglo-Saxon world'.[2] The coincidence between his foreign policy and Hitler's blinded him to the nature of the Europe of the New Order; he looked at the outward form and not at the inner reality. As he himself became more autocratic he welcomed the autocratic aspects of Hitler's rule as a wholesome aspect of European reconstruction. In May 1941 he told an American journalist that 'this is not a war like other wars; it is a revolution from which a new Europe—rejuvenated, reorganized and prosperous— must come'.[3] But to the real nature of that revolution he remained quite blind. Hitler spurned all offers of collaboration. France was never prepared to offer him what he wanted and could indeed scarcely ever have been in a position to do so. Hitler's policy towards France, deeply suspicious and unrelentingly hostile, did not change.

The further French protests of 21 August against the German plan were personally expressed by Huntziger in an interview with Hemmen. They were twofold. In the first place the French felt that no policy they might pursue could now guarantee monetary stability in France. The value of the franc had to be preserved in the dangerous situation in which the government found

---

[1] Y. Bouthillier, op. cit., ii. 16.
[2] W. E. Edge, *A Jerseyman's Journal* (Princeton, 1948), p. 207.
[3] G. Warner, *Pierre Laval and the Eclipse of France* (London, 1967), p. 278.

itself, but German policy made this impossible. Secondly, the threat of massive German purchasing power which could be deployed at any moment seemed to nullify any rational economic policy at all on the part of the French government. 'M. Hemmen indicated that the French money payments would be spent in France: but with that money the Germans will be able to buy the whole of France.'[1] Hemmen justified the charges by reference to the reparations imposed on Germany by the Versailles treaty, reparations which had not been payable through any possible trading mechanism.

The payment demanded is very heavy, and Germany knows by experience how ruinous such charges are. That is why the German government has seen this question from an economic point of view, since at the same time that it has demanded these payments from France, it has proposed to her an economic system which frees France from the anxiety of ruin.[2]

This standpoint became the officially accepted one; memories of reparations and the French occupation of the Rhineland were easily stirred, 'in this way France was prevented from being threatened by the same inflationary tendencies that had developed in connection with the occupation of the Rhineland by French troops'.[3] The counterpart of this view was that Germany herself was also protected against inflationary forces by the strict control of the exchanges. In reality France and Germany were both threatened by inflation. Without attributing to the inflationary pressure in France the dire consequences feared by the Vichy government it is difficult to see how a general and constant inflationary tendency could have been avoided in the French economy.

The system could never be watertight, however close the watch on the exchanges. The occupation costs had to be provided for the most part out of currency creation by the Bank of France. It was not in fact difficult for the government to borrow money. There were few outlets for investment and hoarding was dangerous. Interest rates were lower than at any period since the First World War. But the vast sums could only be provided regularly and completely by credits paid directly by the Bank of France into occupation accounts. It could be argued that this was not in theory very different from the practice of financing rearmament by credits from the Bank of France, a practice going back to the secret agreements between the government and the Bank in 1911. If the money circuits had functioned properly what was in fact deficit financing by the Bank of France on behalf of the occupying power would have been covered by short-term and long-term loans at the low rates of interest which developed. But the circumstances of military occupation were such that these circuits functioned very imperfectly. As the occupation continued even treasury bills, rapidly taken up in the early stages, were taken up less and less quickly.[4]

[1] DFCAA., i. 169. [2] Ibid., p. 166.
[3] K. Ringel, *Frankreichs Wirtschaft im Umbruch* (Leipzig, 1942).
[4] P. Dieterlen and C. Rist, *The Monetary Problem of France* (New York, 1948), p. 62.

The war effort itself had been much less inflationary than in the First World War. That war had begun with the assumption that the gold reserve of the Bank of France would prove sufficient to back up any possible war effort. Rationing began only in 1917, and then only in a very limited way. Taxes were never high enough. These mistakes had been realized for what they were by 1939. Taxes on capital and on personal incomes were all increased and in the case of personal income-tax the method of collection improved while the war was on. War profits were taxed from the outset, whereas in the First World War they had not been taxed until 1917.[1] Thus although 25·1 per cent of France's total war expenditure of 263,000,000,000 francs between 1 September 1939 and 31 August 1940 was provided by advances from the Bank of France, 28·9 per cent was provided by income from taxation.[2] At the time when the clearing agreements were proposed and the franc under-valued little inflation had as yet taken place in France.

The circumstances of the clearing agreements themselves encouraged the French government to inflate if they so wished to do.[3] That was one method by which they could right the exchange which they regarded as so unfavourable. The political and social views of the two Finance Ministers, Bouthillier and Cathala, made the adoption of so wholesale a remedy unthinkable, although not all Pétain's ministers shared their opinions.[4] Bouthillier wished to hand over a 'healthy' economy at the end of the European war come what may. As part of his health treatment he raised the limit of exemption from death duties in November 1940.[5] Part of this revenue was recouped by reducing the financial provision for free secondary education.[6] It must also be said that when German orders in France were placed on a more formal footing it was possible for the French government to raise prices on those particular orders well above the level of domestic prices and try to get the German negotiators to accept these prices. Bouthillier was not at all averse to limited solutions of this kind. Cathala, his successor in office, seems to have considered the possibility of a deliberate inflation as one way out of France's difficulties, but to have rejected it on the grounds that the defence of the franc was not only a guarantee of the future but a 'national duty'.[7]

[1] H. Laufenburger, *Crédit public et finances de guerre, 1914–44; Allemagne, France, Grande-Bretagne* (Paris, 1944), p. 15.
[2] Ibid., p. 23; A. Munz, op. cit., p. 10.
[3] 'Generally it can be said, that apart from a few small measures of the German occupying powers influencing methods of banking in France, not only were the powers accruing to Germany by the right of occupation not overstepped but that they even remained enforced at their lowest level', A. Emmendörfer, *Geld- und Kreditaufsicht in den von Deutschland während des zweiten Weltkrieges besetzten Gebieten* (Düsseldorf, 1957), p. 106.
[4] Y. Bouthillier, ibid., ii. 64.
[5] 'I would have wished to put an end to this erosion of private property so necessary to society and so useful to the state', ibid., p. 398.
[6] '. . . [secondary education] which by its nature and by its aims must only be followed in a healthy state by a feeble minority of adolescents' (ibid., p. 350).
[7] P. Cathala, *Face aux réalités* (Paris, 1948), p. 64.

Notwithstanding the financial strictness of the Vichy governments and their stern rejection of the easy way out of their difficulties, inflation could not be kept at bay.[1] Wages paid by the German armed forces and their auxiliary organizations in France were much higher than the wage levels permitted in the French economy. As Germany's position in the war worsened, French entrepreneurs increasingly demanded payments in cash so that they could not later be inculpated. The black market, extensively used from the beginnings of the occupation for the purchase of strategically important goods by Germany, was almost entirely a cash market.[2] The purchases made on the black market were not all official purchases by any means. In spite of all attempts to stop them soldiers also operated extensively on the same market.[3] Price control became less and less effective. Except at huge administrative cost this may well always be the case in occupied territory. Where considerable scarcities existed already German requisitions, however acquired, were bound to place an increasing strain on their own price controls.

TABLE 6

*Money in the French Economy**

(000,000,000 francs)

Period	Fiduciary issue	Bank deposits	Other liquidities	Total	Indices	
					Total liquidities	Official wholesale prices
To end of August 1939	142	65	4	211	100	100
,, ,, 1940	221	122	11	354	168	142
,, ,, 1941	270	152	76	498	236	171
,, ,, 1942	383	182	35	600	285	201
,, ,, 1943	500	222	37	759	360	233

*ISEA., *Mouvement économique en France de 1938 à 1948* (Paris, 1950), p. 72.

Holdings of liquid assets were also encouraged by the arbitrariness of the system imposed on France. Before 1939 the use of the cheque had been much less developed in France than in Germany. The French government decreed on 22 October 1940 that no payments of over 3,000 francs could be in cash. But, since the original reason for the failure to use banks in France was mistrust, the circumstances of the occupation only increased this mistrust. For political reasons, and also no doubt because taxes went up, tax avoidance also increased during the occupation. In spite of a drop in the volume of French

[1] Munz does not absolve the French government from blame in the inflation, but he produces little evidence for their blameworthiness. A. Munz, op. cit., p. 116.

[2] Ibid., pp. 85–7.

[3] Hoover Institute, Papers of Militärverwaltungsbezirk Bordeaux, Box 2, Letter from Mayor of Dax to Kriegskommandantur, 7 October 1940; Box 7, Letter from Prefect of Basses-Pyrénées to mayors of all occupied communes, 23 April 1941. See also M. Baudot, op. cit., *passim.*

production the increase in the holding of liquid assets was greater than the increase of official prices, for what they were worth. The whole period of the occupation was one of tremendous monetary abundance and pressure on prices. The value of a gold 20 franc piece on the black market increased eight-fold between August 1939 and January 1943.[1]

Yet even with this growing liquidity France might still have avoided the severer aspects of inflation had her economy remained with the same volume of unutilized resources as in August 1940. It was the eventual catastrophic decline in French productivity which gave the inflation an unstoppable momentum and created the financial havoc of 1946. Low productivity became a defence against exploitation and as it developed so did inflation increase.

Nor should it be thought that it was possible for these phenomena to have no effect inside Germany. Trade between Germany and Greece ultimately became impossible on the basis of the exchange rate stipulated in the clearing agreements between those countries. A special company had to be created to equalize prices, its costs being provided for by additional import levies in Greece.[2] The huge number of foreign workers in Germany created constant problems in exchange control by their remittances home. Belgian workers in Germany were able to get goods in short supply in Germany from Belgium by various ways and sell them at high prices. By using their maximum possible right of currency transfer they could remit the proceeds to Belgium by way of the Deutsche Bank.[3] In 1943 serious efforts were made to compel a decrease in the price of goods coming into Germany from the occupied territories and from the General-Government of Poland.[4]

On 26 August the French government abandoned its refusal to pay occupation costs. The attempt to modify them had met with blank opposition from Hemmen; the French had no alternative but to pay, and to try as far as possible to mitigate the consequences.

The French government, as resolved to respect its engagements as to prevent the country suffering the trials of an inflation engendering unhappiness and disorder, asks the German government that there should be a joint examination as to how the credits destined for the occupation troops should be employed. It believes its duty in all loyalty to state that it neither could nor would lend itself to a use of this credit provoking by a disorderly price rise that monetary deterioration against which no social order is proof.[5]

The following day in a personal interview with Hemmen, Bouthillier received Hemmen's view of the future Europe.[6] But speculation was not

---

[1] ISEA., *Mouvement économique en France de 1938 à 1948* (Paris, 1950), p. 72.
[2] H. S. Bloch and B. F. Hoselitz, *The Economics of military occupation* (Chicago, 1944).
[3] FD 2581/44, Mbh. f. B. u. Nf. to Deutsche Bank, 'Missbrauch des Lohnüberweisungs-verfahrens', 13 June 1944.
[4] FD 2627/44 (h), Beauftragter für den Vierjahresplan to Reichskommissar für die Preis-bildung, 15 September 1943.
[5] DFCAA., i. 173.   [6] See above, p. 48.

confined to the German side. 'Since the last war', said Bouthillier, 'some Frenchmen had understood that the principles of liberalism which had made the future of the nineteenth century were worn out. To have wished to reconstruct Europe on worn out principles had been one of the fatal errors of western statesmen.'[1]

In September Pétain himself pursued the same line of thought. 'When it should come to an examination of those principles which assured the victory of her adversaries, [France] will be surprised to recognize everywhere there is a little of her own good, her purest and most authentic tradition.'[2] They were not afterthoughts. Even in July Pétain could still hope that if the French economy were integrated into 'a continental system' of exchanges this would recreate the agricultural and peasant France, the source of all discipline and social order, that he wished to see.[3] The primacy of action as a release from all problems seemed to him a rediscovery by fascism of an older rural wisdom. But to suppose that the acceptance of this belief was in any way to face reality was ludicrous. Diplomatically and economically the only actions that the French puppet state could take were those responding to the strings pulled by the German government. Nor was such a creed a sufficient anodyne to fulfil its purpose as a comfort to those whom he considered his social inferiors.

Once the French government had agreed to pay the occupation costs, economic exploitation as it was understood by Hemmen could begin. The delay had already led to a number of unofficial contacts between businessmen on both sides. On the day in which the French delegation gave in over this issue at Wiesbaden, Göring issued his decree, 'Planned Utilization of the Economy of the Occupied Western Territories for the German War Economy'.[4]

It is a political necessity in order to fulfil orders placed for the further conduct of the war that the capacity and raw materials of the occupied western territories should be employed in a planned way and to do as much as possible to support German armaments production and to increase war potential.[4]

To this purpose there would be three seperate Central Contracts Offices (*Zentralauftragsstelle*) in Paris, one for each branch of the Armed Forces. This corresponded of course to the system in the German domestic economy where each of the armed services ordered its armaments quite independently of the others.[5]

Two days later the Reichs Economics Ministry added further details when the decree was published.[6] The decree had a wider scope than its earlier version. Göring's decree had insisted on a strict priority for all Wehrmacht

---

[1] DFCAA., i. 182.   [2] R. Aron, op. cit., p. 215.   [3] Ibid., pp. 197 ff.

[4] BA., R 7 VIII 207, Reichsbeauftragter für den Vierjahresplan, 'Planmässige Ausnutzung der Wirtschaft der besetzten westlichen Gebiete für die deutsche Kriegswirtschaft', 26 August 1940.

[5] A. S. Milward, op. cit., pp. 23 ff.

[6] BA., R 7 VIII 207, Reichswirtschaftsministerium, 'Planmässige Ausnutzung der Wirtschaft der besetzten westlichen Gebiete für die deutsche Kriegswirtschaft', 28 August 1940.

orders; the aim of exploitation in the first place was to increase Germany's fighting power. The later version had wider economic implications. 'Furthermore it is to be remarked that the capacity of these territories may in principle only be used for production which is important in war or for such production whose dispersal from the territory of the Reich would set free war production capacity there.'[1] This was an elastic extension of the principle laid down by Otto von Stülpnagel, the Commander-in-Chief in France, who had interpreted the Armisticeg Areement as strictly confining German production in France to production for war purposes.[2] The formal method of allocating contracts was to begin on 15 September. The Central Contracts Offices would be jointly controlled by the Economics Ministry and the High Command of the Armed Forces. Their personnel would be drawn from three sources, the officials of the War Economy and Armaments Staff of the Army already in France, the economic section of the military administration, and the Armaments Inspectors. Any contract of a value greater than five thousand Reichsmarks would have first to be cleared and approved by the new body.

The Central Contracts Office for the Army was serving many masters. In so far as the contracts it allocated were connected with German armament industries ultimate responsibility lay with the *Wirtschafts- und Rüstungsstab Frankreich* of the *Wehrwirtschafts- und Rüstungsamt* of the Army Supreme Command, established in Paris from 3 July. But its work also necessitated close co-operation with the High Command in Paris. The personal relations between the *Wirtschafts- und Rüstungsstab Frankreich* and the Central Contracts Office were good, and in fact the same person was often responsible for the same work in the two bodies. All three branches of the armed forces had representatives of their own ordnance boards in Paris, and when Todt was appointed Minister of Armaments and Munitions he too sent a Commissar to Paris. The High Command narrowly avoided having to accept a department of the Four Year Plan Office in Paris.[3]

In spite of the rather loose interpretation of the Armistice agreement and the sweeping nature of Göring's decrees economic policy in the occupied zone was confined within the bounds of German domestic economic policy, to secure whatever was necessary for the success of the Blitzkrieg. On 30 August the French were given to understand that there was no question of the manufacture of completed armaments for German purposes.[4] In a letter to General Huntziger, von Stülpnagel repeated his earlier decision. He defined German orders as being solely those necessary to prosecute the war.[5] The whole tone of his letters was such as to convey that there was no thought of systematic exploitation. Certainly this letter represented von Stülpnagel's own view. He repeated it in a letter of protest to General Jodl, Chief of the Operations Staff

[1] BA., R 7 VIII 207, 28 August 1940.   [2] DGFP., Series D, x, no. 267.
[3] H. Böhme, op. cit., p. 172.   [4] DFCAA., i. 212.
[5] Ibid., p. 215.

of the High Command of the Armed Forces, on 14 September. If France were to be a milch cow she must be given more fodder. At the same time he reiterated his opinion that there were severe dangers in an economic exploitation going beyond the terms of the Armistice Agreement.[1]

Hemmen's own instructions were clearly not to regard the agreement on occupation costs as setting the seal on the Armistice Agreement. Rather the signing of that agreement was the thin end of the wedge by which Germany hoped to prise open a wider passage in to the French economy. He had never supposed that even within the restricted area of German demands it would be possible to treat the occupied zone and Vichy France as two separate areas. Both for French and German purposes the country must remain economically unified.[2] Before the agreement had been signed the German administration was proceeding on the assumption that planning for the use of raw materials would ignore the demarcation line.[3] On 4 September at a meeting of the armaments sub-commission Colonel Hünermann, the representative of *Wehr Wirtschafts- und Rüstungsamt* at Wiesbaden, spoke of German interests in the French aircraft industry, and made it clear that Germany was thinking of regular production programmes which would embrace the unoccupied zone as much as the occupied one.[4]

In early August the German army of occupation had stopped direct requisitions of foodstuffs and raw materials in favour of an organized system of quotas which had been proposed to the French government.[5] More orderly as such a procedure was, it was also a method of introducing a much stricter supervision over the French economy. The German administration insisted that such a scheme would imply a comprehensive rationing of supply, while the French government desperately wanted at least to avoid bread rationing. It was partly to meet this threat that the French government passed the law of 16 August which empowered them to form the 'comités d'organisation'. In principle these committees would superintend the provision and distribution of all raw materials and foodstuffs and some manufactured products within the French economy. There were originally supposed to be only thirty of these committees but eventually their number far exceeded this.[6]

The origins of these committees, the way in which they were formed, and even, in certain cases, their purpose remain obscure. The pressure to form them came from two different directions. They had an obviously useful purpose in erecting a defensive barrier against potential German depredations. Since the Vichy government had formed a clear idea of those precise areas of French production which had the greatest interest for the German government, they could hope, by establishing an over-all control in those fields, to

---

[1] IMT., xxxvi. 480; PS–1756; E. Jäckel, op. cit., p. 94.
[2] DGFP., Series D, x, no. 184.
[3] BA., R 7 VIII 207, 'Wirtschaftsbericht des Wi. Abt. beim Mbh. in Frankreich', 4 September 1940.
[4] DFCAA., i. 216.   [5] Ibid., p. 305.   [6] Y. Bouthillier, op. cit., ii. 275.

restrict and define whatever German demands were coming. But the committees also represented quite faithfully the general social and political views of the government, and their purpose was not a wholly defensive one. Before the war there had been a profound difference in the extent to which economic information had been collected and tabulated in the French and German economies. This difference reflected the long French tradition of economic liberalism. The German administration was astounded to discover that even the basic statistical information necessary to evaluate the progress of the economy, let alone that sufficient to establish systems of economic control as complex as those in Germany, was quite lacking.[1] By instituting committees of control in the economy the Vichy government could not only hope to remedy this defect but also to pander to its own anti-liberal views. The 'comités d'organisation' represented Vichy France's timid step in the direction of the fascist corporate state; they represented the bureaucratic triumph of the right in the same way that the more highly organized committee systems in Italy and Germany did.

It is most unlikely that the institution of the 'comités d'organisation' represented any real change in the personnel who controlled French industry. When the committees which controlled war production in Germany were evolved in 1942, although their powers were very extensive, the people who sat on them were in many cases the leaders of the business 'groups' formed in the early years of National Socialist government.[2] The leaders of those 'groups' in their turn had often been the most prominent members of the manufacturers' associations before the National Socialist take-over. In so far as the law of 16 August represented yet another of the Vichy government's own admissions that it was not wholly out of sympathy with the less revolutionary economic policies of its opponents it may well have merely established French industrialists more firmly in control of the French economy at the price of publishing information to the government, the whole being also conceived as a measure of national defence.[3]

The committees formed in this way were basically concerned with decisions on priorities in a period of scarcity. Inevitably they would be closely involved in any general scheme of rationing. On 10 September the French government again had to bow to main force, and a general scheme of rationing was accepted which was applicable to the whole of France as well as to all German soldiers and administrators there.[4] Hemmen's threats of 22 July had been

---

[1] A. Sauvy, 'Heurs et malheurs de la statistique', *Revue d'histoire de la deuxième guerre mondiale*, lvii (1965).

[2] A. S. Milward, op. cit., pp. 19 ff.

[3] The organizations formed for the control of the agricultural sector of the economy were closely based on the previously existing corporate organizations wherever this was possible. H. Kistenmacher, *Die Auswirkungen der deutschen Besetzung auf die Ernährungswirtschaft Frankreichs während des zweiten Weltkrieges* (Tübingen, 1959), p. 8.

[4] DFCAA., i. 309.

fulfilled. The law by which the scheme was introduced moved the French economy one stage further along the path of corporate organization. The principle of rationing had been established by the powers which the government had taken at the end of February to control the distribution of petrol and of certain luxuries. The laws published in the *Journal Officiel* on 12 September and 13 September established a rigorous central control on the utilization of all raw materials in the economy.[1] Such control had been partly instituted by the decree of 20 May of the Commander-in-Chief. The German administration would now only give up the powers of requisition conferred by that decree in return for certain administrative concessions.[2] The Ministry of Industrial Production created under its control a 'Central Office for the Allocation of Industrial Products'.[3] This department received orders from Division Two of the Economic Branch of the Civil Administration. Individual commodities were controlled by sub-sections of the Central Office, the 'comités de répartition'. In this way a channel of economic command from the occupied territory to the Vichy government was opened.

There were no such 'self-governing' bodies in the occupied zone, priorities there being established directly by the German administration. Nevertheless priorities established, and decisions taken, by the 'comités de répartition' were given general validity in the occupied zone by the fact that the ultimate authority was the same. The total personnel of the 'comités' amounted to more than six thousand. For the occupying power these arrangements were a major step to the elimination of Vichy's economic independence and to the control of the whole of the French economy. As the September report of the High Command in Paris indicated, 'By this step a foundation has been laid on which French industrial production and distribution can be directed in a unified way under German control throughout the whole of France from the point of view of a war economy.'[4]

As far as the French government was concerned, their failure to produce any modification in the German attitude after the presentation of the demand for occupation costs led them to adopt more limited aims. On 26 September, as a result of semi-official conversation between the two heads of the sub-committee for armaments at Wiesbaden, the French delegation had their impression that, in respect of aircraft orders, Germany had no intention of ignoring the aircraft industry south of the demarcation line, confirmed.[5] Furthermore they received a tacit admission that since this was the case Germany would also need to supply French industry with the necessary materials.

[1] NA., T.501, 150, 'Organisation de la répartition des produits industriels'.
[2] DFCAA., iv. 276.
[3] 'Office central de répartition des produits industriels', FD 5148/45, Mbh. in F., 'Grundsätze für die Warenbewirtschaftung'.
[4] BA., R 7 VIII 207; NA., T.501, 150, 000696, 'Wirtschaftsbericht über die Lage im Bereich des Chefs der Militärverwaltung in Frankreich', September 1940.
[5] DFCAA, i. 206.

The best policy for France now seemed to be a determined effort to secure concessions from Germany at every stage of the negotiations at Wiesbaden by a relentless process of bargaining. In this way the meetings of the Armistice Commission could be turned into an effective barrier against German economic penetration. Everything could be delayed up to the point where Germany threatened to use her ultimate sanction and from time to time concessions could be wrung from the adversary, an adversary whose demand was, in the last resort, vital to keep the French economy going.

The adoption of this policy may be said to indicate that Hemmen's position at Wiesbaden had become clear to the French government. The military affairs discussed at Wiesbaden had become less and less important over the previous month, and it had now been demonstrated that Germany's intention was to use the meetings of the Commission to further her economic policy. On 12 September General Huntziger was recalled to become Minister and Secretary of State for War. The French delegation was divided into two parts, a military delegation and an economic delegation, the latter headed by de Boisanger, Governor of the Bank of France.[1] The economic delegation reported directly to the Directorate of the Armistice Services in the Ministry of National Defence. On 16 September the French delegation was instructed to prolong all negotiations on German contracts in France in an attempt to secure concessions parallel to those France was now being obliged to make.[2]

At the same time the French government tried to repair some of the ultimate damage which the clearing treaty would do by imposing a so-called profits tax on French exports. Since the difference in price levels between France and Germany was so great, and since Germany finally allowed French exporters to value their goods in pre-war German prices, there was still a considerable profit incentive to the French entrepreneur to export to Germany, especially in view of the diminished outlets elsewhere. In any case French exporters under the terms of the proposed agreement would be paid in French francs in France at the equivalent of overvalued Reichsmarks. One aspect of the proposed tax was to force the French entrepreneurs to go through a long and complicated series of formalities with their own central government.[3] German opposition to such a tax, however, was based much more on its tendency to raise prices to German consumers. Combined with French attempts to raise prices of those raw materials supplied on contract to a level well above that of the pre-war period, it called forth one of Hemmen's most menacing threats.[4] Nevertheless the French were eventually able to establish an export tax but at an extremely low level. In fact, faced with this threatening situation, French taxation on profits developed considerable subtlety in the first year of the occupation. Firms established after 25 June 1940 and making goods which could be considered to be replacements for destroyed or

---

[1] DFCAA., i. 1.   [2] Ibid., p. 443.
[3] P. Arnoult, op. cit., p. 169.   [4] DFCAA., ii. 99.

deteriorating fixed capital were exempted from all temporary profits taxes.[1] Both the coal and the textile industries actually received subsidies in various forms, and all mineral mines, except those of coal or iron ore, were exempted from profits taxation if the rhythm of their production was such as to diminish their future output.[2]

The French proposal to introduce an exports tax and their determined refusal to allow German customs officials on the frontiers of Vichy France with Switzerland and the Mediterranean meant that the final form of the clearing treaty still remained in doubt. Germany was in a position of such bargaining strength that it seemed worth while to hold out for the whole of her demands. There was no longer any need to delay the placing of orders in France since most of the necessary machinery of economic control had now been imposed on the French.

But the delay in forcing the French government to sign the treaty meant that the alternative policy of the Four Year Plan Office was not yet ruled out of order. The Raw Material Staff, which had been set up by the Four Year Plan Office to seize and transport stockpiles of strategic raw materials found in the captured territories, had functioned since the invasion. On 17 September Göring laid down general principles of economic policy to be followed in the occupied western territories.

The aim is the strengthening of German war potential. For this purpose all mines, iron works, rolling-mills, firms producing primary materials, and also important manufacturing firms such as machine-tool factories, locomotive and wagon works, and so on should be used at their full capacity and firms unimportant for war shall have their production reduced or be closed. Raw materials important for war which will not be used, as well as machine tools, especially such as came from works which have been closed or damaged, after a careful examination as to whether they could not be more purposefully used in the occupied territory will be transported to the homeland. The consumption of the population is to be shrunk to the lowest possible level.[3]

Even at this stage Göring was not wholly reconciled to this carefully organized pillage. Echoes of the desire to loot are still heard. 'The supply of the troops off the land is to be secured as first priority, purchases by soldiers should not pettily and unnecessarily be made more difficult.'[3]

Hitler, although keen to secure the necessary deliveries from France, was in favour of a tough occupation policy. The High Command in France, perhaps on Hemmen's prompting, had represented to him that the existence of the demarcation line was extremely damaging to the French economy. Hitler's reply was that relations with France were to be seen only from the political viewpoint, '. . . it must be all the same to us if the renewal of economic life in

---

[1] H. Laufenburger, op. cit., p. 94.   [2] Ibid., p. 95.
[3] BA., R 7 VIII 207; N.A., T.501, 150, 000696, 'Wirtschaftsbericht über die Lage im Bereich des Chefs der Militärverwaltung in Frankreich', September 1940.

France is prevented. The French have lost the war and consequently they must pay for the damages.'[1] If there were French objections the rest of the country would be occupied. 'All concessions that we make to the French must be paid for dearly by means of deliveries from the unoccupied zone or the colonies.'[1] General Keitel, Chief of the High Command of the Armed Forces, thought that the only way the subsequent duplication of economic effort could be resolved was for the Economic Delegation to move to Paris and be subordinated to the High Command there. In that way Göring's complaints might also be stilled.

Even while this was under consideration the trade negotiations dragged on side by side with economic policy as outlined by Göring. One day after the French government had concluded agreements on trade between unoccupied France and Germany in bauxite, alumina and magnesium they were faced with precise demands for the manufacture of aerocraft for Germany in the unoccupied zone.[2] Meanwhile the German delegation to the Armistice Commission refused to reveal anything about the general principles underlying the allocation of contracts to France or even to reveal the mechanism by which they would be controlled. The matter, said Hemmen on 4 October was, too large an issue for him to comment on it, it was under discussion at Berlin.[3] The following day Hemmen made certain concessions on the operations of the demarcation line and revealed the further concessions he would make once the present negotiations were successfully completed. Where goods had not been specifically mentioned in the Commander-in-Chief's initial order of 20 May, complete freedom of exchange would be allowed. For those goods, which, by that order, were subject to military requisition, there would still be freedom of movement across the demarcation line, provided there was a uniform rule governing their distribution in the French economy, that is to say providing they were in the province of a 'comité de répartition'.[4] Agreement had by now been reached on the supervisory powers of the German commissars attached to the French economy; their powers were very limited.[5]

On 7 October a further order by Göring covered contracts which would be placed in France. In his position as Commander-in-Chief of the Air Force he would be particularly involved. The Central Contracts Office created by the decrees of 26 and 28 August had been installed in Paris since mid September.[6]

The increased level of armaments compels us to try to speed up the surrender of contracts by German industry, especially in the civilian sector, through the channels created for the arrangement of contracts in the occupied territories, to those occupied territories where there is ready capacity.[7]

[1] Hemmen Papers, 'Conférence chez le Generalfeldmarschall Keitel, 20 Septembre 1940', IMT., EC–409.
  [2] Ibid. i. 363.   [3] Ibid. ii. 32.
  [4] Ibid., p. 26.   [5] Ibid., p. 11.   [6] K. Ringel, op. cit., p. 47.
  [7] BA., R 7 VIII 207, Reichsbeauftragte für den Vierjahresplan, 'Auftragvergebung an die Industrie in den besetzten Westgebieten', 7 October 1940.

But Göring still revealed himself as very cautious about placing armaments contracts in France. The danger of sabotage, he remarked, was very great. On 18 October the Reichs Economics Ministry proposed to the *Wirtschaftsgruppen* that they undertake a study along the lines of Göring's order to see what degree of production for civilian needs could be dispersed to France.[1]

From 16 September when the French delegation at Wiesbaden received formal instructions that their tactics must be to negotiate German concessions, before themselves conceding contracts, they continued to negotiate on this basis in spite of the increased German pressure to utilize manufacturing capacity in France. The proposal that Germany should operate a customs control on Vichy France's foreign frontiers remained unacceptable; it was a more direct threat to the sovereignty that the Armistice Agreement had left to France than was the demarcation line.[2] Pétain took with him to Montoire, when he met Hitler, a list of the most vital supplies needed by France, to use them in any bargaining that took place there, but there is no evidence that it was ever shown or mentioned to the Führer.[3] On the domestic scene the French government continued to defend itself against the worst. On 10 October the French Assembly put into force a law blocking capital exports.[4] The only other occupied country where such a law came into force was Denmark, and the German opposition to it was quite mild. Apart from a demand to transfer certain aircraft corporation shares to the Junkers aircraft corporation, according to the German delegation to serve as a guarantee for the satisfactory completion of contracts, and the demand to surrender French capital holdings in the Yugoslav Mines de Bor and in the Romanian oil industry, German capital penetration into France had not shown signs of being too great a threat.

Nevertheless, the incident of the Mines de Bor had seemed very alarming to the French government, and could be read as though Göring's decree of 2 August were still the main guide-line for German occupation policy. A German administrator had already been appointed to take control of the mines when the delegation at Wiesbaden were presented with a demand for the surrender of all French shares in the company.[5] The Yugoslav copper-mining industry was in fact almost entirely controlled by French capital. In 1939 the Mines de Bor had played a big part in the British attempt to prevent Yugoslavia trading copper ore to Germany in return for military equipment, and the German government had been made very aware of the slightness of the links so carefully forged in the previous years.[6] Under the terms of an agreement between the Allies and Yugoslavia signed on 20 December 1939 and finally agreed on 11 January 1940 the French would take the copper

---

[1] BA., R 7 VIII 207, Rwm., 18 October 1940.   [2] DFCAA., ii. 58.
[3] Ibid., p. 190; E. Jäckel, op. cit., p. 10.
[4] O. Ulshöfer, op. cit., p. 76; Y. Bouthillier, op. cit., ii. 112.
[5] DFCAA., i. 247.
[6] W. N. Medlicott, *The Economic Blockade* (London, 1952), ii. 262.

supply of Bor to such an extent that deliveries to Germany would be delayed over a long period.[1]

Of all the non-ferrous metal ores where shortages of supply might ultimately develop in the German economy copper was in much the shortest supply in 1940. The determined German pressure on the question of the Mines de Bor probably reflected therefore the strategic situation as well as an over-all policy of attack on French capital holdings in south-eastern Europe. It was certainly not a sign of the programme of capital penetration of French interests in that area set out in Clodius's memorandum of 30 May.

Very much the same immediate interests motivated the demand for French shares in the Romanian oil industry later. Even the short campaign against France had revealed the danger in Germany's oil-supply situation. Throughout 1939 and 1940 a large number of different Allied plans had been put forward to divert Romanian oil supply away from Germany.[2] British and Netherlands capital represented 39·8 per cent of the participation in the Romanian oil industry, French capital 16·6 per cent, and United States capital 12·5 per cent.[3] Although the French government had certainly not slavishly fallen in with British plans for economic warfare, both this warfare and the sabotage that took place in the Danube valley must once again have pointed up the weaknesses that remained in Germany's supply position.

On 20 September and again on 26 September the German delegation repeated its demand for French shares in the Mines de Bor.[4] On 4 October the French delegation refused to give in to this pressure.[5] But this position was not maintained because of a later decision by Laval. The shares were eventually sold through a French bank in Czechoslovakia. The shareholders and directors of the company received no compensation above the price of the shares, paid in francs under the terms of the clearing agreement.[6] The sum of money involved was actually a very large one, 1,800,000,000 francs, and represented much the largest of Germany's capital encroachments in the first year and a half of the occupation.

No matter how diligently the French government defended itself, no matter how assiduously it sought concessions from its opponents, it could not ultimately postpone the signing of the clearing agreement. The agreement had been more or less accepted in principle when proposed. On 29 October the German government had agreed to pay pre-war Reichsmark prices to French exporters. They had also agreed to the imposition of the export tax on French products going to Germany, first proposed on 17 September.[7] Perhaps

[1] W. N. Medlicott, op. cit., ii. p. 264.
[2] For these plans see ibid., i. 250–9 and *passim*.
[3] Ibid., p. 250.   [4] DFCAA., i. 363 ff., 421.
[5] Ibid. ii. 32.
[6] Y. Bouthillier, op. cit., i. 113; P. Arnoult, op. cit., p. 284; Laval's own version may be read in *Laval Parle* (Geneva, 1947), pp. 169–81.
[7] DFCAA., ii. 254.

influenced by the aftermath of Montoire the French government finally signed the long-sought agreement on 14 November.[1]

It cannot be said that the Vichy government was unaware of the implications of the conclusion of the agreement. Their appreciation of German needs could not have been more exact. The haze of doubt which had surrounded German intentions after the conclusions of the Armistice had been the result of silence and indecision on the German side and some wishful thinking on the part of the French government. But the situation had now been reduced to its bare bones. Germany was no longer interested in a peace treaty, her interests were only to sustain the momentum of her Blitzkrieg by certain limited but vital incursions into the French economy. The memorandum submitted to René Belin, the Minister of Industrial Production, on 19 November from the Economic Delegation at Wiesbaden could not be a more exact appraisal of what those incursions would be.[2] The clearing agreements were not signed in ignorance but in full knowledge of what the subsequent developments were likely to be.

Economically, as well as politically, the German delegation had the whip hand. The policy of negotiating a series of concessions on each contract proposed had not been an especially successful one for the French. The only concessions so far achieved were German promises to supply sugar and potatoes. To delay negotiations on all Germany's economic proposals was in part to play into German hands. Already the Central Contracts Offices had been approached independently of the French government by French entrepreneurs. The Germans had only to wait, '. . . they know that French industrialists and businessmen want to sell their products. At the moment we are stocking phosphates, bauxite, iron ore, and colonial produce; in many respects Germany represents for many products the only immediate market.'[2] Little by little the pass, so furiously defended by the government, would be sold by the entrepreneurs themselves. The terms which they were being offered were much more favourable than those offered to the rest of the French population. Already the Algerian iron-ore mines at Ouenza had negotiated privately with the Germans. So also had the French bauxite mining companies.[3] Both of these were well out of the physical reach of the occupier—indeed Algerian iron-ore could be transported to Germany only with Italian or Vichy French co-operation. The French government could only bow to the inevitable.

The defeat and occupation of France turned her into a European trading power. Every year from 1940 to 1944 Franco-German trade played a more important role in German foreign trade. Since the network of clearing

---

[1] P. Arnoult, op. cit., p. 180. It is Arnoult's opinion that the political climate after Montoire was responsible; see also, id., 'Les finances de la France sous l'occupation' in P. Arnoult et al., La France sous l'occupation (Paris, 1959), p. 51.

[2] DFCAA., iii. 104.   [3] Ibid. i. 149.

treaties imposed on Europe by Germany forced almost the whole of French foreign trade with other occupied and Axis powers to pass through the central clearing accounts in Berlin the consequences for French trade were even more drastic. The secret negotiations between the Vichy government and the British government to maintain France's colonial and Mediterranean supply lines suggest that the Vichy government did not immediately realize how narrow its range of economic choice was.

TABLE 7

German Trade with France (including French Colonies) as a Proportion of Total German Trade by Value*

	Imports from France as a percentage of total imports	Exports to France as a percentage of total exports
1938	3·7	4·5
1939	2·6	2·8
1940	4·6	0·3
1941	11·1	4·6
1942	16·6	7·3
1943	17·1	6·5
1944 Jan.–July	18·3	5·6

* A. Munz, op. cit., p. 71.

Inasmuch as the military decision had been so clear cut, much closer contacts between the French and German economies were inevitable. Germany's victory in the west brought France reluctantly and on highly unfavourable terms back into the German trading network from which she had been increasingly excluded in the 1930s. France had to be integrated into the German *Grossraumwirtschaft*. The way in which this integration was achieved was a curious compromise between Germany's previous economic and trading policies and the desire for booty from the vanquished enemy. As the trade figures show, Franco-German trade in wartime was flagrantly unequal, nor did it show any trend to become more equal. It was conducted by means of massive payments from France to Germany every ten days under the guise of occupation costs. German purchasing organizations in France had sums accredited to them directly from the French occupation cost payments. Under the terms of the agreement financial transfers were only possible in one direction, from France to Germany.

Yet this unequal treaty did not satisfy those in the National Socialist party who hoped to acquire more booty. As a method of economic exploitation it was regarded as over-sophisticated. It may therefore be said that it was not merely the military events of 1940 which brought the French and German economies closer together, but the method by which Germany then proceeded with the economic exploitation of France. Although the seizure of booty as a stage of economic exploitation was very brief in France it did not completely disappear in August 1940. The seizure of machine tools in French aircraft factories, machine tools which would in 1943 have been of great value to Germany if still in France, continued. Many of the most modern machine tools in the Renault, Gnôme et Rhône, Hispano-Suiza, and Turbomeca works were pillaged in this early period.[1] Other methods of exploitation had been possible and were not entirely forgotten after 14 November.

On 6 August 1942 Göring made a speech to all Reich Commissars and Commanders-in-Chief in occupied territories. He made plain his discontent with the way France had been treated.

If a German car is seen in front of a French restaurant or café its number is immediately taken. But let a line of French cars be swallowing petrol behind the building and not a soul bothers. The other day I had the list of people who are still entitled to petrol brought to me. It's really incredible. And people pretend they are there for the German armaments industry. I am convinced that nowhere in France are there armaments orders which come anywhere near the orders in Germany. . . . basically I consider all of occupied France as a conquered country. It seems to me that in earlier times the thing was simpler. In earlier times you pillaged. He who had conquered a country disposed of the riches of that country. At present, things are done in a more humane way. As for myself, I still think of pillage, comprehensively.[2]

[1] CCDR., iv, A. I. 44.
[2] 'Göring et la "collaboration": un beau document', *Cahiers d'histoire de la guerre*, iv (May 1950).

IV

THE FRENCH ECONOMY DURING THE BLITZKRIEG (1940–1941)

IT could be argued that the encroachments on French economic life between June and November 1940 reduced France to a vassal state, like Slovakia or Croatia, in a way that the armistice itself had not done. The political wrigglings of the Vichy government in 1941 seem scarcely to have been felt by Hitler. Neither the sudden dismissal of Laval from power, nor Darlan's later reversal of policy and the war in Syria, had any real impact on German economic policy. Although the wind blew more warmly on Franco-German collaboration in spring 1941 it did not thaw Hemmen's attitude at Wiesbaden.

Germany's economic course had been set in August 1940, and events in France could not change it. All that was left to the French government was a stubborn economic resistance to German demands on their country. Nevertheless, the German war economy functioned in such a way that it was more and more driven towards the exploitation of France. So narrow were the margins on which Germany was operating that the temptation to solve shortages and widen bottlenecks by raiding French resources rather than by disturbing the delicate balance at home was overwhelming. The Blitzkrieg economy in Germany was an uneasy social compromise; rather than strain this compromise Germany had growing recourse to the French economy. The variety of German orders placed in France therefore grew although the general principles of German policy were in no wise changed. Nor, although the administration in the Hotel Majestic would have preferred a more lenient treatment of the conquered territory, was there much further debate in Germany about economic policy.

This debate was only reopened when the Blitzkrieg on Russia failed. In January 1942 Fritz Todt, the Minister of Armaments and Munitions, began the reorganization of the German war economy. The Blitzkrieg was abandoned and the German economy geared to a full-scale war. After Todt's death on 8 February his successor Albert Speer continued the work of reorganization with even greater determination. Part of this reorganization involved the centralization of German economic policy in a Ministry approximating as nearly as was possible in German conditions to a Ministry of War Economy. Amongst the victims of this growing Ministry was the *Wirtschafts- und Rüstungsamt* of the High Command of the Armed Forces. By this change military power over economic decisions in Germany was severely curtailed.

From the moment when this wholesale conversion of the German economy and its administration to the needs of a war of mass-production started, both the limited utilization of the French economy and the machinery by which this utilization was carried out began to change. Germany's increasing interest in the French economy before January 1942 indicated the strains of her own Blitzkrieg economy. After that date the greater degree of intervention in France was the result, not so much of *ad hoc* decisions, as of a conscious and deliberate change of policy.

The Führer-Decree, 'Armament, 1942', of 10 January which marked the ultimate break with the economics of Blitzkrieg, implied the need for increased utilization of occupied territory as one way of achieving Germany's new levels of production.[1] In 1942 the economic exploitation of France once more became an anxious search for a solution. But before then there was little change and the meetings of the Armistice Commission at Wiesbaden came to the participants to represent the performance of a series of sad and well-worn formalities.[2]

But it was through the medium of these formalities that the French and German economies became ever more closely linked. Indeed, it is only the existence of some long-term conception of a future European economy, however vaguely conceived, which can explain Germany's persistence at Wiesbaden in the face of the delaying tactics of the French. The only times when German threats were so violent as to force the French to concede the issue immediately were when French tactics appeared to menace Germany's immediate military interests. Those interests were sacrosanct, but behind them, running like a constant thread through the long negotiations, Germany's longer-term purposes seem from time to time to appear.

The existence of these more remote intentions may also explain the relative leniency of Germany in the matter of booty. Of course the seizures of booty were extensive, but not in comparison with what happened in eastern Europe. That there was an initial period in all the occupations when booty was the principal return to Germany has been already hinted at by other writers. Von Streng, in his tendentious defence of German agricultural policy in the General-Government, regards the period when booty was the main aim of German policy as ending in 1940, whereas Gerber considers it to have ended with the failure of the German Blitzkrieg.[3] In France there is no clear division between the ending of the policy of booty and the beginning of that of 'requisitions'.

---

[1] FD 3049/49 (Folder no. 1), 'Ministerium Todt'; *Kriegstagebuch des Oberkommandos der Wehrmacht (Wehrmachtführungsstab) 1940–45*, ii. 1265.

[2] So much so indeed that post-war French governments were unable to bring themselves to complete the publication of the documents appertaining to them.

[3] H. Von Streng, *Die Landwirtschaft im Generalgouvernement* (Tübingen, 1955); B. Gerber, *Staatliche Wirtschaftslenkung in den besetzten und annektierten Ostgebieten während des zweiten Weltkrieges unter besonderer Berücksichtigung der treuhänderischen Verwaltung von Unternehmungen und der Ostgesellschaften* (Tübingen, 1959).

The desire to seize booty was always there and, as in the case of machine tools, looting continued on a diminishing scale throughout the occupation.

How valuable was booty to the German economy? Apart from the difficulty of distinguishing between booty and 'requisitions' this question is very difficult to answer since there is no comprehensive record of the value of goods that could incontrovertibly be considered as booty. It must be agreed that goods and services taken or used without payment in any form whatsoever can be legitimately classed as booty. Some such goods were specified in the decree of the Commander-in-Chief of 20 May 1940, other goods had always been considered as legitimate prizes, and a further category was added by the terms of the Armistice itself. These categories were mostly armaments and war equipment specified in the Armistice agreement, and raw materials, especially stockpiles of scarce raw materials of strategic value. It was the opinion of General Thomas, the head of the *Wirtschafts- und Rüstungsamt*, that the stocks of non-ferrous metals captured in western Europe as booty might have been the main cause of the absence of any serious shortages of such materials in Germany in 1941.[1] By the end of 1940, 135,000 tons of copper had been acquired in this way.

The concept of booty must be drawn wider than this. In Table 8 those bounds are set wider. But the result is still an underestimation of the value of German booty in France. The use or confiscation of goods in France belonging to those countries in a state of war with Germany should be included, but the problems of valuation seem insuperable. Only the Belgian gold reserves confided to the French government for safe-keeping and later partly surrendered to Germany are included in this heading. The value of goods confiscated from Jewish owners is not known. Nor is it known what proportion of output of the farms operated by Ostland G.m.b.H. was reserved solely for German purposes. The seizure of persons and their transfer to Germany is not included since for the most part they were paid and cannot be classified under booty. Nor should the organized requisition of goods against payment, however arbitrary the payment, be considered as booty.

In that respect the question arises as to whether fines and confiscations imposed by the German authorities should be included. That the occupation costs paid by France were far greater than necessary to maintain the German administration in France might suggest the inclusion of such fines, but they had some basis in law other than international legal conventions seeking to define booty. Where no payment was involved the use of goods and services has been defined as booty; to distinguish between legally sanctioned but unpaid transfers of goods and mere seizure would in the circumstances be too nice. It might be argued that the problem of the seizure of persons could be resolved in the same way, but most such seizures involved some payments by Germany and it is impossible to distinguish those that did not.

[1] G. Thomas, op. cit., p. 245.

Within these definitions of booty, which are no less arbitrary than others, additional sums could be added to Table 8. The cost of acquiring the booty might justly be limited to the cost of transporting it. The administration necessary was already being paid for by the French government. In the case of the transfer of the Belgian gold reserve from Africa to Germany the French government did request payment for the fuel used. The total value of booty obtained from France appears very large. But it should be set in perspective against the calculations in the last chapter of France's total contribution to the German economy.

TABLE 8

German Booty from France 1940–1944*

	(1938 francs)†
Military equipment	52,355,000,000
Transport and communications equipment: seizures	39,787,628,600
Transport and communications: use of services	16,398,024,800
Raw materials	14,380,094,400
Manufactured and semi-manufactured goods	13,072,485,400
Belgian gold reserves	9,047,619,048
Agricultural products and foodstuffs	6,886,669,000
Works of art and valuables‡	1,800,000,000
Entertainments (radio, cinema, etc.)	795,594,400
Total	154,523,115,648

* CCDR., i, *passim.*

† 1939 francs converted to 1938 francs at 1·05 : 1. Current francs converted to 1938 francs at 0·538 : 1, a necessarily much more arbitrary procedure not accounting for the changing value of the franc throughout the war years.

‡ Objects not recovered by 1950.

A measurement of this kind contains much that would not formerly have been considered booty. Whether or not the Germans paid for the manufactured and semi-manufactured products obtained from France, the impact on the French economy was certainly different from that of the seizure of machine tools at the same period. Defined by the older sense of booty, the seizure of food, objects of value, military equipment, and so on, the total value of German booty would be less than in this table. But the futility of such a procedure for recouping the expenses of war as economies grew more complex was precisely the reason why booty in that sense ceased to be an established method for the payment of soldiers. That some productive effort, presumably beneficial in the circumstances of 1940, was necessary for the French economy to produce manufactured products, whether paid for or not by Germany is true. But exploitation, as conceived by the German government, was adapted to the circumstance of dealing with a modern industrial economy. In so far as French output for German purposes was not paid for, this represented the survival of a more primitive form of exploitation, in the modern world fairly to be considered as booty.

G

In fact the seizure of military and transport equipment represents over half the total of German booty. Booty was responsible for 15 per cent of the industrial products obtained from France, 24·5 per cent of the raw materials, and 10·5 per cent of the foodstuffs and agricultural produce. Because the placing of German contracts in France developed so slowly in 1940 and 1941 it is very probable that until the end of 1941, in spite of the complicated negotiations at Wiesbaden, Germany's main profit from the French economy was accounted for by booty. Throughout 1941 its role must have been a diminishing one and from the end of that year it became quite secondary to German orders and purchases in France.

By the time the French government had established its defensive positions and the clearing agreement had been signed, a number of more or less independent agreements between French entrepreneurs and German buyers had already taken place. In the case of the French aircraft industry the occupiers withheld recognition of the relevant 'comité d'organisation' for over two months in order to keep their liberty of manœuvre with the entrepreneurs.[1] After March 1941 the French negotiators persuaded their government that France must make a general and comprehensive settlement with Germany in which all German contracts could be lumped together.[2] For this purpose Bichelonne, Secretary-General for Industry and Internal Trade, drew up a memorandum attempting to express the value of German orders placed in France by that time.[3] German demands on the French economy had widened to include the beginnings of textile manufacture in France for German purposes, particularly for parachutes, and over 5,000 radio sets for aeroplanes. Otherwise aircraft, aluminium, bauxite, iron ore, non-ferrous metals, and a certain amount of colonial produce were the goods most in demand.

By 12 February 1941 96,000,000,000 francs had been paid to the German account with the Bank of France. Of this sum only 45,000,000,000 francs had been spent.[4] This was not so much the deliberate accumulation of a threat as an indication of the narrowness of German needs. The lightness of the economic demands made on Darlan in February supports this.[6] Nevertheless, in each of the main fields of German interest there was a general pressure to increase the demands on France and to make certain that they were met. The most costly and the most complicated of these demands was for aeroplanes.

One of the three conditions for reflating the French economy which Hemmen had laid down to Huntziger in their interview of 22 July 1940 had been the right to employ French aircraft factories in the unoccupied zone.[5] Huntziger's assent was given only in principle to this idea. Before the war industries sub-committee could discuss this request, however, the French

[1] DFCAA., iv. 70.
[2] Ibid., pp. 271 ff.
[3] Ibid., p. 276.
[4] Y. Bouthillier, op. cit., ii. 64.
[5] DGFP., Series D, xii, no. 11.
[6] DFCAA., i. 75.

government gave visas to a party of German engineers intending to carry out a preliminary survey of French aircraft factories south of the demarcation line.[1] In the same month the German Air Ministry installed a branch of the Quartermaster-General's department in Paris.[2] By 30 August French manufacturers had been approached with orders for completed aircraft although the German delegates at Wiesbaden seemed rather surprised to hear of it.[3]

At the end of September Germany began formal negotiations at Wiesbaden to place contracts for the manufacture of war material in the unoccupied zone, and of these contracts much the most valuable were those for aircraft and aircraft motors.[4] France's objections to such a plan were political, for the manufacture of completed armaments might well be said to infringe her neutrality. Economically there were overwhelming reasons for welcoming the German offer. The French aircraft industry had employed 230,000 on the eve of the invasion and almost the whole of these were now unemployed.[5] But when finally revealed the German plan had a much less welcome aspect. On 4 October Hemmen revealed that the Junkers firm wished to produce aircraft motors in France under their own strict technical control. To guarantee this control the French would be asked to provide a proportion of the shares in the French companies in question. Although these shares would remain French property they would be held by the Junkers corporation until the expiry of the contract.[6] Naturally enough the French government viewed this demand with the greatest anxiety.

One motive behind the German request for shares was the administrative resistance of the nationalized aircraft companies in France to the original German approaches. These unofficial approaches spoke of 2,500 aircraft to be completed including both French and German models.[7] Changes in the administration of the nationalized companies were introduced to enable them to centralize all these potential orders.

We were surprised to find [said Hemmen in the later course of the negotiations] that when it came to the commercial realization of this programme we were met by difficulties everywhere, and, to be precise, especially in the nationalized firms. We remarked that the directors continually asserted that they had to consult their government; the result was a loss of time. As for some directors with whom we were very satisfied we found they were recalled or removed to be replaced by other directors who probably had quite different instructions. The French government applied itself to reorganizing the firms, our programme was totally upset, . . .[8]

The demand for shares applied only to the nationalized companies.

The German demand appears to have divided the French. Bouthillier claims that Laval argued at the Council of Ministers on 14 November in

---

[1] Ibid., p. 84.	[2] CCDR., iv, A. 1. 44.	[3] DFCAA., i. 213.
[4] Ibid., p. 363.	[5] CCDR., iv, A. 1. 44.	[6] DFCAA, ii. 34.
[7] Ibid., p. 173.		[8] Ibid. iv. 57.

favour of its acceptance.[1] General Weygand and General Huntziger were in favour in so far as they thought such an agreement might be the beginnings of aircraft manufacture in France for French purposes. However, on 18 November the French flatly refused to transfer any shares while at the same time expressing their willingness to undertake aircraft manufacture.[2]

Once the agreement in principle had been established there began an examination of the extent to which the French could cope with German orders. That, of course, all depended on the extent to which they would be allowed to manufacture for French purposes. Göring's orders were that if France were to be allowed to produce for her own needs she must undertake a fundamental simplification of the types of aircraft she required.[3] Germany would continue to produce the same bewildering quantity of prototypes. As regards motors German requirements were put at 660 a month, about half of the output of May 1940, when the French industry was at full capacity. In fact production of motors for German purposes was never to approach this level throughout the war. From December onwards details of the programme began to be agreed on paper, and the completion began of those aircraft left partially finished in June for delivery to Germany, although no formal agreements concerning the unoccupied zone had yet been signed.

On 29 January 1941 the German delegation, stirred to greater urgency by the fact that German aircraft manufacturers were falling well short of the targets set for the planned invasion of Russia, and by the severe losses in the Battle of Britain, brought heavier pressure to bear. 'The desired goal must be reached,' said Hemmen, 'whether thanks to French goodwill or by all the means in Germany's power.'[4] Two months of shilly-shallying had infuriated Göring. 'You must understand that for us it is a matter of vital necessity and that it is absolutely impossible for us to wait. England is doing all she can to put at her disposal an entire continent which will be charged with replenishing her air force. We have to do the same thing as far as our means permit.'[4] Again Hemmen insisted on the transfer of shares as a safeguard. At the same time he gave repeated assurances that the transfer was not an attempt to take over capital control of the French industry. These share movements would have nothing in common with the surrender of French capital holdings in eastern Europe. The inner cabinet in France drew the conclusion that Germany had tried to manage without France but that their needs were such that they had realized French help to be indispensable.[5]

On 2 February de Boisanger informed Hemmen that the French government would in no circumstances make over any of the capital in its nationalized concerns.[6] Ten days later detailed discussion of the German orders began again, this time under threats so direct that the French government could

[1] Y. Bouthillier, op. cit., ii. 208.   [2] DFCAA., ii. 461.   [3] Ibid. iii. 310.
[4] Ibid. iv. 57.   [5] Ibid., p. 68.
[6] Ibid., p. 84.

only hope to secure some part of its own aircraft-building programme at the same time. A rather feeble attempt was made to confine manufacturing for German purposes to the occupied zone and for French purposes to the unoccupied zone. It was quickly snuffed out. 'We are in agreement', said General Forster, the German negotiator, 'that it is necessary to combine rigorously the industries of the two regions. That is an absolute principle with us and we foresee a common programme for the whole of the French and German industries, from the point of view both of equipment and personnel.'[1] Germany accepted the French refusal to transfer shares, and also accepted the principle that a large part of the raw materials for the German part of the 'common programme' would have to come from Germany. In general each party should provide the raw materials for its own finished output. The existence of the 'comité d'organisation' was recognized by Germany, but at the same time the German negotiators demanded a special mixed supervisory commission, since the contracts were so valuable. Not only this, but they also demanded some say in the nomination of directors of the national aircraft factories.[2]

The proportion in which aeroplanes would be produced was five for German needs to every one for French needs. France, however, would have no absolute right to any particular number of aircraft, German quotas had first to be fulfilled.[3] If the quotas were fulfilled there would be 3,000 aircraft for Germany, and 600 for France. This of course did not include the separate manufacture of aircraft motors for German purposes; 1,350 were foreseen over the same period as the contract for completed aircraft. The weakness of the programme was in its provision for raw material supply. To manufacture the necessary alloys would require 120,000 tons of coal monthly; Germany would be in a position to supply only 4,000 tons monthly.

Bouthillier gives the impression in his memoirs that it was only in April that work really started on fulfilling these contracts. He also conveys the impression that a far higher proportion of the total output than one-sixth went to French use. Yet not only had some contracts been placed before spring 1941, but a large proportion of the contracts placed in France by the German Air Ministry were neither for completed aircraft nor for motors. Although at least 175 aircraft and 662 motors had been delivered by 1 July 1941,[4] and these represented the greater part of the deliveries in total value, the incidental equipment was no small matter. In the months of May and June the value of the contracts placed grew by a further 100,000,000 Reichsmarks beyond its level at the end of April.[5] In the same period of time the number of workers in France employed on work for the German Air Ministry increased from 45,000

---

[1] FD 4796/45, Deutsche Waffenstillstandskommission, Gruppe Luftwaffe.
[2] DFCAA., iv. 194.   [3] FD 4796/45, op. cit.
[4] CCDR., iv, A. 1. 44.
[5] FD 5590/44, Reichsluftfahrtministerium, 'Kurzbericht 27', 5 September 1941.

to 62,800, including those in the relevant metallurgical industries. After July 1941 French deliveries to Germany averaged about 60 aircraft a month the quantity increasing in early 1942, as the programme reached its peak, to over 100 aircraft a month.[1] The quantity of engines produced for German needs was about 250 a month. In 1941, 4,800 tons of aluminium and aluminium alloys were delivered on Air Ministry contracts, and in 1942, 9,200 tons.[1]

Extensive though these German aircraft contracts were they still left manufacturing capacity free for France. French estimates suggest that even in 1942

TABLE 9

*Value of Reichs Air Ministry Contracts in France on 30 April 1941**

	(Reichsmarks)
Aeroplanes	259,320,433
Engines	136,936,546
Raw materials (aluminium, magnesium, etc.)	45,980,450
Intercommunication apparatus	49,183,128
Armaments and munitions	25,308,735
Machine tools, etc.	14,480,966
Semi-manufactured alloy products	13,997,695
Signals and navigation equipment	22,604,221
Ground equipment	7,421,020
Other indirect contracts	90,000,007
Total	665,233,201

* FD 171/45, Reichsluftfahrtministerium, 'Ausnutzung der Industrie in Frankreich für die Deutsche Luftaufrüstung', 15 July 1941.

37 per cent of the work force in the industry was working for French purposes.[1] In 1943 the whole industry would be employed for Germany. It is therefore necessary to observe that even in a case such as aircraft manufacture, where from the outset German policy had been to use French capacity, the German effort remained limited in scope for the first two years of the occupation. There were severe obstacles to increasing the quantity of German aircraft made in France, even had the desire to increase that quantity been present. After Albert Speer became Minister of Armaments and Munitions, and German aircraft production was increased, he was reluctant to utilize French capacity too far. One reason was the extensive modifications to aircraft specifications in Germany. Such modifications required constant close contact between the producer and the ultimate user; 'in an occupied area, where one cannot be sure that the management and workers in the industry will work with enthusiasm, it is impossible'.[2] The importance of obstacles of this kind is amply demonstrated by the fact that in August 1941, when French deliveries were already falling behind schedule, Germany preferred to use French labour

[1] CCDR., iv, A. 1. 44.
[2] Speer Report no. 30, Intelligence Report EF/AM/6, 'Interrogation of Albert Speer'.

in German aircraft factories. The arrival of prisoners of war from the Russian front in large numbers enabled Germany to use them as replacements for French prisoners of war employed in German agriculture. Between 80,000 and 100,000 of the Frenchmen so released were then employed in work for the German air force in Germany.[1]

The other aspects of the French economy in which Germany was interested were approached by the same tortuous path as the French aircraft industry. The implications for the level of employment and economic activity in France were less striking, and the sums involved were usually smaller. But for Germany these aspects were often just as vital.

Negotiations between L'Aluminium français and German industrialists began on 9 July 1940.[1] On 11 July representatives of the German firm Vereinigte Aluminiumwerke visited French works.[3] It was not only the German aluminium manufacturers who were interested in placing contracts in France, it was an important matter for the German Air Ministry also. On 23 July Göring ordered an inquiry into the way German aluminium production could be increased by the utilization of the newly occupied territories.[4] The first of the German negotiators, Dr. Westrick, was in fact the managing director of Vereinigte Aluminiumwerke. Later, when the committee system in Germany was introduced by Todt and Speer, Westrick was appointed Chief of the Special Ring for Light Metals, and hence remained responsible for the placing of aluminium orders in France even if no longer for their actual execution. The French manufacturers submitted their proposals at the end of July. The initial German demands envisaged a possible export to Germany of 400,000 tons of bauxite annually. The figure ultimately agreed on at the end of August was 250,000 tons.[5] The contract was agreed in principle with the Vereinigte Aluminiumwerke but almost immediately transferred to the Junkers Aircraft Corporation.

In general terms the contract covered not only bauxite for German purposes but also aluminium, alumina, and magnesium. By its terms French industry was bound to work at full capacity. Where the result was a total production greater than foreseen by these agreements such production would have to be offered to German purchasers. This last provision was an indication of German dissatisfaction with the agreed figure. In October, while the final details were being settled, they began to complain of its inadequacy, even threatening to send engineers into the French bauxite mines to see if output could not be

[1] FD 5590/45, Reichsluftfahrtministerium, Tagesmeldung 7a, 'Einsatz französischer Kriegsgefangener in der Rüstungsindustrie', 27 August 1941; J. Billig, 'Le rôle des prisonniers de guerre dans l'économie du IIIᵉ Reich', *Revue d'histoire de la deuxième guerre mondiale*, xxxvii (1960).

[2] DFCAA., i. 149. [3] Ibid., p. 195.

[4] FD 288/45, Mbh. in F., Wi.Abt., Generalluftzeugmeister to Generaldirektor H. Koppenberg, 23 July 1940.

[5] DFCAA., i. 178; iv. 276.

increased.[1] Faced with these demands the French government responded by asking 195 francs per ton instead of the preferred German price of 60 to 65 francs. The main pressure for a price increase of this kind came, naturally, from within the government, which hoped to reimburse itself for the low exchange rates. The entrepreneurs themselves would have been happy with a lower price. This further interference by the Vichy government in what at the outset had been an unofficial affair drove Hemmen to the point of threatening to take over the mines altogether.[2]

The French entrepreneurs were not especially pleased with this government interference in price setting, and the negotiations below government level seem to have continued. Vereinigte Aluminiumwerke signed a contract independently of these negotiations with the French Compagnie des Bauxites for a delivery of 60,000 tons of bauxite monthly, at a price of only 75 francs to the ton. The intermediary was a merchant bank, the Banque Monod. However, the French Armistice Commission delegation stuck to their policy and resolutely refused to recognize the acts of their own industrialists.[3] Finally, the contract was concluded at prices slightly above the original German offer in return for a German promise of small coal deliveries, and on 19 December the French government issued the licence for the export of 259,000 tons of bauxite to Germany, thus renewing the export trade prohibited in 1939.[4]

In January 1941 Germany opened negotiations for a renewal of the contract. Both sides claimed that they had not been adequately supplied under the previous contract, but on their side the Germans maintained that there had been no contractual relationship governing the coal supply they had promised.[5] Once again the same pattern of apparent urgency succeeded by apparent disinterest succeeded, in its turn, by extreme urgency ensued. After desultory discussions the German delegations began suddenly in March to apply heavy pressure on the French. On 10 March Hemmen demanded a further contract for the manufacture of aluminium, this contract to be successfully negotiated by 15 March. The contract was to assign 75 per cent of French output to German needs.[6] The German delegation estimated that the gap between French aluminium production and domestic consumption plus exports to Germany was so great that the French must somewhere be accumulating a secret stock of the metal.[7] There were attempts on the German side to take over Canadian and British holdings in the bauxite mines, and even a plan for joint Franco-German investment in an aluminium works in Provence.[8] There is little evidence that Germany took these projects very seriously and as early as 25 March France was offering 2,500 tons of aluminium monthly in return for guarantee of the coal deliveries.[9] It was, however, necessary for the French to agree to a German right of veto on the

[1] DFCAA., ii. 75.   [2] Ibid. ii. 99.   [3] Ibid., p. 254.
[4] Ibid., p. 342.   [5] Ibid. iv. 44.   [6] Ibid., p. 206.
[7] Ibid., p. 223.   [8] Y. Bouthillier, op. cit., ii. 216.   [9] DFCAA., p. 250.

presidents of the councils of administration of French aluminium works and also on the managing directors.

Deliveries on the first bauxite contract fell far below German expectations. They had not been completed up to the required quantity even by the end of 1941. One reason for this was the increasing German demand for French aluminium. If the bauxite incorporated in alumina and aluminium deliveries to Germany is included in the total, bauxite deliveries to Germany in 1941 amounted to approximately 70 per cent of total French output. Processed bauxite and completed aluminium represented 152,000 tons of crude bauxite exported to Germany in 1941.[1] Exports of unprocessed bauxite in the same year were 232,055 tons.[2] Although these figures did not measure up to German hopes, they represented a more than twofold increase in the quantity of bauxite Germany had obtained from France in 1938.[3]

The first aluminium contract had specified deliveries of 23,000 tons over a six-month period, and in its initial stages the new contract would represent a roughly similar monthly total. Alumina deliveries were to be at the rate of 16,000 tons over six months under the first contract and 2,000 tons a month under the second. The deliveries of alumina, although erratic, ran at approximately the agreed levels. Aluminium deliveries, as bauxite deliveries, fell behind.

To get sufficient quantities of bauxite from France was an especial problem for Germany, since the whole of French bauxite resources and a large part of the aluminium manufacturing capacity were in the unoccupied zone. Where the resources which Germany wished to secure were in the occupied area the problem was a great deal simpler. The system of control imposed on the iron-ore mines of Lorraine effectively meant that their production was as strictly controlled as that of the mines in the annexed areas. Hermann Roechling, the Saar industrialist, who was tacitly allowed to take several steelworks under his control, could receive orders directly from the occupying authorities.[4] On 30 July 1940 Mining-Assessor Corell was appointed to a similar position over the iron-ore mines in Normandy and Brittany.[5] The mines in Algeria negotiated directly with the German purchasers, and the French delegation to the Armistice Commission were more or less forced to accept in principle the result of that negotiation.[6] There remained the possibility of trying to raise the price to Germany.

[1] FD 474/45, Mbh. in F., Wi.Abt. 11/a, 'Ausnutzung der französischen Wirtschaft für Deutschland', 3 February 1942.

[2] FD 288/45, Mbh. in F., Wi.Abt. 11/a, 'Bauxit, Förderung und Lieferung in den Jahren 1921 bis 1943'; CCDR., v, M.P. 10. FD 474/45, op. cit., gives a figure of 198,000 tons.

[3] CCDR., v, M.P. 10.

[4] IMT., NI-3751; see also Commandant en Chef français en Allemagne, Tribunal Supérieur de Rastatt, 'Jugement no. 27/210 de l'affaire Roechling'.

[5] BA., R 7 VIII 207, Mbh. in F., Chef Militärverwaltung to Reichswirtschaftsminister, 30 July 1940.

[6] DFCAA., iii. 105 ff.

The agreement between the Ouenza mines and the Rhein-Ruhr Werke was a short-term contract for the delivery of 500,000 tons. The selling price was 100 francs a ton, an arrangement quite satisfactory to the Société de l'Ouenza in the circumstances.[1] The ore was ready for shipment in the Algerian port of

TABLE 10

French Production of Alumina and Aluminium and Deliveries to Germany (including Deliveries for Use in the Occupied Zone)*

(tons)

Month	Production of alumina	Production of aluminium	Deliveries to Germany		
			Alumina	Aluminium	Aluminium included in other contracts
1940					
Sept.	9,626	4,128	270	1,312	
Oct.	10,354	4,970	3,199	4,866	
Nov.	10,793	5,241	3,286	5,194	
Dec.	10,786	5,418	600	2,630	
1941					
Jan.	8,249	4,929		1,746	
Feb.	8,955	4,563	534	2,862	62
Mar.	10,733	5,228	4,220	2,724	180
Apr.	9,907	5,156	2,405	1,734	385
May	12,341	5,453	40	2,595	1,183
June	10,821	5,464	2,960	2,239	1,125
July	11,251	5,975	680	2,366	1,487
Aug.	12,772	5,992	1,700	2,140	1,670
Sept.	11,481	5,799	700	1,890	1,073
Oct.	12,914	5,230	2,920	1,204	1,321
Nov.	12,941	4,298	4,485	251	932
Dec.	12,565	4,132	5,994	139	1,002

* FD 475/45, Mbh. in F., Wi.Abt. 11/a, 'Gesamtproduktion an französischen Aluminium und Tonerde'.

Bône and would be shipped through Italy. Given the state of the British blockade of Vichy France there was certainly very little difficulty in transporting supplies of this magnitude across the Mediterranean.[2] At the same time as the short-term agreement had been signed the German negotiators had tried to secure a long-term contract guaranteeing supply from this source. The French government refused to countenance these longer-term negotiations and insisted that in respect of the short-term negotiations the price paid by Germany should be 200 francs a ton, slightly more than the price recently

[1] DFCAA., iii. 190.
[2] W. N. Medlicott, op. cit., i. 558.

paid by Italy.[1] The German price, which had been agreed by the firm, was based on the average iron-ore prices over the period 1928–37. The French negotiators claimed the much higher prices associated with the rearmament boom of 1938–40. Finally on 6 December the original contract was ratified at an agreed price of 160 francs to the ton. Germany was thus in a position to receive supply from all French iron-ore sources by December 1940.

It took about the same period of time for Germany to secure control over French phosphate resources. There had been a complicated network of agreements between French phosphate producers and their German customers before the war. At the start of September 1940 Germany requested their renewal in the form of contracts.[2] On 23 September this demand was extended into a request for regular supplies of phosphate from French North Africa.[3] Each of the French North African territories had a larger output of phosphates than metropolitan France and each had been a substantial supplier to Germany before the war.

TABLE II

*Production of Phosphates in French North Africa and Quantities Exported**

(tons)

	1936			1937		
	Production	Exports		Production	Exports	
		To Germany	To France (combined)		To Germany	To France (combined)
Algeria	604,500	165,465		597,629	..	
Tunisia	1,611,123	126,170		1,938,329	..	
Morocco	3,539,304	69,310		4,037,725	..	
		360,945	834,438		447,323	972,551

* FD 281/45, Mbh. in F., Wi.Abt. 11/a, 'Produktion der Nordafrikanischen Phosphate'; and ibid., 'Verladungen von Phosphat während des Jahres 1396'.

The largest French phosphate mines, those of Beauval and Hargicourt-Templeux were both in the occupied zone, the one near to Doullens in the department of Somme, the other a line of three mines further to the east stretching from Somme into the department of Aisne. The majority of the smaller mines were also in the occupied zone. Their costs, however, were much higher than the North African mines, and many of them were small enterprises with extremely limited possibilities of expansion, especially in view of the fact that lower-cost supply from North Africa was continuing to arrive. The contract signed in the week beginning 21 October for 50,000 tons of

[1] DFCAA., iii. 190.
[2] Ibid. i. 194.
[3] Ibid., p. 400.

phosphate monthly to be supplied to Germany was probably only fulfillable if Germany not only received her pre-war volume of supply from North Africa but also a considerable part of previous North African exports to France.

The German Ministry of Economics called together on 31 October the firms engaged in the import of phosphates and forced them to form jointly a company which could act as trade representative and importer for all of them. At the same time the share of the trade was strictly apportioned between the five firms involved. This was not done without angry protests from the firm of Henry Flohr, which was allocated 7 per cent of the trade.[1] This firm had built up the phosphate trade between French North Africa and Germany between 1924 and 1933, but in the draft agreements for the new trading company was offered originally only 2·2 per cent of the trade. It was the head of this firm who had first secured the draft contracts on 3 September, before the Armistice Commission took up the question, by direct negotiations with the Comptoir des Phosphates d'Algérie et de Tunisie. This contract had stipulated the sale of 120,000 tons of metallurgical phosphate from Algeria and Tunisia. The French Delegation to the Armistice Commission would not recognize this particular contract unless it were tied to a German guarantee of deliveries of sugar and potatoes to France.[2] When the potatoes began to arrive in December the French negotiators finally ratified the contract.[3]

It soon became clear to both parties in the first months of 1941 that the expected 50,000 tons of phosphate to be shipped monthly from North Africa was too high a total to be reached. It had to compete for shipping space with the 12,500 tons of metallurgical phosphates scheduled for delivery every month under the draft contract signed in September, and also with the iron ore, theoretically to the quantity of 40,000 tons monthly, from the Mines d'Ouenza. On 1 September 1941 therefore a new agreement was signed covering both iron ore and phosphate shipments from North Africa. Under the terms of this agreement the total tonnage of German deliveries was reduced fron 102,500 to 60,000, 36,000 tons of phosphate and 24,000 tons of iron ore.[4]

At the beginning of 1942 the French Admiralty claimed it could now manage to guarantee passage to only 44,000 tons monthly, 20,000 tons of phosphate and 24,000 tons of iron ore. In fact for most of the year the average maintained was slightly higher.[4] This failure to sustain the original level of contracted supply could not be compensated for by increased output in France itself in spite of an extension of activity in the French quarries. Production in the Beauval mine averaged 983 tons per month in the first quarter of

[1] FD 281/45, Mbh. in F., Wi.Abt. II/a, 'Bericht über die Gründungsversammlung der Roh-Phosphat-Handels-Vereinigung', 1 November 1940.
[2] DFCAA., ii. 344.   [3] Ibid. iii. 240.
[4] FD 281/45, Mbh. in F., Wi.Abt. 11/a, 'Bericht über die Phosphat- und Eisenerzlieferungen aus Nordafrika für Deutschland', 17 November 1942.

1941, 1,883 tons in the second quarter, and 3,293 tons in the third quarter, but the possibilities of such a production expansion were too limited.[1]

TABLE 12

*Deliveries of Phosphate from the Beauval Mine**

(tons)

	For French purposes	For German purposes
1940 Sept. to Dec.	4,625	4,330
1941	12,151	23,760
1942	17,646	32,000

* FD 281/45, Mbh. in F., Wi.Abt. 11/a, 'Compagnie française de phosphates, Rapport Général du Commissaire aux Comptes', 30 July 1943.

The French rubber industry signed an agreement on 10 September 1940 with the Reichs Office for Rubber, restricting its use of a raw material likely to be even scarcer in France than in Germany.[2] By the terms of this agreement the French tyre industry was limited to 40 per cent of its peace-time activity, measured by its consumption of raw rubber. Of the restricted output half was to be for French internal consumption and half for German use and exports. The French government also freed 5,000 tons of raw rubber from its stocks in the unoccupied zone for delivery outside the frontiers of that zone. An agreement of this kind was necessarily vague in its bearing on the future. French raw rubber supplies came from Indo-China, and there was little either the French or German governments could do to ensure their arrival. Of the 68,000 tons estimated arrivals, 18,000 tons only would be for French use.[3]

In fact the quantities of rubber arriving were insufficient to meet the needs of German contracts placed in France. From 1941 Germany began to supply France with small quantities of both natural and ersatz rubber. These quantities were rather greater than the quantities of rubber exported from France to Germany. But it must be remembered that large quantities of rubber tyres were seized as booty or used solely for German purposes. A further agreement restricted the allocation of tyres so that 70 per cent was for German purposes.[4] The supply of rubber left to France in 1941 was about 12·8 per cent of her normal peace-time supply.[4]

Some of Germany's demands on the French economy were not met by threats and negotiations but by the seizure of booty in the early stages of the occupation. This was particularly the case with vital non-ferrous metals and their ores, large stockpiles of which were seized in all the western occupied

[1] FD 281/45, Mbh. in F., Wi.Abt. 11/a, letter from Feldkommandatur 580, 15 April 1942.
[2] DFCAA., i. 249.
[3] Ibid. iii. 288; CCDR., vi, M.P. 13.   [4] CCDR., vi, M.P. 13.

territories. By a combination of seizure and negotiation Germany was consequently able to extend her control over a much greater total supply of those raw materials essential to her war economy.

Although the main German demands were for primary products and for the use of French aeroplane factories, as the Blitzkrieg economy began to feel the strain of the preparations for the attack on Russia, Germany's interest in French manufacturing capacity widened. The greater need for ammunition and explosives created in Germany an interest in the manufacture in France of armaments other than aeroplanes, while the policy of dispersing the production of consumer goods from Germany to France in order to liberate manufacturing capacity in Germany gave rise to the Kehrl plan for textile manufacture in France.

The French government's decision of 24 July 1940 had conceded that, in principle, armaments for German purposes might be manufactured in France provided they were not completed armaments. The concessions made in the case of the aircraft industry had left that principle not worth the paper it was written on, and acted as a standing invitation to the occupiers finally to sweep aside the vaguely worded clause in the Armistice Agreement covering this question. In January 1941 Germany proposed an agreement whereby the powder and explosives factories in the occupied zone would manufacture one million anti-aircraft shells and one million anti-tank shells for Germany over the space of eighteen months.[1] In March German demands for the manufacture of explosive in the occupied zone were renewed.[2] These preliminary negotiations were to form the basis of the much more concrete arrangements of 1942.

The Kehrl plan, signed on 1 February 1941 and named after an official of the Ministry of Economics, governed the exchanges between France and Germany in the textile industries to 30 September 1941.[3] It was to prove the forerunner of other such plans. Before the deliveries stipulated on both sides had in fact been completed a further textile agreement had been signed to run from 22 January 1942. To some extent the Kehrl plan, like most of the initial contracts of this kind, was a regularization of what had previously occurred. The agreement covered the period of time from 25 June 1940, since that was the date when the first contacts had been established between the occupiers and the French woollen industry. It also included in the stipulated deliveries of woollen goods from France to Germany and to the occupying troops the quantities of wool seized as booty in the early stages of the occupation.[4] The actual weight of goods exchanged by the agreements appears to favour France, but Germany was providing primary goods and France returning manufactured products.

---

[1] CCDR., iv. 1.   [2] Ibid., p. 190.

[3] Ibid. vi, M.P. 15, Annexe 1.

[4] FD 306/45, Rm.f.B.u.M., Rüstungs- und Beschaffungsstab Frankreichs, 'Deutsche/französisches Abkommen über die Verwertung der Textilrohstoffe durch die französische Industrie'; Hoover Institute, Militärverwaltungsbezirk Bordeaux, Box 1.

France was bound by the plan to deliver a total of 150,000 tons of textile goods to Germany. The actual deliveries effected are difficult to estimate since French sources confine themselves more strictly to the terms of the plan, whereas German sources include all incidental confiscations and purchases for German purposes. German estimates are that in 1941 Germany obtained 71,000 tons of wool and woollen goods, 64,000 tons of cotton and cotton goods, 70,000 tons of rags, and small quantities of silk and linen.[1] French estimates suggest 47,600 tons of wool and woollen products (32,000 tons under the terms of the plan), and 23,200 tons of rags (16,500 tons under the terms of the plan).[2]

Thus, as far as it was possible, Germany satisfied her demands on the French economy in 1941 by way of the Armistice Commission at Wiesbaden and by relying on superior military and diplomatic power to strengthen her hand in commercial bargains. On the whole her policy was successful in spite of the scope for lengthy negotiation which it left to the French. But it was not the sole policy by which Germany attained her ends. Where it seemed necessary to supplement it, it was supplemented by capital penetration into French industry and by the taking of booty. These alternative policies therefore were not entirely eclipsed.

Those French writers who have touched on this subject have paid a great deal of attention to the penetration of German capital into French industry. Perhaps this reflects the gloomy forebodings of the French government in March 1941. They, at least, were convinced that Germany's ultimate intention was to secure the totality of the French economy.[3] Where Germany did extend her control in a more direct way to the French economy this was done in a very piecemeal fashion, on each occasion to meet a specific situation or even to regulate problems which had been newly created by the war. When placed in its European setting German policy does not indicate that Germany intended to maintain any proprietary links with French firms after the war. French industry in the New Order would take its place, not a very significant or dynamic place, as a junior partner of German industry.

Enterprises belonging to Jews were subject to the same treatment in France as in other occupied territories. Since the French government itself actively discriminated against Jewish businesses before being so prompted by the occupiers, the initiative for this policy was not wholly German. Nevertheless, in this respect German policy in France was very like policy elsewhere, and if the laws were enforced in a slightly milder way that was because France was controlled by a military government. Firms could be taken over if the owner was a Jew or if the decisive votes or majority shareholders in a corporation

[1] IMT., 267–EC.
[2] CCDR., vi, M.P. 15, 'Convention franco-allemande du 1er février 1940', and 'État récapitulatif des prélèvements allemands', pp. 44 and 61.
[3] DFCAA., iv. 273.

were Jewish, or even if one-quarter of the capital was Jewish.[1] But there was no attempt in France to seize socialized property in the ownership of the state, as there was in Russia, or to take over complete temporary control of the firm by instituting a special trust (*Fideikommiss*), as in Poland and the General-Government, or to create large mixed governmental and private companies to run whole industrial sectors, like *Ostfaser* in Poland; only a very few French firms were forced to accept the absolute technical direction of a German firm (*Patenschaft*).[2] In general the Jewish businesses seized in France were relatively small affairs, although numerous. The only large firm that seems to have been submitted to the absolute technical direction of a German firm, apart from the steel works of Alsace-Lorraine, was Thomson-Houston (Paris), which was forced into signing a set of agreements with the Allgemeine Elektrizitäts Gesellschaft on 8 October 1943.[3]

The reasons behind German capital penetration into French industry were various. One was a decision by the Commercial Policy Department of the Foreign Office on 25 June 1940. In their outline of policy to be pursued towards France '. . . the surrender to Germany of French capital interests in those countries to be incorporated or attached to the Greater German economic area' was specifically mentioned.[4] French economic influence in the Balkans had remained high in the inter-war period in spite of German economic policy and was no doubt partly a reflection of the traditional French foreign policy in that area. A much vaguer concern of the Commercial Policy Department had been 'reparation for the economic injustice to Germany arising from the Armistice of 1918 and the Treaty of Versailles'.[4] Inasmuch as the peace settlement had changed the industrial structure of the two countries, its work had been reversed by the military verdict of 1940. Such considerations were the starting-point of an agreement such as that responsible for Francolor. Thirdly, capital penetration might in some cases increase the production of goods of particular interest to Germany where this could not be achieved by other means. There was never any concerted attack on French capital, but the determination to reduce French influence in Europe to that of a small power was unmistakable and lay behind every German move.

The best example of the first of these categories is the German pressure to obtain shares in French oil companies in Romania and in transport companies on the Danube. The prelude to the German moves was the negotiations which began on 16 July 1940 concerning German attempts to use French railway wagons for the carriage of oil westwards from Romania in return for a guarantee to France of a small but regular supply of Romanian oil.[5] These discussions persisted into October when they were swallowed up by larger issues.

[1] O. Ulshöfer, op. cit., p. 20.
[2] For a brief discussion, rather favourable to Germany, of the various systems of control practised by Germany see B. Gerber, op. cit.   [3] IMT., RF–106, v. 585.
[4] IMT., NG–3699; H. Böhme, op. cit., p. 277 has a fuller account of the document.
[5] DFCAA., i. 63.

When Pétain went to meet Hitler at Montoire, among the documents which he took with him which were not presented to the Führer was a declaration that the French would suspend the payment of occupation costs as a protest against their size.[1] M. de Boisanger intended to present a similar remonstrance to Hemmen on 20 November but refrained from doing so because Hemmen hinted at the important political consequences that might follow the Montoire meeting. The following day Hemmen mentioned the possibility that part of the French occupation costs could be paid by the transfer of share capital, and in particular capital in the Romanian oil industry. The French response indicates that their main fear was still internal inflation. Could not the sums of money be used for investment in the Romanian oil industry, thereby taking some steps to solve what might be considered a joint Franco-German problem? The discussion is one of the most interesting of all those at the Armistice Commission, as it reveals not only the deep conservatism of the Pétain government (whose fears for the external threats with which they were now menaced were matched by those for the inflationary threat at home), but also the determined ferocity with which the German delegation were prepared to pursue a matter where the needs of the Blitzkrieg coincided rather than conflicted with the reconstruction of Europe.

We are still at war [said Hemmen], and we need an immediate influence on the production of petrol in Romania. We can not therefore wait for a peace treaty.[2] ... Besides [he added], it is not politically desirable that France should invest capital in Romania; useful employment for that capital will certainly be found in France itself for the work of reconstruction.[3]

The shares which Hemmen particularly wanted were those of the Concordia Company, a subsidiary of the Belgian company Petrofina. Another company, Steaua Romana, had its shares held by the Romanian government, the Anglo-Iranian company, and merchant bankers many of whom were French.[4] Since the affair of the Mines de Bor the French attitude towards real transfers of this kind had been very hostile. The only such transfer had been the shares of the Banska Hutni, whose retention in French hands would have presented almost insuperable administrative difficulties, since it now operated within the territory of four separate jurisdictions, Germany, the General-Government, Bohemia–Moravia, and Slovakia.[5] Nevertheless, Bouthillier was placed on the horns of a dilemma, should he allow the share transfers to be discounted against the occupation costs in the clearing balances in the hope that the threat of inflation might be slightly reduced, or should he preserve the 'national patrimony' against a better day? Since the French government feared that German interests would not be confined to the Balkans they decided to resist German pressure. In December the Deutsche Bank tried to purchase shares

[1] P. Arnoult, op. cit., p. 30.　　[2] DFCAA., ii. 505.　　[3] Ibid., p. 511.
[4] W. N. Medlicott, op. cit., i. 250; P. Arnoult, op. cit., p. 324.
[5] Y. Bouthillier, op. cit., ii. 113.

in the Banque Commerciale Roumaine from a French bank. And in January the German government widened their interests into shares in Romanian transport companies.

The extension of German demands may well have been a response to British economic warfare in the Danube valley. In September 1939 the British government had begun to buy up all available and purchasable means of oil transport from Romania to Germany.[1] The large French group, *S.F.N.D.*, 'the Danube flotilla' as it was known, comprised more than ninety vessels. It had been hurriedly transferred against the wishes of the Romanian government at the moment of the French collapse. The Romanians had managed to detain some of the vessels and Germany now demanded both the ships and the company. In retaliation for French delays they seized sections of oil pipeline intended to complete the line from Donges to Montargis to use as a pipeline from Ploesti to Giurgiu.[2]

But at the same time as German demands were stepped up, so did the terms of their offer change in another way. Among the paper the invading forces had captured in Holland were large quantities of French government bonds of the 1939 4 per cent rearmament loan. These the Germans now offered in return for petrol and bank shares in Romania. In the first week of March 1941 the French government agreed to cede, in return for these bonds, shares in the Romanian oil industry, in the Banque Commerciale Roumaine, and in the Banque Générale de Crédit Hongroise.[3] When the Deutsche Bank finally acquired the whole of Concordia, payment was made in City of Paris loan certificates.[4]

Meanwhile the French threat to suspend payment of the occupation costs had been put into practice for two instalments at the beginning of December 1941.[5] The whole issue was to be reawakened by Darlan's attempts at a closer agreement with Germany. The idea of a reduction in the occupation costs in return for political concessions by France was closely tied by Hemmen to the possibility of France's paying some portion of those costs in share capital.[6] At a meeting of the full Economic Delegation on 16 May 1941 de Boisanger claimed that the burden of the costs had now become quite insupportable for France, and on 21 May Couve de Murville, president of the finance subcommittee of the Armistice Commission, repeated this warning.[7] Neither the instalment of 20 May nor that of 30 May was paid by France. On 3 June Hemmen suggested that if the arrears were paid a term of two months could be set for the negotiations and during that period France might pay at the rate of only 15,000,000 Reichsmarks a day of which 5,000,000 might be transfers either of shares or of gold from the Bank of France.[8] The memorandum of

[1] W. N. Medlicott, op. cit., i. 254.   [2] DFCAA., iii. 391.
[3] Ibid., iv. 173.   [4] P. Arnoult, op. cit., p. 330.
[5] Ibid., p. 33.   [6] DFCAA., iv. 417.
[7] Ibid., pp. 421-43.   [8] Ibid., p. 482.

25 June 1940 had laid down the transfer of part of the French gold reserve as another specific aim of German policy.[1]

The French cabinet was again divided over this offer.[2] To decide on the better policy meant to decide on the ultimate outcome of the war, although whatever decision was taken Germany's massive accumulation of purchasing power would continue. Darlan's view seems to have been that, given the size of Germany's credit with the Bank of France, the only possibility left to the French was to prevent the Germans using it exactly as they wished by a judicious policy of concessions. On 3 July Germany offered an agreement in which the sum to be paid in transfers of this kind was smaller, 3,000,000 Reichsmarks out of 10,000,000.[3] The agreement in respect of the transfers was accepted finally for three months, to run from 11 July to 10 October, thereby imposing an upper financial limit of 1,800,000,000 francs. Since all the conditions of both sides were not met the agreement remained provisional. As far as Germany was concerned the right to demand 20,000,000 Reichsmarks a day in occupation costs if she so wished remained untouched; indeed the French acceptance of the new terms in July was treated 'dilatorily' by the Foreign Office.[4] The French government had been allowed to publicize the reduction in the occupation costs to 15,000,000 Reichsmarks a day. The German Foreign Office was therefore not certain how easily this could revert to 20,000,000 Reichsmarks if the negotiations proved unsatisfactory to Germany. Economic sanctions would be against Germany's own interests, seizures of personal holdings of securities or jewelry would antagonize the population, 'which to a large extent works for us'.[4] The issue could only be resolved by awaiting a moment when it was easier to demand the original sum once more from France.

In spite of the inconclusive nature of this agreement and Germany's general lack of interest in concluding it, a considerable sum in share values was transferred to Germany as one of its results and further sums passed as a result of bullying and bargaining on the German part. The French intention in accepting the proposals had been to pay in capital holdings in the Balkans and Poland.[5] Over the subsequent period France ceded shares in the Huta Bankowa, Tubes de Sosnowice, Mines de Sosnowice, and Houillières de Dombrowa, all in Poland, together with Zincs de Silésie now in Germany.[6] This list became much longer in 1943 by the addition of further companies in Romania and Poland.

If share transfers of this kind fitted in with the concept of a New Order and were made with one eye on the peace, German capital investment in France was often made for short-term reasons. The project to construct gas

[1] H. Böhme, op. cit., p. 277.
[2] DFCAA., iv. 590; Y. Bouthillier, op. cit., ii. 64.   [3] DFCAA., iv. 607.
[4] DGFP., Series D, xiii, no. 222.
[5] Y. Bouthillier, op. cit., ii. 65.   [6] P. Arnoult, op. cit., p. 316.

generators in France was conceived as a way of reducing French oil consumption even further. Of the augmented capital in October 1942 of les gazogènes Imbert 7,500,000 francs came from the German firm of the same name.[1] In autumn 1941 Krupp and I. G. Farben tried to get hold of the small wolfram mine at Montmins, but failed to do so by official approaches. Not to be thwarted they tried more devious methods, 'Kyllmann gave it as his opinion that the I. G. would never get anywhere along the legal paths they had pursued. A confidential agent of Krupp is travelling to Paris today and he considers it perfectly correct to make yet another attempt to get hold of Montmins through "special channels" and by "special means".'[2] The attempt was successful. In January the Bankhaus Worms acting for I. G. Farben acquired a majority of the shares of the Montmins mine through its subsidiary the Société d'études minières. In May 1942 I. G. Farben purchased the molybdenum mine at Chateau Lambert.[3] In these cases the larger German firms were ensuring their raw material supply by vertical integration.

Much the best known of the German investments in France, however, is the creation of Francolor. To understand what lay behind the creation of Francolor it is necessary to go back to 1914. At that time the massive technical superiority of the German dyestuffs industry over all others meant that it controlled almost 90 per cent of the French market. This stranglehold was quite broken as a result of the First World War, and the French dyestuffs industry as it existed in the inter-war period was essentially a creation of the immediate aftermath of the German defeat. German investments in France were confiscated and, in this instance, used to create a dyestuffs industry under French national control. This policy of confiscation was supported both by the reparations clauses of the Treaty of Versailles and by a highly discriminatory tariff. All raw materials and plant which could be used to build up the French domestic industry were admitted into France free of duty under the sixth article of the Treaty of Versailles and were taken from Germany at knock-down prices as reparations. The tariff on German dyestuffs exports to France, however, was four times the French minimum tariff, and all exports not classed as reparations had in addition to pay a supplementary reparations duty of 26 per cent of their value. The biggest works of the Compagnie Nationale, at Villers-Saint-Paul (Oise) was built on the ruins of the former German Höchst works.

The state of industrial war in which the French, by virtue of their control of the occupation zone and the German plant situated in that zone, had every advantage, certainly in respect of industrial espionage, was brought to a temporary close by a forty-five year treaty between the new French industry and the German firms signed in 1920. The treaty allowed the German industry a

[1] CCDR., iii, A. 1. 8.

[2] FD 5148/45, Fachabteilung Ferrolegierungen, Stahl- und Leichtmetall-Veredler der Wirtschafts-Gruppe Chemische Industrie, 'Notiz über Telefon-Gespräche mit Bergassessor Kyllman, Krupp A. G.', 15 November 1941.

[3] Ibid., 'Molybdän Frankreich'.

share in the profits of the new French firms in return for technical help in establishing them.[1] These arrangements collapsed completely during the French occupation of the Ruhr. The Compagnie Nationale was taken over by a private firm, Établissements Kuhlmann, which unilaterally revoked the now inapplicable treaty in 1924. The German manufacturers regarded the French as being entirely to blame for this breakdown. By 1927 the German share of the internal French market was a mere 9 per cent.[2] In that year the cartel was refounded on the basis of the shares in the market of the respective industries over the period 1924–7. The Swiss industry had usurped the German place as the major supplier of chemical imports to France and the French colonies and France had begun to export dyestuffs herself. The arrangements of 1927 recognized the level to which French exports had risen, 11,000,000 Reichsmarks a year. To this cartel Switzerland was admitted in 1929 and Britain in 1931.

There were nine dyestuffs works in France at the time of the French defeat, bound more or less closely by capital arrangements in the Centrale des matières colorantes.[3] The German industry itself had meanwhile become associated in the cartel of I. G. Farben. Like other large German firms I. G. Farben was invited by the Reichs Ministry of Economics to submit recommendations for the reorganization of the European economy in so far as it touched on its special interests.[4] The gist of their recommendations was that all further development of the French chemical industry which might encroach on German export markets should be stopped forthwith. These proposals were not specific to France, but there were certain proposals of a more detailed nature which were. There was no possibility of undoing the developments of the previous twenty years in other European countries. 'But that may make it appear more

[1] FD 2203/45, Bundle D (NTLL.), I. G. Farben, 'Entwicklung und Stand der französischen Chemiewirtschaft unter besonderer Berücksichtigung der deutschen Ausfuhrinteressen, gegliedert nach Verkaufsgebieten, sowie Wünsche spezieller Art für bestimmte Produktionsgebiete'.

[2] R. Denzel, *Die Chemische Industrie Frankreichs unter der deutschen Besetzung im zweiten Weltkrieg* (Tübingen, 1959), p. 116.

[3] Établissements Kuhlmann; Société anonyme des matières colorantes et produits chimiques de Saint-Denis; Compagnie française de produits chimiques et matières colorantes de Saint-Clair-du-Rhône; Société des produits chimiques et matières colorantes de Mulhouse; Établissements Steiner, Vernon; Société anonyme pour l'industrie chimique, Mulhouse–Dornach; Mabboux et Camell; Société des matières colorantes de Croix-Wasquehal; and Prolor. Of these, the fourth and sixth had been in Germany before 1914. Only the second and fifth were not based on German potential taken over during the war. The first six were integrally bound in the Centrale des matières colorantes, the last three more loosely associated. In addition, at Saint-Fons, near to Lyons, there was the Société pour l'industrie chimique à Bâle, belonging to the Swiss section of I. G. Farben.

[4] W. Schumann and G. Lozek, 'Die faschistische Okkupationspolitik im Spiegel der Historiographie der beiden deutschen Staaten', *Zeitschrift für Geschichtswissenschaft*, xii (1964). For the recommendations submitted by the Zeiss firm see W. Schumann, 'Das Kriegsprogramm des Zeiss-Konzerns. Ein Beitrag zum Problem des staatsmonopolistischen Kapitalismus und der faschistischen Politik der "Neuordnung" Europas und Ostasiens während des zweiten Weltkrieges', ibid., xi (1963).

justifiable in planning a European *Grossraumwirtschaft* to destine the German chemical industry once more to the leading position which its technical, economic, and scientific rank warrants.'[1] Accordingly I. G. Farben proposed that the Reich should take over 50 per cent of the capital of the French dyestuffs industry to prevent any further impediment to German exports to France and to prevent French competition in third markets. In particular the dyestuffs division of Établissements Kuhlmann should be taken over with the other dyestuff firms of Centrale des matières colorantes. This would except the two firms in Mulhouse, which would be considered henceforth purely as German firms. They had in fact been placed in the hands of trustees immediately after the occupation of Alsace. The Société anonyme des matières colorantes et produits chimiques de Saint-Denis, which had not been founded as a result of French government policy after 1918, would also be excepted. The effect of the proposals would therefore be to break up the Centrale des matières colorantes and recreate the former Compagnie Nationale, but as a Franco-German company under German domination. The new company would have the sole right to introduce new products on the French market. Its production would be confined to the French and colonial markets. All duties on products not produced by the new company would include preferences for Germany and the tariff itself would have to be bearable.

These proposals were forwarded to the Ministry of Economics on 3 August 1940. The French industry was not to be put out of business, it was to become a tightly controlled subsidiary of the larger German trust. This was in keeping with I. G. Farben's view of the French chemical industry as a whole.

The co-operation between the German and the French industries which is indispensable to securing a planned economy is best achieved through the creation of *long-term international syndicates*, for the most part through the tightening of present conventions, for which a clear agreement with the French industry is a precondition. In contradistinction to the previous forms of Franco-German chemical agreements these syndicates must be placed under a tightly unified leadership, which, considering the greater importance of the German chemical industry, must lie in German hands and have its seat in Germany.[2]

The French manufacturers approached I. G. Farben two days after the proposals had been submitted to the Ministry of Economics.[3] The two sides met at Wiesbaden on 21 November 1940. The German delegation announced that they considered the 1927 cartel to be utterly broken. Germany would recover her pre-1914 leadership in the chemical industry, the French industry would be confined to the domestic and colonial market, and a new Franco-German firm would be created to share that market.[4] Any French competition in German Markets was henceforward out of the question.

---

[1] FD 2203/45, Bundle D (NTLL.), 'Entwicklung . . . der französischen Chemiewirtschaft . . .'.   [2] Ibid., p. 44.   [3] DFCAA. ii. 520.   [4] Ibid., p. 462.

You should not therefore be surprised that while respecting your existence we should ask you to take your appropriate place within the framework of I. G. [said Hemmen]. For you will have your place, but not so that you may permit yourselves the uncontrolled competition of before the war. Besides, that is the line of our general economic policy towards France. We have already applied the same principles to other industries.[1]

That was the way in which the French should understand the meeting between Hitler and Pétain. The German desire was to co-operate with the French not on the basis of the past but on the basis of the future.

Note that, set in the framework of our programme of European reorganisation, these proposals are economically very advantageous for you. They are in your interest. They are in the interest of the I. G. They are above all in the interest of Europe, since, essentially, it is a question of reorganising the continent of Europe.[1]

The French resistance to these proposals was very stiff. When the negotiations recommenced at Paris on 20 January 1941 the German plans, which at the outset had been almost exactly those which I. G. Farben had itself first formulated, had been modified. I. G. Farben no longer proposed to pay for their 50 per cent participation in the new company in cash but by transferring 12,750 of its own shares at a nominal value of 1,000 Reichsmarks each, thus overcoming one of the biggest objections in principle of the French government.[2] In addition. the new company would still be able to export to Belgium, Spain, and Portugal provided it did not exceed the level of French sales there in recent years.[3] Before the French negotiators gave in they were able to force still further concessions from the Germans. At a meeting on 12 March 1941, at which the representatives of the economic section of the German military administration in France and of the French government were present, the German negotiators finally abandoned their claim that the new company should have a complete monopoly of innovations on the French market and that its direction should be entirely German. The French government accepted that 51 per cent of the capital should be German, but it was agreed that the president of the council of administration should always be French and that Germany would not use the agreement as a precedent for demanding majority capital holdings in other French industries.[4]

I. G. Farben bound itself not to export to the French internal market and colonies goods manufactured by the new company, Francolor. In return I. G. Farben would be freed from competition in other markets.

Given the tight interconnection between the French economy and that of the immediately neighbouring countries the field of action of Francolor has been enlarged

---

[1] Ibid., p. 527.

[2] FD 2203/45, supplement B (NTLL.), I. G. Farben, 'Francolor-Vertrag'.

[3] R. Denzel, op. cit., p. 135; P. Arnoult, op. cit., p. 306; Y. Bouthillier, op. cit., ii. 185.

[4] FD 2203/45, supplement B (NTLL.), I. G. Farben, 'Protokoll der Sitzung betreffend Bildung einer deutsch-französischen Farbstoffgesellschaft, abgehalten in Hotel Majestic, Paris, am 12 März 1941'.

in the sense that the company will also participate in sales to Belgium, Spain, and Portugal, considered in some measure as an extension of the internal market. The *I. G.* is well aware that it could be in the course of a long-term development in the interest of the two parties that, after the war, an export of French dyestuffs to one or other of the overseas export markets could equally take place. This point of view has been expressed in the wording of article fifteen of the constitution.[1]

The original plans of the German trust in regard to the French dyestuffs industry were thus considerably changed in the course of trying to implement them and the French industry came rather better out of the affair than it might have been expected to do. But in its general outlines German policy towards the French chemical industry had not changed, and the founding of Francolor is one of the most significant indicators to the shape of the European economy under the New Order.

The final agreements over Francolor did not by any means mark the end of German interest in the French chemical industry nor even in the dyestuffs industry. It is clear from Director ter Meer's account of the Francolor agreement that it was regarded by the German company as the thin end of a wedge rather than as a final settlement.[2] His report regretted the failure to secure an absolute monopoly of the market to the new company. The important textile centre around Lyons was still supplied by the Swiss branch of I. G. Farben at Saint-Fons.[3] In order to secure that particular market for Germany a drastic reduction of raw materials and intermediate products supplied to the Swiss industry would be undertaken. The principles of intervention in the chemical industry in its other branches remained what they had been in the case of the dyestuffs industry; provided French industrialists were prepared to accept a wholly subsidiary role in the European market, German participation in the industry took the form of a capital investment.

The inter-war period had seen a sharp competition between French and German manufacturers in the field of artificial fibres. In 1919 German producers had signed an agreement with Swiss producers whereby the French subsidiaries of the Swiss firms were brought under German control. But as the manufacture of artificial fibres increased in France, so did the French manufacturers bring successful pressure to bear on the government to increase the tariff. In 1929 they united in the Comptoir des textiles artificielles. Fearing that it would be totally excluded from the French market I. G. Farben took counter measures. In 1931 it formed an association of eight firms, the Association Vistra, to produce in France the Vistra thread which had been one of I. G. Farben's most successful exports. However, pressure from the French cartel forced two firms to drop out of the agreement and the others to weaken their

---

[1] FD 2203/45, supplement B (NTLL.), I. G. Farben, 'Constitution de la Francolor', 3 November 1941.

[2] Ibid., 'Aktennotiz. Betrifft: Établissements Kuhlmann–I. G. Besprechung in Frankfurt/M. am 15 März 1941', 17 March 1941.

[3] See p. 101, n. 3.

ties to the German company.[1] After 1937 German exports of artificial fibres to France showed a sharp downward trend in the face of this domestic competition. After the French defeat the German manufacturers showed themselves once more eager to renew their foothold in France. On 28 December 1940 the French government agreed to the formation of France Rayonne, to manufacture artificial textiles. The position of the German negotiators was very strong, for Germany's chemical industry meant that in wartime circumstances she had an extensive degree of control over the necessary raw materials. Germany agreed to supply cellulose and sulphur products in return for one-third of the capital of the new company. Like the settlement arrived at in the dyestuffs industry, the terms seem to suggest that it was Germany's intention to leave France, although much reduced, still part of the new Europe, able to play a small part in neighbouring economies but fundamentally a mere subsidiary of the greater industrial power of Germany.

As in other spheres of German economic policy strategic and military factors came to dominate as the war continued, and it is to these that the German plans to develop a larger artificial rubber industry in France must be attributed. The Michelin tyre company turned down an offer of German financial participation in 1941, and it was partly this rebuff that induced *I. G. Farben* to undertake the building of an artificial rubber works in France.[2] The acute shortage that wartime developments brought about in the supply of rubber to France meant that French industrialists were nothing loath to take part in this investment programme, especially when it became clear in 1942 that Germany would not be able adequately to supply France with the artificial product.[3] In March 1942 I. G. Farben and the French firm of Rhône-Poulenc agreed to the construction of an artificial rubber factory which, beginning in spring 1945, would produce at a level of 12,000 tons a year.[4] Even in October 1943, however, the French authorities had not finally sanctioned these plans.[5]

Where German contracts were not wholly dictated by immediate military needs they too indicate a future Europe within which France would be included as an industrial power subsidiary to Germany, not simply a member of a peripheral ring of raw material suppliers.

In his memoirs Bouthillier estimates the value of German contracts in France in December 1940 at 60,000,000,000 francs, including 5,500,000,000 in the textile and leather industries and 4,000,000,000 francs in the engineering industry.[6] This looks like a gross overestimate. Very few contracts had been

[1] FD 2203/45, Bundle D (NTLL.), 'Entwicklung . . . der französischen Chemiewirtschaft. . .'.
[2] FD 2203/45, supplement A G2 (NTLL.), I. G. Farben, 'Aktenvermerk über eine Besprechung im Reichswirtschaftsministerium am 14.10.1941'.
[3] Ibid., Rwm. to I. G. Farben, 9 March 1942.
[4] Ibid., 'Aktenvermerk über eine Besprechung im Lyon am 11 März 1942'.
[5] Ibid., I. G. Farben to Rwm., 26 October 1943.
[6] Y. Bouthillier, op. cit., ii. 177.

finally agreed on by December 1940. In April 1941 the value of German contracts in France was 1,500,000,000 Reichsmarks.[1] About 40 per cent of this total was represented by contracts placed with the French aircraft industry.[2] One year later the value of German contracts in France stood at 2,360,000,000 Reichsmarks.[3] By autumn 1942 the level would have passed 4,000,000,000 Reichsmarks.[4] In December 1941 alone 207,000,000 Reichsmarks worth of contracts were placed in France.[4]

On 29 November 1940 the Reichs Ministry of Economics encouraged German firms to distribute orders in France through the new Central Contracts Agency (*ZAST.*). 'Since for a certain space of time no resumption of the manufacture within the Reich of those products which are susceptible of being dispersed is foreseeable, it is in the interests of the firms to utilize every possibility of dispersal by contract as quickly as possible.'[5] This exhortation was backed up on 9 December by threats to close down the production of certain consumer goods in Germany altogether in order to achieve a more satisfactory flow of contracts abroad.[6] It was also on 20 November that a decree of the High Command in France had constituted the French 'comités d'organisation' as 'Warenstellen' and appointed the heads of these committees, the 'répartiteurs', as heads of the 'Warenstellen'.

The process of dispersal of manufacturing contracts had a momentum of its own, especially as the ordnance departments of the Armed Forces became more and more anxious about the slightness of Germany's reserves of military equipment. At the start of 1941 General Thomas asked Keitel to influence Hitler's attitude more favourably towards France. 'It is becoming increasingly apparent that in order to obtain the greater production which the war imposes on us we must exploit France with all its resources more exhaustively than hitherto.'[7] More lorries could be manufactured in France and greater quantities of raw materials purchased. The biggest obstacle to economic co-operation between France and Germany was the continued separation of the two most northerly departments, which only created ill-will but was economically inefficient. Keitel's reply, after he had consulted Hitler, was an unfavourable one.[8]

But the High Command in France did not abandon hope. On 27 March they returned to the charge.

---

[1] Hoover Institute, Militärverwaltungsbezirk Bordeaux, Mbh. in F., Wi.Abt., 'Das französische Preisproblem', 17 April 1941.

[2] FD 171/45, Reichsluftfahrtministerium, 'Ausnutzung der Industrie in Frankreich für die Deutsche Luftaufrüstung'.

[3] FD 671/46, Mbh. in F., Wehrwirtschafts- und- Rüstungsstab Frankreichs, 'Lagebericht April 1942', 15 May 1942.   [4] IMT., no. 267–EC.

[5] BA., R 7 VIII 207, Rwm., 'Allgemeine Bekanntmachung der Mobbeauftragten der Wirtschaftsgruppen der Eisen und Metall verarbeitenden Industrie an alle Betriebe', 20 November 1940.

[6] Ibid., Leiter der Hauptableitung II, 9 December 1940.

[7] *Kriegstagebuch der OKW.*, i. 997.   [8] E. Jäckel, op. cit., p. 152.

There would be nothing to bring against this state of affairs from the German stand-point [they wrote] if the principal task of the military administration in the economic sphere, as at the beginning of the occupation, was still to transport from France, foodstuffs, raw materials, and machines, and otherwise to limit itself to securing the maintenance of law and order necessary to the life of the inhabitants. However, this phase of *booty* (Ausräumung) has in the meantime been replaced by the phase of *exploitation of the economic strength* of France. The French economy has been drawn into the greater German economic plan.[1]

The almost imperceptible stages by which French economic independence had been reduced tend to conceal the scope of what had been done. The principle on which Hemmen had been told to act, that the Armistice must not be allowed to block Germany's economic demands on southern France, had been carried through consistently. Hemmen had an easier task than in any other of his negotiations. Every month that passed after the Armistice rendered the real relationship of France towards Germany a weaker and weaker one. Every German negotiation was conducted from a position of massive, and increasing, strength. By May 1941 the economic clauses of the Armistice Agreement no longer effectively governed Franco-German economic relations, so extensive were the concessions going beyond the agreement which Hemmen had secured. A commissar for foreign exchange, a commissar for the Bank of France, and a certain measure of control over all the frontiers of the unoccupied zone were concessions whose aim was to secure for Germany 'some influence over the whole of French economic and financial life, that is to say over that of unoccupied France including the overseas territories and to align them with their German interests'.[2]

The clearing treaty had been based on Germany's unilateral valuation of the respective currencies; capital transfers between the two economies were possible only in one direction, and unilateral denunciation of the treaty was possible only for Germany. France was obliged to submit a periodic declaration of the state of her gold and foreign exchange reserves. The Belgian gold reserve, which had been transferred to the Bank of France for safekeeping, and by then transferred to Africa, had been partly surrendered to Germany. By May 1941 160,000,000 Reichsmarks of Belgian gold had arrived in Berlin. The French government had been forced into selling foreign holdings as part payment of the occupation costs, had been forced into innumerable small concessions in the commercial agreements which had been made, and was obliged to provide full information about all its negotiations with third parties.[3] Germany in return had relaxed the controls on the circulation of

[1] BA., R 7 VIII 207, Mbh. in F., 'Notwendigkeit der wirtschaftlichen Eingliederung der Departements Nord und Pas de Calais in den Geschäftsbereich des Militärbefehlshabers in Frankreich', 27 March 1941.
[2] Hemmen papers, Pièce 501/M/LM, Telegram, Délégation pour l'économie, no. 241, 24 May 1941.
[3] In the case of Britain it did not do so.

persons imposed by the Armistice, had granted certain concessions on prices to French exporters, had allowed the French to keep for their own air force one aeroplane out of every five manufactured, and promised, a promise so far unfulfilled, to make negligible deliveries of sugar and potatoes.

In February 1941 the Reichs Economics Ministry was pursuing a policy of placing contracts in Belgium, both because it seemed politic to relieve the unemployment there, and because delivery times were much shorter there.[1] In the same month they opened negotiations with Elmar Michel with a view to placing more contracts in unoccupied France and were sharply reproved by the Foreign Office on 28 February for infringing their authority.[2] General von Hanneken, of the Economy and Armaments Staff, writing to the Reich Industrial Organizations in March, indicated that French entrepreneurs were actively looking for orders from Germany, that Hitler wanted to encourage the placing of such orders, particularly in unoccupied France, that the French government was not unwilling, and that if orders were not placed it was largely due to the continuation of peace-time attitudes of mind among German manufacturers.[3] In June the end of the policy of looting of machines from French factories was foreseen as the growth of manufacture for German purposes there had begun to make that policy absurd.[4]

The report of the military administration for 1941 was quietly self-congratulatory.

The manufacturing and production capacity of French industry which, at the Armistice, had large supplies of raw materials and finished goods at its disposal, has, to a very great extent, been made to serve German war production; it has rendered valuable service to the Reich and to the Armed Forces by raising considerable quantities of goods and sums of money as well as by placing a considerable output at their disposal.[5]

Germany had obtained from France 48,000 tons of copper, 9,000 tons of lead, over 2,000 tons of tin, 200,000 tons of bauxite, 32,000 tons of pure aluminium, 26,000 tons of alumina, and 2,000 tons of magnesium. France had been allowed to retain for her own purposes only 30 per cent of the normal output of the woollen industry, 16 per cent of the normal output of the cotton industry, and 13 per cent of that of the linen industry. In the same year France had provided to Germany over a million tons of wheat and oats, 1,100,000 tons of hay and straw, 160,000 tons of meat, and large quantities of fruit, vegetables, wine, and fish.

One corollary of this growth of the economic exploitation of France was measures to protect the French labour force. In 1941 125,000 workers left

---

[1] BA., R 7 VIII 207, Rwm., 'Verlagerung von Bergbau-Aufträgen in die besetzten westlichen Gebiete', 19 February 1941.
[2] Hemmen papers, Pièce 27, 23198 DJM/1. 3 March 1941.
[3] BA., R7 VIII 207, Mbh. in F., von Hanneken to Reichsgruppe Industrie, 17 March 1941.
[4] FD 667/49, Mbh. in F., 'Lagebericht des Wehrwirtschafts- und Rüstungsstabes Frankreich für Juni 1941', 30 June 1941.   [5] IMT., 267-EC.

France for Germany attracted by employment and higher wages. On 22 February the Reichs Economics Ministry pleaded for the retention of skilled workmen in France and their protection from any form of draft.[1] In April Darlan, as Deputy Prime Minister and Minister of Foreign Affairs, managed to secure a promise of the return to France of French miners who were prisoners of war in Germany, provided they were not already employed in mines in Germany.[2] The decree 'Armament, 1942' of 10 January 1942 reversed this policy. Four days after it was promulgated Michel demanded an official declaration from the French government encouraging workers to go to Germany.[3] On 19 March 1942 Hitler informed his new Minister for Armaments that Fritz Sauckel would be appointed Commissar-General for Labour with powers quite independent of those of the Minister for Armaments.[4] Two days later the official promulgation of the decree appointing Sauckel stipulated that one of his main tasks was to secure a large number of foreign workers for Germany.[5] In October 1941 the High Command of the Armed Forces had sought an intensification of the programme of manufacture in France and a general attempt to increase the level of productivity in French industry.[6] The new Minister of Armaments had no intention of abandoning this policy, indeed he was appointed to increase German production by whatever means as quickly as possible. In 1941 Germany moved away from the idea of booty to the idea of an organized exploitation of the French economy. In 1942, when the Blitzkrieg had been rejected as an economic strategy, that exploitation would be greatly increased both in scale and in intensity.

[1] BA., R 7 VIII 207, Rwm. to Reichsgruppe Industrie, 22 February 1941.
[2] J. Billig, op. cit. [3] R. Aron, op. cit., p. 476.
[4] FD 3353/45, vol. iv, 'Führerkonferenz', 19 March 1942.
[5] FD 3049/49 (Folder no. 2), 'Führer-Erlass über einen Generalbevollmächtigten für den Arbeitseinsatz', 21 March 1942.
[6] BA., R 7 VIII 207, OKW., 'Versorgungslage der Rüstungsindustrie Frankreichs', 1 October 1941.

V

THE LEVEL OF EXPLOITATION INCREASED

'THE Blitzkrieg is over,' wrote General von Hanneken on 15 January 1942, 'as for the economy, it is a matter of the first priority that it should be clearly reconstructed on the basis of a long war.'[1] The strategic plan by which the new Europe was to be created had failed. If Germany were still to achieve the reconstruction of the Continent, or if the National Socialist revolution were to survive at all, a new economic strategy was necessary. This strategy could only be the reorganization of the economy to meet the demands of the total war which Hitler had wished to avoid. A complete war economy, a war economy which involved every sector of the economy in production for war purposes, had to be created in Germany.

In the early months of 1942 this reorganization of German strategy was confined to the domestic front. Its impact on France was slight, because there were so many unutilized reserves in the German economy. The very fact of reorganization itself was able to produce a rapidly increasing rate of production in Germany which only began to slow down in early summer. As it began to slow down, the question of the exploitation of the occupied western territories came once again into the foreground of considerations. Ought not a much greater demand to be made on French resources? What was a fundamental change in German domestic policy, took the form in France of an intensification of previous policies. The aim of German policy there, by whatever improvizations and pressures possible, was to increase the level of exploitation, in order to sustain the change of direction in Germany's domestic economy.

The beginning of the massive transfers of French labour to Germany has usually been considered as a break in German policy. But, in reality, it was a quite logical intensification of previous policies. In 1940 and 1941, of all the factors of production in France, labour was the most apparently underutilized for German purposes. An intensification of the exploitation of French productive resources led quite naturally to attempts to use more French labour. The question that would ultimately divide the German administration so sharply, the question of *where* the French should work, certainly became important in 1942. But the answer was relatively simple while French labour resources were so under-utilized.

In 1942 the exploitation of the French labour force became a main part of

[1] FD 1434/46, no. 170, OKW./Wi.Rü.Amt., 'Umstellung der Rüstung', p. 42.

German policy. But at the same time all the previous methods of exploitation were diligently pursued. French industry was used much more intensively for German purposes. Raw materials, for which German demand increased dramatically with the changed plan of 1942, were obtained in much greater quantities. Certain categories of booty, especially the scarcer metals, were ruthlessly tracked down, even to the smelting of church bells. And in this period of ruthless exploitation Germany twice took the opportunity to increase the sums of cash demanded as occupation costs.

But the economic changes in Germany could not be confined to that country. No economic strategy was feasible without some discussion of its purpose, and to the answer that its purpose was simply the survival of Germany, the question could legitimately be put, 'what kind of Germany'? The National Socialist revolution had been a European revolution and nowhere more so than in its economic policy. The early stages of the exploitation of France had been perfectly in keeping with the National Socialist ideas of the future Europe. So long as it was possible to increase the level of exploitation in France in 1942 and 1943 by using up previously under-utilized resources these questions of principle could be avoided. When increasing difficulties in exploitation were met in autumn 1943 new policies were called for. Any discussion of new policy raised the question of the National Socialist New Order and France's place in it.

It would be pleasant to argue that Germany attained a ceiling of exploitation in France in these years, beyond which economic exploitation was not possible, and even more pleasant to argue that it was not economically possible even to sustain economic exploitation at the level it had reached by summer 1943, and that for these reasons German policy there, and elsewhere in Europe, had to be reconsidered. Certainly the history of German labour policy in France provides some fuel for the liberal argument that in the long-run economic exploitation of occupied territory is either not possible or unprofitable. The formidable fact, however, is that in 1943 Germany was directly utilizing for her own purposes at the very least 40 per cent of French resources, and probably more. In so far as German policy had to be changed in autumn 1943 this was not so much because it was, economically, a failure. Rather it was because events in Germany, the changes in economic policy which had taken place there in 1942, spread their implications to occupied Europe.

Those changes had mainly been the work of Albert Speer, and of the Ministry of Munitions after Speer's appointment as Minister in February 1942. Inasmuch as they were a managerial and administrative revolution in the German economy they were subject to attack on the grounds that they were politically suspect. But the defence of necessity was overwhelmingly convincing. The greater the power of the Ministry of Munitions in Germany, the more those powers were extended to the occupied territories. The Armistice Commission declined in importance in 1942 as the French state became less important and as the creation of a full war economy in Germany under centralized control meant that the German Ministry of Munitions itself began to take an interest in France. Thus the administrative changes in Germany also had their effect in diminishing the sovereignty of the Vichy government. German economic policy in France was less and less discussed with the French and more and more imposed on them, to the extent that, in 1943, Speer himself seemed the arbiter of France's economic destiny. At that moment the internal disputes about the economic organization of the National Socialist Order were inevitably carried into France.

As Germany's hold on the eastern territories began to slip, France became of ever greater significance to the German New Order, and its relationship to the Europe of the future, a question which could be safely left in abeyance during the Blitzkrieg in Russia, became a vital issue. As the attack of the National Socialist party on Speer's economic ideas became more pronounced in Germany, so Speer, by the pressure of the necessity of organizing an economic defence of Germany against economies so much more powerful, was forced into acting on a European level rather than merely a domestic one. To do so was to come into direct conflict with his critics in the National Socialist party over an issue where they were not silenced by the argument of necessity, the issue of the future European order. In August 1943 Germany was face to face, not with the collapse of the policy of exploitation, but with a choice of policies. The implications of this choice were vital to the future of the National Socialist revolution.

The initial reaction of the occupiers to Laval's return to power on 19 April 1942 as Minister of Foreign Affairs and of the Interior was one of mild hope. 'Above all, in the practical tasks of making France useful for German war potential the change of government may well turn out useful.'[1] Neither the new prime minister nor his new Minister of Finance, Pierre Cathala, were prepared to further Sauckel's purposes, and the mood of qualified optimism lasted no more than a month. 'Reconstruction of the French government brought no perceptible change in the opinion of the population. The future of Franco-German relations, even in industrial circles where there is an interest in co-operation with Germany, was judged ever more sceptically.'[2] By and large the question of who ruled in Vichy had now become one of little or no importance to Germany. Given the political policy which Germany had continued to pursue in 1942 it was unthinkable that there could be any genuine economic co-operation with the French government.

In September 1941 there were 1,226,686 foreign workers in the Reich; 72,475 of them were French.[3] In autumn 1942, including prisoners of war working in the economy, there were 5,093,000 male foreign workers;

[1] FD 671/46, Mbh. in F., Wi.Rü.Stab., 'Lagebericht', April 1942.
[2] Ibid., May 1942.
[3] CCDR., ix, D.P. 1.

1,341,000 of them were French.[1] In September 1941 there were about as many French workers in Germany as Danish workers, about half as many as Dutch workers. In autumn 1943 male French workers were 26·3 per cent of the male foreign labour force in Germany, the largest single ethnic group.[2] The rapid increase in the use of foreign labour was a consequence of the disruption of Germany's strategic plans, rather than a part of them; it was a way of avoiding the problems inherent in a full mobilization of the domestic labour force which would otherwise have been inescapable in 1942. Thus it was the creation of a full war economy in Germany in 1942 which brought the utilization of French labour from a peripheral position in German occupation policy to a central one. The increase in the internal debt of the Third Reich, Hitler declared in May, would be no difficulty since it would be amply compensated for by the acquisition of foreign territory and by the incorporation of 20,000,000 foreign workers into the German labour force at lower cost than the employment of Germans.[3]

Even before Sauckel's appointment the pressure on the French government had increased. On 14 January 1942 Michel tried to insist on an official declaration by the French government encouraging workers to leave for Germany.[4] The first indications of the compulsory recruitment of labour for Germany came on 6 March in Belgium, but this decree was later modified.[5] The first Sauckel 'action' did not begin until April. It had no definite quotas to fulfil, nor was it concerned solely with foreign labour. Nevertheless it met immediate criticism from the occupying authorities. The military administration looked ahead with foreboding to Sauckel's proposed visit to Paris in May to negotiate with Laval. The effect of German propaganda in France was much weaker than that of the enemy. Laval's agreement with the Germans to permit labour recruitment in the unoccupied zone had done nothing to change this. The food supply was inadequate, and there was every reason to suppose that the morale of the French would get worse under this new threat.[6]

In February the Commander-in-Chief of the Army in France, General Otto von Stülpnagel, had resigned after several protests against the shooting of hostages and the deportation of political prisoners. His replacement, General Carl-Heinrich von Stülpnagel, his cousin, the former head of the Delegation to the Armistice Commission, proved no more pliable than his predecessor. In the negotiations in May he upheld the view that the forced deportation of French workers would be contrary to the principles of international law.[7] Hitler appears to have decided in early May, however, that the

---

[1] FD 301/46, Mbh. in F., Wi.Abt., 'Der Beitrag des französischen Raumes zur Kriegswirtschaft'.

[2] Of the 1,714,000 female foreign workers included in the total the Russians and Poles form larger ethnic groups than the French.   [3] *Hitlers Tischgespräche*, p. 311.

[4] R. Aron, op. cit., p. 476.   [5] F. Baudhuin, op. cit., p. 304.

[6] FD 671/46, Mbh. in F., Wi.Rü.Stab., 'Lagebreicht', April 1942.

[7] E. Jäckel, op. cit., p. 224.

conscription of workers in France was to begin. On 6 May Speer recorded in his minutes of an armaments conference with the Führer:

At the suggestion of Gauleiter Sauckel, the Führer agrees that conscription be introduced for occupied France, Belgium, and Holland. In no circumstances will he allow prisoners of war and conscripted Frenchmen to be placed on the same level (as regards pay). He points out that it was not we but the French who declared war and that they must therefore also bear the consequences.[1]

At the same time as the removal of Russian, French, and other workers to Germany was decided, Hitler also decided that in Czechoslovakia the labour force would be left in place except where there was surplus manpower. Instead of further conscription of workers there 'the Czech armament firms should operate full-time in three shifts so as to obtain a greater volume of war production'.[1] As far as the French were concerned it was a matter of meeting Sauckel's demands and at the same time trying to stave off the compulsory drafting of their labour force. It is against this background that Laval's dramatic offer of the 'relève', the exchange of French workmen for prisoners of war in Germany, must be seen. It was a method of avoiding the ultimate catastrophe, no more. The idea was to obtain the return of a prisoner of war for every three workers who departed for Germany.

The incentive to leave for Germany was theoretically high, even without the rather melodramatic appeal. The price and wage controls which had been imposed on the French economy worked, as is always the case with such arrangements, much more effectively on wages than on prices. The arbitrary prices used both in foreign trade and in requisitions by the military, the existence of a relatively higher-paid group in the labour force who worked for the occupying authorities, the presence of a large number of occupying troops, and the cumbersome methods of the control of food supply, all tended to the creation of a black market which increased effective prices still more. The increase in employment in Germany together with the continuing under-employment in many sectors of French industry in this setting ought to have eliminated the need for compulsion, and at first Sauckel hoped it would do so. The number of workers which Sauckel wanted was variously estimated, even by himself, at between 350,000 and 500,000. In the event two separate agreements were negotiated, one in early May and one at the end of May each stipulating that 250,000 workers must go to Germany before the expiry of a fixed period, otherwise the compulsory powers would be used.[2]

On 16 June the conferences in Paris began again and on this occasion Speer also took part. Speer's presence indicates that the discussions ranged outside

[1] FD 3353/45, 'Führerkonferenz', 6–7 May 1942.
[2] CCDR., ix, D.P. 1; IMT., v. 484, *France During the German Occupation 1940–1944* (Hoover Institution), iii. 101 ff. (It should be said that Cathala's testimony in these volumes is as tendentious as the volumes themselves.)

the bounds of the labour programme alone. It was in the same week that Speer began to incorporate the machinery for controlling German production in France into his own ministry and in the same week that a more extensive programme for the dispersal of manufacturing for German purposes to western occupied territories was begun. At that time Speer was in full agreement with the plans for the utilization of French labour, indeed he regarded it as an essential part of Germany's war effort. Some over-all planning was necessary, however, to make sure that these various aspects of German policy remained compatible with each other. It is difficult to believe that the Vichy government were not able to have a closer insight into over-all German plans than their representatives later claimed to have had.

The 'relève' was announced on 22 June in a speech on the radio by Laval. The appeal to French workers to leave for Germany was surrounded by many hints of the dreadful consequences that would follow should they not follow their government's exhortations. In the light of Hitler's decisions in the previous month the negotiation of the 'relève' was a victory for Laval. But the terms of the 'relève' were in fact less favourable than the prime minister gave his radio audience to understand. The prisoners of war who would be returned to the French labour force in the proportion of one to every three workmen leaving for Germany were in fact to be returned to work for German purposes, the volume of which was increased by decree on the day after Laval's speech. The concession made by Germany in the negotiations was a very small one, and in so far as it enabled the German administration to redistribute the French labour force, whether in Germany or France, to suit German purposes it added an element of flexibility to the German plans which they had previously lacked. That this was the purpose of the presence of both Speer and Sauckel at the negotiations is shown by the intensification of measures to concentrate French industrial output in fewer units of production and to close down factories altogether.[1]

The machinery by which this would be carried out was the so-called 'combing-out committees', which would decide where superfluous labour was located. Since the main German interest was skilled labour these committees, to get satisfactory numerical results, turned their attention to the larger works where larger pools of skilled labour existed. This had a twofold effect. Firstly, it impeded the measures for concentration of French production, and it was undoubtedly one of the reasons why these measures had such little effect throughout the war. Secondly, it tended to deprive of skilled labour precisely those French works which were set to receive an ever-increasing quantity of contracts from Germany. The nationalized aircraft factories at Les Mureaux were estimated to require between 300 and 400 more workers in July to meet contracts from Messerschmitt. From 1 June Junker 52 planes were entirely produced in France, and to meet the increased output 1,000 more workers

[1] FD 671/46, Wi.Rü.Amt, Wi.Rü.Stab., 'Lagebericht', 2 June 1942.

were required at the Amiot plant in July.[1] The shortage of skilled workers was felt particularly in Paris.

The 'combing-out committees', combined with the moral pressures of the 'relève' and the manifold administrative pressures of the occupying authorities, were quite unable to secure the necessary quantity of skilled workers. By the end of July it had become evident that if Sauckel's demands were to be met it could only be by compulsory measures. In fact the increase in German contracts to occupied countries in some ways increased the need for compulsion. No increase in output for German purposes in Scandinavia or in eastern Europe was possible without an increase in the exports of German coal. This was possible only with an increase in the number of miners. A satisfactory increase was promised in August 1942 by Sauckel, whose intention was to provide it from Russian labourers. If Sauckel were to conscript a further million Russian labourers for Germany, and his intention was no less, compulsory and arbitrary powers were essential.

In this connection the Führer states that the problem of providing labour can be solved in all cases and to any extent; he authorizes Gauleiter Sauckel to take all measures required.

He would agree to any necessary compulsory measures in the east as well as in the west if this question could not be solved on a voluntary basis.[2]

This can be taken as the starting-point of the second 'Sauckel action', this time based clearly on force and compulsion. The decision was communicated to the French government on 22 August. On 29 August Bichelonne, the new Minister of Industrial Production, was told that the German labour offices must be supplied with lists of all unemployed and under-employed French workers, and that the French government would be required to make the hiring of all new labour dependent on the German labour offices.[3] The worst fears of the French seemed now to have come completely true.

The French government was asked to introduce immediately a new labour law to apply to everyone between the ages of 18 and 55, which would create a general liability for labour for the whole of that age group. The law which was subsequently passed, on 4 September, was slightly less drastic. Compulsory labour was to be required only of men between 18 and 50 and unmarried women between 21 and 35. All workers effectively employed for a period of less than 30 hours a week also had to report this fact to the local labour office. The conditions of contract for those workers who left voluntarily for Germany were improved, their families would receive one half of their previous nominal wage in France in addition to the remittance from Germany.

Measured simply by numbers both the first and second Sauckel actions

---

[1] FD 671/46, Wi.Rü.Stab., Rüstungsinspektionen — IA, 'Lagebericht', July 1942.
[2] FD 3353/45, Rm.f.B.u.M., 'Führerkonferenz', 10–12 August 1942.
[3] E. Homze, *Foreign Labor in Nazi Germany* (Princeton, 1967), p. 182.

were successful. Sauckel claimed to have brought an average of 340,000 new workers a month into the German war economy in the first nine months of his spell of office.[1] Of this new intake 80 per cent was foreign. But the biggest part of this influx of new labour was unskilled workers from Russia, whereas the trend away from labour intensity inherent in the German war economy required more skilled workers. The most likely source of these remained France. In Sauckel's eyes the French labour law of 4 September did not give him sufficient powers.

On 30 October he attended the meeting of the Central Planning Committee to discuss labour utilization and complained volubly of the protected position of the French:

A telegram burst into my last negotiations in France to the effect that the Laval government could not be threatened under any circumstances. The Führer has declared as follows. If the French are not obliging I will rope in again the 800,000 prisoners of war, if they are obliging, then the Frenchwomen can follow their men to Germany and work there. Naturally I have an interest, he said, in preserving the Laval regime. The government will remain, it now depends entirely on us, and after Laval has taken over wordy phrases from my proclamation and spoken to the French he can do nothing more. At the most he can be overthrown by Pétain. On that question I would emphasize that there is still an over-supply of young men whom we could employ somewhere in Germany. We demand of our people that they strip their living standards to the minimum. We cannot permit a state of luxury to persist in France such that small bistros still have orchestras of 25 musicians and two waiters are employed at every table.[2]

His powers were extended to give him a greater chance of 'combing-out' skilled labour from French factories. These decisions were but the prelude to much more important ones to be made in December. The background to these decisions was the unremitting demand for more labour transmitted through the agency of the Minister of Armaments himself. On 6 November the Central Planning Committee considered the depletion of iron-ore stocks. The remedy was to increase iron-ore output in Lorraine from its current average of 2,800,000 tons a month to about 4,300,000 tons a month. This could only be done by further massive drafting of labour. The increase of German output in winter 1942/3 meant a whole series of such sudden calls on Sauckel's ingenuity.[3] On 15 December it was decided to remove a further 300,000 men from the economy into the Wehrmacht.[4]

After his meeting with Hitler on 3 January 1943 Speer was left in no doubt about Hitler's policy towards France:

The Führer expressly orders that in no circumstances should it be permitted for France to be less heavily burdened than Germany. Germany must sacrifice her blood

[1] Ibid., p. 143.
[2] FD 3353/45, Rm.f.B.u.M., 'Bericht der 21 Besprechung der Zentralen Planung betreffend Arbeitseinsatz', 30 October 1942.
[3] FD 3353/45, vol. cxlv, Minutes of Zentrale Planung, 6 November 1942.
[4] *Kriegstagebuch der OKW.*, ii. 1141.

for the war. We must demand of France much heavier economic tasks than hitherto. If any signs of resistance are shown by the conscripted French workers they are to be treated as civilian internees and deported accordingly. At the slightest sign of sabotage the severest action is to be taken. Any idiosyncrasies about humanity are quite out of place.

The Führer is in agreement with my suggestion that all questions concerning the utilization of French industry in connection with armaments are to be dealt with directly from the Ministry of Armaments and Munitions.[1]

On the day on which Hitler handed down these orders Speer telephoned Sauckel from the Führer Headquarters and informed him that it was no longer necessary to proceed so circumspectly with regard to skilled workmen employed in France. Sterner measures could now be taken to utilize the French labour force more efficiently.[2] Of course the implications of Hitler's decisions were not confined to Sauckel's programmes in France, they fell also on the manufacture of armaments in France. The more extensive powers accorded to Speer were in order to control the increased manufacturing programmes in the occupied territory and were ratified by Göring on 10 January.[3]

Therefore when Sauckel arrived once more in Paris on 10 January the inherent contradictions in the German programme of exploitation had become more apparent. Sauckel's plan was to obtain a further 250,000 workers, 150,000 of whom were to be skilled or semi-skilled, from France before 15 March. Five days before his arrival he had already communicated to his labour offices in France the terms of Speer's message to him from the Führer Headquarters, that it was no longer necessary to have the same scruples about removing skilled workers from the French economy.[4] That there were ample reserves of skilled labour available which could be drawn on without endangering Germany's production programme in France was not in doubt, although Sauckel's own administrative offices in France certainly exaggerated the extent to which this was so, an exaggeration reinforced by Sauckel's own tendency to simplify economic issues beyond reason. 'Since it can be reckoned that at the moment in the French economy there are at least 450,000 workers in the metal-processing trades on an average every third man is to be released. In practice this principle should be employed elastically according to whether a factory is carrying out urgent armament contracts or not.'[5]

The estimates made by the German labour offices suggested that compared to Germany certain sectors of French industry were employing far too much

[1] FD 3353/45, vol. xxix, 'Führerkonferenz', 3–5 January 1943.

[2] IMT., xxvi, 556(13)—PS, USA—194.

[3] FD 3049/49, Folder no. 2, 'Über die Steigerung des Rüstungspotentials in den besetzten Gebieten', 10 January 1943.

[4] CCDR., ix, D.P. 1.

[5] NA., T.71, Roll 5, 398130, GbA., 'Anordnung für den Beauftragten für den Arbeitseinsatz in Frankreich zur Bereitstellung von 150,000 französischen Fachkräften und 100,000 Hilfskräften für deutsche Rüstungsbetriebe in der Zeit vom 15 Januar bis 15 März 1943', 11 January 1943.

labour. Some 128,000 were said to be employed in stone and earth quarrying and processing, 230,000 in the chemical industry, 182,000 in forestry and wood processing, and 513,000 in civilian construction, whereas employment in all these sectors combined in Germany was far less.[1] These estimates can scarcely be believed. Total employment in these sectors in Germany even five months later, was 1,487,000, and that only in the area of the Old Reich.[2] The majority of the French workers were to be drawn out of the metal industries. If these were taken to include iron-ore mining and iron and steel manufacturing Sauckel's figures indicated that total employment in France was 958,000 as compared to 280,000 in Germany. The comparison of course was ludicrous. The categories were dissimilar and the calculation included every one remotely connected with metal trades of any kind in France, while the figures for Germany seem to be just wrong. So bad, however, were French statistics of employment by industry that it was not possible, on 12 January, to demonstrate the falsity of the German claims. The French estimate of total employment in the metal industries was 338,000.[3]

Sauckel at this stage had no intention of trespassing on factories which were genuinely working in the German interest, and he wished to avoid any conflict with the policy of dispersal of German contracts to France. In fact one aspect of his plans was the institution of an extensive labour training programme in France which would ultimately create two skilled workmen for every one that was taken away.

If Germany were narrow minded she would not extend this scheme to France because such a procedure certainly brings with it an increase in the supply of skilled labour in France. Germany does this consciously and makes no difficulty in any way because she is convinced that France should participate in the tasks that await the new Europe in peace time.[4]

The purpose of this industrial training would be that more German contracts could be placed in France.

Laval refused to countenance such a proposal. 'It is no longer a matter of a policy of collaboration,' he protested, 'but on the French side of a policy of sacrifice and on the German side of a policy of compulsion.' Sauckel was moved on to a more generous plane. Had Laval been in charge of French destinies in 1939 rather than Daladier and Blum, who had aligned themselves with 'the English plutocrats and American Jews', this catastrophe would not have overtaken Europe. 'The German people, like the French people, awaited a new Europe, a long peace, and a true understanding. The Germans know that if every twenty years another war should be launched our two nations would suffer under the onslaught of the rest of the world.'

[1] Ibid., 398133, GbA., 'Vermerke über Dienstreise nach Paris usw. vom 10 bis 16.1.1943'.
[2] Deutsches Institut für Wirtschaftsforschung, op. cit., pp. 141–2.
[3] NA., 398153, GbA., 'Besprechung im Hotel Raphael 12.1.43'.
[4] Ibid., 398176, GbA., 'Besprechung zwischen Gauleiter Sauckel und dem Regierungschef Laval am 12.1.1943 in der Deutschen Botschaft Paris'; IMT., RF 1509–809F.

So flimsy were the preparations for the training scheme, so hectoring the manner in which Sauckel delivered his demands, so ominous the future for France in spite of Sauckel's assertions to the contrary, that the French government now felt obliged for the first time to refuse completely all co-operation. Co-operation of this kind, especially since the great changes in the North African situation, seemed not to be worth the new Europe. Would there be anything left of France to take into the new Europe? 'I represent', interrupted Laval, 'a country which has no army, no navy, no empire, and no more gold. I represent a country which still has 1,200,000 prisoners of war in Germany, a country where 900,000 workers, whether in Germany or in France, in the last resort work for Germany.'[1] In principle the labour draft was acceptable to him, but only in return for substantial concessions on the German side. 'I have really gone as far as possible, it is materially and morally impossible for me now, given the present situation, to send 250,000 French workers to Germany unless the necessary climate in which to do so is created.'[2]

Laval was prepared to offer an extension of the 'relève', at the improved rate of two prisoners of war for every worker leaving for Germany.[3] Since the total occupation of France the diplomatic value to Germany of the French prisoners of war had greatly diminished. Their value as labour, however, had increased, especially as the 'relève' had not brought Frenchmen to Germany in sufficient numbers. Laval also tried to exploit the uncertainties of German policy by offering 100,000 workers to Germany combined with a doubling of French output for Germany in France.[4] Neither he nor Bichelonne wished to withdraw support from the German war effort, but both wished that support to entail a reinvigoration of the French economy rather than its apparent ruin. Considering the bullying methods of Sauckel and his position of vastly superior force Laval resisted with tenacity.

Certainly Sauckel himself felt he had brought very little worthwhile back from Paris. In the course of his discussions the French had continually raised the idea that the present system of recruitment for Germany was arbitrary and unjust. If much greater numbers were to leave then they should be recruited on a 'demographic basis'. This would involve compulsory labour. No voluntary system could provide such numbers. Any compulsory system would have to be controlled by the French government.[5] Sauckel reported to Hitler that he now had the definite impression that the French government would refuse to co-operate in any programme and would insist on being seen to be compelled to act against their wishes. 'They are playing the role of the abandoned friend who wished for the best but now feels himself obliged to withdraw to another position.'[6] This would not matter provided Germany could enforce her executive will at a lower level in the French hierarchy.

[1] NA., 398176 GbA.   [2] Ibid., 398192 GbA.
[2] IMT., xxvii, NG–3035.   [4] E. Jäckel, op. cit., p. 269.
[3] CCDR., ix, D.P. 1.   [6] NA., T.71, Roll 5, 398133, 'Vermerke . . .'.

Although on the surface the results of Sauckel's discussions were very few, in reality everything had been decided. The various parties to the negotiations had been forced to examine German policy critically and to take up an unequivocal position. Laval and Bichelonne were prepared for economic co-operation with Germany if it were to their own economic advantage; if it were to their disadvantage they would resist. The military administration in France made their reservations about Sauckel's plans clear. They were only prepared to accept the labour draft as a necessity, for it disturbed law and order and it meant a fall in armaments output in France. Sauckel for the first time took up a position that the vital criterion was one of labour productivity. The French were not working properly in France, they must be moved to Germany. The Speer Ministry alone tried to compromise. Under the pressure of events Speer was moving towards the idea of greater production for Germany in France. Under interrogation after the war he said that the real exploitation of France only began at the end of 1942.[1] But so long as the main task of the Ministry of Armaments was to increase output in Germany they had also to give priority to the additions to labour supply which the Sauckel programme seemed to guarantee.

In these circumstances the position of the French government was hopeless. They decided to give in to Sauckel's pressures, but in what seemed the most just way; they would conscript labour on a 'demographic' basis. By a circular of 2 February prefects were ordered to carry out a general census of all Frenchmen born between 1 January 1912 and 31 December 1921. The preamble made it clear that the intention was to preserve from conscription certain age groups and those workers already employed in vital occupations. One day after the census began the French government was forced to move more quickly along the same path by introducing the law on compulsory labour service (*Service du Travail obligatoire*) of 16 February. Labour direction was made compulsory for all born between 1 January 1920 and 31 December 1922. The length of compulsory service, which might be in the army, in agriculture, or even in the 'chantiers de jeunesse' was two years. The recruitment of labour for Germany would take place within this category, and the indiscriminate recruitment which had been continuing for so long was stopped. That is to say that departure for Germany could be enjoined on those born in 1920, 1921, and 1922, none of whom would as yet have performed their military service, instead of on those who might have already performed it.

These were not the only categories to make up Sauckel's quota until 15 March. There would be a further extension of the 'relève' by which 150,000 workers would be exchanged for 150,000 prisoners of war. Furthermore a programme of 'transformations' of French prisoners of war in Germany was begun. They were to be given the same wage as though they were civilian

[1] Speer Report no. 30, Intelligence Report EF/AM/6, Interrogation of Albert Speer, 21 July 1945.

workers and were to have the right to two weeks' leave in France every year. By the end of April 157,000 workers had left France under the terms of the second Sauckel 'action' and, allowing for the month's delay, the quota had been almost completely filled. To that extent the policy of compulsion began by proving itself more successful than that of encouragement. But it depended on the executive of the French government. It may well be that the law of 16 February introducing compulsory labour service was an admission by Sauckel that his only chance of success was to act through the French government and to bend their executive powers to his will. In three age groups Germany could now legally recruit workers and demand the assistance of the French government.

The skilled workers were selected by the 'combing-out' committees. There can be no doubt that at this stage Speer was in favour of these committees; the need for skilled workers in Germany made them imperative. In the Central Planning Committee discussions on 16 February, however, both he and Milch showed some anxiety about the effect of these operations on German contracts in France. Speer described his policy as moving further away from finishing processes and closer to the full exploitation of more basic industries, but pointed out that the manufacture of component parts was increasing all the time in France because of subcontracting from Germany. This was particularly so in the aircraft industry. It was, said Milch, not a policy of choice but one of necessity:

If we were not forced to produce in France, since many facilities, space, machines, and so on cannot be transferred to Germany, if the housing of workers were not so difficult and so on, then we might prefer to transfer everything to Germany and let all the work be done here. But we would have too great losses in production, apart from the restiveness of the men.[1]

The Speer Ministry would have liked to see the control of skilled workers carried out under the auspices of the German firms responsible for the sub-contracts so that the labour force might be deployed usefully in the 'Patenfirma', rather than misused. Nevertheless, it was clearly decided that 'it has been established that an absolute protection of armament factories in occupied countries is not admissible'.[1] By the new laws armaments production in France might be affected by as much as 30 per cent. Only beyond that point would policy be reconsidered.

On 5 March Sauckel, Laval, and Michel again conferred in Paris, and Sauckel made it clear that, given the continually rising demand for labour in Germany, further contributions from France would eventually be necessary. Laval begged for time and Sauckel proposed a month's respite with departures then recommencing at the rate of about 100,000 a month.[2] Nevertheless

[1] FD 3353/45, vol. clxi, minutes of Zentrale Planung, 16 February 1943.
[2] CDR., ix, D.P. 1.

before the close of March a further request for 50,000 non-skilled workmen was submitted. By 9 April the French authorities were aware of Sauckel's new demands. A further 120,000 men would have to be provided in May and 100,000 in June. The census had revealed that in the three age groups liable to conscription, only 245,000 workers were in fact available for transfer to Germany and 88,000 of them had already left.[1] In May therefore the task began of hunting down the remainder.

Only 21,000 of the intended quota of 120,000 left in May. Hemmen wrote from Paris that the mere mention of a visit by Sauckel was enough to provoke a fresh wave of resistance.[2] In order to keep pace with the programme, departures would now have to be at the rate of 6,000 workers a day throughout June. At the end of May the French government decreed the call-up of the whole of the age group born in 1922, none of the exemptions mentioned in the decree of 16 February would apply to that group. Nevertheless the rate of departure averaged only 2,600 a day. From the end of June the number of departures diminished steadily and the resistance increased just as steadily.

Sauckel attributed this decrease to a failure of executive will by the Germans. There were ample labour reserves in France, he argued. By the end of the year a further 500,000 Frenchmen could be brought to Germany.[3] In an angry meeting with Sauckel on 6 August Laval refused to submit to this further demand. He did so in the full knowledge that Germany herself was casting about for a new method of exploitation and that in the Speer Ministry there were growing doubts about the usefulness of Sauckel's activities. On 9 August Sauckel complained to Hitler of Laval's attitude. 'It is no longer possible to free oneself from the suspicion that Laval is exploiting these difficulties because, as seems to be the case with everyone in this country, he has a totally false idea of the military and domestic situation of the Reich.'[4] Without some support from the French government Sauckel did not have the executive strength to enforce his will. Although therefore he secured Laval's agreement in principle to the departure of a further 500,000 before the end of the year, the result, as he told Hitler, of 'tough, hard, and protracted negotiations',[5] he had little confidence in Laval's intentions to put the agreement into practice. This was why in August he attempted to construct a link between the *Gau* labour offices in Germany and the departmental labour offices in France.

Sponsorship of this kind was futile in face of the massive resistance of the civilian population to deportation. The most persuasive testimony to this resistance are the figures themselves. It will be seen from Figure 1 that the effective French addition to the German labour force in Germany was made almost entirely between October 1942 and the end of July 1943. After that date it was statistically insignificant.

---

[1] *France during the German occupation 1940–1944*, i. 61.
[2] E. Homze, op. cit., p. 189.   [3] IMT., xxvi. 154, 556(39)–PS, (RF–65).
[4] R. Aron, op. cit., p. 631.   [5] IMT., xxvi. 158, 556(43)–PS, (RF–67).

Although the transference of French labour to Germany on a large scale took place over a short period of time, it was immensely valuable to the German economy. Between October 1942 and March 1943 it was responsible for nearly 10 per cent of the net addition to the active labour force in Germany. These were the months when the index of total armaments production in Germany,

TABLE 13

French Workers in Germany

Period	No. of departures for Germany from France (excluding Nord and Pas-de-Calais)*	No. of departures from Belgium (including Nord and Pas de Calais)†	No. of departures from the Netherlands†	Presumed proportion of French workers as a percentage of total new employment in Germany over that period‡
1 June–30 Sept. 1942	32,530	..	..	1·0
1 Oct.–31 Dec. 1942	163,726	..	..	6·9
January 1943	60,063	22,000	14,000	11·4
February 1943	63,627	17,000	12,000	9·4
March 1943	126,569	31,000	17,000	9·9
April 1943	18,000	23,000	8,000	1·7
May 1943	19,000	13,000	22,000	2·3
June 1943	74,000	12,000	43,000	11·3
July 1943	30,000	16,000	29,000	5·4
August 1943	10,000	6,000	10,000	1·8
September 1943	5,000	5,000	..	0·6
October 1943	3,728	1,901	2,951	0·4
November 1943	3,602	1,516	1,735	..
December 1943	5,623	2,445	7,573	..
January 1944	2,582	1,183	2,145	..
February 1944	2,876	1,832	1,913	..
March 1944	5,222	3,143	2,532	..
April 1944	8,228	2,778	2,761	..

  * CCDR., ix, D.P. 1.
  † FD 3040/49, Section IV, Sc. 425, Rm.f.R.u.Kp., Planungsamt, 'Werbung von Arbeitskräften aus den besetzten Gebieten für den Arbeitseinsatz in Deutschland', 20 June 1944; 'Heranführung ausländischer Arbeiter aus Belgien und Nordfrankreich, Frankreich und Holland', 5 July 1944.
  ‡ Ibid., GbA., 'Die in der gesamten Wirtschaft eingesetzten Arbeitskräfte nach Wirtschaftssektoren'. It should be noted that the GbA.'s figures for new employment are really new registrations in employment. Each change of occupation is therefore counted as a new workman in a new job. These percentages may therefore be underestimates.

after remaining level from July 1942, took its second leap upwards. Seen in the European context of massive transfers of workers from all economies to Germany the phenomenon is more striking. It was a most comprehensive example of the value of conquest.

Its value is the more striking because at no time could it be said that the removal of labour was Germany's only policy of exploitation or even her primary policy. Throughout the whole period of this massive transfer the previously established policies of exploitation were successfully continued.

On 5 February 1942 the French government ratified the *Metallplan* which governed the transport of scarce metals to Germany. In fact the rate of removal slowed in 1942 but this was not due to any easing of German policy, rather to the increasing difficulty in obtaining such metals. It was for this reason that on 1 December the Führer ordered that 'it is to be examined internally—without attracting particular attention in France—how much

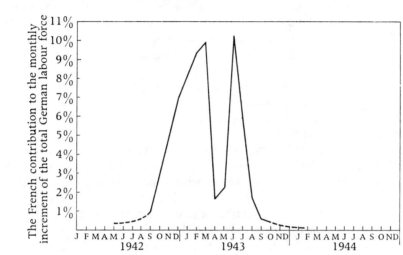

FIG. I. The importance of French labour in the German war economy.

copper could be obtained by ruthlessly removing church bells and monuments'.[1] By the end of March 1942 16,715 machine tool units had been transported to Germany, and by the end of July the total was over 17,000.[2] In June 1942 50,000 more vehicles were confiscated in the occupied western territories for use in the Reich.[3]

After the Allied invasion of Morocco and the successful implementation of the German plan, already in existence for a long time, for the total military occupation of France, Germany's financial demands on France also increased. The legal excuse was the greater cost of administering the greater area. At the outset of the occupation the costs had been fixed at 20,000,000 Reichsmarks (400,000,000 francs) a day, and from May 1941 France had begun, unofficially, to pay at the rate of 15,000,000 Reichsmarks a day. On 15 December 1942 a new German demand was presented for payment at the rate of 25,000,000 Reichsmarks (500,000,000 francs) a day.[4] The timing of this demand, coinciding as it did with the much greater demands for French labour, led Laval to make his despairing, and, in the event, fruitless, journey to the Führer

[1] FD 3353/45, Rm.f.B.u.M., 'Führerkonferenz', 1–3 December 1942.
[2] FD 671/46, Wi.Rü.Stab., 'Lagebericht', March 1942. G. Thomas, op. cit., p. 275.
[3] FD 3353/45, Rm.f.B.u.M., 'Führerkonferenz', 4 June 1942.
[4] P. Arnoult, op. cit., p. 88.

Headquarters in East Prussia. The day after Hemmen had presented his memorandum Göring explained that the increased sum was necessary not only for troops and increased fortifications in France, but also for black-market operations which would require 'about 1,000,000,000 Reichsmarks in the next five months'.[1]

On 17 December the French government, rightly convinced that they were being asked to finance a considerable part of the German war effort against other powers, refused the new demands.[2] Laval, however, had already agreed in principle, hoping to postpone an actual decision by his visit to Rastenburg. 'You attached a particular importance', Hemmen wrote to him on 17 December, 'to emphasizing that you considered these payments as a French contribution to the common defence of Europe.'[3] On 12 January 1943, with many reservations about the implications and methods of the payments, Laval agreed to commit France to paying at the new rate, that is to say one day after his stormy meeting in Paris with Sauckel.

The reservations which Laval expressed were not entirely hollow ones. The negotiations about the general purpose of the occupation costs and their effect on the financial management of the French economy did begin at the end of January. Danger of inflation was the problem that both the French and German governments had in common and that danger was obviously much increased by the new payments. The official price indices show no particular upward movement at this time, but on the black market gold coins reached their highest value of the whole period of the occupation.[4] In spite of the drop in production total liquidity was increasing much more rapidly than official prices. In spite of low interest rates, however, it was still possible for the French government to borrow on short term without difficulty. At the end of August 1939 the composition of the total French public debt had been such that three-quarters of it was long-term borrowing. By the end of 1942 421,000,000,000 francs were held on short-term and medium-term loans, 350,000,000,000 on long term, and during 1943 this trend continued undisturbed.[5] In these circumstances the news of the German defeat at Stalingrad may well have come at a valuable psychological moment for the French economy.

Hemmen's suggested remedy for the dangerous state of suppressed inflation in France was that the occupation costs should be covered by a long-term 'defence' loan raised by the French government. This would effectively remove the excess currency which was circulating. As for Laval's other objections to the increased costs, most of which would have involved some demolition of the clearing apparatus, they received short shrift from Hemmen. Nevertheless the negotiations were prolonged by Couve de Murville throughout February

[1] E. Jäckel, op. cit., p. 266.   [2] P. Cathala, op. cit., annexe V.
[3] P. Arnoult, op. cit., p. 92.   [4] INSEE., *Le mouvement économique* . . ., p. 72.
[5] Ibid., p. 71.

and March, until he departed secretly to North Africa. The main result might be said to have been the end of the independence of the Bank of France, for the payment of the new sums was imposed on that institution by an act of authority by the Minister responsible on 30 March.

As far as the significance of these events for the future was concerned Laval was no more able to obtain any satisfaction from Hitler about France's future role when he saw him on 29 April than he had been on his visit in January. Nor did his letter of 9 March demanding that this role be defined achieve any result.[1] He had become an almost complete prisoner of German policies, and they were themselves more and more in doubt in 1943. The financial sub-commission of the Armistice Commission, and even the Armistice Commission itself, became quite unimportant after the total occupation. The negotiations of February and March were carried on outside the framework of the regular meetings of the Commission. Not until the collapse of Italy and the German take-over of the Italian occupation zone east of the Rhône valley were financial questions again raised. On 4 November 1943 Germany demanded that she receive the occupation costs of 1,000,000,000 francs monthly that had been paid to Italy under the terms of the Franco-Italian Armistice and the arrears of 2,800,000,000 francs out of a special payment of 3,000,000,000 francs.[2]

From the discussions which took place in November 1942 in the Commercial Policy Committee of the Foreign Office it is evident that, given the decisions which had been made at the beginning of the occupation, Germany had no alternative but to increase the occupation costs or to issue more *Reichskreditkassenscheine*. The latter alternative was not a very satisfactory one since it reduced the extent to which the German economy was insulated from price changes elsewhere. The Commercial Policy Committee itself had never been responsible for the strict accountability of the occupation costs. The Armed Forces wrote down the sum they needed, supposedly for administration, to which was added the cost of black-market operations, propaganda, secret service expenditure, and so on. Finally, the cost of the occupying troops themselves was added, and that, by November, was merely about 20 per cent of the weekly total.[3] The conclusion reached was that French occupation costs would have to be increased by 10,000,000 Reichsmarks a day, from 15,000,000 to 25,000,000.

These demands, prepared in November, were submitted to the French on 15 December. The German explanation that their account at the Bank of France was now extremely low should be taken at face value. They were sufficiently alarmed to consider issuing more occupation currency or even

[1] A. Scherer, 'La Collaboration' in *La France sous l'occupation*, op. cit., p. 35.
[2] P. Arnoult, op. cit., p. 107.
[3] Hemmen papers, 'Sitzung des Handelspolitisches Ausschusses vom 26 November 1942', NG–4526.

altering the exchange if Hemmen's negotiations should prove unsuccessful.[1] The depletion of the account was of course due not only to the growth of French exports to Germany but also to the great increase in military activity, particularly the building of the Atlantic Wall. Laval conceded the new costs on 12 January 1943, but only after a visit to Hitler in Poland.

Not only did Germany continue to take cash and other booty from France while removing the skilled labour force, but production in France for German purposes increased over the period, even between September 1942 and July 1943, the period of the massive labour departures for Germany. German demands for essential raw materials from France increased and the tendency to manufacture armaments in France also increased. Thus, far from previous policies of this kind having to be modified to meet the new labour programme they were in many cases intensified.

On 19 March 1942 Hitler decided to stop mining in the Dogger iron-ore mines in Baden and to abandon construction of the coking plant and smelters at Kehl which would have been dependent on those ores. The conquest of the minette ore fields had made these costly operations superfluous. The output of minette ore would have to be further increased.[2] By June an expansion in French alumina-processing capacity had also been carried through contingent on this increase in steel production in Germany and in France.[3]

The pressure on the French government to permit more munitions output in France became stronger in 1942. In May Laval signed an agreement permitting powder production for Germany to take place in the unoccupied zone.[4] But the concessions were insufficient to meet the demands of the German Ministry of Munitions. It would have been surprising had they been so, for towards the end of June the rapid increase in armaments and munitions production which had followed upon the new decisions about the war economy taken in January had begun to slow down. In these circumstances the Speer Ministry first began actively to consider the policies of producing munitions both in France and in the Ukraine. On 23 June Speer broached these problems with Hitler:

Informed the Führer of the Thoennissen arrangement (dispersal of orders to France), and in this connection of my endeavours to be on good terms with the French government in the interest of a rapid execution of these orders.

From this he ought not to come to any conclusions as to my general political attitude towards the French problem, which I explained to him in detail. The Führer agrees with a friendly handling of the French through me.[5]

Although the so-called 'powder plan' appeared to be of little importance from the production point of view, it was of extreme importance as marking

---

[1] Hemmen papers, 'Vermerk über die Handelspolitisches Ausschuss-Sitzung im AA', 7 November 1942', NG-4198.
[2] FD 3353/45, Rm.f.B.u.M., 'Führerkonferenz', 19 March 1942.
[3] FD 671/46, Wi.Rü.Stab., 'Lagebericht', April 1942.   [4] E. Jäckel, op. cit., p. 222.
[5] FD 3353/45, Rm.f.B.u.M., 'Führerkonferenz', 23 June 1942.

the first steps in the Speer Ministry's attempt at a different solution of the problem of the economic exploitation of France. It raised issues of principle which were much more important than the mere quantities of extra explosives to be produced. It was also the first stage in what was eventually to become a tacit alliance on policy between Speer and the military administration in France. For these reasons it re-opened the old question of the separation of Nord and Pas-de-Calais from the rest of the country, a constant source of complaint by the occupying authorities themselves.

Hitler sanctioned the munitions production programme in the Ukraine on 4 June and that in France on 28 June.[1] The 'powder plan' for France entailed the release of 139 French officers and 364 skilled workmen from captivity in Germany, and the installation of anti-aircraft protection for the factories involved. It also entailed a realignment of the priorities for the allocation of fuel and nitrogen in the French economy. The second of these changes was only permitted under the express reservation that there must be no cuts in the allocation of nitrogenous fertilizers, but that the actual production of nitrogen itself must be increased in 1942. The coal and nitrogen would in fact have to be largely supplied from the two northern departments, as would some of the additional alcohol needed. It is clear that Speer made an attempt to persuade Hitler once again that, in the interests of economic rationality, the boundaries should be readjusted. But Hitler remained firm. 'The Führer decides that a territorial or economic allocation of Pas-de-Calais and Nord to the Military Command in France cannot be made. Any necessary relief of an economic nature may be claimed from the High Command at Brussels.'[2]

Although, in so far as the matter was one involving spheres of authority, the Military Command in Brussels was reluctant to lose control over two such economically valuable areas, in so far as it was a question of general economic policy to be pursued in occupied areas they also were wholeheartedly in favour of dispersing manufacture away from Germany.

The unchanged readiness of the population to work, the unutilized production capacity in industry, the abundantly available labour supply, and the favourable transport situation of the firms would tend to an increased distribution of contracts to Belgium and northern France and thus to a greater development of the German war economy, if, through a scanty allocation of the quotas of necessary materials, even the raw materials and auxiliary materials which are produced here, narrow limits were not imposed.[3]

The 'friendly handling' of the French by Speer did not extend to the lengthy wranglings of the Armistice Commission. It was not, in any case, part of Speer's character to be able to tolerate long-drawn-out bargains of the kind

[1] FD 3353/45, Rm.f.B.u.M., 'Führerkonferenz', 4 June 1942; ibid. 28–9 June 1942.
[2] Ibid. 28–9 June 1942.
[3] FD 671/46, Mbh. in. B. u. Nf., Rüstungs-Inspekteure Belgien, 'Lagebericht', 1 July 1942.

that were made there; the situation was urgent and the Commission itself by now very weak. The attempts of the French government to secure further military production for themselves were swept aside by the expedient of empowering Speer to negotiate without going through Wiesbaden.

The present obliging attitude towards the wishes of the French with regard to military equipment is impracticable. The Führer decides that the French powder plan, whose fulfilment is absolutely necessary within the framework of the new powder programme, must proceed according to the conditions laid down. The Armistice Commission must remain aloof from these negotiations, since, with its soft attitudes, it is inclined to compromise.[1]

In fact the anti-aircraft defence of the factories would have to be carried out by French gunners although Germany was prepared to provide some guns. It would be nonsense, Hitler decided, to move prisoners of war in Germany back into military service in France. Contracts in existence suggest that the Speer Ministry had its preparations well under way as early as 10 July and that the French attempts at bargaining had already been ignored before the Führer himself swept them aside.[2]

In spite of this cavalier treatment Laval was able to insist on some parts of his objections. The final negotiations for the powder plan broke down over the question of anti-aircraft protection. But Laval had already accepted all the main points of the German programme in a note to Hitler on 6 August.[3] The arrangements were that French factories would provide 45,000 to 50,000 tons of powder, some of which would be reprocessed from war stocks of American origin, by 30 September 1943. The release of the prisoners of war to take part in this production programme therefore went ahead in August.

How far had French economic resources been deployed for German purposes on the eve of the first really large-scale movements of labour from France? It is possible to provide a general answer to this question from the imperfect statistics of the Economic Section of the High Command in Paris.

The most important advantages (other than the financial ones) from the French economy were the supply of foodstuffs, iron ore and iron, non-ferrous metals, machinery, vehicles, and textiles, mostly paid for out of the money received as occupation costs, and the existence of 1,100,000 French prisoners of war still in Germany in August 1942. It may reasonably be doubted whether this last was really of any great economic advantage at that stage as the men, where they were employed at all, were generally employed at an extremely low level of productivity. The total sum of money paid in occupation costs in 1942 before 1 August was 3,345,000,000 Reichsmarks. The only important category in Franco-German trade which can be certainly

[1] FD 3353/45, Rm.f.B.u.M., 'Führerkonferenz', 23–5 July 1942.
[2] FD 967B/45, OKH., Heereswaffenamt, Dienststelle Paris, Contract with Société des Aciéries de Longwy, 10 July 1942.
[3] FD 3353/45, Rm.f.B.u.M., 'Führerkonferenz', 10–12 August 1942.

evaluated was machinery, where the agreements were stipulated on a price basis rather than a weight basis. German purchases of French machinery in 1942 up to the month of June were as follows:

TABLE 14

Supply of Machines from Occupied France to Germany*
(January to June 1942)

Type	Value (current Reichsmarks)
Internal-combustion engines, heat engines, motors, pumps, compressors, armatures	53,400,000
Machine tools, tools	43,260,500
Hoisting gear, winding gear, construction machinery, steel and rolling-mill apparatus	8,192,000
Ball-bearings	6,103,600
Fire-fighting equipment	2,770,000
Office machines	1,829,500
Textile machinery, paper machinery, food preparation machinery	1,286,900
Gears and pinions	1,210,000
Others	1,452,300
	119,504,800

* FD 301/46, Mbh. in F., Wi.Abt., 'Leistungen der französischen Wirtschaft für Deutschland, Stand 1.8.42'.

In the first half of 1942, therefore, about $3\frac{1}{2}$ per cent of the value of the occupation costs was represented by the total of machinery purchased from France. Of the other major items of German need almost all flowed from France in increasing quantities in 1942. Under the terms of the arrangements which had been made through the Armistice Commission France was bound to deliver 823,000 tons of wheat, over a million tons of oats, almost a million tons of straw, 759,000 tons of hay, and 285,000 tons of meat, in addition to 686,290 hectolitres of wine. In addition a further commercial agreement provided for the delivery of large quantities of fruit and 3,200,000,000 further hectolitres of wine. Actual deliveries were considerably smaller than these quantities.[1] Roughly 3,000,000 tons of minette ore should have been delivered in the first six months of 1942; actual deliveries were about 2,750,000 tons. About 300,000 tons of bauxite should have been delivered in the same period, actual deliveries were about one half of this total. Since the beginning of 1941 France had delivered 52,586 lorries to Germany, and a further 15,000 used lorries had been purchased.[2]

[1] CCDR., vii, P.A. I.   [2] FD 301/46, 'Der Beitrag des französischen Raumes ...'.

But this is to take no account of the many less important categories. It is surely reasonable to suppose that the great advantage of Germany's position was that within the limitations of the hardships she was prepared to enforce on France she could acquire whatever she might wish and which could actually be obtained from France. By imposing her will on the occupied economy Germany was able to obtain goods, many of which had not been usual

TABLE 15

Comparisons of Output of Selected French Products for German Purposes in 1942 and 1943*

Goods	Quantity	1942	1943	Percentage of French production	
				1942	1943
Iron ore	1,000 tons	7,246	8,494	57	50
Foundry pig iron	1,000 tons	153	184	70	69
Strip mill products	1,000 tons	626	728	62	69
Bauxite	1,000 tons	231	484	36	53
Cement	1,000 tons	1,440	1,926	99	99
Soda	1,000 tons	103	124	33	40
Sulphuric acid	1,000 tons	..	29	..	8
Colophony	1,000 tons	33	33	59	61
Turpentine oil	1,000 tons	9	9	58	62
Rabbit skins	1,000,000 pieces	37	44·8	61	60
Walking shoes	1,000 pairs	2,655	1,962	32	28
Working shoes	1,000 pairs	1,130	1,531	36	38
Locomotives	units	135	186	70	76
Goods wagons	units	5	1,975	..	47
Generators	1,000 units	13·2	22·5	30	35
Armoured cars	units	3,336	176	95	85
Lorries	units	35,421	16,533	90	92
Special vehicles	units	200	748	65	88
Alarm clocks	1,000 units	376	587	42	64
Wrist watches and pocket watches	1,000 units	423	538	59	71

* Collected from FD 301/46, 'Der Beitrag des französischen Raumes . . .'.

items of trade between the two countries. On 31 July 1942 3,665 locomotives belonging to French Railways were available in Germany together with 199,000 goods wagons and 2,300 passenger carriages. A monthly average of 13,000 clocks and watches was produced in France for Germany in 1941, and in 1942 the quantity was planned to increase to 40,000, about 70 per cent of the entire French production. A further programme for the delivery of 14,000,000 razor blades to the German armed forces was in the course of completion in August. That quantity represented about 60 per cent of total French capacity. Since the armistice 382,000 tons of phosphates had been

TABLE 16

*Value of German Orders to French Engineering Industries**

(current Francs)

Category	1941	1942	1943	As percentage of total output in France
				1941 1942 1943
Handling and hoisting machinery	223,000,000	773,000,000	797,000,000	(about 40 per cent of total tonnage was for German purposes)
Cars, lorries, etc.†	3,284,300,000	3,811,800,000	3,171,000,000	
Cycles†	174,400,000	121,700,000	79,100,000	
Meters and control apparatus	5,179,000‡	211,313,000	41,829,000	7 7·5 13
Electrical and radio-electrical construction	1,112,000,000	2,515,000,000	4,285,000,000	15·4 26·3 39·6
Foundings	102,880,000	327,823,000	335,946,000	
Heavy forgings and die-stampings	339,000,000	180,000,000	238,500,000	
Office machines	24,848,814	50,160,766	94,789,448	
Machinery for food, plastics, chemical, and textile industries	143,000,000	287,000,000	355,000,000	(about 25 per cent of total output was for German purposes)
Thermal, hydraulic, and pneumatic machinery	477,000,000	877,000,000	874,000,000	
Agricultural machinery†	23,326,560	29,377,497	128,050,750	
Railway material	550,923,000	1,090,869,000	1,668,415,000	17 26·7 54·1
Optical and precision instruments	186,717,120§	348,569,100	331,406,236	
Precision instruments for industry (non-specialized)	849,358,665	822,550,717	1,472,855,358	47·1 50·6
Machine tools, tools, welding	300,000,000	610,000,000	650,000,000	14 25 23
Steel tubes	270,000,000	50,000,000	80,000,000	
Aeroplanes and aeroplane motors	1,216,751,000‖	2,919,532,000	10,810,548,000	55** 63** 100**

* CCDR., vols. iii and iv, A. 1, 3, 4, 5, 6, 7, 10, 11, 12, 13, 15, 16, 18, 35, 38, 44.
† 1938 francs.   ‡ Fourth quarter only.   § Includes 1940.   ‖ Second half of year only.
** Percentage of total work-force employed on German orders.

delivered from North Africa. About 75 per cent of the capacity of the French soda industry was working for German purposes, and deliveries of calcined soda between 1 January 1941 and 30 June 1942 were 137,705 tons. The Military Command had actually appointed a 'Special Commissar for French Soda and Caustic Soda Production' to supervise French production on German contracts.[1] The Kehrl Plan had produced 70,800 tons of woollen goods, 64,300 tons of cotton goods, 32,400 tons of linen goods, 12,000 tons of rayon and silk goods, 3,500 tons of jute goods, and 70,000 tons of rags. The over-all value of contracts placed in the clothing industry between October 1940 and July 1942 was 184,000,000 Reichsmarks. Production plans for August foresaw the delivery of 350,000 pairs of shoes to Germany or the Wehrmacht together with considerable quantities of leather and hides. A total of 2,250,000 tons of cement had been delivered for German constructional purposes in France, and 4,500,000 Reichsmarks worth of precious stones and pearls obtained in one way or another, together with 2,500,000 Reichsmarks worth of jewelry.

[1] R. Denzel, op. cit., p. 57.

Moving forward from the standpoint of autumn 1942 there was a considerable increase in the quantity of almost all these products going to Germany in 1943, in spite of the Sauckel actions. The Economic Section of the Military Administration were prepared to suppose that as much as 50 per cent of total French non-agricultural production by value was for German purposes by the end of 1943.[1] This would be to measure very generously in an area where a great deal of scope for vague measurement exists. The information obtainable from the statistics of the Central Contracts Office itself indicated a percentage considerably lower than this. None the less a great deal of French output for Germany did not come under the aegis of the Central Contracts Office. In particular the very extensive use of French service industries by the occupiers would not be indicated in their figures.

Tables 17 and 18 do not give a complete picture of the extent and value of French food production for Germany. No account is taken there of the amount of food consumed by French workmen in France working for Germany. Nor is any account taken of the operations of the widespread black market in food. Wages paid to French workers on German construction projects, as, for example, the West Wall, in which construction was particularly active in 1943, were much above the level of permitted wages in France, and this was one of the most potent sources of black-market operations. The estimate of the military administration as to the number of French workmen employed in France for German purposes must be treated with great caution. In spring 1944 the estimate was that 1,378,000 were working directly on German orders or on goods produced entirely for German purposes, and that 1,387,000 were indirectly employed in the same way. The first figure must be regarded sceptically, because no single body effectively supervised all production for German ends, and because, also, of the general deficiencies of French labour statistics at that time. The second figure would be inherently difficult to estimate even were those statistics available. Where the multiplier effect of German orders was particularly felt, as in the French aircraft industry, it is impossible to say who was 'indirectly' employed in fulfilling those orders.

The Statistical Department of the Speer Ministry also made an attempt at a complete estimate of the degree of the German exploitation of France; and, although their results indicate a lower level of exploitation, that level is still high enough to make the estimate of the military administration (that 50 per cent of French capacity was being used for German purposes) seem not too fanciful. The Statistical Office calculations (Table 19) were confined to the original occupied zone excluding the departments of Nord and Pas-de-Calais, and to those industries for which the *Office Central de répartition des produits industriels* had kept statistics. It therefore omitted the food-processing industries, the building industry, and the aircraft industry, three of the industries most dependent on German orders. In Table 19 the 'crude estimate' indicates

[1] FD 301/46, Mbh. in F., Wi.Abt., 'Der Beitrag des französischen Raumes . . .'.

deliveries of French industry to Germany as a percentage of total deliveries, or column three as a proportion of column two. Obviously this would be much too low an estimate, not only because of the industries omitted from

TABLE 17

Comparison of French Output of Agricultural Products for German Purposes in the Harvest Years 1941–2, and 1942–3*

(tons)

Product	For German purposes 1941–2	For German purposes 1942–3
Bread grains	485,000	714,000
Fodder grains	458,000	686,000
Meat	140,000	227,000
Vegetables	98,000	107,000
Fruit	59,000	118,000

TABLE 18

Value of French Agricultural Output for Consumption in Germany in Harvest Year 1942/3*

(000,000 Reichsmarks)

Meat	285	Seed	33
Bread grains	134	Fruit	32
Fodder grains	100	Wine	30
Horses	70	Potatoes	25
Butter	56	Vegetables	24
Alcohol	49	Hay	18

* Ibid. (excluding Nord and Pas-de-Calais).

the calculation but also because total French production involves a considerable element of double counting, such as the deliveries of raw materials or semi-finished products to makers of completed products. These elements of double counting are absent from the estimates of deliveries to Germany. The 'adjusted estimate' eliminates these elements of double counting from total French deliveries by applying to them the methods by which German production was estimated. This estimate itself is obviously still too low. The 'adjusted and inflated estimate' therefore makes an arbitrary increase of 10 per cent in the value of deliveries to Germany to cover those industries for which statistics were lacking, and to cover various other items of trade and services which might properly be included. It is therefore only a general approximation. The general indication is that 40 per cent of French industrial production was for German purposes by autumn 1943. Although in the agricultural sector, output for German purposes was a smaller proportion of the total, since German utilization of French services or French labour may both have been over the level of 50 per cent, and since the *Planungsamt* calculations took no

TABLE 19

*Proportion of Delvieries for Germany of Total French Deliveries**

(Approximate estimates for the occupied zone,
excluding Nord and Pas-de-Calais)

Month	Total deliveries (1,000,000 RM)	Deliveries for Germany (1,000,000 RM)	Crude estimate per cent	Adjusted estimate per cent	Adjusted and inflated estimate (approximate) per cent
1942					
January	457·9	93·7	20·5	31	34
February	444·0	84·7	19·1	29	31
March	426·3	94·8	22·2	33	36
April	539·0	106·3	19·7	29	32
May	523·7	119·2	22·8	34	37
June	555·5	116·0	20·9	31	34
July	536·1	111·6	20·8	31	34
August	478·3	97·7	20·4	30	33
September	537·2	125·4	23·3	35	38
October	544·9	112·4	20·6	31	34
November	512·4	105·1	20·5	31	34
December	520·9	120·0	23·0	34	38
1943					
January	488·4	104·8	21·5	32	35
February	500·7	131·2	26·2	39	43
March	531·4	114·2	21·5	32	35
April	538·6	124·5	23·1	35	38
May	554·0	135·4	24·4	36	40
June	569·0	152·5	26·8	40	44
July	537·2	133·6	24·9	37	41
August	454·5	128·0	28·2	42	46
September	514·4	132·3	25·7	38	42
October	522·6	125·6	24·0	36	39
Jan. 1942 to Oct. 1943	11,287·0	2,569·0	22·7	34	37

* FD 3037/49, Section 1, Sc. 72, Rm.f.R.u.Kp., Planungsamt, 'Wie stark wird die Produktionskraft der französischen Industrie für deutsche Zwecke herangezogen?', 22 February 1944.

account of southern France, the estimates made by the military administration probably ought not to be very much reduced. The general level of exploitation must have been between 40 per cent and 50 per cent of French capacity in autumn 1943.

If these estimates are accepted only as vague approximations to reality, and it would be unwise to ask for more, they still give a startling picture. Just less than one half of the work force in employment in France was, on that basis, employed for German purposes. Since there were in autumn 1943 between 1,300,000 and 1,400,000 French workers in Germany, not counting

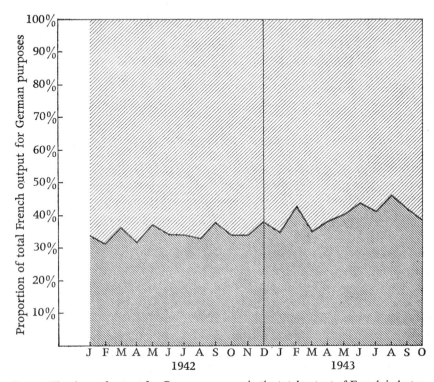

FIG. 2. The share of output for German purposes in the total output of French industry.

those who remained classified as prisoners of war, and since it is reasonable to suppose that these workers were, to say the very least, as productively employed for German purposes as those in France, it would appear that in all probability Germany was employing for her own economic purposes over half of the employed French labour force.

To the makers of German economic policy France, by 1942, had become an integral part of the German war economy. The changes which took place in the supervision of economic affairs in France were less and less concerned with the problem of the best way to exploit France and more and more concerned with administrative convenience on the German side and the battle for power within the German hierarchy. France had become merely one of the battle-grounds over which they fought. The decline of the Armistice Commission as the forum where exploitation was argued had begun before the occupation of the whole country. As France became more economically dependent on Germany the problem of exploitation became less a problem of foreign affairs, and in the course of 1942 two new figures, Speer and Sauckel, became more important to the French than Hemmen

In February of that year Hemmen was asked to report to the Foreign Ministry on the question of whether he still considered his Delegation a useful one. The justification was mainly in terms of past successes. Of the future he said little:

> If, during the year and a half which have gone by, my Delegation has been able, in spite of many difficulties and obstacles, to continually and successfully extend its negotiations outside the framework of the Armistice agreement and thus to continually make new demands on France in aid of our war potential and our food supply, it has, because of this, taken upon itself, so to speak, the role of a Franco-German governmental committee. But it is precisely its character of an Armistice Delegation which has given it that authority which is the more necessary, since it has, unlike the Military Command, no means of pressure at its disposal. As an Armistice Delegation it constitutes for the French a permanent reminder of the actual military situation.[1]

That one year and a half of negotiations had indeed created a situation where the control of economic life in unoccupied France had passed out of the hands of the Vichy government. This was so to such an extent that Hemmen himself was worried lest Germany, by refusing to accept the greater extent of its own responsibilities, should kill the goose that laid the golden egg. The French efforts to obtain concessions from Germany in return for the concessions they themselves were forced to make were 'perfectly comprehensible *from a purely economic point of view*, and not even unjustifiable in any way' in view of the damage being done to the French economy, whose preservation was as important to Germany as to France.[1] Mounting prices, the depletion of raw material stocks, the increasing national debt, and the lack of foreign trade, all weakened Germany's future chances of exploitation.

Although the Economic Delegation was retained, the changes in German domestic economic policy inevitably had their repercussions in France. Hitler's decision to organize a full war economy meant that in Germany economic decisions began to pass out of the hands of the military. In May 1942 the Economic and Armaments Office of the High Command of the Armed Forces, which by default of other organizations had retained much responsibility for the management of the war economy, was divided and its most essential functions transferred to the Ministry of Armaments. It was an evident defeat for the soldiers. From 20 July, as a result of the orders of 26 June, the *Wehrwirtschafts- und Rüstungsstab Frankreich* was divided into the *Wehrwirtschaftsstab Frankreich*, which remained under the control of the High Command of

---

[1] Hemmen papers, Pièce 2, Waffenstillstandkommission, 1026/42P, 7 February 1942.

the Armed Forces, and the *Rüstungsstab Frankreich*, which was placed under the direction of the Speer Ministry.[1] In fact the direction of both offices in France remained in the hands of the same person, but the Armament Inspectors, who were concerned with the day-to-day details of German armament manufacture in France became ultimately responsible to the Ministry of Munitions. Speer's intention was to put into practice in France the same processes of rationalization of production and concentration of manufacture that he had introduced in Germany. It was through these new channels that Speer began his negotiations over the 'powder plan' with the French government in June.

The very existence of the German military administration in France was called into question after the occupation of southern France in November. The river Rhône now became the dividing line between the German and Italian zones of occupation. Although there were always German troops on the left bank of the Rhône the legal rights of a 'belligerent occupier' were vested in the Italian government. Hitler had twice told Pétain in November that he regarded the events in Morocco as having led to the abrogation of the Franco-German Armistice.[2] Certainly he considered dissolving both the military administration in Paris and the Armistice Commission.[3] Finally, in December, Germany and Italy agreed to keep the Armistice Commission in operation. It remained as a symbol of French sovereignty, but, as Hitler told General von Stülpnagel, French sovereignty was only to be recognized 'in so far as it serves our purposes'.[4] On 19 December Hemmen was named as Delegate of the Reichs Government for Economic and Financial Questions to the French Government. He retained his position on the Armistice Commission.

The changed situation in the west and the constant demand for armaments, a demand which only the Speer Ministry now seemed capable of meeting, were no doubt behind the transfer of much greater powers in the Netherlands to that Ministry on 26 November. The problem there was simpler, in so far as the Netherlands had remained under civil administration. But the intention was to reduce the powers of the economic administration in the Netherlands to make decisions from a Dutch point of view; their decisions were now to be based on over-all considerations of the German war economy itself. On 24 February 1943 the same thing was done for the same purposes in Belgium. The decree of 2 September 1940 had instituted the same 'Warenstellen' in Belgium as in France. These organizations, and the later 'gildes principales', curious intrusions into Belgium's extremely liberal economic organization, bore striking resemblances to their French cousins. They represented a large

---

[1] G. Thomas, op. cit., p. 318. Hoover Institute, Militärverwaltungsbezirk Bordeaux, Box I, Mbh. in F., Wi.Abt., 'Organisation der Wehrwirtschafts- und Rüstungsdienststellen in Frankreich', 11 August 1942.

[2] M. Domarus, *Hitler Reden und Proklamationen 1932–1945* (Neustadt a. d. Aisch, 1963), ii. 1952.

[3] E. Jäckel, op. cit., p. 260.   [4] Ibid., p. 261.

administrative apparatus, employing members of the middle class who might otherwise have had less satisfactory employment, and evolved into a useful defensive bulwark against German demands. Any legislation threatening the semi-independence of these offices in Belgium was bound also to be aimed at France.

So it proved. In March the Speer Ministry introduced its system of production control by committee, the so-called 'self-responsibility and autonomy of German industry', into France also. The system was thus introduced in the one month of the whole occupation when almost twice as many French workers were transported to Germany as in any other. The groundwork for these changes had been laid by a Göring decree on 10 January 1943:

In the further course of the present war every possibility of an increase in German armaments potential in the occupied territories must be completely exhausted by every means. This must take place under a single point of view through central control by *one* person. I therefore decree within the powers allotted to me by the Führer the following:

> (i) The Commissar-General for Armaments Tasks and Reichsminister for Armaments and Munitions has to undertake completely by every means at his disposal the exploitation of every possibility of an increase in German armaments potential in the occupied territories.[1]

These orders had given Speer powers to dictate policy to the economic administrations in occupied territories. The new arrangements in Belgium were the result of this. In March the head of the Planning Office of the Speer Ministry, Hans Kehrl, came to an arrangement with Michel by which these orders could be implemented in France. It was necessary to establish direct links between the production committees in Germany and the 'Warenstellen' in France. Ultimate responsibility for the economic policy in France, *vis-à-vis* the French government, had still to remain with the Economic Section of the military administration, as they alone could have a total view of the situation in France, and it was still necessary to pay 'certain attentions' to the remaining sovereign powers of the French government.[2] On the other hand, it was essential that some over-all planning embracing the German and French economies should be introduced, especially in view of the labour transfers. The solution proposed was that a series of liaison officers between the German production committees and the French 'Warenstellen' should be given powers by the military administration and the Speer Ministry to co-ordinate production policy. Effectively the new liaison officers (*Verbindungsmänner der Reichsstellen*) would receive their orders from the Ministry of Munitions in Germany, and the German administration in Paris would have the right to be advised

---

[1] FD 3049/49, Folder no. 2, 'Anordnung über die Steigerung des Rüstungspotentials in den besetzten Gebieten', 10 January 1943.
[2] FD 5148/45, Mbh. in F., Wi.Abt., 'Chef des Verwaltungsstabes an den Reichswirtschaftsminister', 10 March 1943.

and to refer policies with which they disagreed back to Berlin for possible reappraisal. The initiatives for economic policy in France would now come from Speer in the first place.

The 'Warenstellen' had had an essentially negative function to fulfil so far. They had creamed off a regulated percentage of the output of certain products for German needs. This negative approach to the problem of exploitation was now to be replaced by a much more positive one. In future it would be their task to plan the permissible quantity of output of any goods, taking into account both French and German demand, now to be considered as a unity, and then to organize its production and distribution. Instead of being committees which existed solely to extract booty from the French economy they were to become planning committees in the full meaning of the term.

This production planning—covering both product and firm—which is already practised in a few important areas, must also take account of native demand, since production planning is total and unitary and the proper interests of the French administrative offices in controlled management must be respected. However, the only thing that is to be conceded in this respect, and its production then secured, is what is necessary to sustain the capacity to work of the working population.[1]

Any question of negotiating contracts through the Armistice Commission had been swept aside completely by an agreement of this kind. It reflected the complete hollowness of the pretence with which the Vichy government continued to surround itself. It might no longer have existed for all the attention that was to be paid to it even in matters concerning economic production for its own citizens. 'The required respect is to be paid to the remaining sovereignty of the French government, but with the aim of making the productive capacity of the newly occupied territory as fully serviceable as possible.'[1] It was to serve that purpose that the changes were being made. Since the newly occupied areas of France were not under the control of the Commander-in-Chief in Paris, but, as an operational area, under that of General von Rundstedt as Commander-in-Chief in the west, the problems of economic management were now administratively simpler. But the administrative changes only solved this difficulty incidentally; they drew their inspiration directly from what had previously happened in Belgium and the Netherlands. The whole industrial economy of western Europe was now to be mobilized for the defence of the Reich. Germany's demands on the occupied western territories were no longer to be limited and specific, they were now nothing less than the utilization of the occupied economies as though they were part of the German economy.

Such a conception meant that the occupied economies could themselves make certain claims on the German economy, especially for raw materials.

<hr>

[1] Ibid., 'Grundsätze für die Warenbewirtschaftung'.

In particular co-ordination of the control of goods is only achievable if the Reich's production managers in the occupied territories take into account in their production plans the volume of German contracts distributed. In that respect by contracts should be understood the totality of German contracts, whether dispersed from the Reich or originally placed in the occupied territory.[1]

The same economy in the use of labour and raw materials must be enforced in France as in Germany. Unutilized French stocks must be considered as unutilized German stocks, and the liaison officers would be directly responsible for seeing that no discrepancies existed in the two economies.

From March 1943, therefore, the French economy was much more directly aligned with that of Germany than before. Theoretically, economic policy in France should have shown a noticeable break at this point. The break, however, is much more noticeable in German intentions than in what actually occurred in the French economy. The last German hesitations about using French industrial capacity had been dissolved in the fiery heat of the massive military campaigns in the east. If there had once existed a vision of a de-militarized France, a peaceful producer of primary products for the German economy, that vision had fled. France was now treated without scruple as an important industrial adjunct to the German economy.

These changes in German thinking about the role of France were only a part of a general change of attitude towards occupied territory. Even in the General-Government a munitions industry was to be created. Unfortunately the previous treatment of that area had been such as sadly to impede any such development.

At the same time, the Führer's attention has been emphatically drawn to the inadequate armament possibilities in the General-Government. Owing to the bad feeding conditions of labour, and the consequent necessity for them to buy food in the black market, causing a waste of time of about half the working hours, and owing to the inadequate distribution of coal, etc., it is not possible to make proper use of the armaments industry already existing in the General-Government.

Dispersals from the west are for these reasons out of the question, although the armaments industry of Poland would be quite capable of having its share. The Führer heard these explanations with great concern and expressed the opinion that a change had only to be brought about by changing the person responsible, i.e. the exchange of Dr. Frank.

Following this report, the memorandum of General Schindler was produced, which corroborates the facts. The Führer demands that the armaments industry in the General-Government must get its share—the construction of a sound armaments industry in the General-Government must be made possible.[2]

The creation of a 'European' armaments industry, managed by Speer, was at stake. France, although obviously the most important of all the occupied

[1] FD 5148/45, Rwm., 'Warenbewirtschaftung in Frankreich / Einschaltung der Reichsstellen', 27 March 1943.
[2] FD 3353/45, Rm.f.B.u.M., 'Führerkonferenz', 3 April 1943.

· territories in such a plan, was not being treated differently from the others. The clear distinctions which had existed in German occupation policy between the treatment of Poland and the Ukraine, and the treatment of Belgium and France, in 1941 and 1942 were disappearing. If Pétain had hoped to avoid the 'polonisation' of France his hopes were illusory. In so far as France had any claim now to better treatment that claim resided only in her greater economic utility. On 15 May Hitler issued orders that the army commanders in the Ukraine were to give all possible help to the project to begin armaments production there.[1] The Ukrainian iron industry was to have its labour force protected against the labour draft in the same way as the skilled workers in France employed on German contracts were protected. On the same day Hitler sanctioned the extension to southern France of the programmes for tank production, heavy armaments production, and infantry armaments production, and the provision of anti-aircraft protection for the workers employed there.[1] In the Ukraine as in France, 'anything detrimental to the armaments industry must be avoided'.[1]

But the development of armaments manufacture in the occupied territories was not the only aspect of this change of policy. Economic circumstances in Germany also demanded the dispersal of consumer goods production for Germany to the occupied areas. If France and Germany were to be treated as the same economy, with the exception that French demand was always to be held much lower than that of Germany, why should not the restrictions on consumer goods production in Germany be compensated by an increase in their manufacture for Germany in France? There had already been arrangements of this kind and, in the case of clock and watch manufacture or the 'Kehrl-Plan' for textile manufacture, they had been important. Speer was beginning to think in wider terms along these lines and he was encouraged to do so, although not perhaps for the same motives, by Hitler. In April 1943 a further move was made to restrict the manufacture of consumer goods in Germany. Hitler, as always, displayed great sensitivity to this problem and hoped that goods would be allowed to 'disappear' rather than be publicly prohibited. There was also the possibility of filling these deficiencies by the use of the occupied territories. 'The Führer specially drew attention to the fact that the occurrence of shortages in the Reich must be remedied at the expense of the occupied territories. When, for instance, armament workers are short of bicycles, one must, to begin with, fall back on bicycles in Holland, Belgium, Denmark, etc. The same holds good for tramcars and other items.'[2]

Although, by the side of military production, raw materials, and foodstuffs, French consumer goods production for Germany in 1943 does not appear high, its tendency was to increase. The value of contracts for consumer goods placed in France after spring 1943 may well have been increasing more rapidly

---

[1] Ibid., 13–15 May 1943. [2] Ibid., 27 April 1943.

TABLE 20

Deliveries of Selected Consumer Goods from France to Germany*

Product	Quantity	Total French output			Deliveries to Germany			Percentage of total output delivered to Germany			Development of deliveries to Germany (2nd half 1942 = 100)		
		2nd half 1942	1st half 1943	2nd half 1943	2nd half 1942	1st half 1943	2nd half 1943	2nd half 1942	1st half 1943	2nd half 1943	2nd half 1942	1st half 1953	2nd half 1943
Plate glass	1,000 tons	41·9	38·6	39·6	0·8	1·6	1·3	2	4	3	100	200	163
Hollow glass	1,000 tons	8·8	12·1	9·7	0·9	0·5	2·0	10	4	21	100	56	222
Bottles	1,000 units	70·4	62·1	53·5	5·4	6·7	3·9	8	11	7	100	124	72
Domestic porcelain	tons	579·0	370·0	550·0	189·0	244·0	500·0	33	66	91	100	129	265
Domestic stoneware	1,000 tons	7·0	4·9	4·9	4·0	1·8	3·8	57	37	78	100	45	95
Sanitary ware	1,000 units	200·0	170·0	83·0	107·0	80·0	53·0	54	47	64	100	75	50
Brushes: from natural bristle or hair	1,000,000 units	13·2	12·0	9·8	1·3	2·5	4·5	10	21	46	100	192	346
Brushes: from vegetable material	1,000,000 units	13·0	13·1	9·9	2·3	3·0	4·8	18	23	48	100	130	209
Furniture	1,000 cu. m. of wood	112·6	78·2	84·4	30·0	30·0	60·0	27	38	71	100	130	200
Hutment equipment	1,000 cu. m. of wood	90·0	72·0	72·0	90·0	72·0	72·0	100	100	100	100	80	80
Barracks	1,000 cu. m. of wood	198·0	202·8	190·6	150·0	160·8	154·6	76	79	81	100	107	103

* FD 301/46, Mbh. in F, Wi.Abt., 'Der Beitrag des französischen Raumes . . .'.

than the value of contracts for other products. As French consumer goods production fell the share which Germany took increased.

The policy of producing consumer goods in France in 1943 may also therefore be said to have had some measure of success, although the general average of consumer goods production for German purposes as a part of total French production remained much lower than that of other sectors of French production. The closer connection between the two economies also meant an increase in certain German exports to France in 1943. This increase did nothing to benefit the French population. In so far as it created employment by providing the necessary raw materials and fuel, it only made up in most cases for deficiencies which became increasingly evident in French domestic supply, due to the severance of Franco-North African trade and declining output of some domestic raw materials.

Was the economic exploitation of France beyond the 40 to 50 per cent level possible? The estimates which indicate an increasing exploitation in autumn 1943 take no account of the one area where German policy had become an evident failure. In August 1943 only 10,000 workers left for Germany, the lowest total in any month since the beginning of the Sauckel actions. In September only 5,000 left. The more costly and determined the German efforts to secure labour, the smaller the numbers obtained. After August the share of French production going to Germany also began to decline. Had the ceiling of possible economic exploitation been reached?

Hemmen thought that might be the case; neither Sauckel nor Speer thought so. German contracts to France in 1943 amounted to about 4,400,000,000 Reichsmarks and were greater than the total of the previous two and a half years combined. Deliveries of raw materials, semi-finished goods, and food-stuffs, valued at 1,800,000,000 Reichsmarks in 1942, stood at 3,200,000,000 in 1943.[1] The purely financial contribution made by France had increased by 40 per cent. The financial contribution and those payments into the clearing account used by Germany to pay for imports together showed an increase of 80 per cent. Together they were two-thirds of the French budget. This increased level of exploitation had only been achieved by stringent controls to avoid the threatened inflation at the beginning of 1943 when it had seemed that France might 'go the way of Greece'.[1] In 1944 Germany would have to reckon with much greater transport difficulties in France, and, more than that, with the utter hostility of the population, not only to Germany, but also to its own government. The black market, the knowledge that food could still be bought for sufficient cash, had created in addition a serious social problem in France which further alienated the population.

This pessimistic outlook was not shared by Sauckel. He never moved from the position he had taken in his telegram to Hitler on 27 June

---

[1] Hemmen papers, 'Die Entwicklung unserer wirtschaftspolitischen Beziehungen zu Frankreich im Jahre 1943 und ihre aussenpolitischen Rückwirkungen', 1764–PS.

L

1943.[1] There was still room to extend further contracts from Germany to France. At least a million more Frenchmen could be made available in Germany. Given better organization of the French food supply and a more direct supervision over French labour this would in no way block the policy of placing more contracts in France.

Speer also had no doubts that further exploitation was possible, but only by admitting that the labour policies pursued in 1943 had arrived at a dead end. They must be scrapped. If Germany were to survive, the principles which underlay the administrative changes of February and March must be preserved, her survival was contingent on the organization of a European war economy embracing all the occupied territories. Sauckel's policies must be abandoned in favour of a new policy based on the economic rationality of new circumstances. That new policy was to be based on Speer's own conception of Germany's role in Europe, the central manufacturing core of a large free-trade area. It was the dream of German economic expansion which had so long prevailed in German industrial circles. To Sauckel and the National Socialist Party it appeared as yet another compromise, for immediate ends, with the fundamentals of the revolution. Therefore what Speer proposed, although to him a rational policy drawn from necessity, was in fact an attack on the National Socialist ideas of the 'New Order', a blow at the National Socialist revolution in Europe.

[1] IMT., xxvi. 154, 556 (39)–PS, (RF–65).

VI

WHAT KIND OF EUROPE?

'I WANTED to form a coal combine, for example,' said Speer after the war, 'to which Germany, France, Belgium, Holland, and Bohemia, etc., were to belong, a similar combine for iron ore, for aluminium, for motor vehicles, or for power-generating.'[1] These cartels were to be an extension into the rest of Europe of the organizational methods which had been so successful in increasing German domestic war production. The control of production by the best managerial abilities within the relevant industry, although an ideal not always attained, had proved a valuable device in Germany. As Germany's needs led to heavier demands on the occupied areas it seemed this might also be the way to increase production there. There would, of course, have to be certain restrictions on the nationality of the managers controlling some parts of these cartels. Nevertheless, if the occupied territories were to be really useful there must be over-all planning of their output on the same basis, and following the same procedures, as in Germany.

I wanted finally to put the 'European Production Planning' at the head of these individual combines as a covering organization [Speer said]. I was of the opinion that, if the military developments had not brought any further setbacks, the other countries, such as Sweden, Switzerland, or Portugal, would at least have their feelers in this organization. An organization of this sort could have settled more political disagreements in a short time than all diplomatic attempts. When, for example, I have a unified plan for ores in a unified tariff zone, and the ore is therefore distributed everywhere according to the requirements, then minette is no longer a bone of contention for war.

It would have been the supposition that the tariff was lifted from this large economic area and through this a mutual production was really achieved. For any deeply thinking individual it is clear that the tariffs which we have in western Europe are unbearable. So the possibility for producing on a large scale only exists through this scheme.[2]

When the industrialist von Delbrück had been asked in September 1915 by the Reichs Chancellor Bethmann-Hollweg to consider a plan which would include France within a customs union with Germany, he had expressed similar opinions. 'We are no longer fighting for the mastery in the internal market,' he wrote, 'but for mastery in the world market, and it is only a Europe which forms a single customs unit that can meet with sufficient power

---

[1] Speer Report no. 30, Intelligence Report EF/AM/6, interrogation of 21 July 1945.
[2] Ibid. The curious English is that of the original interrogation.

the over-mighty productive resources of the transatlantic world.'[1] This was
the conclusion at which liberal capitalism in Germany had arrived.[2]

The members of the Prussian Ministries, when consulted in 1915 on the
possible forms of a central-European federation between Germany and the
Austro-Hungarian Empire, expressed fears that such arrangements might
exclude Germany from the rest of Europe, where she was bound to dominate.
Von Falkenhausen of the Ministry of Agriculture wrote of creating a new
European power which would match the United States, Russia, and the
British Empire, and which would be dominated by Germany.[3] In the 'Principles' which Kuhlmann extracted from the Habsburg Foreign Minister
Czernin in October 1917 Austria-Hungary was forced to acknowledge the
strength of German ideas of a larger economic unit; by that date of course it
could only be in central Europe. The German plans for the exploitation of
the Russian iron and manganese ores at Krivoi Rog in the Second World War
are plainly foreshadowed by the representations of the *Verein Deutscher
Eisen- und Stahlindustriellen* at the time of the preparations for the treaty of
Brest-Litovsk.[4]

Speer's views on the industrial organization of Europe, although primarily
inspired by the immediate need to increase war production, fitted, therefore,
quite comfortably into the line of German liberal capitalistic thought stretching from the work of Rudolf Delbrück to the Common Market. They were
not excluded from that line of succession in any way by the regrettable tinge
of nationalism which coloured them.

I planned that, as much as possible, German cars should be made in Germany, and
I wanted to draw from the components industry in France, even at the risk that,
consequently, for example, fewer Citroëns or Renaults would be produced. In Germany without air-raids we could have raised our production 30–40 per cent while
the French were to have maintained their level.[5]

Considering that Speer's task was to win a war, he was less nationalistic than
many thinkers in his company. His European plans reawakened past forms
of German plans for Europe. They awoke, also, a vision, not too distorted,
of the Europe of the next decade.

Inasmuch as Hitler's foreign policy seemed to offer the reality of a European
economic unit dominated by Germany it had attracted the support of many
whose economic ideas were based on a solid historical derivation. While
Hitler was successful such ideas had lived harmoniously with the more revolutionary views of the National Socialist Party. When Hitler's failure forced

---

[1] F. Fischer, *Griff nach der Weltmacht* (Düsseldorf, 1961), trans. *Germany's Aims in the
First World War* (London, 1967), p. 248.

[2] It is interesting that it should have arrived there so much earlier than in rival economies.
Outside Germany the desire to compel by force other powerful states to be liberal has been
confined to relatively recent history.

[3] F. Fischer, op. cit., p. 250.   [4] Ibid., p. 483.

[5] Speer Report no. 30, Intelligence Report EF/AM/6.

Germany to consider more immediately the problems of European organization the harmony disappeared. When the New Order was in the process of being formed, these differences of opinion could wait on the event. When, however, it was a question of organizing the territory that Germany actually possessed, and for defensive purposes, this was not possible. The economic power of Germany's opponents meant that some European economic entity, larger than the German economy, had to be created.

The disputes which arose over its creation were rooted in the very nature of the National Socialist revolution in Germany. One aspect of that revolution was German society's last stand against capitalism. The economic ideas of the National Socialist Party had a lineal descent from the many social and economic protests against industrial capitalism. The ideas were championed, against Speer's plans, by Fritz Sauckel, the Commissar-General for Labour, a former Gauleiter. Fanatical, revolutionary, and irrational, he might well in an earlier age have been the leader of a millenarian anti-capitalist movement. His 'socialism', like that of the National Socialist Party itself, was not so much a logical extrapolation from the development of capitalist society as a primitive rejection of that society. He rightly suspected Speer's Europe of the future as being the Europe which the major German business interests would have wished to create. The coincidence between his economic standpoint and that of the men who created the independent economic empire of the S.S. was very close. The revolutionary nature of his ideas is best revealed by his refusal to compromise on them in the practical circumstances of autumn 1943, and their primitive nature may be judged from his insistence on the value of the oldest kind of booty, appropriate only to the conquest of the simplest societies, the seizure of men.

The dispute between Speer and Sauckel, protagonists not merely of two different ways for Germany but of two different ways for Europe was already simmering in 1943. But at that time Speer was immersed in the problems of organization in Germany itself. It was the realization that no amount of economic reorganization within the frontiers of the Reich itself was sufficient that brought Speer into conflict with Sauckel's already established policies. Speer, the rational pragmatist, became the advocate of a policy which could only be seen by the Party as a compromise. Sauckel became the advocate of a continuing National Socialist revolution in Europe, a revolution which could brook no compromise for merely practical purposes.

Sauckel's meeting with Laval and Bichelonne in the German embassy in Paris on 6 August 1943 had been a difficult one, lasting from a quarter to five until half past ten.[1] The testimony of Gaillochet, the under-secretary at the Ministry, about this meeting is borne out by the tone of Sauckel's later letters to Hitler.[2] He complained that the French government had refused all help

[1] *France during the German occupation*, op. cit., I, p. 48.
[2] IMT., xxvi., 158, 556 (43)–PS (RF–67).

in further labour recruiting. On 26 August Sauckel was again in Paris and attended a meeting of the German labour organizations there. By this time the drastic fall in labour recruitment in August had become clear. Sauckel blamed the abandonment of its authority by the French government for these results. At a local level the French bureaucracy was now actively opposing any further attempts at labour recruitment. Given the distaste of the military administration for Sauckel's measures, the problem of executive force was a very serious one, especially as the growth of the resistance movement in France was so stimulated by the labour draft.

The resistance of the French government to Sauckel had been strengthened by the interest shown by the German administration in Paris in alternative policies. On 28 May Speer and his officials had taken the preliminary steps in abandoning their support of Sauckel's policies.[1] In July Bichelonne had approached Michel with proposals for increasing the volume of production in France for 'the European war economy'.[2] Bichelonne's proposal was that the Germans should not only classify as protected labour the workers in agriculture, mines, and certain armament factories but also all who were concerned in the production of component parts, semi-finished goods, or raw materials of value to German war production. In return France would make a much greater productive effort in aid of Germany.

Although the initiative in France came from Bichelonne it did not take the Speer Ministry by surprise and it was not unwelcome. The Speer Ministry itself had been extending its powers into France in order to supervise and control the increasing amount of production there, and in summer 1943 it may only have been the administrative jealousy of others which had prevented Hitler from allowing Speer even greater powers there.[3] There had been a growing conviction in the Speer Ministry that some new approach to the occupied territories must be made. In April Speer had attempted to organize some armaments production in the General-Government and by doing so had called in question the whole of National Socialist occupation policy there, which had been to strip the whole area of any manufacturing capacity and to turn it into a primary producing area for Germany. In May the so-called Iwan Programme for the manufacture of munitions in the Ukraine was given protection from Sauckel's actions. 'Just as in all other occupied and annexed territories, anything detrimental to the armaments industry must also be avoided here. The responsibility for armaments rests with me and thus also the decision as to what has to be done before authority can be delegated to my intermediate agencies.'[4]

[1] FD 3037/49, Section I, Sc. 132, Rm.f.B.u.M., 'Chronik der Dienststellen des Reichs-ministers Albert Speer', p. 57.

[2] FD 3040/49, Section IV, Sc. 425, Rm.f.B.u.M., Chef des Rüstungs- und Beschaffungs-stabes Frankreichs to Mbh. in F., Verwaltungsstab, 30 July 1943.

[3] G. Janssen, *Das Ministerium Speer; Deutschlands Rüstung im Krieg* (Frankfurt a. M., 1968), p. 151.   [4] FD 3353/45, Rm.f.B.u.M., 'Führerkonferenz', 13–15 May 1943.

The success of armaments manufacture in Poland and the Ukraine was not very striking. On 30 May Hitler declared that it was unsafe to evacuate armaments factories to the General-Government.[1] Nevertheless, some production was obtained in both areas. If armaments could be manufactured in territories destined to play a wholly agricultural role in the New Order, could not war production in a wider sense take place in France where, on a small scale, there had always been some armaments manufacture for Germany? Bichelonne's approaches therefore should not be seen merely in the context of Franco-German relations. They were part of a general change in the relationship between Germany and the whole of occupied Europe.

The Ministry of War Production had become increasingly determined during 1943 to reduce the amount of consumer goods production in Germany. The policy of manufacturing consumer goods for German purposes in France had been first implemented on a small scale in 1941 with the 'Kehrl Plan' for textile manufacture. Hans Kehrl himself moved into the Ministry of War Production and became Head of the Planning Office in autumn 1943, when he and Speer began to develop this policy much further. Speer's own opinion of the capacity of the French to produce armaments was very low, and a variety of difficulties ranging from that of organizing the supply of spare parts to the danger of sabotage justified this opinion. If, however, it were possible to suppress completely the production of consumer goods in Germany in order to increase armaments manufacture there and, while doing this, to increase the volume of war production in its wider sense in France, such a policy would fit well with Speer's own conception of the future Europe. Germany would remain a specialized manufacturing centre receiving supply from the peripheral states.

When, therefore, Bichelonne proposed that he and Speer should meet to consider an increase in the dispersal of contracts from Germany to France, Speer was not merely eager to comply but saw the meeting as a potential turning-point in the policy of his Ministry. He urged Hitler to permit the meeting to take place and to accept whatever consequences might flow from it. Circumstances contrived to make the meeting of even greater importance than either Speer or Bichelonne could have first imagined. On 2 September the functions of the Reichs Economic Ministry in respect of production were transferred to the Speer Ministry. The Economics Ministry retained only very limited powers.[2] The title of the Speer Ministry was widened into that of Ministry of Armaments and War Production to recognize these changes. Speer now effectively controlled economic policy in the annexed eastern territories and in the Protectorate. Three days later his powers were extended

---

[1] Ibid., 'Führerkonferenz', 30 May 1943.
[2] FD 3049/49, Folder no. 2, 'Erlass des Führers über die Konzentration der Kriegswirtschaft', 2 September 1943.

to Alsace and Lorraine, to Luxembourg, to the General-Government, and to the district of Bialystok.[1]

On 9 September the news of the Italian defection broke in Germany. This news dramatically simplified the relationship of the Italian and German economies in the German war effort. The burden of supplying Italy with coal and other raw materials need no longer be supported except where it was necessary for armaments production. Italian armaments factories could be controlled and supply to the rest of the Italian economy ruthlessly cut off. On 12 September this was decided between Speer and the Führer.

The Führer is impressed by the amount of supplies so far delivered to Italy. The discounting of these supplies, he thinks, constitutes a considerable relief for the whole of our armament industry. In view of the situation generally it has been decided that these supplies should only be continued in the future if in the interest of our own armament industry.

Planning Office: to see to it that the materials saved by cutting down supplies to Italy are used only in the direct interest of our own armament industry.[2]

Whereas the Italian decision to seek an armistice did not damage Germany's prospects of greater armaments production it did potentially affect the total supply of other goods to Germany. This was the more worrying in view of the constant Russian advances in September. It was becoming increasingly obvious that the chance of getting any substantial return from the occupation of Russia was fading away.

The official contacts at a high level between the French and German governments had been astonishingly few and bizarre. Not the least bizarre, in historical perspective, had been the extraordinarily uncommunicative exchanges between Pétain and Hitler in a railway carriage at Montoire. The German representative at Vichy, Krug von Nidda, had scarcely fulfilled normal diplomatic duties. Laval's impulsive visit to the Führer's headquarters after his dispute with Sauckel had been menacingly unceremonious. Speer now insisted that Bichelonne be received with the honours due to a minister of an allied State. The possible co-operation between the two was to be the basis of Speer's European plans.

The Führer agrees to the visit of Bichelonne [Speer recorded on 12 September]. He thinks that Bichelonne should be treated with courtesy and in a friendly manner. The Führer agrees in principle to my proposal to plan production on a European basis, possibly by setting up a production office. He also agrees that France should be represented in this planning on an equal footing with the other nations. He also takes

[1] IWM., Kehrl Documents, 'Anordnung des Führers zu dem Erlass über die Konzentration der Wirtschaft', 5 September 1943.
[2] FD 3353/45, Rm.f.B.u.M., 'Führerkonferenz', 11–12 September 1943. FD 3049/49, Folder no. 2, 'Anordnung des Führers über die Bestellung eines Bevollmächtigten des Grossdeutschen Reiches in Italien und die Gliederung des besetzten italienischen Gebietes', 10 September 1943; 'Erlass des Führers über die Sicherung der Kriegswirtschaft in Italien', 13 September 1943.

it for granted that Germany, as the leading power in Europe, will retain undisputed leadership as far as production planning is concerned.[1]

The necessity to increase war production, the desire to organize a territorial base within which the factor endowment of the war economy might be comparable to that of the war economy of the United States or Russia, the desire to centralize under one direction the control of German war production, and the territorial losses in the east and in Italy all contributed to the importance of the Speer–Bichelonne meeting. But there were also other causes, related to the organization of production, which pushed Speer in the same direction.

In particular there was the growing effectiveness of the strategic air offensive against Germany. The transport of semi-finished products and component parts over long distances was becoming more and more difficult. No illusions existed that the Allies would not bomb factories in France. But it was also clear that the weight of Allied air attacks on Germany would increase whatever the future policy. The manufacture of completed goods in France would reduce the amount of transport necessary in the completion of any particular article and that in itself constituted some economic defence against air attack. Arguments based on this reasoning had been advanced on 30 July by the Speer Ministry's representatives in France to the military administration in response to Bichelonne's letter of 15 July.[2]

Behind all these considerations lay the certainty that the policy still at that time in operation in France was failing. Continued increases of production for German purposes in France were incompatible with continued labour drafts on such a scale. Before the Speer–Bichelonne meeting several remarkable proofs of this failure were demonstrated. Out of one hundred men drafted from a workshop for the training of apprentices in Troyes only eleven turned up at the station for transport. Ten of these disappeared on the way to the frontier.[3] Out of 1,500 men conscripted in one conscription area about 300 arrived in Germany.[3] But this must be seen as quite a good result, for in September only about 10 per cent on average of the men detailed to go to Germany actually arrived there. The consequence was special police searches to round up those who did not appear for transport at the appointed time. These produced still more grotesque results. One such 'action' supported by the local field commander to round up 5,618 escapees produced twenty-three.[4]

[1] FD 3353/45, Rm.f.B.u.M., 'Führerkonferenz', 11–12 September 1943.

[2] FD 3040/49, Section IV, Sc. 425, Chef des Rüstungs- und Beschaffungsstabes Frankreich to Mbh. in F., Verwaltungsstab, 'Vorschlag der französischen Regierung für die Produktionssteigerung der französischen Wirtschaft', 30 July 1943; this view may be compared with Speer's remark in February 1943, 'In France we are more and more turning towards giving up finishing processes, and stressing the sub-contracting. It is the foundries and similar works, e.g. in the aluminium industry, which we wish to use to capacity.' NCA., viii. 180, Minutes of Zentrale Planung, 16 February 1943.

[3] FD 3040/49, Section IV, Sc. 425, GbA. to Beauftragten für den Vierjahresplan, 11 September 1943.

[4] Ibid., Anlage 5.

Such circumstances and such operations were not to the taste of the
military. Armament industries, canals, railways, chemical plant, gasworks,
and power stations all had to be protected against sabotage by large numbers

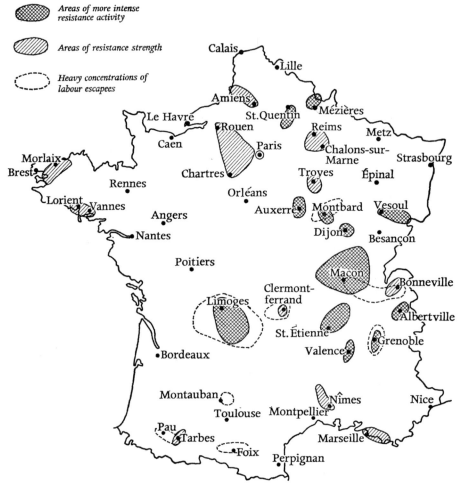

MAP 2. Areas of strength of the resistance movement in August 1943.
(FD 3040/49, Section IV, Sc. 425, Mbh. in F. Abt./c.)

of men.[1] Sauckel's actions had become one of the principal driving forces
behind the 'maquis'. The security police considered that the bands of armed
marauders in the Ardennes were mostly young men evading the labour service
laws in France and Belgium.[2] They were constantly replenished by workers

[1] FD 3040/49, Section IV, Sc. 425, 'Schutz gegen Sabotage'.
[2] Ibid., Chef der Sicherheitspolizei, 'Neuregelung der Arbeitseinsatzmassnahmen in den
besetzten Westgebieten', 24 November 1943.

going home on leave from Germany. Their numbers were now too great for them to be rounded up in such a terrain.

Six months later in the Central Planning Committee Hans Kehrl, looking back at the climate of opinion in September 1943, reviewed the situation in the following terms:

The circumstances which at that time occupied Minister Speer and led to the agreement with Bichelonne were the following. If now, even by the use of violence, I cannot bring people from France to Germany in the necessary quantity, a fact which is clear from developments, and at the same time I run the risk that through fear of violent seizure people leave the firms where they are at present working, then only the lesser evil is left for me, that I try to employ these people in France or Belgium. Thus I no longer need a German force to bring them over the frontier. In this way began a change in production policy. Until that time Minister Speer had, in essence, dispersed armaments production which was running into bottlenecks in Germany because in those areas German production capacity did not suffice. 'Now', he said, 'I will not only transfer production in those areas to France, but also indisputably important war production which otherwise could be carried out in Germany by German labour. That is in order to free German labour in Germany and to bring about this production in France, Belgium, and Holland.' We have dispersed in some areas up to 50 per cent of total German demand to the west, and production is succeeding there.[1]

It may be said therefore that the prospects for the meeting between Speer and Bichelonne were very good ones. But the meeting was more fruitful even than all these trends suggested it would be. That was because of the personal liking and trust which the two men developed for each other. They were indeed very similar. Both were very young for the positions which they held. Both were inclined to think of politics as a matter to be regulated by rational calculation and efficiency. Both were men inclined to judge by practical results rather than abstract principles. Both were extraordinarily able. Both, by the chance of war, had come to ministerial office from outside the political ranks. 'In 1943', Speer told his interrogators, 'I gave Bichelonne, the French Production Minister at that time, complete power to work independently in his country. Bichelonne was of the same age as myself, and we understood each other very well. I had confidence that he would keep his agreement.'[2]

Some of the details of the agreements reached at the meetings between 16 and 18 September, including the crucial question of the classification of those industries which would be protected from the labour draft, were in fact settled without the presence of the officials by the two men themselves. Working arrangements between the two men were the smaller part of their mutual agreement. They shook hands together on the future of Europe. 'The French Production Minister Bichelonne, with whom I spoke about these matters, and I myself thought further ahead. The next phase interested us already at that

[1] FD 3038/49, Section II, Sc. 246, Minutes of Zentrale Planung, 1 March 1944.
[2] Speer Report no. 30, Intelligence Report EF/AM/6.

time. We said, we are both young and we must strive for a solution which is a rational, permanent affair.'[1]

Bichelonne's original letter had mentioned the employment in France of 215,000 more workers for German purposes.[2] Speer's own preparatory notes for the meeting indicate that he regarded this as insufficient; he wished to offer Bichelonne more than Bichelonne had hoped for. The administrations in Brussels and Paris had suggested that the total increase in employment for German purposes ought to be 440,000.[3] Even to bring the labour force on present contracts up to a complement sufficient to guarantee the completion of those contracts on time would require 150,000 additional workers. Speer therefore proposed to suggest that if the French government could guarantee this initial increase within one month the labour drafts would be stopped. It was here that he ceased to be fully empowered to negotiate, because any such offer to the French government depended on clear instructions from Hitler to Sauckel, and Speer was in no position in this matter to guarantee to Bichelonne everything that he would have wished. The total increase of 440,000 was to be spread over a period of thirteen weeks.

Any increase in production in France depended not merely on additional labour inputs but on an increase in the output of coal and iron. Part of this coal could be supplied by Germany, but the experience of the previous two years showed that this was unlikely to be a very large amount. Beyond the labour increases necessary to fulfil existing contracts, therefore, the main increases in employment in France would have to be in coal mining and in the iron and steel industries. Within five months there would have to be an increase of 30,000 underground workers. As a result of air attacks the monthly production of crude steel in the Ruhr and Upper Silesia had fallen from 3,150,000 tons to 2,900,000 tons. With fuller utilization of the productive capacity of the occupied territories it should be possible to reach a level of 3,670,000 tons a month.[4] Although the Italian electro-steel industry could still be forced to contribute something to this total, the main contribution would have to come from France.

At their meeting on 17 September Speer and Bichelonne agreed that once the details of the final programme were settled its control in detail would be left in the hands of the French Ministry of Industrial Production. Although the allocation of the various aspects of the programme among the different firms involved would not be determined by the Speer Ministry, the liberty of action accorded to the French was greatly circumscribed by the continued need to operate through the 'Warenstellen', and, even more so, by the development of more direct links between French and German firms, such as the

[1] Speer Report no. 30, Intelligence Report EF/AM/6.
[2] FD 3040/49, Section IV, Sc. 425, 'Vorschlag der französischen Regierung . . .'.
[3] Ibid., 'Besuch Minister Bichelonne, Besprechungs-Notiz für Minister Speer', 16 September 1943.
[4] Ibid., Kehrl to Dorn and Humbert, 23 November 1943.

'Patenfirmen' arrangements, which Speer saw as arising naturally out of the agreement. The agreement on the precise nature of the programme itself was a compromise between Speer's wishes before the meeting and Bichelonne's limited proposals of July. At all costs there had to be an increase of coal production in France. On the German side an increase of 300,000 tons output a month in the northern coalfield was considered possible. On the French side 200,000 tons a month was thought more realistic.[1] Whatever result was achieved it was agreed that 15,000 workers more were necessary in the northern coalfield and 15,000 in the other fields. The full production programme in the coal-mines was to be implemented over the space of five months.

On the German side it was agreed to make a larger iron quota available to the French coal-mining industry. Through an increased utilization of scrap this would be possible, although it also depended on an increased output of iron ore and iron in France as well. In order to increase productivity at the coal face better rations would be made available to the underground workers. Once the increased output had been achieved coal allocation to the French chemical industry would be increased. But there would also have to be much stricter control over the distribution of coal within the French economy as a whole, involving the closing down of many smaller enterprises. Although the additional intake of labour into the coal-mining industry was to be of the same order as Speer had intended before the meeting the total increase in employment for German purposes in France was to be 600,000, 385,000 more than Bichelonne's original proposal. Of these 150,000 would be for the fulfilment of existing contracts. This inflation of the original estimates revealed both the mutual confidence of the two negotiators and the great deterioration in the German situation since July. It also revealed considerable optimism on the German side.

It was this extraordinary increase over the original estimates that made a completely new approach to labour classification in France essential. There already existed in France a system of protecting labour from the labour draft; the so-called 'V-Betriebe', and those works actually producing armaments for Germany, the 'Rü-Betriebe', had their labour force guaranteed against drafting. But the definition of these two categories was very strict, nor did they cover many of those industries to which Speer now wished to divert German contracts. Bichelonne was officially forbidden by his cabinet colleagues to discuss Sauckel's activities. But the personal confidence which the two ministers had in each other overcame this barrier. Their officials temporarily dismissed, Bichelonne's secretary Charbonneau alone remaining, they pursued more confidential negotiations further. 'The final conversations took place before the late meal in the Reichs Government Guest House, after

---

[1] Ibid., Mbh. in F., Wi.Abt. II, 'Notiz über die Schlussbesprechungen anlässlich des Besuches von Minister Bichelonne bei Minister Speer am 17.9', 20 September 1943.

the Minister had once more spoken alone with Bichelonne, who had asked for this private talk to deal with the Sauckel "actions". An official conversation on these points had been forbidden him by his government.'[1] The policy agreed was to denominate all firms employed in war production, in the widest sense, as 'S-Betriebe'.[2] This appellation would guarantee absolute immunity against Sauckel's activities. Sauckel had given his assent to this principle on 16 September but he had at that time no idea of the wide range of firms which would be given this appellation. Nor was he given the opportunity to find out.[3] The original German intention was that the criterion for classifying a firm as an 'S-Betrieb' would be the proportion of its total activity devoted to German purposes. The criterion which emerged from the meeting was that of whether or not the firm was engaged in a 'programme' of war production.[4] Since Speer's intention was to undertake the manufacture of consumer goods in France this definition was a very wide one. Gaillochet's testimony is that one classified firm made gramophone records; Sauckel discovered one that made labels for champagne bottles.[5] In general, railways, road transport, water transport, mines, electricity production and distribution, forestry, quarries, and some sections of the construction industry were covered, as well as factories engaged on German contracts. The classification was also valid in the two northern departments.

'For French industry the increased dispersal means an extraordinary opportunity, for it can maintain and increase its peacetime productive capacity while German industry must reorganize itself for armaments.'[6] Such was the verdict of the military in Paris. It was an ingenuous judgement, for the agreements also implied a much greater control over the distribution of raw materials within the French economy. Such materials would now be even more strictly allocated according to German needs. The agreement also cemented German economic control over the former unoccupied zone and in addition, of course, over the former Italian zone. Bichelonne's view was that there now existed a possibility of genuine co-operation. The 'comités de répartition' would no longer have as their prime responsibility the control of raw materials in order to cream off a surplus for Germany wherever possible, but the preparation of manufacturing 'programmes' for the whole of France. His reservations were very few. There were indeed great advantages in the agreement for France, if it were compared with any other possible outcome.

For Germany it cleared the way to an even greater concentration on armaments production and a better deployment of the labour force. Goebbels celebrated in his diary the fact that German civilian production would soon

[1] FD 3037/49, Section I, Sc. 132, 'Chronik der Dienststellen . . .', p. 147.
[2] 'Sperrbetriebe.'   [3] G. Janssen, op. cit., p. 126.
[4] France During the German Occupation 1940–1944, i. 49.
[5] FD 3040/49, Section IV, Sc. 425, Sauckel to Speer, 10 March 1944.
[6] Ibid., 'Notiz über die Schlussbesprechungen . . .', 20 September 1943.

come to a standstill: 'The total war which I have demanded for years will then become a reality.'[1] The only doubt left was whether the agreement could work. Speer dismissed Bichelonne with an exhortation.

One and a half years ago in Germany we drew up a plan for doubling production. We know the difficulties, and optimism is necessary to overcome them. We were able to stick to the programme and we got results. I believe you should not go too much into detail but should work. The will overcomes everything. We do not want written conditions which are too severe. We want to find out through work where the difficulties are. We are bringing advantages; you must bring French industry to unreservedly effective results. Difficulties can be overcome through good co-operation. We have the wish to co-operate and if the affair goes through successfully France will be making a substantial contribution, and we shall be very thankful to you if you get under way, because you will permit us to free soldiers for the eastern front.[2]

All that remained was for Hitler to ratify the agreement. This he did on 1 October at his next meeting with Speer. The change in German policy had been successfully completed.

Reported on the conversation with Minister Bichelonne. The Führer agrees with the policy of placing consumer goods production in the occupied countries and especially in France. He considers the risk of a possible stoppage of production in these countries through strikes, unrest, and the like as one which could be borne.
The Führer also agrees with the labour policy in the occupied countries (protected firms, priority granting of labour).[3]

In order to consolidate the unity of the French economy Speer introduced into France a new executive branch of his Ministry before his meeting with Bichelonne. The Länderbeauftragten were charged with local duties very much like those of the former Armament Inspectors, but they dealt directly with the production committees in Germany and communicated decisions directly to French factories, merely informing the administration in France what those decisions were.[4] The actual powers of the production committees had in principle been extended beyond the frontiers of the Reich by the decree of 1 June 1943. Bichelonne's address to the meeting of the presidents of Chambers of Commerce in Paris on 1 November shows how he had been influenced by the organizational methods of Speer and how similar their outlook was. Each industrial programme would be under the central direction of a prominent manufacturer in that industry whose job it would be to co-operate with the German authorities. The same address shows to what extent the agreements were a defensive arrangement for the French economy; they

---

[1] *The Goebbels Diaries* (London, 1948), p. 396.
[2] FD 3040/49, Section IV, Sc. 425, 'Notiz über die Schlussbesprechungen . . .'.
[3] FD 3353/49, Rm.f.B.u.M., 'Führerkonferenz', 30 September/1 October 1943.
[4] FD 2627/44, Rm.f.B.u.M., 'Dienstanweisung für die Länderbeauftragten', 15 September 1943.

constituted an open invitation to every local manufacturer to set himself up
as a manufacturer of consumer goods to meet German orders.[1]

When Speer addressed the assembled Gauleiters at Posen on 6 October he
again went out of his way to stress the singular importance of the new policy.
In part the speech, an extraordinarily long one for Speer, and considering the
nature of the audience, an extremely frank one, was a sketch of the rise to
power of his own Ministry.[2] But that rise to power was a reflection of Germany's total strategic position and Speer wished to point the moral. If consumer goods production were to be stopped in Germany the main opposition
would come from the National Socialist Party itself. The social motives behind
the Blitzkrieg economy had not disappeared, even though that economic
strategy itself had gone, and in carrying out his plans Speer was taking the
fight to the internal enemy and attacking the Party itself.

After illustrating the success of the production committees in concentrating
armaments production on those firms best and most economically able to
produce, Speer revealed his intentions to do the same thing with consumer
goods industries. Of the six million workers employed in consumer goods
industries in Germany between one and one and a half million were to be
transferred into the armaments industry. The transfer could be made because
of the unutilized reserves of productive capacity still remaining in the occupied
territories.

If it was not possible for the French Government before this war under the pressure
of the coming war, to change French industry into an armaments industry, then I
believe our endeavours to make an armaments industry out of French industry will
also be impossible. We have, nevertheless, in French industries, unusual and unused
reserves for the production of consumer goods. . . . I am completely aware that this
utilization of the French consumer goods industry, with which France will agree
because of the benefits bound up with it, carries advantages, mainly the fact that the
consumer goods industry will be in full swing at the end of the war and could be
fully exploited, while our consumer goods industry at home would by this time have
practically come to a standstill.[2]

The reaction to this speech was extremely hostile, but Speer felt secure
enough to push forward unhesitatingly in spite of Sauckel's complaints over
the ambiguity of the agreement about the 'S-Betriebe'. The Speer decrees
instituting protection for all necessary firms in France were published on 11
October. From 15 October to 19 October Sauckel was again in Paris to try
to modify their effect. But the main purpose of his visit was to agree with
Laval on a further programme of labour transfers to begin in January 1944.
Their discussions were kept secret, but Laval later stated that Sauckel had

---

[1] Procès-verbal de la réunion Ministre Bichelonne–Présidents des Chambres de Commerce,
1 November 1943.
[2] FD 3353/49, vol. lxxxi, Rm.f.R.u.Kp., Speech by Speer at Posen, 6 October 1943.

made no effort to secure the completion of the 1943 labour programme in view of the changed circumstances.[1] Indeed, by December 3,301 firms had been classified as 'S-Betriebe', representing a total labour force of 723,124. Of this total 425 firms had less than 70 per cent of their total output earmarked for Germany. There were plans for classifying a further 390 works with a work-force of 44,600.[2] Only 5,000 workers were transferred to Germany in September and less than 4,000 in October. In March 1944 Sauckel complained

TABLE 21

Value of Contracts in Certain Branches of French Industry*

(current Reichsmarks)

	September and October	November and December
Small metal goods and allied industries	5,097,000 (the major part of the increase due to clock production)	16,863,000
Metal foundings	2,890,000 (mainly increased production of stoves)	6,100,000
Ceramics	1,661,000	3,027,000
Chemical industry	39,112,000 (cosmetics responsible for 53,000,000)	76,639,000
Paper industry	1,490,000	2,293,000
Leather and leather goods	5,230,000 (shoes responsible for 23,000,000)	28,673,000
Textiles	19,715,000	42,287,000
Clothing	3,560,000	9,894,000

* FD 5238/45, Zentralauftragsstelle Frankreich, 'Bericht November und Dezember 1943'.

that there were in all 4,070,000 workers in classified occupations in France of whom only 890,000 were in armaments firms.[3] But according to the Speer Ministry estimates the figure should have been a much smaller one.[4]

Between September and December the pattern of German contracts changed significantly, although their total value showed only a small increase. The value of contracts placed in the iron and steel industry, where the Wehr-macht was the most important contractor, fell. There was also a fall of two

[1] E. Homze, op. cit., p. 194.
[2] FD 3040/49, Section IV, Sc. 425, Rm.f.R.u.Kp., Amstgruppe Beschaffung, 'Vermerk', 7 December 1943.
[3] NCA., v. 760, Sauckel to Hitler, 17 March 1944.
[4] Ibid., p. 763, Speer to Hitler, 5 April 1944.

million Reichsmarks in the value of contracts in the shipbuilding industry, where the Navy was the most important contractor. In the machine building industry there was a drop of almost ten million Reichsmarks. Contracts in the building industry fell by four million Reichsmarks. These figures were compensated by the increased value of contracts going to industries producing consumer goods.

However, Hitler's support for Speer's plans was not unwavering. Sauckel, who had himself been a Gauleiter, received the strong support of the Party and was also the beneficiary of Bormann's intrigues against Speer. Even Robert Ley, the head of the Reichs Labour Front and one of the most ardent of the advocates of 'total war', thought Sauckel's European solution more 'far-sighted' than Speer's.[1] In October Hitler placed financial restrictions on the utilization of Italian industrial capacity, although he continued to encourage the manufacture of armaments in Bohemia.[2] Hitler's own view of the shape of the future Europe was not yet a completely resigned one. The defensive East Wall was to be a permanent structure only on the northern part of the front.[3] In these circumstances Sauckel's refusal to accept the new policy was a constant threat to it.

It was towards the end of November that the grandiose nature of Sauckel's plans for the following year became clearly apparent. He had conceived the idea of transferring one million men, no less, from France to Germany in the course of 1944. On 21 November Speer expressed his resolute opposition to such a proposal and the Führer himself agreed that it was impossible.[4] By now the Speer Ministry had increased still further its estimates of the additional numbers it wished to employ in France and was thinking in terms of between 700,000 and 800,000 men, together with a further 80,000 to be employed on the West Wall.

On 23 November Sauckel again came to Paris to announce his projects to the French government. It was as direct a challenge to Speer's policies as Speer had made to his. His demands were twofold. Firstly, at the same time as a continued rise in employment was taking place in France it should still be possible to transfer 80,000 workers a month to Germany.[5] The level of employment of women in France was no higher than in Germany, the level of labour productivity was much lower, and the 'S-Betriebe' only exaggerated these tendencies. Secondly, he insisted not only that there should be no pay increases in France but that the level of wages there should be brought back to the 1939 level. Wage increases narrowed the vital differential

---

[1] E. Homze, op. cit., p. 222.

[2] FD 3353/45, Rm.f.R.u.Kp., 'Führerkonferenz', 14–15 October 1943; ibid., 13–15 November 1943.

[3] Ibid., 30 September–1 October 1943

[4] FD 3040/49, Section IV, Sc. 425, Rm.f.R.u.Kp., 'Niederschrift über Führerkonferenz 21.11.43', 22 November 1943.

[5] Ibid., Kehrl to Speer, 4 December 1943.

which induced foreign workers to work in the Reich. The consternation produced by these demands was as great among the German military administration as among the French government.

In a long and impassioned letter to the Führer on 2 December Sauckel set out his own views on the situation and made a public declaration of belief.[1] The minimum acceptable increase in the total of foreign workers in Germany was three million. One million of these would have to come from France, one million from Italy, a quarter of a million each from Belgium and the Netherlands, and the rest from the eastern territories. Were Germany to renounce a labour quota from France she would be in the position of conscripting workers from neutral and allied countries while sparing workers from a potentially enemy country. In any case there remained a vast labour surplus in France. Should not France be made to suffer rather than Germany?

> In very many French factories the forty hour week is still the ruling practice. The tempo of work cannot be compared with that in Germany. My German offices in every part of France made extraordinary complaints about missing and understaffed shifts, so that I would put forward the thesis that a Frenchman working in Germany is responsible for one third more output than when he is working in France.

German plant was obviously more modern than French plant, so, irrespective of the tempo of work, there was every probability that Frenchmen would be more productive in Germany. Speer himself was of the opinion that the French workers were the most productive of all the foreign workers in Germany.[2] Their only rivals were Russian women, but they were, naturally, mostly employed as agricultural labour. But the opportunism of Sauckel's arguments on productivity was revealed by the way his organization in Germany continued to allocate labour to small and unproductive concerns in Germany, even to those consumer goods industries which Speer wanted to close. They did so as a challenge to the big business interests which they believed, rightly, to be represented so powerfully in the Speer Ministry.

Not only were Sauckel's estimates of the numbers of foreign workers he had secured too high but his estimates of future demand were too high as well. There was little difficulty in finding the logical defects in his arguments.[3] But his argument's strength was not its logic, it was designed to make a more visceral appeal to Hitler. There was no better policy for the Speer Ministry to pursue than to go ahead with its plans more quickly. This they did by means of the two decrees of 3 December and 14 December. The main difference between the latter and the former was the inclusion of a firm promise of protection for the 'S-Betriebe'.

---

[1] Ibid., GbA. to Hitler, 2 December 1943.
[2] Speer Report no. 29, Intelligence Report no. EF/LN/2.
[3] FD 3040/49, Section IV, Sc. 425, Rm.f.R.u.Kp., Speer to Kehrl, 'Stellungnahme zu dem Bericht des Gauleiter Sauckel', 10 December 1943; ibid., Planungsamt, 'Entwurf eines Schreibens an Herrn RM. Speer', 15 December 1943.

I am determined [began the first decree] to make the total productive capacity of the occupied western territories available to the greatest possible extent to the German war economy, and to this end to carry out a planned and centrally controlled dispersal of contracts in place of the present method which is based on free discretion.[1]

From 15 January 1944, in all territories in the west, the production committees would have control over the volume of German orders of all goods. What could be produced in those territories must be produced there and not in Germany. A new chance was to be offered to the industry of western Europe to return to its pre-war level of output. 'In order to create the material prerequisites for greater production I will take care that the necessary labour strength for war production shall be left in the western territories.'[1] The quality of the promise resided in its boldness not in its firmness. On 16 December, Hitler, at Speer's next conference with him, was not so prepared to renounce the Sauckel programme.

> Reported to Hitler on differences with the Commissar-General for Labour. From my point of view the main thing is to exploit French industry better for Germany so that approximately one million additional workers can be employed there. Sauckel, however, takes the view that labour must be brought into Germany in the first place.
>
> Hitler declares that the dispersal to France is very important to him because of the possibilities of increased iron production connected with this dispersal. In spite of this it is his opinion that the additional call-up of Frenchmen for Germany should not be given up. One should therefore try to combine happily both points of view.[2]

Hitler himself suggested nominating certain factories in France as protected works and thus making them immune from the labour draft. Speer reminded him that this was already the practice in France and Hitler insisted that the 'S-Betriebe' should remain sacrosanct. If, however, Speer could do without the labour in France he should make it available to Sauckel. Speer thereupon protested that what was involved was the whole problem of the consistency of behaviour of the German executive in France. He had arranged an interministerial conference with Himmler, Keitel, Sauckel, and, perhaps, a representative from the Foreign Ministry to discuss the whole issue on 3 January. Hitler was to be informed of the results of their discussions and he himself would then give a final ruling. All policies ultimately rested on Hitler's decision. In this instance he had been unable to forestall events and the decision would have to be made. It was obviously not possible for 'both points of view' to be 'combined'.

On 20 December Sauckel restated his policy, without any changes, in a teleprinter message to Speer and claimed that he had already taken the pre-

---

[1] FD 2192/44, Rm.f.R.u.Kp., 'Erlass über Auftragsverlagerung in die besetzten Westgebiete', 3 December 1943; FD 2627/44, Rm.f.R.u.Kp., Rüstungsobmann, 'Abschrift. Erlass I über Auftragsverlagerung in die besetzten Westgebiete', 1 February 1944.

[2] FD 3353/45, Rm.f.R.u.Kp., 'Führerkonferenz', 16–17 December 1943.

liminary steps with the French government.[1] The following day the Central Planning Committee decided firmly against further labour drafts. 'It is imbecility if I call up one million men in France', said Speer, 'I end up with two million workers less there and fifty to a hundred thousand more in Germany.'[2] In preparation for the conference with Hitler the Planning Office of the Speer Ministry drew up a comprehensive, and favourable, balance of the contribution of the occupied western territory to the German war effort.

TABLE 22

Estimates of Contribution of Occupied Western Territories to German War Production (January 1944)*

(percentage of total production by weight and number)

Hard coal	25	Electro-steel§	25
Coke	20	Sheet steel	25
Iron ore†		Tubes§	25
(fe content)	30	Lorries	20/25
Crude steel	15	Wood-burning gas	
Bauxite	40	generators	50
Alumina	18	Clothing	40
Nitrogen	25	Stoves	25
Soda	25	Alarm Clocks	80
Castings	20	Working Shoes	25

* FD 3040/49, Section IV, Sc. 425, Rm.f.R.u.Kp., Kehrl to Speer, 3 January 1944.
† Total German supply includes imports from neutrals.
§ Italian production alone.

Should the industries of the western territories be used even more fully it would mean a real acquisition to the German armaments industry of between 400,000 and 500,000 workers from this development alone, irrespective of the massive redeployment of labour resources within the German economy which Speer hoped to achieve and which the Gauleiters hoped to prevent. But the question had also to be faced whether any further total general expansion of war production in Germany alone was feasible. Was it possible to transport such a high proportion of the total coal and iron supply to the Reich itself when Allied strategy was directed at the destruction of communications? Was it possible to increase the output of energy within the Reich itself? Was it sensible to attract, by such a policy, further air attacks on to Germany? Was it possible to house three million more foreign workers in Germany in 1944? Was it possible to feed them?

Speer, Sauckel, Keitel, Milch, one of the three members of Central Planning, Backe, the Minister of Food, Lammers, the head of the Reichs Chancellery, and Himmler met in Hitler's presence on 4 January. Sauckel estimated that between 2,500,000 and 3,000,000 more people in employment were

[1] FD 3040/49, Section IV, Sc. 425, Sauckel to Speer, 20 December 1943.
[2] G. Janssen, op. cit., p. 128.

necesary to maintain present levels of production allowing for the recoupment of losses, although the basis for this estimate remained vague. Speer required 1,300,000 men more in the armaments industry. Hitler added a further 250,000 to total requirements to carry out special air raid duties. Sauckel proposed that the total of 4,050,000 could be obtained by securing the same quantities of foreign labour as forecast in his letter of 2 December, that is to say, including one million French workers. In addition, a further 500,000 could be obtained from Italy, raising the total labour draft for 1944 from Italy to 1,500,000, and Speer's plans could be held responsible for releasing a further 500,000 workers for redeployment in Germany. The major effort would thus have to be made outside Germany. Hitler agreed with these proposals. It was necessary to stabilize wages in occupied territories, to improve conditions for foreign workers in Germany, and to allocate foreign labour more rationally. But if the four million workers could not be secured the S.S. and other German agencies were to support Sauckel with all their efforts. The only restriction on Sauckel's activities was to be that the 'S-Betriebe' in France were to remain protected.[1] There, it was still necessary to 'combine happily both points of view'. Sauckel had no chance of securing his required quota from France even if the 'S-Betriebe' had not existed. But the maintenance of the protected works there made the decision even more confused. Psychologically, the decision had gone against Speer. And even in a material way, too, some damage had been done to the French programme, for Sauckel had little intention of respecting for long the agreement over 'S-Betriebe'. It was not necessary to trouble Hitler with administrative details, Lammers reported to Sauckel, he was now behind the whole programme.[2] Hitler also emphasized that the coming invasion meant that in future the army commanders in France must have the power to decide which economic activities had absolute priority.[3]

Fortified by these decisions Sauckel returned once again to Paris to institute his programme. The labour laws, he suggested, should be extended to cover men aged between sixteen and twenty and women aged between eighteen and forty-five. The working week should be extended to forty-eight hours. Officials who impeded the carrying out of the programme should be shot.[4] These proposals were accepted in a protocol signed by Sauckel and the German administration on 14 January. The project of a law embodying these proposals was presented to Laval on 19 January with a schedule of the degree to which various French industries would be affected by the labour draft.

---

[1] FD 3040/49, Section IV, Sc. 425, Lammers to Speer, 'Abschrift; Führerkonferenz, "Arbeitseinsatz 1944"', 8 January 1944. According to Speer himself this concession was extracted at the last moment after the formal closure of the meeting. This would explain the later confusion over what Hitler had decided.

[2] Ibid., Lammers to Sauckel, 8 January 1944.

[3] Ibid., 'An Obersten Reichsbehörden', 11 January 1944.

[4] Ibid., Mbh. in F., Wi.Abt., General Wäger to Kehrl, 19 January 1944.

Germany, the proposed law stated, had prevented the French state and economy from falling into ruins and had preserved French culture against the threat of bolshevik chaos.[1] The industrial sectors which would be most heavily affected were jewellery, foodstuffs, and clothing, all of which would lose more than 30 per cent of their labour force.[2] Service industries, the building industry, and the ceramics industry would all lose between 20 and 30 per cent. Only mining, not including quarries, agriculture, forestry, and fishing, would be completely spared.

While these negotiations were under way the number of 'S-Betriebe' in France was rapidly extended. There had previously existed two different systems of classifying firms engaged on production for Germany, the so-called 'Rü-Betriebe' and 'V-Betriebe'. The former classification had been bestowed by the armaments inspectors and the latter by the local organizations which took over some of their powers. In December 1943 these two classifications had covered 1,970 firms with 500,873 workers.[3] On 17 January they were all included under the same provisions as the 'S-Betriebe', thus bringing the total number of protected workers to well over one million.[4] This extension followed the agreement on 12 January over a further programme of contract dispersals to France.[5]

The French government objected strongly to both the preamble and the terms of the law which Sauckel proposed. Laval bluntly stated his conviction that it was absurd to expect to recruit 90,000 workers a month from France. If compulsory labour service for women were to be introduced it would have to be confined to France. The law on penalties was quite unacceptable. Decreases in wage and price levels were out of the question. These objections by the French government were all fully reported back to the Speer Ministry by the military administration which had every sympathy with them.[6] This sympathy was reinforced by the opposition to the plans shown by the Military Commander in Brussels.[7] Sauckel's strength, however, resided in his influence with the Party. The great publicity given to his speech to the Gauleiters in Weimar, a deliberate riposte to Speer's earlier speech in Posen, caused Speer to protest to Hitler that Sauckel must be brought to order and, in so far as policy in the occupied territory was concerned, subordinated entirely to the control of the Ministry of War Production.[8] At the end of January Sauckel by means of his own private police organization in Belgium

[1] Ibid., GbA., 'Gesetz zur Behebung von Notständen und zur Sicherung der Lebensgrundlagen des französischen Volkes während des Krieges'. [2] P. Cathala, op. cit., p. 258.
[3] FD 3040/49, Section IV, Sc. 425, Rm.f.R.u.Kp., Amtsgruppe Beschaffung, 'Vermerk', 7 December 1943.
[4] Ibid., Mbh. in F., Wi.Abt., 'Erlass', 17 January 1944.
[5] FD 3037/49, Section I, Sc. 72, Rm.f.R.u.Kp., Rüstungsobmann in Frankreich, 'Vermerk' 22 January 1944.
[6] FD 3040/49, Section IV, Sc. 425, Mbh. in F., Jehle to Kehrl, 20 January 1944.
[7] Ibid., Mbh. in B. und Nf., Abt. Arbeit., 16 January 1944.
[8] NA., T–73, Roll 19, 1336951.

began to draft Belgian railway workers to Germany.[1] He told the military in Brussels that he intended to extend protection only to those workers in the 'armaments industry' and not to those in 'the war economy'.

The new French labour law was promulgated on 1 February 1944, extending the age groups covered by the law of 4 September 1942 to the further categories on which Sauckel had insisted. The draft would be based on a system of 'combing-out' (Auskämmung) of surplus labour in all factories and workshops. This would be carried out by the 'combing-out commissions', teams of French and German experts who would investigate the level of productivity in French factories. The question of the relative level of wages in France and Germany was deferred until a later meeting. Compulsory labour service for women was to be confined to French territory.[2]

The legislation on prices and wages which Sauckel had demanded at the conference of 4 January was drafted for submission at the beginning of February. It is a document which bears heavily Sauckel's own stamp, no mere administrative instrument, but an argumentative exposition of the problem. 'The basic law of the Greater German National Socialist Empire consists of the maintenance of the stability of the level of prices and wages', it began.[3] Thanks to this stability the general population had been able to maintain the same living standards it had had on the first day of the war. The initial impact of the German occupation on other territories, however, had been to cause unemployment. Through the extension of National Socialist economic policy to these areas the standard of living had been maintained and the threat of 'bolshevization' avoided. This had not been achieved without opposition. 'Liberal interference, reckless striving for profit, and lack of discipline have unfortunately led to a state of affairs in most occupied European countries where, through a lack of suitable rules and laws, irresponsible and mercenary elements have driven prices higher and higher, in spite of the circumstance that these countries in expectation of a war were fully supplied with goods of all kinds and still are so now.' The main sufferers from these developments were the mass of the working people, the main beneficiaries unscrupulous liberal businessmen. 'There can be no doubt that such a development can only be greatly desired by the enemies of the Reich, plutocrats as well as bolsheviks.' The destruction of social order and the conversion of the masses to communism was the natural result. 'All experiments, which have been made in very large numbers in Germany since 1919, show that the method of chasing rising prices with rising wages is completely useless, and must indeed even be termed harmful and catastrophic.' How could such a situation best be handled?

[1] FD 3040/49, Section IV, Sc. 425, Mbh. in B. und Nf., Wi.Abt., letter to Kehrl, 27 January 1944.   [2] IMT., xxvi. 556 (55)–PS (RF–70).
[3] FD 3037/49, Section I, Sc. 72, Fernschreiben AA Berlin, Telegramm Nr. 577, 'Entwurf einer Verordnung zur Erhaltung der europäischen Lohn- und Preis Stabilität', 4 February 1944.

There is only one way to master such a development in spite of all difficulties, impediments, and objections, namely, to call categorically to order mercenary elements and criminal dealers and to rewrite the prices which they have driven up on the basis of the true and genuine costs and of the real production relationships plus a fair profit. It is easier to put a stop to several hundred thousand price breakers and criminals, especially if these people should forfeit through their fines milliards of francs or lire, than to withhold the possibility of existence from several hundred million of Europe's workers and, on account of the ever increasing price level, give them a lying and completely unrealistic promise of support through a doubtful wage increase. In the one case irresponsible merchants and dealers will be justly brought to book and made to suffer the consequences of their economic misbehaviour; in the other, over a hundred million workers in Europe will be driven irretrievably into despair, bitterness, and ultimately into Bolshevism, their goodwill and even their capacity to produce will be destroyed, and their otherwise valuable capacity for work will be lost, in contradistinction to the true aims of the war and the maintenance of the possibility of existence in Europe. The discontented masses would become a burden to the European Order.

The solution must be fair prices firmly guaranteed. For one thing only in that way could it still be worthwhile in the New Order for workers to go to Germany and transfer their wage back to their native land. France had become during the war a glaring example of social injustice where the worker was deprived of a decent means of existence. His position could only be restored if wages and prices were again brought into a 'correct' relationship.

This concept of a 'true' relationship between prices and income, a relationship different from the one which actually existed, was no other than the time-honoured anti-capitalist traditional belief in a 'fair' price. That Sauckel was concerned with using rhetoric to Germany's advantage cannot alter the fact that his rhetoric was very different from Speer's. The ideas for which Gottfried Feder had been so ardent a publicist in the early years of the National Socialist Revolution did not fade away with him.[1] The Europe of the future was to belong neither to communists nor to 'plutocrats'.

At his next meeting with Laval, on 8 February, Sauckel offered his personal assurance that at the end of the year he would ask Hitler to request no more labour from France if only the necessary million men could be found. Nevertheless, they should bear in mind the fate of the Italian fascist government as a dire warning of what might result from a war on French soil. French labour working in Germany would be protecting France from these horrors. However unpleasant the work might be, and, as he said, he knew from the experience of his own life what existence in a foreign country meant to a man, Sauckel was determined to carry through the whole of his task.[2] In fact the numbers of workmen brought to Germany showed no worthwhile increase;

[1] G. Feder, *Das Manifest zur Brechung der Zinsknechtschaft des Geldes* (Munich, 1919).
[2] FD 3040/49, Section IV, Sc. 425, Rm.f.R.u.Kp., Planungsamt, 'Abschrift der Niederschrift über die Pariser Besprechung Sauckel–Laval, 8.2.44.', 29 February 1944.

in spite of a special organization of over 2,000 men backed by the security police and the S.S., the number of men obtained was no greater than in the period when movement had been entirely voluntary. Between September 1943 and April 1944, inclusive, less than half as many workers were obtained from France as in the one month of June 1943.

TABLE 23

*Number of Workers Conscripted for Labour in Germany**

	Belgium and France (Nord and Pas-de-Calais)	Rest of France	Netherlands
1943			
August	6,000	10,000	10,000
September	5,000	5,000	
October	1,901	3,728	2,951
November	1,516	3,602	1,735
December	2,445	5,623	7,573
1944			
January	1,183	2,582	2,145
February	1,832	2,876	1,913
March	3,143	5,222	2,532
April	2,778	8,228	2,761

* FD 3040/49, Section IV, Sc. 425, Rm.f.R.u.Kp., Planungsamt, 'Werbung von Arbeitskräften aus den besetzten Gebieten für den Arbeitseinsatz in Deutschland', 20 June 1944; 'Heranführung ausländischer Arbeiter aus Belgien und Nordfrankreich, Frankreich und Holland', 5 July 1944.

The failure of Sauckel's policy had been easy to foresee, but was Speer's policy any more successful? Judgement is difficult in view of the fact that it was only given a more or less unimpeded trial between September and Hitler's decision of 4 January. After that date the confidence both of the French workers and the French government in the 'S-Betriebe' was very low. On 20 April 180 workmen in an 'S-Betrieb' in Tarbes hearing of an impending visit by a Sauckel commission rushed into the river Adour.[1] The existence side by side of the two policies meant insurmountable difficulties for both. But it would be unrealistic to blame the continuation of the Sauckel 'actions' for the poor result of the Speer–Bichelonne agreements. These agreements were more humane, and even more sensible, than the alternative policies, but economically they were only slightly more justifiable. They were based on a false appreciation of the level of labour productivity in France, a falsity which Sauckel was quick to see. It should be remembered that France was being exploited to a point where 40 per cent of her total output was for German

[1] FD 3040/49, Section IV, Sc. 425, Rm.f.R.u.Kp., Chef der Rüstungs- und Beschaffungsstab Frankreichs, 23 April 1944.

purposes when the agreements were negotiated. Bearing this in mind the fact
that the agreements resulted in any further increase at all for German purposes argues their success.

When the policy of labour conscription for Germany failed the Speer–
Bichelonne agreements showed a new way ahead. But could they do more
than slightly increase the level of exploitation of the French economy? It was
impossible that they could fulfil the grandiose visions of two Ministers themselves. Three and a half years of exploitation had created a different economy
in France, slow to respond to any stimulus for change, an economy designed
for survival until the end of the war. Human labour, the one factor of production which had seemed certain in July 1940 to be in excess supply, came,
by 1944, to be the critical factor in the economy. Speer's hopes for a labour
increase in French industries were no more realistic than Sauckel's hopes for
a massive movement of labour to Germany.

Between 1 November and 31 December 1943 Bichelonne had promised a
net intake into French coal-mines of 10,000 men. There was a crude intake
of 3,040 and a loss of 2,307 in that period.[1] French coal production in September 1943 had stood at 3,426,000 tons, and in October it was 3,200,000
tons. The average for November and December was 3,510,000 tons, and for
January and February 1944 3,420,000 tons.[2] The labour intake into the iron
and steel industry was no more successful. In the two major steel-producing
regions, the northern coalfield and the department of Meurthe-et-Moselle,
output recovered from the decline of August and September but remained
about the levels it had reached in spring 1943. The combined output of the
two regions in September was 158,465 tons, in October 167,242 tons, in
November 163,647 tons, and in December 165,345 tons.[3] French domestic
consumption of power was not reduced at all over the period. Transport
difficulties increased all the time. Through air attack and through sabotage
300 railway locomotives a month were put out of action, and the total stock
had been reduced from 16,000 to 8,000. The losses of wagons were more
severe, and there was insufficient labour to repair them.[4]

However limited the scope for manœuvre the only possible approach was
a thorough examination of all the available possibilities. This the Planning
Office hoped to achieve by a more exhaustive statistical investigation on the
basis of which further comprehensive plans for the utilization of French
capacity could be drawn up.[5] But their failure to realize their initial plans gave

---

[1] Ibid., Rm.f.R.u.Kp., Conference between Kehrl, Jehle, and Studt, 16 February 1944.
[2] FD 3045/49, Section IX, Sc. 292, 'Bericht 2', Dr. L. Westrick to Continentale—Öl A.G.,
17 May 1944.
[3] FD 1670/45, Reichsvereinigung Eisen und Wirtschaftsgruppe Eisenschaffenden Industrie, 'Rohstahl-Erzeugung'.
[4] FD 3040/49, Section IV, Sc. 425, Rm.f.R.u.Kp., Chef der Rüstungs- und Beschaffungsstab Frankreichs, 23 April 1944.
[5] FD 2627/44 Rm.f.R.u.Kp., Rüstungsobmann in Frankreich, 1 March 1944.

Sauckel greater room for criticism. Was the increased hardship for Germany worth while, given the meagre results obtained in France? Would it not be better to abandon the whole plan and recruit for Germany from the 'S-Betriebe'? On 1 March Sauckel himself came to the meeting of the Central Planning Committee. The meeting was a direct confrontation of the two policies and a most bitter one.

Sauckel blamed the failure of conscription in the west after September on the conviction among the inhabitants of the occupied countries that the Speer–Bichelonne agreements meant that policy had totally changed. 'It has gone so far—I can assure you of this—that certain prefectures in France have received instructions not to carry out my orders, since it is even being asked in the German administrative offices whether Sauckel is a clown or not.'[1] Already he had been reproached by German officers for not recruiting more men in the east. Had he done so there would now be less Russians to fight against. But he had been prevented from doing so by Speer's European plans. These plans were based on wholly false premises. There were still enormous reserves of labour in France and Italy. 'Italy is an absolute European scandal and for the most part so is France. Gentlemen, the French work badly and live at the cost of the German soldiers and German production and even at the cost of the German food supply, and it is just the same in Italy.' The plans for total war in Germany were wholly misplaced, the situation was wildly exaggerated by the Speer Ministry in order to achieve its own ends. Less women were at work in Britain than in Germany. To mobilize more women in Germany would in any case be very easy, but it would be wholly undesirable. 'Several times on the fourth of January I expressly asked Hitler that, if he would give me full powers à la Stalin to mobilize people, I could still perhaps put one million women at his disposal. The Führer brusquely, sharply, and repeatedly declined. He used the phrase that our long-legged slender German women could not be compared with the short-striding, primitive, hale Russian women.' In these circumstances it was certain that no more German labour could be obtained.

The only possible step therefore, he argued, was to continue to secure foreign labour. This could be done by a wholesale attack on small firms in France where productivity was very low, and on the protected firms which had become a mere ruse to thwart German plans.

How, then, shall I carry through the redeployment of French labour? In this instance the German offices must all work together and if, in spite of all promises, the French do not take effective measures then we on the German side must make an example of someone and in certain cases on the basis of this law we must stick a prefect or a mayor who doesn't go along with us up against a wall, otherwise no Frenchman will ever go to Germany.

---

[1] FD 3048/49, Section II, Sc. 246, Rm.f.R.u.Kp., Minutes of Zentrale Planung, 1 March 1944; see also FD 3353/45, vol. 196, Rm.f.R.u.Kp.

The reproach that such tactics only increased the strength of the resistance was quite unjustified. Kiev, from which 100,000 men had been taken, had remained the quietest area in Russia; Minsk, from which hardly a man had been taken, had been the worst area of all for partisans. The reality in France was that the resistance fighters were composed of bands of unemployed to whom the English distributed weapons by plane.

To this farrago of violence and ignorance it was difficult to make any reply. Sauckel's words were not his own personal idiosyncrasies, they were the voice of the continuing revolution. It seemed wiser to allow him some nominal concessions in respect of recruitment in the protected factories; if there were cases of very low productivity there the ban on recruitment should not be absolute. But Sauckel was not to be appeased by administrative temporizing; he was concerned more with ideology than administration. And in the circumstances of March 1944 this attitude was not entirely out of place.

It is actually the case [he replied] that the French worker in France lives better than the German worker in Germany, and the Italian worker, in that part of Italy which we occupy, even when he is out of work, lives better than when he is working in Germany. That is the basis of my request on the subject of German nutrition to improve the nourishment of German workers by a 'factory-snack'. If I am in Paris I naturally go to Maxim's. You can witness prodigies of feeding there. I have talked about it with the Führer. It is always the idea in these countries that only the really rich rabble who can go to Maxim's are well provided for.[1]

A wholesale attack on the policy of contract dispersals to France could certainly not be successful within the setting of the Central Planning Committee. The French had been promised the programme would go through, said Kehrl, and it would go through. It was, in any case, the only remaining way ahead for Germany, and had begun because Sauckel's policy had been itself a failure. Laval's refusal to give any further help to German recruitment would have occurred even without the Speer–Bichelonne agreements. As for Sauckel's plans to reorganize the pattern of employment in France itself, it was clearly impossible, witness the difficulty in getting sufficient labour even into the protected firms. The only glimmer of agreement in the meeting was on the subject of industrial training in France. Here the practical needs of the Speer Ministry for more skilled workers and Sauckel's views about liberal French society could find a common meeting-place. A continuous industrial programme to train skilled workers to replace those brought to Germany was acceptable to both sides. It was not surprising, Sauckel argued, that Bichelonne could not get sufficient workers for the new programmes, the social conditions in French mines were so bad that no one would work there.

The result of the meeting of 1 March was therefore a deadlock. Except in so far as it was agreed to investigate the possibilities of industrial training, and to fix a required labour strength for all the 'S-Betriebe', the situation in

[1] Ibid.

France remained unchanged. Sauckel was not content with this result. On
10 March he submitted a list of 'useless' protected firms to Speer and asked
permission for the 'combing-out commissions' to begin their work there.[1] The
following day Speer complained to Hitler that Sauckel was challenging his
authority and the decisions of 4 January.[2] Sauckel's reply came on 17 March
when he wrote directly to Hitler asking permission from Hitler to attack the
'S-Betriebe'.[3] On 21 March Speer ordered that all labour surpluses in the
protected factories should be used to fill deficiencies in other such factories.[4]

On 6 April Saur handed Hitler Speer's reply to Sauckel's protests during
an armaments conference.

Having read the letter the Führer summarizes as follows: 'that is my own
opinion completely'. In order to eliminate the doubts of Gauleiter Sauckel he asked
that Reichsminister Speer's department should check up thoroughly whether the
workers in 'S-Betriebe' work for the armament industry and are able to produce
satisfactory results.

When asked the next day the Führer agreed to inform Gauleiter Sauckel through
Reichsleiter Bormann but pointed out that nothing must happen in this matter
without his consent.[5]

At the same meeting Hitler refused to allow the transfer of French workers
to Alsace to accompany firms which might be moved there. Presumably the
refusal was based on racial grounds.[6] The whole tendency of the meeting was
to sustain Speer's views. There was to be an increased level of armaments
manufacture in Slovakia and a particularly important drive to increase production in Hungary, where the same system of 'S-Betriebe' would be introduced. Nevertheless, reading between the lines of the minutes, it is not difficult
to see that the Führer's support for these policies was more half-hearted than
it had been in September 1943. However untouchable the 'S-Betriebe', the
psychological climate for any genuine 'European war economy' had been
destroyed by the decision of 4 January to support Sauckel's plans.

Indeed, in spite of the apparent conviction with which Hitler had agreed
with Speer's letter he summoned a further general conference to discuss the
whole labour situation on 24 April, at which Bormann, Sauckel, and Robert

[1] FD 3040/49, Section IV, Sc. 425, Sauckel to Speer, 10 March 1944.
[2] IMT., xli. 442.
[3] NCA., v. 760, Sauckel to Hitler, 17 March 1944.
[4] FD 3040/49, Section IV, Sc. 425, Rm.f.R.u.Kp., Speer to Mbh. in F., Chef Wi.Abt.,
21 March 1944.
[5] FD 3353/45, Rm.f.R.u.Kp., 'Führerkonferenz', 6-7 April 1944.
[6] The Führer was more explicit on 19 April. 'On the grounds of fundamental political
considerations, the Führer can under no circumstances give his assent to workers from west
European countries being transferred, in the course of the industrial dispersals, to the new
underground factories in Alsace, Lorraine, and Luxembourg. Arrangements must therefore
be made to set up a special exchange of manpower procedure, which, applied to the measures
for industrial dispersal, must exercise a combing-out action on the personnel to be evacuated
to such sites, so that western labour is exchanged for workers from the east and south-east',
ibid., 19-20 April 1944.

Ley were all present. As a result of their discussions the conference was prolonged the next day in the presence of Speer.¹ Sauckel's burden of complaint
had not changed, except in so far as he exaggerated the conditions in France
still further. Nor was his optimism diminished; he still hoped the 'combing-
out commissions' would produce a further 250,000 men from France. The
result of the conference was a further retreat from Speer's original standpoint. He retained the ultimate authority over 'S-Betriebe' but he was told
to allow Sauckel's commissions in, under his own authority, to undertake the
'proofing' of the protected firms. 'The Führer considers it absolutely necessary
to prevent a misuse of the "S-Betriebe" and wishes a "proofing" of them as
well as a decisive "combing-out".'

This decision was even more ambiguous and temporizing than the earlier
ones. It was interpreted quite differently by the parties concerned. Sauckel
insisted that he had the right to investigate freely labour in firms whose output was, in the first instance, for France, although they might because of their
ultimate connection with war production for Germany be classified as 'S-
Betriebe'.² Speer was prepared to concede that Sauckel could undertake a
'proofing' of the 'S-Betriebe', especially in cases where the immediate output
was not for Germany, but that any 'combing-out' must be resisted.³ Nevertheless, the extensive powers given to Sauckel in Italy to impose a wage freeze
and to use Italian soldiers and detainees as civilian workers could not help
but affect the situation in France. 'After the Führer had especially outlined
the difficulties in Italy the Commissar-General for Labour asked him if, since
he must still fulfil his programme there, he should proceed on the principle,
"God helps those who help themselves". The Führer agreed to this.'⁴

Armed with this useful principle Sauckel attended a meeting with Déat,
the new French Minister of Labour and National Solidarity, and Bichelonne.⁵
Déat, the leader of the fascist Rassemblement National Populaire, who had
been forced into the government by German pressure, had, like Bichelonne,
not changed his earlier opinions on Europe in spite of the continued German
military reverses. 'It would be madness', he said, 'to believe today that there
could be any salvation for France outside co-operation with Germany and
Europe.' He was therefore ready to agree to any scheme which called up the
whole of the age group of those born in 1924 and 1925 even if they were in
protected factories. Such a call-up would give a total of 500,000 men. But
it would be better to keep them in France until they were properly disciplined.

¹ FD 3040/49, Section IV, Sc. 425, Rm.f.R.u.Kp., Leiter des Zentralamtes, 'Vermerk über
eine Besprechung von Arbeitseinsatzfragen beim Führer am 25.4.1944', 26 April 1944.
² Ibid., Rm.f.R.u.Kp., Telegram, Rüstungs- und Beschaffungsstab to Kehrl, 8 May 1944.
³ Ibid., Rm.f.R.u.Kp., Chef der Rüstungs- und Beschaffungsstab to Sauckel, 10 May
1944.
⁴ Ibid., Rm.f.R.u.Kp., Chef des Zentralamtes to Kehrl, 10 May 1944.
⁵ Ibid., Mbh. in F., 'Besprechung mit den deutschen Dienststellen am 8.5.44 in der
deutschen Botschaft, Paris', 9 May 1944; 'Niederschrift der Sitzung in der deutschen Botschaft am 8 Mai 1944, 18.30 Uhr, Einsatz französischer Arbeitskräfte im Reich', 12 May 1944.

He hoped that he might instil into French youth a more statesmanlike European view by indoctrinating them at home. The French people, for historical reasons, could not be expected to give such a shining example of the National Will as their neighbours. There was the possibility that they would be unable to obtain the promised number and thus to bring the French people into 'the European struggle'. Bichelonne did not agree with Déat. To his mind, a young worker in the Renault factory was making a bigger contribution to Europe at the present moment than he would make in Germany. The European war economy was even now only coming to fruition with the concentration and centralization of French industry. Finally, Sauckel agreed that miners and transport workers should be exempt from the new measures, although they would otherwise apply to the protected factories. General Studt of the military administration predicted a vast influx into the resistance movement, a view which Abetz, the ambassador, seemed to share.

The French government did not have to temporize very long. The flow of workers in May was no greater than before. On 6 June Sauckel threatened Laval that if he had not signed the necessary decrees by the following day German soldiers would carry out the recruiting themselves.[1] It was a singularly ill-timed threat. On the same day they were faced with much grimmer duties.

The immediate result of the invasion was to still the argument in a rather indirect way, by diverting all transport to military needs. In principle, recruitment of labour survived; in practice, it was impossible. In fact on the eve of the invasion of France Hitler had attempted to bring Speer and Sauckel to terms with each other. The attempt did not promise very much.

I drew the attention of the Führer to the fact that I will endeavour to clear up all my important differences with Sauckel and will submit to him for final decision differences which cannot be adjusted.

The spectacle of heated and protracted quarrels, which, moreover, on the lower levels, have passed from the sphere of business to personal disputes, is not consonant with the gravity of the hour.

My aim in this matter is to have it clearly understood that the main responsibility for everything in armaments and war production—including labour—rests in fact as well as in theory with me.[2]

So grave was the transport situation that the issue was decided by that alone. Allied air attacks had been concentrated for weeks before the invasion on the destruction of the French system of communications. The French railway system was 90 cer cent useless for German economic purposes and road transport was exceedingly dangerous owing to the resistance movement.[3]

---

[1] E. Homze, op. cit., p. 199.

[2] FD 3353/45, Rm.f.R.u.Kp., 'Führerkonferenz', 3–5 June 1944.

[3] FD 3045/49, Section IX, Sc. 146, Folder No. 1, Europakreis, Monatsbesprechung, 29 August 1944.

It therefore was only possible as far as France was concerned to produce on the spot with the minimum possible movement of raw materials.[1] The only question that remained was whether or not French industry should be evacuated as territory was lost.

The principle that there should be no evacuation of labour from factories temporarily at a standstill because of the transport problem had been accepted by Hitler on 5 June. The maximum possible production as near as possible to the front must be achieved. Following this principle it was decided to try to make better use of the productive capacity of Romania.[2] Dr. Voss, President of the Skoda works, had visited Romania in April and reported to the Planning Office that the economy was on the point of collapse.[3] At the same time it was decided that the utilization of the economy of occupied Italy must be sustained until the last possible moment. Its loss would mean a 15 per cent fall in German armaments production.[4] This simplification of the situation also meant the end of the military administration in Brussels. The economic contribution of Belgium to the war effort had been far less sustained than the French. Coal production there had declined by over 25 per cent between 1940 and 1943,[5] and the constant complaints about the administration there, which emanated from Paris as well as from the Speer Ministry, could be acted upon without hesitation in the new circumstances, especially as General von Falkenhausen was politically very suspect. Speer lent his voice to the movement against von Falkenhausen, who was replaced by Josef Grohé, Gauleiter of Cologne and Aachen, as head of a civil administration. In these circumstances Sauckel's concession to Speer to abide by his decisions in all matters of war production was an extremely hollow one.[4]

The military administration in France did not long survive that in Brussels. Many of its most important members, including Elmar Michel himself, were more or less involved in the attempt on Hitler's life.[6] There was even an echo of the bitter German internal divisions when some of the S.S. administration, which only towards the end of the occupation had secured a foothold in Paris, were briefly imprisoned. General von Stülpnagel was hanged by the People's Court in Berlin after the failure of the plot. General Karl Kitzinger became head of the military administration. His reign was a short one. On 26 August the military administration was formally wound up and the Commander-in-Chief placed under the command of the Commander-in-Chief in the west. At the end of July the occupation costs were increased for the last time, to a level of 35,000,000 Reichsmarks (700,000,000 francs) a day. When the new payments had not been completely met by 12 August Hemmen threatened to seize the Bank of France.

[1] NCA., vi, 766.   [2] FD 3353/45, Rm.f.R.u.Kp., 'Führerkonferenz', 3–5 June 1944.
[3] FD 3045/49, Section IX, Sc. 146, Folder No. 1 Europakreis, 'Die ungenügende Leistung der rumänischen Kriegswirtschaft', 20 May 1944.
[4] FD 3353/45, Rm.f.R.u.Kp., 'Führerkonferenz', 3–5 June 1944.
[5] F. Baudhuin, op. cit., p. 292.   [6] E. Jäckel, op. cit., p. 334.

The dispute between Speer and Sauckel continued over another issue. The dictates of economic strategy were that production should take place on the spot until the territory was overrun by the enemy. The dictates of the revolution were that the territory should be stripped bare and what was of value transported to Germany. On 14 September Hitler officially proclaimed a policy of scorched earth in face of the enemy advance.[1] But, as was so often the case in the National Socialist government, these decrees reflected a previous controversy over precisely this question, in this case, of course, in the occupied territories. After the breakthrough at Avranches on 1 August Hitler ordered the area in front of the advancing troops to be laid waste.[2] Similar orders were given covering a much larger area in the General-Government. Speer wished to substitute for such policies a policy of temporarily crippling works which were likely to be captured rather than putting them entirely out of action, and he succeeded in persuading Hitler to adopt this idea on 18 August.[3] The 'scorched earth' decrees were not therefore introduced until a large part of France had been lost.

Nevertheless, the threat of destruction was always present, especially as the transport situation effectively blocked any large-scale evacuations. On 9 August Speer had guns and ammunition issued to the *Länderbeauftragten*.[4] Because of Speer's insistence that production should take place until the last possible moment the reversion to booty was much less violent than it might otherwise have been. The volume of booty seized in the closing stages was fairly small, although in the case of machinery it was important. In July the transfer of firms from France to Baden and Alsace was still continuing.[5] Once the transport restrictions in the military interest were imposed these movements of firms stopped. First priority for wagon space in any retreat had to be given to military equipment.[6] After that, priority was given to fixed capital which could produce goods of particularly vital importance and where 50 per cent or more of the productive capacity was in the danger zone. Third in order of priority came fixed capital in the same category with over 30 per cent of the productive capacity in the danger zone. Where the shortfall in production as a result of the loss of such fixed capital could be made up by the employment of additional labour in the Reich then these urgent priorities ceased to

---

[1] FD 4734/45, Rm.f.R.u.Kp., 'Verbrannte Erde'.

[2] G. Janssen, op. cit., p. 304.

[3] 'The Führer agrees to the measures suggested by us for paralysing instead of destroying plants or power stations which might temporarily be occupied by the enemy', FD 3353/45, Rm.f.R.u.Kp., 'Führerkonferenz', 18–20 August 1944.

[4] FD 2627/44, Rm.f.R.u.Kp., Der Rüstungsobmann in Frankreich, 'An die Länderbeauftragten für Frankreich', 9 August 1944.

[5] FD 155/45, Rwm., Badischer Finanz- und Wirtschaftsminister, Lists of firms transferred from France to Baden/Alsace.

[6] FD 3037/49, Section 1, Sc. 11, Rm.f.R.u.Kp., Planungsamt, 'Sitzung beim Gb. für die Reichsverwaltung über Abstimmung der Auflockerungsmassnahmen der Obersten Reichsbehörden im Osten und anderen Gebieten aufeinander', 25 August 1944.

apply.[1] Measures of this strictness confined indiscriminate looting to a minimum. Even so some fixed capital was moved. The *Länderbeauftragten* were ordered to prepare lists of machines to be moved to the east of France in August.[2] And, on the orders of the Commander-in-Chief, the ladies in the Hotel Chambord were transported back to Germany, but only up to 30 per cent of the total stock.[2]

The history of the long dispute between Speer and Sauckel indicates that, had it not been for the exigencies of the war economy, Sauckel would have had his way. As it was, Hitler's unquestioning support for the Speer–Bichelonne agreements lasted only for three months. From the beginning of 1944 he was prepared to lend an ever-readier ear to the voice of the Party. Not, it seems, out of genuine ideological conviction, but out of a shrewd and perfectly correct sentiment that the policy of manufacturing consumer goods in France was not working very successfully. Faced with two policies, neither of which were likely to be very successful, there was no harm in throwing in his lot with the Party's ideology, providing that, by so doing, he did not harm too greatly the war economy. In any case the enormous growth of the resistance movement in France, which paralysed the German executive there, revealed the 'European war economy' for the sham it was. Neither Sauckel nor Speer after September 1943 was effectively able to increase to any great extent the level of exploitation of France by Germany.

TABLE 24

Development of Labour Force in French Consumer Goods Industries*

(excluding Nord and Pas-de-Calais)

	1943 1 Oct.	1 Nov.	1 Dec.	1944 1 Jan.
Textiles and clothing	318,000	317,000	317,000	316,000
Leather and shoes	94,000	94,000	94,000	94,000
Chemical industry	220,000	219,000	221,000	220,000
Wood working	47,000	48,000	49,000	49,000
Building materials and ceramics	68,000	68,000	68,000	68,000
Mechanical, electrical, and optical industries	474,000	479,000	488,000	490,000

* FD 3040/49, Section IV, Sc. 425, Mbh. in F., Wi.Abt. As a greater proportion of the raw materials supplied to French consumer goods industries in 1944 was specifically allocated to manufactures for German purposes the proportion of final output for such purposes was almost certainly greater.

Before the return of Night primeval and of Chaos old to French statistics it is possible to see a falling-off in French production for Germany under the

[1] Ibid., Rm.f.B.u.M., 'Erlass über Rückverlagerung aus dem Westen', 3 September 1944,
[2] FD 2627/44, Rm.f.R.u.Kp., 'Länderbeauftragten-Sitzung', 8 August 1944.

terms of the Speer–Bichelonne agreements. The value of deliveries from the factories which had been originally classified as 'Rü-Betriebe', and which were making a more or less direct contribution to the German armaments industry, reached a peak of 175,300,000 Reichsmarks in March 1944.[1] In April it fell to 155,900,000, in May to 140,900,000, and in June it stood at 127,900,000 Reichsmarks. In the period when the agreements held undisputed sway the net intake of labour into French consumer goods industries scarcely increased at all.

Since the level of exploitation of the French economy was so high already, the failure to go further is not surprising. The significance of the dispute is that in any discussion as to how the level of exploitation might be increased the fundamental disagreements on economic policy which existed in the National Socialist Party itself were revealed. The attempt to create a wholly isolated economy in Germany had always been an impossibility. If the revolution were to survive it could survive only on a European scale. But to do that it had to agree on a European policy. The Party was composed of too many divergent elements to do so. The attempt at an agreement on the organization of a genuine 'New Order' was hopeless from the outset. The National Socialist revolution had its origins in the whole period of rapid economic growth in Germany after 1815 and was the product of social tensions generated by that growth. Its applicability to any state with a different historical experience of economic growth was very vague. To attempt to define a 'New Order' acceptable to Europe as a whole was therefore impossible. It could only reveal the fundamental disagreements on economic policy within the National Socialist revolution itself.

[1] FD 3037/49, Section I, Sc. 72, Rm.f.R.u.Kp., Planungsamt, 'Lieferung der ca. 1500 Rüstungsbetriebe nach Deutschland im Wege der echten Verlagerung im Gebiet Frankreich', 31 July 1944.

VII

THE EXPLOITATION OF
THE FRENCH COAL INDUSTRY

SINCE the early nineteenth century the industrialization of France had been based on coal more than on any other fuel, and by 1939, although the quantity of oil consumed was increasing, coal was still the main industrial fuel. In spite of this, since the early nineteenth century French coal production had been insufficient to meet consumption. On the eve of the war France was the most important importer of coal in the world.

Although other economies, whose domestic coal production was lower than that of France, had a higher *per capita* consumption of coal,[1] France was the fifth largest coal consumer in the world, preceded only by economies able to supply their own needs in entirety. Over 30 per cent of average annual domestic coal consumption was imported. Since France was particularly deficient in coking coals over 55 per cent of coke consumption was accounted for by imports. French coal imports were almost 20 per cent of total world imports of coal.

The central feature of the western European coal trade was the fierce competition on the French market. The two principal competitors were Britain and Germany, and if allowance is made for the fact that in 1940 imports from Germany were abnormally low, it would not be unreasonable to say that the competition between these two suppliers on the French market was vital to the export trade of both in every year between the two wars. Other suppliers were much less important. The export of coal from Belgium to the industrial areas of northern France had been a feature of French economic history for well over a century, and usually Belgium was the third largest seller on the French market. But to some extent this trade was part of a series of complementary movements of coal which involved short-hauling across the frontiers of France, Germany, Belgium, Luxembourg, and the Netherlands. These complementary movements were responsible for part of the small French export trade, about 1,000,000 tons a year. The remainder of French exports consisted of movements of smaller quantities over a similar distance into Switzerland and Italy. Poland rarely provided more than 5 per cent of the total French supply in any year.

---

[1] Denmark, for example. International Labour Office, Studies and Reports, Series B, no. 31, *The World Coal-Mining Industry* (Geneva, 1938), i. 69.

From the German point of view the strategic implications of this situation were immense. Exports to France were the largest single part of German coal exports, about 20 per cent. But German exports to Italy and Holland were a much larger fraction of the total coal import of those countries than they were of total French coal import. The Italian war economy could only function on German coal, and although Italy's imports from Britain were relatively small, in time of war the burden of making up the deficiency fell on Germany.

TABLE 25

*Imports of Coal by European Countries from Greater Germany,
Poland, and Britain*

(annual average of 1936–8 in thousand tons)

Importer	From Greater Germany†	From Poland	From Britain	Total	Percentage imports of Greater-German and Polish origin
Denmark	689	299	3,262	4,250	23·2
Norway	230	402	1,453	2,085	30·3
Sweden	605	2,431	2,931	5,967	50·9
Finland	129	262	1,215	1,606	24·4
Italy	7,615	1,414	1,533	10,562	85·5
Netherlands	6,348	300	1,114	7,762	85·7
Belgium	4,291	504	713	5,508	87·1
Switzerland	949	131	291	1,371	78·8
France	6,494	1,468	7,507	15,469	51·5

* FD 4228/45, Institut für Weltwirtschaft, 'Die Kohlenversorgung Europas durch Grossdeutschland unter den gegenwärtigen kriegswirtschaftlichen Gesichtspunkten', October 1939.
† Includes Austria, Sudetenland, and Saarland.

In this respect the annexation of Poland was most important. If Germany could succeed in turning the territorial remainder of Poland into an agricultural state the coal consumption of that country could presumably be reduced. However, the principal part of Polish exports went to Sweden. After the German annexation of Upper Silesia these erstwhile Polish exports to Sweden became for Germany a valuable way of paying for imports from Sweden which were vital to her own war ceonomy. Coal was one of the few raw materials Germany could hope to export in wartime. It was accordingly very difficult to reduce the quantity of coal exported from pre-1939 Polish areas or even to change the direction of those exports.

A study by the Institut für Weltwirtschaft written immediately after the defeat of Poland therefore proposed that deficiencies in coal supply to western

TABLE 26

*Output of Principal French Coalfields**

(tons)

Region	1930	Per-centage of total	1935	Per-centage of total	1936	Per-centage of total	1937	Per-centage of total	1938	Per-centage of total
Pas-de-Calais	25,309,308	47·0	19,145,976	41·4	9,056,320	42·1	18,372,021	41·4	19,123,690	41·1
Nord	9,715,682	18·0	9,876,545	21·5	9,354,277	20·7	8,815,926	19·9	9,114,795	19·6
Lorraine	6,073,798	11·3	5,646,471	12·2	5,455,335	12·1	6,143,698	13·9	6,739,210	14·5
Saint-Étienne	3,672,468	6·8	3,348,410	7·3	3,241,144	7·2	3,130,493	7·1	3,273,638	7·1
Blanzy	3,116,571	5·8	2,751,777	6·0	2,731,466	6·1	2,628,439	5·9	2,716,471	5·8
Alès	2,273,536	4·2	2,327,142	5·0	2,311,235	5·1	2,323,904	5·2	2,439,691	5·2
Total French production†	53,884,035		46,207,342		45,226,646		44,318,183		46,502,047	

* FD 1808/44, Reichsamt für wehrwirtschaftliche Planung, 'Beiträge zur Wehrwirtschaftsstruktur Frankreichs', May 1940.
† The total figures for French production are not the totals of the columns as all mining areas are not separately listed.

Europe which might be caused by any German annexation of those areas could only be remedied by a reduction in the internal consumption of coal in Poland.[1] If coal consumption in western Europe were no higher than at the cyclical peak of 1936–8, British supply could, by this means, be dispensed with, were it not for the dependence of France on British coal. It was, therefore, the French economy that would be the stumbling-block in any rational reorganization of the European coal economy to exclude Britain. Too much should not be made of this kind of planning. It had little or no impact on the direction of the war, and, in any case, grossly underestimated the actual wartime demand for coal in Germany. But, as early as 1939, one of the greatest economic problems of the occupation had loomed in only too distinct a form over the horizon.

The annual output of coal in France after the return of the Saarland to Germany averaged about 46,000,000 tons. Total annual consumption of coal

TABLE 27

French Coal Imports from Germany*

(tons)

1941	282,000
1942	1,470,000
1943	3,064,000

* These are the figures given in CCDR., v, M.P. 3. The 1941 figure includes imports from Moselle. The German figures vary. FD 474/45, Mbh. in F., Wi.Abt. II/a, 'Ausnutzung der französischen Wirtschaft für Deutschland', 3 February 1942 gives a figure for 1941 of 341,000 tons. FD 3041/49, Section VI, Sc. 385, Reichsvereinigung Kohle, 'Die deutschen Kohlenwirtschaft in den Monaten April bis Oktober 1943', gives a figure for 1943 of 2,715,000 tons. Since the figures indicated for 1942 and 1943 in FD 469/45, Mbh. in F., Wi.Abt. II/a, are also lower than the French figures, the French figures may well be overestimates.

was about 70,000,000 tons. In fact over 60 per cent of total French coal output was mined in the two departments of Nord and Pas-de-Calais. Therefore, for the duration of the war the greatest part of what must be considered 'normal' French output took place under the control of the German military command in Belgium. The second most important centre of production, Lorraine, was annexed by Germany and treated as an integral part of the Reich proper. From the start of the occupation, therefore, the administrative boundaries drawn by Germany made any solution of the problem of coal supply only more difficult to achieve.

Vichy France was left in possession of the Saint-Étienne coal basin and the Alès basin. But the other coal-mining basin on the fringes of the Massif Central, that of Blanzy, which included Montceau-les-Mines and Le Creusot, was just inside the occupied zone. Vichy France, consequently, was left with about 19 per cent of total pre-war French coal output.

[1] FD 4228/45 Institut für Weltwirtschaft, 'Die Kohleversorgung . . .', October 1939.

Total coal production in Germany increased during the war, and this increase was not merely due to the expansion of the territorial area. Total available supply increased from 240,300,000 tons in the period from March 1938 to March 1939 to 347,600,000 tons in the same period from 1943 to 1944. Of this increased supply 16,800,000 tons was attributable to increased output in the territorial area of pre-1938 Germany.[1] This result was better than pre-war optimism had foreseen. Unfortunately pre-war forecasts had been even more optimistic in their estimates of the demand for coal. The demand of an

TABLE 28

*French Coal Imports from Belgium**

(tons)

1938	3,552,000
.	. .
1941	1,388,000
1942	1,616,000
1943	1,627,000
1944	2,589,000

* CCDR., v, M.P. 3. There seems a possibility that this report overstates the flow of Belgian coal to France. FD 474/45, Mbh. in F., Wi.Abt. II/a, 'Ausnutzung . . .', gives the 1941 figure as 1,220,000 tons. The incomplete evidence of FD 256/45 and FD 257/45, Mbh. in F., Wi.Abt. II, 'Kohlen-Import nach Frankreich' suggests still lower quantities. The combined total of monthly imports from Belgium in 1941, less the missing totals for January and August, is only 804,757 tons. The total for 1942, less the missing month of December, is 1,001,520 tons. Total imports for the first five months of 1943 appear as only 302,060 tons. These lowest figures are also borne out by N.A., T.501, Roll 150, 474, which gives the total of imports from Belgium in 1941 as 959,715 tons and from Germany as 245,335 tons.

enormous area of Europe was to make itself felt directly on the German coal industry. By August 1942 Paul Pleiger, the Head of the Main Committee for Coal Production, was unable to promise deliveries of all the coal necessary to complete German armaments programmes.

He points out that the demand for coal has risen during recent weeks for Norway, Sweden, and Denmark, for the power industry, for the Krauch plan, and, above all, for gas supplies for the armament industry. The east also requires for the time being considerable additional quantities of coal. The projected output of 750,000 tons of coal per month in the Donetz region after January 1943 will ease the strain later on but during this fourth quarter it can have no effect.[2]

The quantity of coal available for export to France proved much lower than before 1939. At the beginning of the occupation Germany, understandably, made little effort in this regard. From the outset the decision was adhered to that all coal deliveries, including those from Nord and Pas-de-Calais, should be used as bargaining counters at Wiesbaden to obtain political

[1] USSBS., *The Effects of Strategic Bombing on the German War Economy*, p. 94.
[2] FD 3353/45, Rm.f.B.u.M., 'Führerkonferenz', 10–12 August 1942.

TABLE 29

French Coal Production*

(tons)

1940

	Nord and Pas-de-Calais	Rest of France	Total
January	2,907,241		
February	2,754,472		
March	2,967,825		
April	3,128,146		
May	2,067,785		
June	62,710		
July	770,925		
August	1,331,115		
September	1,817,148		
October	2,285,826		
November	2,235,489		
December	2,293,025		
Total	24,621,707	14,663,584	39,285,584

1941

	Nord and Pas-de-Calais	Rest of France	Total
January	2,426,647	1,221,659	3,647,951
February	2,204,122	1,166,779	3,370,901
March	2,396,454	1,250,070	3,646,524
April	2,325,656	1,196,117	3,521,773
May	2,390,113	1,124,465	3,614,578
June	1,778,546	1,148,324	2,926,870
July	2,252,113	1,154,233	3,406,346
August	2,187,766	1,081,434	3,269,200
September	2,253,916	1,178,626	3,552,542
October	2,471,903	1,247,329	3,719,232
November	2,233,282	1,140,988	3,374,270
December	2,563,178	1,246,287	3,809,465
Total	27,583,696	14,155,956	41,739,652

* This table is compiled from the figures of Mbh. in F., Gruppe Bergbau. The figures for output in 1940 are in NA., T.71, Roll 101, 6029104; for December 1943 to March 1944 in FD 278/45, Service national des statistiques, Section de la statistique générale, 'Données statistiques mensuelles relatives à l'économie française, Nos. 24 and 25', 29 June 1944; for January 1941 to August 1943 from FD 469/45, Mbh. in F., Wi.Abt. II/a, 'Kohlenwirtschaft Frankreichs'. By this procedure output appears lower than in CCDR., v, M.P. 3. The total output for 1943 given there is 42,472,000 tons, a decline of 1,300,000 tons as compared to 1942. The monthly averages given in INSEE., *Mouvement économique*, are very close to the figures in this table and are almost certainly derived from the same source. Consequently the final totals given there for 1943 have been used in this table. Blanks indicate that the monthly figures are unknown.

TABLE 29 (*cont.*)

French Coal Production

(tons)

1942

	Nord and Pas-de-Calais	Rest of France	Total
January	2,439,691	1,216,503	3,656,194
February	2,181,572	1,142,075	3,323,647
March	2,356,628	1,208,091	3,564,719
April	2,280,064	1,195,360	3,475,424
May	2,200,798	1,136,553	3,337,351
June	2,334,710	1,144,648	3,479,358
July	2,344,056	1,109,629	3,453,685
August	2,260,351	1,026,137	3,286,488
September	2,327,806	1,069,099	3,396,905
October	2,583,175	1,178,798	3,761,973
November	2,397,603	1,129,232	3,521,835
December	2,441,703	1,166,881	3,608,584
Total	28,143,157	13,723,006	41,866,163

1943

	Nord and Pas-de-Calais	Rest of France	Total
January	2,341,401	1,161,574	3,502,975
February	2,250,338	1,090,928	3,341,266
March	2,456,371	1,194,811	3,651,182
April	2,383,197	1,138,603	3,521,800
May	2,382,892	1,129,441	3,512,333
June	2,353,989	1,081,978	3,435,967
July	2,363,523	1,035,033	3,398,556
August	2,376,850	943,501	3,320,351
September			
October			
November			
December	2,510,512	828,458	3,338,970
Total	27,804,000	12,932,000	40,536,000

[*Table 29 continued on p. 188.*

TABLE 29 (*cont.*)

French Coal Production

(tons)

1944

	Nord and Pas-de-Calais	Rest of France	Total
January	2,444,694	815,176	3,259,870
February	2,383,308	805,514	3,188,822
March	2,571,808	865,846	3,437,654
April			
May			
June			
July			
August			
September			
October			
November			
December			
Total			

concessions.[1] French demands for coal from Germany were for 900,000 tons per month, including supply to the army of occupation.[2] In November 1940 the German delegation agreed to the import of 900,000 tons of coal from Belgium, but this quantity was to be spread over six months.[3] When strategic conceptions changed in 1943 Germany had to make a greater effort, and only in that year were German coal exports to France such as to create the possibility of re-establishing pre-war levels of industrial production.

Given this grave deficiency in supply from Germany, France was left heavily dependent on the quantity and regularity of the supply which the German authorities in Belgium made available. The downward trend in production and in productivity in Belgian coal-mines during the occupation was more marked than in France. Belgian coal output fell from 29,585,000 tons in 1938 to 24,895,000 tons in 1942.[4]

The level of French coal imports from Belgium, according to the French War Damages Commission, did not decline, although it was always much lower than the pre-war level. It may indeed have been lower than hitherto supposed.

Whatever policy the German administration pursued in France, it was faced with a constant and chronic coal shortage. Until 1943 no long-term methods of overcoming this difficulty were considered. After the decisions

[1] DGFP., Series D, x, no. 267.   [2] DFCAA. ii. 190.   [3] Ibid., p. 369.
[4] FD 3040/49, Section IV, Sc. 425, Rm.f.R.u.Kp., 'Niederschrift über Führer-Konferenz', 21 November 1943. See also F. Baudhuin, op. cit., p. 290.

to reinvigorate the French economy the 'comité d'organisation' drew up a long-term plan to increase French coal output to 65,000,000 tons a year by modernization and by the reopening of closed pits.[1] The ultimate intention of the plan was to make France self-sufficient in coal. In 1943 also greater quantities of coal were made available from Germany and Belgium. Although increases of coal output during the war years were obtained, these increases were small, and in 1943 they were not sustained. Although total French output appears much lower that pre-war levels, that is due to the fact that Lorraine coal output was, of course, counted as German.

If the average annual output of the Lorraine coalfield from 1936 to 1938 is deducted from total annual French output of those years and a comparison

TABLE 30

Average annual output of coal in France (except Lorraine) 1936–8	=	39,236,211 tons
Increase over this average in 1941	=	2,503,441 tons
Increase over this average in 1942	=	2,629,952 tons
Increase over this average in 1943	=	1,299,789 tons

made with output during the war years, it can be seen that the increase in output of coal in wartime France was considerable. It can also be seen that domestic French output declined in the year when larger supplies of imported coal were first made available to the French economy. Much the most significant increases in production, however, were achieved outside the main northern coalfield.

TABLE 31

Relationship of Annual Output 1940–3 to Average Annual Output 1936–8

Nord and Pas-de-Calais			All other coalfields (except Lorraine)		
1940	—	3,305,676 tons	1940	+	3,266,165 tons
1941	—	361,980 tons	1941	+	2,865,421 tons
1942	+	197,481 tons	1942	+	2,432,471 tons
1943	—	141,676 tons	1943	+	1,641,465 tons

Higher output in the northern coalfield was the only means of increasing French coal output to a more satisfactory level, and it is clear that the weakness lay there. The High Command in Paris constantly blamed the High

[1] FD 232/45, Deutsche Reichsbank, Volkswirtschaftliche Abteilung, 'Frankreich' 13 October 1943.

Command in Brussels for this weakness and demanded a more unified system of control. But output in the northern French coalfield, although it never rose significantly above pre-war levels, at least did not fall so far below them as output in the Belgian coalfields. Nor was the record of the High Command in Paris very successful. The average output of coal increased by 239,000 tons a month in the area of Vichy France between 1938 and 1942. In the area of the occupied zone it increased by 17,000 tons.[1] The plain fact is that the main part of the increase in wartime coal production in France was achieved in Vichy France and that once Vichy France was occupied production there began to decline.

A comparison with the average apparent consumption of 1934–8 shows that French coal supply, including imports, varied over the war years between 60 and 65 per cent of 'normal' supply.[2] Such a drastic reduction demanded a drastic redistribution of supply. Such a drastic redistribution was almost impossible to achieve, given the pattern of coal consumption within the French economy.

The two most important pre-war French consumers of coal were the steel industry and the railways. Both consumed about 10,000,000 tons a year. Gasworks and coking plants consumed about 4,000,000 tons, power stations about 3,000,000 tons. Of the remaining 35,000,000 tons, 19,000,000 were consumed by other large and medium industrial enterprises, and 16,000,000 by small enterprises and households. Any large reduction in the quota allocated to railways seemed unlikely in wartime for military reasons. In any case, if the French economy was to be economically useful to Germany, then large quantities of coal would still have to be transferred within the economy, and such internal coal movements were almost entirely done by rail. Similarly, if any volume of armament production for Germany was to take place the coal supply to the French steel industry could not be much reduced. The most promising category for reduction seemed to be that of small enterprises and households. The size of this category is interesting evidence of the number of very small family businesses, bakeries, laundries, and so on, which could not function without very large deliveries of coal. Because of the number and nature of such undertakings it was very difficult to separate them from mere households. And if the many inconvenient deliveries which had to be made to them were omitted the normal functioning of the life of the community was as severely disrupted as if reductions were made in the quotas assigned to the larger consumers. The problem of coal distribution within the economy was, in the event, tackled on the basis of expediency; the quotas were readjusted every time a really unmanageable situation presented itself, but never before.

From the outset it was obvious that any pattern of coal distribution within France would have to ignore the new zone boundaries, otherwise the occupied

[1] FD 272/45, Warenstelle für Kohle, 'Erzeugung französischer Gruben'.
[2] See CCDR., v, M.P. 3, for a slightly higher calculation.

zone itself would have been left dependent on a total coal supply of little over 2,500,000 tons a year. It is quite clear that in this respect Germany never had any intention of treating the allocation of coal to the different sectors of the French economy other than as one problem. But the great difficulty, recurring throughout the occupation, was to secure a sufficient movement of coal from the northern coalfield southwards, a difficulty emphasized by the shortage of supply from Belgium.

In principle all the coal mined in Nord and Pas-de-Calais, less what was actually consumed in those departments or allocated to the Wehrmacht, was to be the sole source of supply for the occupied zone.[1] Imports from Belgium were confined to the area of the Ardennes.[2] These principles were infringed from the beginning of the occupation. The iron and steel industry of Lorraine received supply from the north as soon as transport was possible. In addition there were great difficulties in supplying those areas of western France which had formerly been supplied by sea from Britain, partly because of the transport problem but mainly because of the difficulty in restoring production to normal levels on the northern coalfield after June 1940.

The almost complete stoppage of production in June 1940 was not due so much to destruction of capital equipment as to the flight of the labour force out of the path of the occupying army. There was less absolute destruction than in the First World War. Nevertheless, the breakdown of means of communication, the damage to power and water supplies, and the extreme shortage of labour inevitably meant a long period of lower production.

In the occupied territory of northern France part of the industrial work force has fled.

The overland wires have mostly been interrupted by destruction, most of the power stations are not superintended. The water supply suffers from insufficient force.

The coal mines and the coking and processing plants connected with them, lie idle, instances of sabotage are not yet reported.[3]

The mining inspector of the High Command in Paris who made a visit of inspection on 23 June was optimistic. He envisaged a quick return to 60 per cent of normal production. The management and clerical staffs of the mines were largely intact, it was the miners who had fled. 'In spite of that,' he reported, 'I came away with the general impression that most of the companies are ready and capable of getting production going.'[4]

[1] BA., R 7 VIII 207, 'Auszugsweise Abschrift aus einem Wirtschaftsbericht über die Lage im Bereich des Chefs der Militärverwaltung in Frankreich', September 1940.

[2] FD 272/45, Warenstelle für Kohle, 'Erzeugung französischer Gruben'.

[3] BA., R7 VIII 207, Reichswirtschaftsministerium, 'Zustand der besetzten Gebiete Niederlande, Belgien, Luxemburg, und Nordfrankreich', 1 June 1940.

[4] NA., T.501, Roll 150, 584 'Aktenbericht über eine Befahrung des nordfranzösischen Bergbaugebietes'.

Nevertheless, it was clear that some provisional arrangements would have to be made for the supply of Paris. Since mining operations had been much less disturbed in Burgundy, projects were mooted to supply Paris from the Blanzy mines, an interesting reversion to the state of affairs in the early nineteenth century. Production had stopped there on 16 June with the arrival of German troops, but by 6 July was already up to half its pre-invasion level.[1]

It was only in August that output in the northern coalfield reached half the pre-invasion level. There should by that time have been twenty coal trains a day, each of 1,000 tons capacity, into the occupied zone. The trains seldom reached this capacity and the general level of movement outward from the coalfield was about 16,000 tons a day.[2] From the Blanzy basin 6,500 tons came daily and 2,500 tons came from Vichy France in exchange for pit-props. The economy of the occupied zone was therefore running on a total input of 25,000 tons of coal a day, about one-third of its pre-invasion consumption. In spite of this in August the *Reichskohlenkommissar* tried to enforce a decision whereby coal from the northern French coalfield would also have to be used in supplying Alsace and Lorraine. The ostensible grounds were a temporary decline in output in the Ruhr coalfield, but the decision was taken in the first stage of the occupation when ideas on economic exploitation had not yet felt the icy finger of reality. After negotiations in the Reichs Economics Ministry between the High Commands in Paris and Brussels and the heads of civil administration in the Netherlands, Alsace, and Lorraine, the decision was rescinded.[3]

It was forecast that by September thirty-six coal trains a day of the same capacity would be crossing into the occupied zone. In spite of the increased September production coal supply in the occupied zone climbed no higher than 37 per cent of its previous level. As production climbed the magnitude of the transport problem also became apparent. In September there was a clash of priority over coal transport and the transport necessary to move the northern French grain harvest to Paris and, in part, to Germany.[4] From this point onwards all plans for coal allocation had to cope with the basic transport problem, a problem which bombing only exacerbated.

[1] NA., T.501, Roll 150, 618, Ministère des travaux publics, 'Rapport de l'inspecteur général des mines', 6 July 1940, and ibid., 626, 'Rapport sur la visite aux mines de Blanzy 13 July 1940.

[2] BA., R 7 VIII 207. Mbh. in F., Wi.Abt., 'Wirtschaftsbericht August 1940', 4 September 1940, and NA., T.501, Roll 150, 642, Mbh. in F., Wi.Abt., 'Bericht betreffend Bergbau und Kohlenwirtschaft', 26 August 1940. DFCAA., I, Annexe au compte rendu no. 18, p. 184; 'At the present moment there are 2 million tons of coal in northern France, needed neither by Belgium nor Germany, which could be used by France if they could be transported' (Hemmen), 27 August 1940.

[3] NA., T.501, Roll 150, 655, Mbh. in F., Wi.Abt., II., 'Bericht über die Lage der Kohlenwirtschaft,' 3 September 1940.

[4] DFCAA., I, Sous-commission 'transports', 16 September 1940.

The early plans for allocation of coal foresaw a sharp reduction in the supply to households and small businesses. Even with such reductions the numbers of deliveries of this type emphasized to what extent economic life in France had continued for so long on the basis that coal would always be available. It proved much harder to cut back in this sector than the administration had originally hoped, mainly because of the difficulty of distinguishing between households and small businesses. In June 1941 the *Reichskohlenkommissar* complained that the allocation to this sector of 165,000 tons a month meant that French household consumption was almost as high as German, and tried to force a further reduction in the quota on the two High Commands. 'It will be said by the High Command in Belgium and northern France that a reduction in the household quota is not feasible because production will go down since apart from their bad diet the miners will also have to freeze.'[1]

The over-all coal shortage had become severe enough in May to menace the fulfilment of armaments and textile contracts for Germany.[2] Already the fixed quotas were being tampered with so that German priorities would not suffer. Only half the foreseen imports from Belgium arrived in May, in June nothing arrived. On 28 May the coal strike in Nord and Pas-de-Calais broke out, with the consequence that the June output in that coalfield was well below two million tons. In November 1941 ideas of increasing the quota to industry were thwarted by a sharp decline in the import of electric current from Vichy France, most of which was supplied by hydroelectric works. The deficiency had to be remedied by increasing the coal quota to power stations in the occupied zone.[3] Stocks of coal in these power stations had got so low that from 21 December 1941 to 4 January 1942 almost the whole of French industrial production was stopped to spare coal for the production of electric current. Even railway coal was cut back. Older power stations which, unlike more modern ones, consumed high-grade coal, were brought back into service. This redistribution in favour of power stations was to prove a permanent feature of the system, although at the time it was only thought of as a last-minute expedient. By the end of 1942 the total quantity of coal allotted to power stations was actually greater than before the war, and it was to continue to climb, to the detriment of general industrial supply, until the end of the occupation.

In May 1942 coal allocation to gasworks had also to be increased because of the increased demand for gas from firms previously using *mazoute*.[4] By

[1] FD 257/45, Mbh. in F., Wi.Abt. II/a, 'Kohlenversorgung', 24 June 1941.

[2] FD 667/46, Rü-Inspektion 'A' (Paris und Nordwestfrankreich), 'Lagebericht', 24 June 1941.

[3] FD 257/45, Mbh. in F., Wi.Abt. II/a, 'Lagebericht', 21 January 1942; 'Lagebericht', 19 November 1941; and 'Besprechung über die Versorgung der Elektrizitätswerke', 10 December 1941.

[4] Ibid., 'Lagebericht', 22 May 1942.

O

June 1942 gasworks and railways were receiving about 80 per cent of their pre-war supply and power stations over 100 per cent. Industry and house-holds had become clearly established together as the greatest sufferers. In-dustry was receiving 35 per cent of its peace-time supply and small industry and households a mere 25 per cent of that level.[1]

This general pattern of allocation was also applied to Vichy France after the occupation of that area. Coal supply was based on the principle that 68 per cent of the supply should go to the former occupied zone and 32 per cent to the area of former Vichy France.[2] With the change of German economic policy towards France in 1943 this system of allocation appeared less and less satisfactory. Some methods of securing a greater coal supply to French industry had to be devised. The Renault factories at Billancourt, which should have been busy with German war contracts, were in fact reduced to short-time working in April because of lack of coal.[3] The successive adjustments which had been made to the original allocation schemes meant that the general level of coal supply to French industry in the first five months of 1943 was less than three-quarters of its 1941 level, when armaments contracts had been less plentiful.[3] The 1941 level had itself been barely sufficient for any rational exploitation of French industry.

Consumption of coal by the railways had been reduced only slightly by 1943. The result of this was that whereas railways had been responsible for about 14 per cent of total consumption in 1938, they were now responsible for 24·5 per cent. One possibility was, therefore, to reduce railway consump-tion by 5 per cent in favour of general industry. A second possibility was to force the Wehrmacht to disgorge part of the supply which they claimed before allocations within the economy were made. On previous occasions the Wehrmacht had several times surrendered part of its coal stocks in return for other goods which it required. The general overheating of Wehrmacht premises in the previous winter had been well known. The monthly average deductions from the output of the northern coalfield for the Wehrmacht and the Organization Todt, which also had to cover supply to the Channel Islands, was around one-tenth of the monthly average supply from that coal-field to the occupied zone.[4] A third possibility was to further reduce the allocation to households and small industry. This would mean an administra-tive reform of some importance, as in the area of former Vichy France allocation at this level was still done through French regional offices. If the

[1] FD 469/45, Mbh. in F., Wi.Abt. II/a, 'Kohlenversorgung Frankreichs', 25 June 1942.

[2] Ibid., 'Notiz für Herrn Oberstleutnant von Hofacker zur Kohlenversorgungslage in den Westgebieten', 16 October 1942.

[3] FD 256/45, Mbh. in F., Wi.Abt. II/a, 'Stabilisierung und Erhöhung des Industriekohlen-kontingentes in den zum Zuständigkeitsbereich des Militärbefehlshabers in Frankreich gehörenden Gebieten', 24 April 1943.

[4] FD 256/45, Office de répartition du charbon, 'Production et répartition des tonnages des mines du Nord et du Pas-de-Calais'.

consumption of those industries whose average consumption in 1938 had been less than twenty tons a month could be more closely supervised by the High Command, more coal might be made available for those industries which had greater importance for war production. Consumers of this kind, however, were only responsible for 11·5 per cent of total consumption in May 1943, whereas in 1938 they had been responsible for 27 per cent of the total.[1] Restrictions on household consumption and on consumption of electric power were more severe in France than in Belgium or Holland. Consequently there was also a possibility of reducing consumption elsewhere in western Europe and exporting the surplus coal to France.

TABLE 32

Distribution of Coal Consumption between the Largest Consumers*
(monthly averages, thousand tons) (excluding Nord and Pas-de-Calais)

	1938	1942	1943
Gasworks	329	287	288
Power stations	216	274	272
General industry	1,051	658	664
Household and small industry	1,128	519	475
Steelworks in eastern France	297	120	193
Other metallurgical industries	105	41	36
Railways	813	616	689
Engineering	142	62	56
Cement	77	21	38

* FD 272/45, Warenstelle für Kohle, 'Aufgliederung des Verbrauchs'.

All plans of this kind failed to increase substantially the average quantity of coal available for French industry throughout 1943, although they arrested the declining trend and ensured that supply increased somewhat in the months after April. But the redistribution was quite insufficient to increase French industrial output to the desired levels.

Figures of this kind disguise the extent to which, after the occupation of southern France, it proved impossible to reduce coal consumption there as drastically as it had previously been reduced in the occupied zone. Of course the general level of supply there was lower, yet it is clear that industries which were not vital to the war were protected there more successfully than in the north.

Whatever the faults in the system of allocation the only thing that could really have made a fundamental change of policy possible was an increase in domestic coal output. When output decreased at the end of 1943 a more serious crisis was reached. In spite of the increased volume of imports industry was effectively able to obtain only 50 per cent of its November

[1] CCDR., v, M.P. 3.

quota by December 1943. Instead of an increase in coal inputs into armament factories it became necessary, because of the transport situation, to organize an extended lay-off of labour over Christmas and the New Year.[1] In fact greater output would merely have resulted in greater stockpiles. In January 1944 all quotas to railways, gasworks, and power stations which remained unfulfilled at the end of the month were annulled, but this step did not extend to industrial supply where efforts continued to catch up with the backlog of supply from November 1943. The efforts were unavailing.

TABLE 33

*Distribution of Coal Consumption between Large Consumers**

(monthly averages, thousand tons)

	Gasworks	Power stations	Eastern French steelworks	House-hold and small industry	General Industry
1. *Area of occupied zone*					
1938	247	201	297	776	703
1942	219	257	120	335	366
1943	219	262	193	308	379
2. *Area of Vichy France*					
1938	82	15	..	352	348
1942	68	17	..	184	292
1943	69	10	..	167	285

* FD 256/45, Office de répartition du charbon, 'Production et répartition etc.', FD 272/45, Warenstelle für Kohle, 'Aufgliederung des Verbrauchs', and FD 469/45, Mbh. in F., Wi.Abt. II/a, 'Verbrauch'.

Stockpiles increased again in northern France in January 1944.[2] From that month onward the coal crisis deepened. Transport became more difficult to find and productivity declined even further. At the end of March the Planning Office determined that the dispersal of contracts to France must have as its first priority the availability of sufficient coal.[3] Each occupied area had to prepare a series of production plans of which the first had to be based on the minimum possible availability of coal. That might be said to represent the final failure of the Speer–Bichelonne agreements.

It must be emphasized that the shortage of coal in wartime France was in part a function of the failure of the German administration in Belgium. Not only did the production of coal in Belgium proper fall during the war,

[1] FD 469/45, Mbh. in F., Wi.Abt. II/a, 'Industriekohlenversorgung im Monat Dezember 1943'.

[2] FD 257/45, Mbh. in F., Wi.Abt. II/a, 'Kohlenförder — Verteilungs- und Versandprogramm für die nordfranzösischen Gruben', January 1944.

[3] FD 3042/49, Section VI, Sc. 385, Rm.f.R.u.Kp., Planungsamt, 'Auftragsverlagerung in Verbindung mit Kohlenversorgung', 31 March 1944.

thus closing one way out of the French dilemma, but deliveries of what was available were unsatisfactory. In November 1940 an agreement was concluded at Wiesbaden under the terms of which a quantity of Belgian coal up to a maximum of 150,000 tons a month would be imported into the occupied zone.[1] The intention of this agreement had been to respond to what the Germans pretended had been a French demand for 900,000 tons over six months from Germany, but which had in fact been for 900,000 tons a month.[2] In any case the average monthly quantity imported under this agreement was only 5,200 tons between November 1940 and April 1941.[3] This quantity was offset by the deliveries which France was obliged to make to the Lorraine steelworks under the control of Hermann Röchling.[4] Even when the quantity imported from Belgium began to approach the level foreseen in the original agreement it was still far too low. A further agreement was made, to operate from 1 March 1942, by which a supplementary 60,000 tons of coal would be delivered from Belgium in return for foodstuffs, expressly 600 tons of wheat, 340 tons of meat, and 200 tons of fats.[5] In May the available quantity of coal for allocation was 80,000 tons less than in April principally because Belgian deliveries fell far short of the figures in the March agreement.[6] Supplies from Belgium eventually ceased altogether in March 1944.[7]

The attempts to increase supply from Belgium were not the only unsuccessful palliative to be tried; there were also urgent attempts at digging more peat in France. Merely from the standpoint of production these efforts were quite successful. Although investment in peat bogs in the Paris region at Essonne, Juine, and Pont-Sainte-Maxence proved abortive, elsewhere there was much more success.[8] The total output of peat, which had been 23,880 tons in 1940, rose to 60,490 tons in 1941 and 194,000 tons in 1942, by which time a labour force of 5,000 was employed.[9] Unfortunately for these efforts the peat had usually too high a water content to be used in gas-generators, and since that had been the principal intended use the investment was misplaced.

The question must now be asked why the German administration was unsuccessful in increasing the supply of coal in France. There were many minor contributing reasons. The system of administration which left the greatest coal-producing area under the control of Brussels was very unsatisfactory;

[1] FD 257/45, Telegram Röver to Mbh. in F., Wi.Abt. II/a, 'Absatzregelung für die Einfuhr belgischer Kohlen nach Frankreich', 15 November 1940.

[2] DFCAA., ii. 377.

[3] FD 257/45, Mbh. in F., Wi.Abt. II/a, 'Import belgischer Kohlen nach Frankreich', 23 October 1941.

[4] DFCAA., iv. 43.

[5] FD 257/45, Mbh. in F., Wi.Abt. II/a, 7 February 1942, and ibid., 'Lagebericht', 25 March 1942.

[6] Ibid., 22 May 1942.

[7] Ibid., 'Besprechung in Paris', 27 March 1944.

[8] FD 243/45, Mbh. in F., Wi.Abt. I, 'Production de la tourbe dans la région de Paris'.

[9] FD 309/45, File 4, Comité d'organisation de l'industrie des combustibles minéraux solides, 'Renseignements relatifs à la tourbe', 20 July 1943.

the German mining administration in Belgium had a miserable record. The disruption of the most important part of the world's coal trade placed a great burden on the firms responsible for handling war-time traffic. The shortage of pit-props was felt throughout the war. The acute transport problem led to rapid production increases accumulating in stockpiles at the pit-head and so discouraging further effort. But the most important reason was the decline in productivity. The level of output was in fact maintained only by constant increases in the labour force.

The High Command in Paris made several attempts to take over responsibility for coal production in Nord and Pas-de-Calais and on several occasions acrimonious correspondence passed between the two military commands on this subject. Since the supply of coal to the Wehrmacht over the whole area was unified it seemed particularly illogical to maintain the two spheres of administration so strictly when it was a question of supply to the economy in general. At the same time there was a lot of difficulty in getting the Belgian coal syndicate and the French import firms to collaborate.[1] Collaboration was even more difficult between the French import firms and the German coal combines. The 'comité d'organisation' for coal imports decreed that coal could only be imported into France by those firms engaged in the trade before 1 April 1939. German firms engaged in the coal trade maintained that this was a case of discrimination against them, since before the war so many French firms had discriminated in favour of the British that there were insufficient contacts between French and German traders.[2] The reason for the discrimination was that about fifty of the firms dealing in coal imports had over 50 per cent British capital. A large proportion of the imports into France from former Polish territory had been handled by such firms.

The shortage of pit-props began to make itself felt as soon as production began to return to pre-war levels.[3] Pre-war sources of supply of pit-props, particularly from Finland, were now completely interrupted. The industry was thrown back entirely on domestic supply, mainly the forests of the Landes and of eastern France. Small deliveries of coal were made to Vichy France in return for deliveries of pit-props, but by spring 1942 the shortage in northern France was endemic.[4] The large amount of construction work in France undertaken by the Wehrmacht and the Organization Todt led to great price competition for wood, and there was a shortage of forestry workers. The effects of the shortage of pit-props were to exaggerate the crisis brought on by transport difficulties, and those caused by falling productivity also. The

[1] FD 257/45, Mbh. in F., Wi.Abt. II/a, 23 October 1941, 'Import belgischer Kohlen . . .'.
[2] FD 257/45, Stinnes to Röver, 'Vorschläge des deutschen Kohlenexporthandels zur Reorganisation des Importes von fremden Brennstoffen nach Frankreich', 17 June 1941.
[3] BA., R 7 VIII 207, 'Tätigkeitsbericht der Militärbefehlshaber in Belgien und Nordfrankreich no., 13', 25 February 1941.
[4] FD 257/45, Mbh. in F., Wi.Abt. II/a, 25 March 1942, 'Lagebericht'; FD 469/45, Mbh. in F., Wi.Abt. II/a, 'Schwierigkeiten im Grubenholz — Abtransport'.

lack of a sufficient stockpile of timber led to over-exploitation of already
worked seams. It also meant that once any particular transport bottleneck
had been removed the rhythm of work in the mine could only be slowly
restored to normal as it was necessary, once the pit-props arrived, to undertake the essential preparatory work before production at the coal face could
begin. What had become established as the 'normal' pattern of work and
exploitation in the mine was consequently impossible, not merely for short
periods but throughout the occupation.

The transport problem was general in the French economy, but bore much
more heavily on the coal industry because of the extent to which coal was
moved by rail. Substitution of lorry transport was impossible, since oil was
in even shorter supply than coal. Even at the relatively low level of output
of September 1940 thirty-six trains a day would have been necessary to maintain coal supply from the northern coalfield to the occupied zone. There were
not the wagons available and stockpiles were already accumulating at the
pit-head. Part of the rolling stock had been outside French frontiers at the
start of the invasion, part had been withdrawn south of the demarcation line
during the course of the fighting, part simply disappeared over the frontier
in the months after the armistice.

The German demand for 1,000 locomotives and 35,000 wagons in August
1940 was a demand that this stock should be used in the occupied zone while
still remaining the property of French railways.[1] By September a further
demand had been submitted for 2,000 locomotives and 50,000 wagons. By
that time 800 to 900 locomotives and 21,000 wagons had been delivered.[2]
In November the French network had 273,000 wagons at its disposal; of this
number 60,000 were needed to cater to German needs, including military
transport.[3] French complaints at the Armistice Commission meetings that
German policy towards French railways was partly responsible for the coal
shortage were in fact borne out by the officials of the German administration.[4]
By December 1940 the stock of wagons had declined to 252,000, as against
400,000 on the eve of the war.[5] By February 1941 a further 10,000 were out
of action.[6] By June 1941 four or even five weeks' delay in dispatching industrial
orders was being experienced.[7]

The difficulties were not only a function of the shortage of wagons but also
of the complicated system of priorities. Military transports always had top
priority but in the first autumn of the occupation equal priority had to be
given to grain transports. There was always doubt as to the exact priority to
be accorded to coal movements within France. Speer complained about the
military control of French railways to Hitler in May 1942.

---

[1] DFCAA., i. 129, 137.　　　　[2] Ibid., p. 297　　　　[3] Ibid., ii. 484.
[4] Ibid., p. 168; NA., T.501, Roll 150, 702, Mbh. in F., Wi.Abt. II/a 'Wirtschaftsbericht
über die Lage in Bereich des Chefs der Militärverwaltung in Frankreich', 2 October 1940.
[5] DFCAA., iii. 385.　　　　[6] Ibid., iv. 143.　　　　[7] Ibid., p. 496.

In this connection attention is drawn to the large number of 8,000 wagons held in permanent readiness by the military authorities for special purposes in France and Belgium. The Führer gives detailed reasons for these military needs but considers the figure of 8,000 much too high. The Reichsbahn is to go into the matter once again with the military authorities.[1]

Nevertheless, in March 1943 there was a ban on all movements except of troops.[2]

To these complications must be added the gradual but constant depreciation of the capital stock which was ill equipped to face the bombing onslaught when it was deliberately aimed at means of communication in northern France. The stocks of undistributed coal in March 1944 were 475,000 tons. To meet this situation a special emergency programme had to be put in operation, but in its first week it carried only 29,000 tons a day out of the daily quota of 53,000 tons. The opinion of the High Command was that 'the wagon situation remains so bad, that a regular shipment of production can no longer be guaranteed'.[3]

It is harder to arrive at a fair judgement on the decline of productivity in the mines. One thing, however, is clear. The inter-war period witnessed a trend to much higher productivity in coal-mining, and this trend was reversed by the occupation.

Labour productivity in coal-mining rose between 1913 and 1936 by 117 per cent in the Netherlands, by 81 per cent in the Ruhr coalfield, by 50–51 per cent in Belgium, by 22 to 25 per cent in France, and by 10 per cent in Britain.[4] These estimates are almost certainly underestimates, since they are based on output per man-shift and a tendency towards a shortening of the working day can be seen in most of these areas over this period. A series of decrees in 1936 and 1937 applied a forty-hour week to the French mining industry,[5] and in Belgium a forty-five-hour week maximum was introduced in 1937.[6] In all these areas much the greater part of the increase in productivity was achieved after 1929. Between 1929 and 1936 labour productivity rose by 38–43 per cent in the Netherlands and Belgium, by 35 per cent in Germany, by 24 per cent in France, and by 8–9 per cent in Britain.[7]

It is clear that the biggest factor in this increase of productivity was the introduction of mechanization into the mining process, in particular the mechanical coal-cutter and the pneumatic pick. The second most important factor was the rationalization of the mine layout and of the sequence of activities. But this rationalization of the work was often contingent on the

[1] FD 3353/45, Rm.f.B.u.M., 'Führerkonferenz', 30 May 1942.
[2] FD 256/45, Mbh. in F., Wi.Abt. II/a, 'Der Beauftragte für den westfranzösischen Eisenbergbau to Röver', 18 May 1943.
[3] FD 257/45, Mbh. in F., Wi.Abt. II/a, 29 March 1944, 'Lagebericht'.
[4] International Labour Office, op. cit., i. 108.
[5] Ibid., ii. 220.   [6] F. Baudhuin, op. cit., p. 34.
[7] International Labour Office, *The World Coal-Mining Industry*, i. 109.

initial introduction of mechanized mining methods. In 1913 8·5 per cent of Britain's coal output was won by coal-cutting machines. In 1929 this had risen to 28 per cent, in 1936 it was 55 per cent.[1] Owing largely to slowness in introducing mechanical methods into the south Wales coalfield the percentage of coal won by mechanical methods was much lower than in other

FIG. 3. Output per man day worked in French coal-mines, 1938–46 (annual averages).

European countries, and hence over-all productivity was lower. The question must be considered whether this particular factor of the mechanization of hewing could have continued to affect the productivity in French mines after 1939. If it could not, the opportunities for installing mechanical loading and conveying would also diminish. In that case the basic geological fact, which applied with particular force to northern France and Belgium, that as mines get older and deeper they become less productive, would reassert itself.

In the Pas-de-Calais section of the northern coalfield 88 per cent of coal output was won by mechanical means in 1935; in Belgium the proportion was almost 100 per cent.[1] Although the consequence of this mechanization had been to bring down the relative cost of coal to the consumer, differences in costs of coal-mining due to geological differences in the mining

[1] Ibid., i. 106.

regions were not eliminated. The cost per ton of coal mined in France in 1935 varied from 84 to 93 francs in the Saint-Étienne basin, to 74·10 francs in the northern coalfield and 67·65 francs in Lorraine.[1] The element of wage costs per ton was 43·60 francs in Saint-Étienne and 26·88 francs in Lorraine. Germany, therefore, annexed the most geologically favoured of the French coalfields, and some allowance must be made for the effect of this on the subsequent average productivity level in French coal-mining.

A similar disparity existed in Belgium. Productivity was much higher in the newer coalfield of the Campine than in the older basins in the south of the country. Wage costs as a proportion of total costs seem to have been generally over 60 per cent and sometimes over 70 per cent in 1938 in coal-mines in the south, whereas they were often little over 50 per cent in the Campine.[2] As the impact of mechanization in all coal-mines began to taper off the rational economic policy was to transfer labour from the south to the Campine. Such a policy was in fact pursued by the military administration as an attempt to halt the decline in productivity. The personnel employed in the Campine showed a 40 per cent increase in 1943 over its 1939 level.[3] But in the circumstances of occupation this policy had little impact. Output per man there seems to have fallen to the level of the older Belgian coal-mines. Almost a half of the increase in labour was Russian prisoners of war. At the same time, in the Campine, as elsewhere in Belgium, mine-owners seem to have thwarted German policy by, wherever possible, working the less profitable seams. The thickness of the seam worked has a very important bearing on the output per man at the coal face. Although the shift of emphasis from the south to the Campine produced no results during the occupation, this should be taken as an illustration of the extreme difficulty of pursuing rational economic policies in occupied economies, rather than as a critique of the policy itself. In this light it may not be wholly unreasonable to suppose that the annexation by Germany of the Lorraine coalfield had a smaller impact on lowering the average level of productivity in French coal-mines than might be deduced simply by looking at the composite levels of productivity in conditions of peace.

Whether or not the rate of increase in productivity in coal-mines was declining in the immediate pre-war period owing to the reassertion of these geological factors, as mechanization of hewing became almost complete, is difficult to determine. The observed slowing after 1936 could equally well be attributed to the important reduction in the length of the working day made at that time. Figure 4 shows that output per employee rose only in Czechoslovakia after 1936, although in Britain, where, as in Czechoslovakia, mechanization had previously proceeded at a much slower pace, it did not

---

[1] 'Enquête sur les conditions économiques et financières d'exploitation des mines de combustible françaises', *Annales des Mines* (1937), p. 70.

[2] Centre Belge d'études et de documentation, Commission Charbonnière, *Rapport Général* (1944), p. 26.

[3] F. Baudhuin, op. cit., p. 301.

fall so rapidly as elsewhere. It was certainly the opinion of the Belgian mine-owners that this slowing down was due to the inability to mechanize any further.[1] But given the labour legislation of 1936 in both Belgium and France it cannot really be said that this opinion is entirely proven.

Although productivity in both French and Belgian coal-mines declined during the war, it also declined in Britain. Indeed, the main cause of the deficiency in British coal output during the war was not the reduction in the labour force but the lower productivity of the labour that remained.[2] Only the roughest comparison between the productivity trends in Britain and

TABLE 34

*Employment and Productivity of Labour in French Coal-Mines**

	Total workers	Above ground workers	Underground workers	Average output per underground worker (tons per month)
1. Yearly averages 1938				
Nord and Pas-de-Calais	154,381	50,524	103,857	22·6
Rest of France (including Lorraine)	95,059	35,742	59,327	25·6
All France	249,440	86,256	163,184	24·0
2. Yearly averages July 1941				
Nord and Pas-de-Calais	151,657	48,864	102,793	21·9
Rest of France (excluding Lorraine)	77,714	27,974	49,737	23·2
All France	229,371	76,838	152,530	22·3

* The employment figures are from FD 257/45, Mbh. in F., Wi.Abt. II/a, 'An den Vorsitzenden des Westkohlenausschusses', 28 August 1941.

France is possible without better information on the changes in size and the distribution within the mine of the French labour force.

Between the first quarter of 1939 and the last quarter of 1943 the quarterly output per wage earner in British mines declined by 8·9 tons.[3] Output per employee in French mines fell from 16·6 tons per month in December 1941 to 15·4 tons per month in December 1942 to 14·6 tons per month in April 1943, and in May 1943 stood at 14·4 tons per month,[4] representing a quarterly fall in output over that period of 6·6 tons per employee.

Any measure of output per man is an inefficient test of coal-mining productivity. What is really needed is a measure of output per coal-face worker. The nearest approach the surviving French statistics allow to this in the present state, are indications of output per underground worker.

[1] Fédération des Associations Charbonnières de Belgique, *La Belgique devant le problème charbonnier* (Brussels, 1945), p. 88.
[2] W. H. B. Court, *Coal* (London, H.M.S.O., 1951) has a most scholarly discussion of this question. [3] Ibid., p. 110.
[4] On the basis of the employment figures in FD 283/45 (b), Mbh. in F., Wi.Abt. II/a 'Beschäftigungszahl im französischen Bergbau', 7 August 1943.

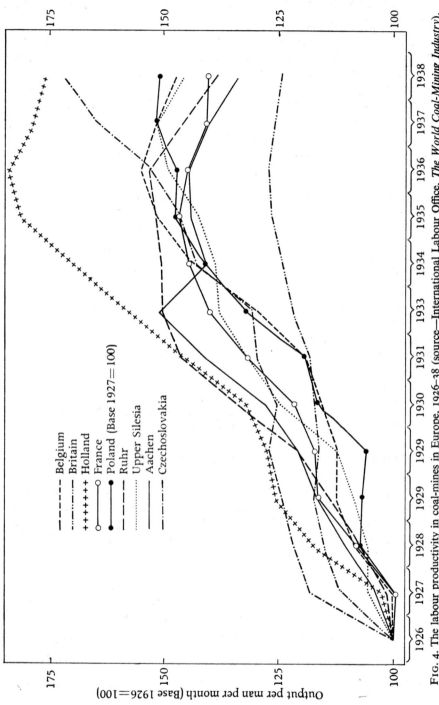

Output per man per month (Base 1926 = 100)

- - - - - Belgium
- · - · - Britain
+ + + + + Holland
○———○ France
●———● Poland (Base 1927 = 100)
- - - - Ruhr
· · · · · · · Upper Silesia
——— Aachen
- · · - · · - Czechoslovakia

Fig. 4. The labour productivity in coal-mines in Europe, 1926-38 (source—International Labour Office, *The World Coal-Mining Industry*).

The fall in productivity had reached more serious proportions by December 1943. By this time 173,000 men were employed underground[1] for an average output per underground worker of 19·3 tons per month. There was a general decline in output per head of about 10 per cent between October 1942 and December 1943.[2]

Since the working week in French coal-mines was increased at the onset of the war and later further increased by the German administration, so that the working day was eventually eight and three-quarter hours long, either the proportion of shifts worked at the coal face declined or output per worker at the coal face declined. Information on the first of these possibilities is lacking, but this lack is perhaps not serious in view of the severe decline evident in output at the face. No calculation is possible about output per manshift at the coal face, but the average daily output at the coal face fell from 1154 kilogrammes in 1938 to 1052 kilogrammes in 1942 to 995 kilogrammes in 1943 and to 700 kilogrammes in 1944. At the end of 1946 it had not recovered to its 1943 level.[3] There was therefore a 39 per cent decline in average daily output at the coal face between 1938 and 1944. In the northern coalfield the total of men employed underground rose by 13,000 between January 1941 and February 1944; the daily output at the face fell from 1073 kilogrammes to 892 kilogrammes.

Production in French coal-mines seems only to have been maintained at the level satisfactory to the occupying authorities by increasing the days and hours worked and by increasing the labour force. It may be that the violent changes in the size and structure of the labour force over the period 1939–45 were responsible for changes in the balance of shifts. There was, however, no significant change, at least in the northern coalfield, in the ratio of men employed at the coal face to men employed elsewhere. Even had there been such a change, there would still be strong grounds for supposing that the output per manshift worked at the coal face also declined.

The problem of low productivity appears to have emerged almost as soon as the mines had returned to relatively full-capacity working and was a cause of serious concern as early as January 1941 in the northern coalfield.[4] By this time coal output in the northern French coalfield was 90 per cent of its 1939 level and in the Belgian coalfield about 100 per cent. January was, however, the first month after the effective establishment of the occupation when coal production did not increase. The statistical information collected by the military administration indicates a fall in output per day worked over the first six weeks of 1941.[5]

[1] CCDR., v, M.P. 3.
[2] FD 3045/49, Section ix, Sc. 292, Reichsministerium für Rüstungs- und Kriegsproduktion, 'Bericht no. 2', 17 May 1944.
[3] CCDR., v, M.P. 3.
[4] BA., R 7 VIII 207, Rwm., 'Tätigkeitsbericht no. 13'.
[5] Ibid., 'Tätigkeitsbericht no. 14', February 1941.

As the work-force returned to its pre-invasion levels the drop in output per man became noticeable. What is not so clear, however, is what connection existed between changes which may have taken place in this period of low output and the subsequent tendency for productivity to decrease. Of the 240,000 workers employed in French coal-mining before the war 75,000 were immigrant workers, of these 51,000 were Polish.[1] The dispersal of this work-force was partly responsible for the slow return to earlier levels of output. Most of the foreign workers were either lost in the initial dispersion or were among the first to be moved to Germany at a later date. If the immigrant workers were younger than the native-born French miners this would have left France with an older work-force in the mines to which less skilled and less willing workers were later added. If the cumulative effect of longer shifts and poorer food on this work-force is then taken into account the movement of productivity over this period does not appear so startling. The greater capital-intensity of coal-mining in the 1930s, together with the change in the relative importance of the industry and the social tensions which surrounded it, were all good reasons for the native-born labour-force to have aged.

The military administration both in France and Belgium never swerved from the explanation that the chief factor in the shortfall of production was lower output per man. On the cause of this they were less united. It was variously attributed to shortages of supply, to inferior labour, to absenteeism, and to poor working conditions.

Shortages of wood began to appear in January 1941. Together with shortages of metal they persisted throughout the war and were later made more acute by the disruption of transport. At the same time the labour force, and particularly the substitute labour drafted into the mines, was of an inferior quality. Both of these factors had a particularly telling effect when many smaller seams were opened up in 1943 in the unsuccessful attempt to boost production. Meanwhile, capital deterioration, as elsewhere in the economy, was not sufficiently compensated for by new investment. With the exception of the Lorraine coalfield the average age of the fixed capital on the surface was thirty years.[1]

So high and so constant was the level of absenteeism that it seems better to attribute the falling productivity rate to the intolerable conditions. The miner's work, and the social conditions in which he lived, had been bad enough before the war. The extra burdens of rationing and longer hours made them unbearable and absenteeism was the only response available. Nothing else seems to explain satisfactorily why so many ran such a risk. After October 1941 stricter measures were taken to increase punishments for indiscipline and for breaking contracts, but they had no effect. Absenteeism is, of course, only a rough indication of time lost unless measured against the time actually worked. The working week was increased from seven and three-quarter hours

[1] CCDR., v, M.P. 3.

per day to eight and three-quarter hours, and by 1943 regular holiday working had become the rule and there was also a certain amount of compulsory Sunday working. The level of absenteeism did not consequently increase to quite the extent the figures suggest.

In the northern coalfield in January 1942 the percentage of days lost in relation to days worked was 10·96 per cent. Of the days lost 9·62 per cent were due to illness, accidents, or 'illegal' absenteeism. In 1943 the percentage of days lost in relation to those worked was between 14 and 16 per cent of which between 10 and 11 per cent were lost for the same reasons. The average rate of absenteeism in Blanzy was 13 per cent in 1938, 14·1 per cent in 1939, 16·1 per cent in 1941, and 14·9 per cent in 1942.[1] Although there is a tendency for the true absenteeism rate to be higher than in pre-war years, it still does not follow that this was primarily due to absenteeism by coal-face workers. The increase in the absenteeism rate during the occupation in the Blanzy mines was steeper for technical personnel than for underground workers. In the northern coalfield the most serious troubles with the labour force occurred with the surface workers. The opportunity of the pit-head workers for sabotage was also greater.

What is much more striking than the increased rate of absenteeism, however, is its quite different pattern. The difference reflects the changes in the economic and social forces bearing on the lives of the miners. Holidays were spread over the whole year by the German administration so that the pre-war peaks of absenteeism in July and August were replaced during the war by different peaks. The increase in 'illegal' absenteeism was relatively small, the increase in absenteeism due to accident and illness was much greater. This increase must partly have reflected the greater age of the work-force, their poor nourishment, and the longer hours worked. But it was also a safer form of resistance to the occupier. Doctors were notoriously ready to give certificates of unfitness to work. German policy depended on the exploitation of human labour in the mines to a greater and greater degree, and the miners both could not and would not respond.

In February 1941 there were hunger strikes in Belgian coal-mines and in May the strike movement spread to the French part of the coalfield. After much labour unrest a full-scale strike began at the Ostricourt mine on 1 June, a strike which had paralysed almost the whole coalfield by 5 June. The prefect of the Department of Nord attributed the strike to communists and feared a wave of communist agitation which would sweep away all authority whether French or German.[2] The whole working population of the district he described as being extremely anti-German and also anti-Vichy. The evidence of political motivation in the strike is slight, the evidence of hunger and bad working conditions among the men is clear. The basic rations for

[1] FD 469/45, Mbh. in F., Wi.Abt. II/a, 'Mines de Blanzy, graphiques des absences'.
[2] DFCAA., iv. 596.

coal-face workers in Belgium and France were much lower than those in Germany. The differential in basic rations between coal-face workers and other consumers in northern France, however, was very much lower than in Belgium.

TABLE 35

Ration of Basic Foodstuffs in Germany, Belgium, and Northern France, 1941*
(grammes per day)

	Germany		Belgium		Nord and Pas-de-Calais	
	Normal consumer	Heaviest worker category	Normal consumer	Underground worker	Normal consumer	Underground worker
Bread	321·4	664·2	225	450	300	450
Meat	71·4	171·4	35	70	51·4	75
Fats	37·6	104·5	15	60	14·3	29
Potatoes	not rationed		500	500	100	100

* BA., R 7 VIII 207, 'Tätigkeitsbericht no. 14', February 1941.

Rations of this order were clearly not sufficient for coal-miners and the justification of the strikes was clear to both military administrations. In February it was the opinion of the Belgian authorities that 'full output in the miners' heavy work cannot therefore be expected in the coal-mines of Belgium and northern France'.[1] The strikes in the Lille area evoked the same response from the authorities in France.

The supply of foodstuffs to the French population has further deteriorated. The quotas in themselves are already barely sufficient. The Frenchman, who is no overeater, would at any rate manage to escape need (except for bread) if the quantities were actually maintained. That, however, is not the case at all. From this stems the food crisis, which puts the capacity and willingness of the French to work seriously in question, and endangers their hitherto peaceful disposition.[2]

From the moment that France was cut off from British coal supply an acute coal shortage was inevitable. That shortage was exaggerated by the German failure to maintain a level of exports to France anywhere approaching her pre-war level. Belgian exports to France were also below their pre-war level; this was in part a function of the decline in output in Belgium during the war. The coal shortage in France was exacerbated by constant transport difficulties which often reduced the supply of the small quantities of coal that were available and also prevented the mines from obtaining supply of their own. A shortage of pit-props seriously disturbed the rhythm of exploitation in

[1] BA., R 7 VIII 207, 'Tätigkeitsbericht no. 14', February 1941.
[2] FD 667/46, Mbh. in F., 'Lagebericht des Wehrwirtschafts- und Rüstungsstabes Frankreich', June 1941.

French mines, and was also a factor in the lower level of productivity which developed there. Owing to the pattern of French consumption it was impossible to increase substantially, at the expense of other sectors of the economy, the amount of coal made available to manufacturing industry.

The most important cause for the failure of German policy in the French coal industry was the lower productivity of the mine-workers themselves. This was so because German policy depended, in the last resort, on increasing their productivity. There was little further mechanization in French coal-mines after 1932, partly because the level of possible mechanical innovation was already high by that date, partly because economic conditions became so unfavourable. These unfavourable conditions were potentially reversed by the war and the occupation. Suddenly the French coal industry was transformed from a depressed sector of the economy to a key industry in both the French and German war efforts. But the policy pursued by the occupiers meant that this potential transformation was not realized. The aim of the German mining administration was not to increase the level of mechanization, nor to improve the financial climate so that greater investment would take place, but to exploit the human element—to make the miners work harder. In this they totally failed. Thus they prolonged the unfavourable conditions in which the French coal industry had operated before the war. Capital equipment and men continued to age and there was a remarkable fall in the productivity of labour. In the early years of the war this could be compensated by drafting in extra supplies of labour; by 1943 this was no longer possible.

VIII

IRON ORE

THE economic ties between the German steel industry and France, since the nineteenth century, had grown ever closer and more complex. This was not only attributable to the fact that France was one of the world's major suppliers of iron ore. The geographical situation of her biggest source of supply, the minette ore field, involved it intimately in the fluctuating historical fortunes of the two countries after 1870. The basin of low-grade phosphoric ores crossed the historical frontiers between France, Lorraine, and Luxembourg. From the invention of the Gilchrist–Thomas process, with the consequent rapid growth in the utilization of phosphoric iron ore, the area developed an economic unity in striking contrast to the political discord in which it was involved.

From the early nineteenth century the ironmasters of Lorraine, and in particular the de Wendel family at Hayange, had depended on supplies of coking coal from the Saarland. When Lorraine was incorporated into the German customs union in 1871 it was no longer obliged to import its coal through a tariff barrier. Between that date and 1914 the Lorraine iron industry accounted for 13 per cent of German iron production and was more solidly based on domestic ores than the rest of the German iron industry. Its impact on the German iron and steel industry as a whole, however, was limited by the fundamental difference in the type of raw material used and by the consequent differences in finished products. In the decade before the acquisition of Lorraine German producers had begun to switch from native ores, becoming rapidly exhausted, to high-grade Spanish and Elban ores. The Lorraine industry remained geared to the use of low-grade ore, of about 35 per cent iron content. With the opening up of the Briey–Longwy section of the minette orefield which had remained on the French side of the frontier, an important steel-making industry grew up on that side of the frontier, and also in Luxembourg. Across these frontiers passed a growing trade.

The re-drawing of the frontier by the Treaty of Versailles drastically altered the proportions of this traffic. Almost the whole of the minette basin was now in French territory. The development before 1914 of the Longwy–Briey and Luxembourg regions had already necessitated an annual average import of 6,500,000 tons of coke from the Saarland and from Belgium. France now became much more dependent on German coal supplies, although some of the newly acquired Lorraine plant never worked at full capacity during the inter-war period. At the same time Germany's dependence on imported iron ore became overwhelming. On an average about 65 per cent of Germany's iron-ore consumption in the inter-war period was imported. The major part of these imports was supplied by Sweden, whose links with the German market became closer and more important throughout the inter-war period. Hence the greater part of the German steel plant remained geared to the use of higher-grade ores than those of the minette basin. Nevertheless, France was the second most important of Germany's foreign suppliers.

TABLE 36

*German Iron-ore Imports from Sweden and France**

(thousand tons)

	Sweden	France
1929	7,382	3,253
1930	6,725	2,780
1931	2,803	1,920
1932	1,577	716
1933	2,257	1,031
1934	4,695	1,631
1935	5,509	5,614
1936	8,248	6,860
1937	9,084	5,740
1938	8,992	5,056

* BA., R. 13 I 450, Wirtschaftsgruppe Eisenschaffende Industrie, 'Gesamtausfuhr Schwedens'.

This dependence on imported ore presented an obstacle to the Blitzkrieg economy. The resurgence of German manufacturing capacity after 1933 meant that, in spite of the carefully regulated foreign-exchange and trading policies, pressure on the balance of payments became very heavy. Coupled with this pressure was the strategic undesirability of having to import so large a part of the annual consumption of what was perhaps the most vital of all raw materials in a war economy.

Although the Blitzkrieg economy was based on stockpiles of essential raw materials, stockpiling had obvious limitations in the case of a raw material so bulky, and consumed in such large quantities, as iron ore. The United States Strategic Bombing Survey estimated German stockpiles of iron ore to have been of nine months' capacity at the start of the war.[1] This estimate is far too high. In 1939 German stocks of iron ore were about 8,000,000 tons, sufficient to cover between three and four months' consumption in Greater Germany.[2]

[1] USSBS., *The Effects of Strategic Bombing on the German War Economy*, p. 102.
[2] J.-J. Jäger, op. cit.

There is no case for arguing that Germany's war economy was dependent on Swedish supply between the invasion of Poland and the attack on France; the Blitzkrieg was an economic strategy designed to circumvent difficulties of precisely this kind. Nevertheless, in the light of National Socialist economic policy, the situation was very undesirable. The Party had therefore attempted to bring pressure to bear on the German steel industry to use larger quantities of very low-grade domestic iron ore, in particular the Dogger and Salzgitter ores. The manufacturers' opposition to this pressure, which would inevitably mean a rise in production costs, was determined. The complicated compromise which was reached, dignified by the name of Four Year Plan, had far-reaching social and political implications. In itself it reconciled many of the warring strains of economic thought within the Party while furthering Hitler's strategic intentions.

A partially state-owned firm, the Hermann Göring Werke, was set up to exploit the Salzgitter ores. The finished product was not of such general utility as other steels, and its cost was well above the level of comparable steels produced elsewhere. In Lorraine, where steel was also manufactured from low-grade ores, the easier availability of the ore and its more favourable chemical constitution led to considerably lower steel costs. It was much easier to obtain a suitable fluxing mixture, with or without the addition of lime-stone, by using minette ore than by using Salzgitter ores. At the same time, mechanized mining, either on the surface or underground, lowered mining costs further in Lorraine than in central Germany because of the geological disposition of the minette field.[1] Four years after the start of the Salzgitter investment programme part of Lorraine was again to be absorbed into the German Empire, with dire consequences for the newest sector of the German steel industry.

Although Germany was not absolutely dependent on Swedish supply to sustain her war economy between November 1939 and June 1940, over a longer period of time dependence on Sweden might have become crucial. The possibility of absolute control over an alternative source of supply made iron ore appear as the most valuable commodity which the French economy had to offer Germany. As soon as German troops had occupied Lorraine, iron ore was placed in a special category of administrative importance. A much more direct system of controls was imposed on the French iron industry than on other industries. Consequently, the evolution of German policy in France is not so clearly distinguishable. Even when more manufacturing contracts were being placed in France the essential problem for Germany was always to secure the necessary quantity of French ore.

Iron-ore mines in the department of Moselle were taken immediately into German control when the area was occupied. From the moment of their

---

[1] United Nations, Dept. of Economic and Social Affairs, *Survey of World Iron Ore Resources, Occurrence, Appraisal and Use* (New York, 1955).

capture the mines became part of the German domestic economy. The production of Lorraine and Luxembourg, excluding the department of Meurthe-et-Moselle, was initially placed under a Commissar-General, Paul Raabe, resident at Metz.[1] Later his control was extended to the department of Meurthe-et-Moselle also. The individual firms continued to run the mines and sell their product, but every aspect of the technical operations of the mines, of labour regulations, of wages, and of investment was strictly controlled by the new office. The distribution of the product was not left to the variable pressures which the German administration could bring to bear on a 'comité de répartition' but was placed in the hands of a German organization, the *Liefergemeinschaft der Eisenerzgruben in Lothringen und Meurthe-et-Moselle*. Although never legally recognized by the mining companies, the *Liefergemeinschaft* drew a considerable part of its revenue from them. Only the mines of Normandy, Anjou, and the Pyrénèes, accounting for about 11 per cent of pre-war French output, were controlled by the German economic administration in Paris.

The average output of minette iron ore in France over the years 1936 to 1938 was 31,711,000 tons. The area of mining covered two departments, Moselle, where the annual average output over the same period was 14,200,000 tons, and Meurthe-et-Moselle.[2] Since the average annual level of French exports was about 15,000,000 tons the output of the department of Meurthe-et-Moselle alone was roughly equivalent to French domestic consumption. Minette iron ore was 89 per cent of total French output.

There were two other distinct regions of iron-ore output in mainland France, where, although output was relatively small, it was important because of its quality. In Normandy and Anjou there were supplies of non-phosphoric ores. Although the Normandy and Anjou ores are usually classified separately, they have a close chemical similarity and a relatively high iron content, from 44 per cent to 53 per cent. Buoyant export markets in Germany, Belgium, and Britain had led to a considerable expansion of mining in both Normandy and Anjou between 1905 and 1913 and between 1925 and 1929.[3] Because the French steel industry was so heavily concentrated on Thomas steel production the importance of these non-phosphoric ores had always been greater for foreign manufacturers than for French manufacturers. Thomas steels were 78·5 per cent of total French production, whereas they were only 42·3 per cent of German output.[4]

The output of iron ore in Normandy in 1938 was 1,632,000 tons, that of Anjou, 386,000 tons.[5] The average annual level of exports from the two areas

[1] Generalbeauftragter für die Eisenerzgewinnung und- Verteilung in den Gebieten Luxemburg und Lothringen. [2] CCDR., v, M.P. 1.
[3] FD 287/45, Mbh. in F., Wi.Abt. II/a, 'Die Eisenerzlagerstätten der Normandie, des Anjou, und der Bretagne', 9 May 1941.
[4] BA., R 13 I 384, Wirtschaftsgruppe Eisenschaffende Industrie, 'Eisenindustrie Frankreichs'. [5] FD 287/45, Mbh. in F., Wi.Abt. II/a 'Die Eisenezlagerstätten . . .'.

combined between 1934 and 1938 was 1,232,000 tons.[1] Of these exports 449,000 tons on average went to Germany and 446,000 tons to Belgium.

Very small reserves of high-grade haematite ore had been mined for a long time in the Pyrénèes. The relative importance of these supplies in the French economy had been declining since 1900, except for a short increase in production during the First World War. This increase was to be repeated in the preparation for the Second World War. Output rose from 10,000 tons in 1938 to 106,000 tons in 1939.

To these sources of supply should be added the output of Algeria and Tunisia. The average annual output over the period 1934 to 1938 was 2,742,000 tons, of which the whole was exported. The main market was Britain, but about 500,000 tons a year went to Germany.

Not only did France lose the total output of the department of Moselle during the war, an output about equal to her very large pre-war export surplus, but usually rather more than 50 per cent of the output of the department of Meurthe-et-Moselle was diverted away from France. The output of iron ore in the department of Meurthe-et-Moselle in 1942 was 11,364,111 tons. Of this 6,462,746 tons were diverted to Germany, 2,426,586 tons going to the Saarland, 2,276,513 tons to the Ruhr, and 1,082,371 tons went to Belgium including Nord and Pas-de-Calais.

The monthly figures for output of minette ore in Table 37 do not exist for dates after 1942. They have therefore been supplemented by the annual figures published in France. There are in fact small differences between the German and French figures for the earliest years but not such as to be particularly troublesome. Only in 1943 did iron-ore production in the department of Meurthe-et-Moselle approach the level of 1938, but even then it was still over 500,000 tons short of that level. In the areas annexed by Germany production of iron ore in 1943 was over one million tons higher than the level of 1939. In every wartime year the level of output compared to that of 1938 was lower in the areas left under French sovereignty than in the areas annexed by Germany. The level of labour productivity, however, in the annexed areas, was no higher than in the occupied areas. Indeed, it was often lower.

The combined output of all iron-ore mines in mainland France, other than those of the minette basin, in 1939 had been 2,312,000 tons.[2] During the war it was never to approach this level. Iron-ore mines controlled directly by the Military Command in Paris therefore responded no better than those under the Commissar-General. The iron-ore mines of western France, which were particularly important to the German economy, since their ore was the only French ore which could be easily substituted for Swedish ore, produced about 60 per cent of their average output of 1938 and 1939. Those of the Pyrénèes

[1] CCDR., v, M.P. 1.
[2] FD 256/45, Comité d'organisation des minerais et métaux bruts to Mbh. in F., Wi.Abt., 10 April 1942.

TABLE 37

Output of Minette Iron Ore*

(tons)

		Meurthe-et-Moselle	'Lothringen'†	Luxembourg	Total
1940	July	..	46,513	114,394	160,907
	Aug.	..	198,983	249,106	448,089
	Sept.	41,357	427,597	522,735	991,689
	Oct.	151,269	546,760	605,093	1,303,122
	Nov.	260,366	575,176	526,140	1,361,682
	Dec.	406,880	621,456	525,940	1,554,276
Total	July/Dec.	859,872	2,416,485	2,543,408	5,819,765
1941	Jan.	456,874	720,521	551,550	1,718,945
	Feb.	505,015	726,559	537,925	1,769,499
	Mar.	597,313	826,087	588,037	2,011,437
	Apr.	634,434	870,718	613,012	2,118,164
	May	726,353	843,572	589,263	2,159,188
	June	723,936	768,132	575,286	2,067,354
	July	872,539	902,178	660,334	2,435,051
	Aug.	889,039	877,430	645,839	2,412,308
	Sept.	928,538	897,364	643,505	2,469,407
	Oct.	1,002,585	955,959	631,262	2,589,806
	Nov.	963,719	931,094	484,456	2,379,269
	Dec.	1,020,240	984,084	439,922	2,444,246
Total		9,320,585	10,303,698	6,950,391	26,574,674
1942	Jan.	972,324	974,724	400,883	2,347,931
	Feb.	857,541	776,889	251,664	1,886,094
	Mar.	921,902	870,927	361,267	2,154,096
	Apr.	836,015	885,347	402,306	2,123,668
	May	829,332	949,169	416,325	2,194,826
	June	912,946	1,067,710	427,889	2,408,545
	July	948,570	1,080,993	455,015	2,484,578
	Aug.	951,338	1,052,703	461,318	2,465,359
	Sept.	995,684	1,088,320	480,187	2,564,191
	Oct.	1,086,196	1,203,256	518,023	2,807,475
	Nov.	997,966	1,106,207	480,361	2,584,534
	Dec.	1,054,297	1,189,537	459,929	2,703,763
Total		11,364,111	12,245,782	5,115,167	28,725,060
1943	Total‡	15,612,000	14,952,000	5,693,000§	
1944	Total	9,000,000	9,588,000	2,088,000§‖	

* FD 4711/45, Bezirksgruppe Südwest der Wirtschaftsgruppe Eisenschaffende Industrie, Geschäftsstelle Metz, 'Erzbergbau, Erzförderung'.

† The territory annexed from France.

‡ INSEE., *Mouvement économique* . . ., p. 224.

§ The weight of ore dispatched. BA., Wi./IA 105, Der Vorsitzer der Rüstungskommission XIIb des R.m.f.R.u.Kp., 'Denkschrift über Minette', Anlage 1, 31 October 1944. The

[*Footnotes § and ‖ continued on next page*

produced more than in 1939 but the quantities involved were so small they could in no way affect the total situation. Expansion of production up to a certain level was in fact easy in the Pyrénèes, being merely a matter of reopening mines closed as uneconomic in the inter-war period. Once this had been done, which was in any case only a continuation of what had already taken place there in 1939, monthly average output did not rise. In 1943 it began to fall when output elsewhere in France was increasing. This phenomenon was repeated in western France, where monthly average output for the first seven months of 1943 was lower than in 1942 and merely 59 per cent of that 1939. In no region of France, in spite of the most strenuous efforts, did Germany succeed in obtaining an increase in production of iron ore. Only in 1943 did the level of output approach pre-war levels.

TABLE 38

*Iron-ore Output in France**

(tons)

		Meurthe-et-Moselle	Anjou/Normandy	Pyrénèes	Total†
1940	July				
	Aug.				
	Sept.	41,357			
	Oct.	151,269			
	Nov.	260,366			
	Dec.	406,880			
Total	July/Dec.	859,872			

quantity of ore dispatched to various regions throughout the period July 1940–July 1944 from Lorraine, Luxembourg, and Meurthe-et-Moselle was, according to the same source:

To:	Ruhr	14,660,000
	Saarland	20,780,000
	Lorraine	26,806,000
	Luxembourg	21,664,000
	Eastern France	15,534,000
	Belgium	14,263,000
	Elsewhere	67,000
	Total	113,774,000

I am indebted to Dr. J.-J. Jäger for this information and for his help on other points.
 ‖ January–July.

  * The figures for Meurthe-et-Moselle for 1940 are from FD 4711/45, Bezirksgruppe Südwest, 'Erzbergbau'. Those for 1941, 1942, and 1943 and for the other regions are from FD 287/45, Mbh. in F., Wi.Abt. II/a, 'Eisenerz Bergbau'. The discrepancies between these and the figures for Meurthe-et-Moselle of Wirtschaftsgruppe Eisenschaffende Industrie (Table 37) are quite small. The figures given in FD 287/45 are only complete until September, and the September and October entries are provisional estimates. The total given for Meurthe-et-Moselle for 1943 is therefore that of INSEE., *Mouvement économique . . .*, p. 224. The

TABLE 38 (cont.)

		Meurthe-et-Moselle	Anjou/Normandy	Pyrénées	Total
1941	Jan.	456,874	35,461	9,217	522,223
	Feb.	505,015	36,244	10,419	542,040
	Mar.	597,313	60,129	12,718	664,427
	Apr.	634,434	85,664	12,945	723,760
	May	726,353	85,795	13,130	812,075
	June	723,936	105,961	12,202	830,059
	July	872,539	117,721	14,064	969,506
	Aug.	889,039	119,778	16,977	1,013,983
	Sept.	928,538	121,965	17,349	1,055,940
	Oct.	1,002,585	129,154	16,232	1,135,711
	Nov.	963,719	123,462	14,392	1,090,722
	Dec.	1,020,240	129,309	14,523	1,152,432
Total		9,320,585	1,150,643	164,468	10,512,878
1942	Jan.	972,324	121,204	13,942	1,098,645
	Feb.	857,541	86,913	13,773	933,689
	Mar.	921,902	99,325	14,274	1,027,602
	Apr.	836,015	112,028	13,850	951,610
	May	829,332	108,930	13,279	939,216
	June	912,946	118,705	13,098	1,033,930
	July	948,570	120,544	12,951	1,069,894
	Aug.	951,338	101,318	12,154	1,072,584
	Sept.	995,684	115,580	12,041	1,131,260
	Oct.	1,086,196	116,196	11,803	1,223,136
	Nov.	997,966	100,102	12,033	1,110,091
	Dec.	1,054,297	111,731	12,514	1,171,542
Total		11,364,111	1,312,583	154,712	12,763,199
1943	Jan.	1,095,453	91,124	12,210	1,198,787
	Feb.	1,137,424	102,119	11,341	1,269,537
	Mar.	1,331,569	107,430	10,871	1,449,870
	Apr.	1,278,328	102,881	13,712	1,386,139
	May	1,339,316	113,761	12,504	1,465,581
	June	1,354,560	115,142	13,131	1,486,328
	July	1,421,431	118,764	13,327	1,551,214
	Aug.	1,353,825	107,470	13,000	1,466,687
	Sept.	1,339,061	94,728	12,700	1,432,145
	Oct.	1,366,793	100,000		1,456,142
	Nov.				1,403,041
	Dec.				1,353,867
Total		15,612,000			16,929,338

final totals given are those of FD 282/45, Mbh. in F., Wi.Abt. II/a, Secrétariat Général de l'Énergie, Direction des Mines, 'Production de minérai de fer'. Users of this document should note that the pencilled addition 'Meurthe-et-Moselle' is an error. The totals given, therefore, are not the totals of the separate lines in the table, but the totals used by the Mbh. in F., Wi.Abt. II/a, to estimate the extent of exports to the Reich.

† Blanks indicate unknown totals.

In spite of the comparative failure of German efforts to increase production, the improvement in 1943 in output of minette iron ore shows the changes in German economic policy in that year. The low levels of output in the preceding years may merely have been a reflection of Germany's lack of interest during the Blitzkrieg and the first, essentially domestic, phase of the reorganization of her own economy, once she had satisfied her immediate needs. All that would have been necessary in that case would have been to provide the French economy with the minimum quantity of iron ore to meet a greatly reduced French demand plus that which was required to meet German contracts in France. More important than the quantity of iron ore mined, therefore, is the variation in the proportion of that quantity taken by Germany over time.

The calculations of the 'Commission Consultative' indicates that this proportion became fixed at between 75 per cent and 80 per cent of total supply in 1941 and dropped to 72·5 per cent in 1943, perhaps to meet the increase in German contracts to France in that year.[1] There is a serious statistical difficulty in deciding these proportions. Records of the quantity of minette iron ore exported from Meurthe-et-Moselle, that is to say from 'French' to 'German' Lorraine, are very fragmentary. Furthermore the 'Commission Consultative' was obliged to estimate the total output per year of the annexed regions, since no statistics were available permitting them to proceed more accurately. On the basis of Table 37, which shows the monthly output of iron ore in the department of Moselle, it is possible to proceed more accurately.

Table 39 shows the quantity of metropolitan French iron ore exported to Germany, if exports to the department of Moselle are omitted. The biggest part of iron-ore exports to Germany went either to the Ruhr district or to the Saarland. Exports to Belgium and Luxembourg are also shown. Deliveries to Luxembourg were in effect deliveries to territory under German sovereignty; but deliveries to Belgium included deliveries to the departments of Nord and Pas-de-Calais, where much of the French metallurgical industry was to be found. On this basis, therefore, omitting French exports to 'German' Lorraine and to Luxembourg, and making no allowance for exports of ore from North Africa the proportion of French iron ore diverted to Germany declined from 1941 to 1943. In 1941 Germany took 51 per cent of total output, in 1942 43 per cent, and in 1943 36 per cent.

How do these percentages change if allowances are made for the missing quantities in Table 39? The *Wirtschaftsgruppe Eisenschaffende Industrie* records show that the Lorraine iron industry and its close neighbour that of Saarland remained the biggest users of minette iron ore, as might be expected. Nevertheless, large deliveries were made to Belgium, including northern France, and to the Ruhr industry. Of the minette ore supplied to Lorraine, Luxembourg, and the Saarland in 1941, 21·2 per cent was supplied to steelworks in

[1] CCDR., v, M.P. 1.

TABLE 39

Production and Distribution of Iron Ore in France

(tons)

		Output	Exports to Germany (excluding exports to Moselle)	Exports to Belgium and Luxembourg (including Nord and Pas-de-Calais)	Elsewhere
1941	Jan.	522,223	..	..	..
	Feb.	542,040	254,181	74,713	1,040
	Mar.	664,427	307,519	85,100	6,785
	Apr.	723,760	397,971	114,084	10,230
	May	812,075	397,718	140,396	10,805
	June	830,059	502,249	165,968	11,020
	July	969,506	678,596	163,109	4,800
	Aug.	1,013,983	699,660	169,853	6,720
	Sept.	1,055,940	641,633	164,010	6,233
	Oct.	1,135,711	622,487	128,630	6,256
	Nov.	1,090,722	489,140	168,765	5,200
	Dec.	1,152,432	419,100	174,052	7,281
Total		10,512,878	5,410,254	1,548,680	16,370
1942	Jan.	1,098,645	296,440	108,025	5,200
	Feb.	933,689	242,730	117,499	5,202
	Mar.	1,027,602	355,226	130,385	4,171
	Apr.	951,610	435,955	150,824	6,253
	May	939,216	503,807	146,563	6,215
	June	1,033,930	556,127	181,609	7,289
	July	1,069,894	598,532	176,173	8,320
	Aug.	1,072,584	651,174	205,706	5,160
	Sept.	1,131,260	579,787	197,415	7,280
	Oct.	1,223,136	533,300	133,629	..
	Nov.	1,110,091	382,954	128,488	..
	Dec.	1,171,542	335,120	150,843	..
Total		12,763,199	5,471,150	1,827,159	
1943	Jan.	1,198,787	439,621	188,207	..
	Feb.	1,269,537	492,619	244,939	..
	Mar.	1,449,870	569,509	177,536	..
	Apr.	1,386,139	661,103	191,571	..
	May	1,465,581	660,758	253,071	..
	June	1,486,328	592,994	304,694	..
	July	1,551,214	635,858	347,248	..
	Aug.	1,466,687	487,996	365,985	5,200
	Sept.	1,432,145	357,388	384,361	5,200
	Oct.	1,456,142	407,932	333,686	4,170
	Nov.	1,403,041	334,917	302,780	4,160
	Dec.	1,353,867	341,580	265,021	11,429
Total		16,929,338	6,082,275	3,359,099	

* FD 282/45, Mbh. F., in Wi.Abt. II/a, Secrétariat Général de l'Energie, Direction des Mines, 'Production de minérai de fer'.

TABLE 40

Distribution of Minette Ore by Area 1942*

(tons)

| Month | From | To | | | | | | | | |
		Ruhr	Saar	Lorraine	Luxembourg	Elsewhere in Reich	Whole of Germany	Belgium	France	Total
Jan.	Lorraine	64,878	149,397	482,953	204,849	647	902,724	13,157	..	915,881
	Luxembourg	31,069	37,014	..	167,424	40	235,547	117,596	..	353,143
	Meurthe-et-Moselle	38,820	193,800	80,660	13,000	..	326,280	85,312	294,110	705,702
	Total	134,767	380,211	563,613	385,273	687	1,464,551	216,065	294,110	1,974,726
Feb.	Lorraine	11,640	167,520	381,960	142,390	1,250	704,760	12,160	..	716,920
	Luxembourg	3,010	38,310	1,600	116,560	20	157,900	19,320	..	177,220
	Meurthe-et-Moselle	11,990	188,810	68,910	11,760	..	281,470	1,520	271,100	554,090
	Total	26,640	394,640	450,870	270,710	1,270	1,144,130	33,000	271,100	1,448,230
Mar.	Lorraine	27,010	185,430	413,900	151,700	1,410	779,450	13,140	..	792,590
	Luxembourg	19,060	43,600	..	172,160	20	234,840	101,200	..	336,040
	Meurthe-et-Moselle	25,990	275,940	71,570	13,000	..	386,500	116,870	304,210	807,580
	Total	72,060	504,970	485,470	336,860	1,430	1,400,790	231,210	304,210	1,936,210
Apr.	Lorraine	63,140	168,820	415,030	190,730	2,280	840,000	12,380	..	852,380
	Luxembourg	36,950	40,890	1,600	152,750	160	232,350	183,170	..	415,520
	Meurthe-et-Moselle	134,530	228,920	70,570	20,480	..	454,500	119,310	319,550	893,360
	Total	234,620	438,630	487,200	363,960	2,440	1,526,850	314,860	319,550	2,161,260
May	Lorraine	24,370	207,360	489,940	226,470	900	949,040	14,320	2,980	966,340
	Luxembourg	24,130	51,650	5,160	186,670	..	267,610	181,930	..	449,540
	Meurthe-et-Moselle	209,780	209,120	115,410	24,840	..	559,150	114,150	288,600	961,900
	Total	258,280	468,130	610,510	437,980	900	1,775,800	310,400	291,580	2,377,780
June	Lorraine	42,550	237,090	496,590	248,570	1,120	1,025,920	14,400	..	1,040,320
	Luxembourg	26,050	56,220	6,520	165,230	..	254,020	199,680	..	453,700
	Meurthe-et-Moselle	224,990	242,600	138,140	40,240	..	645,977	134,120	306,460	1,086,550
	Total	293,590	535,910	641,250	454,040	1,120	1,925,910	348,200	306,460	2,580,570

Month	Region									
July	Lorraine	81,210	258,540	505,610	252,360	1,770	1,099,490	15,540	..	1,115,030
	Luxembourg	42,160	53,030	..	184,500	80	279,770	203,930	..	483,700
	Meurthe-et-Moselle	276,330	228,450	122,340	32,240	..	659,360	139,920	280,630	1,079,910
	Total	399,020	540,020	627,950	469,100	1,850	2,038,620	359,390	280,630	2,678,640
Aug.	Lorraine	149,620	232,710	523,190	216,130	1,830	1,123,480	13,910	..	1,137,390
	Luxembourg	52,110	53,260	6,440	217,050	..	328,860	193,400	..	522,260
	Meurthe-et-Moselle	410,190	186,310	126,570	40,330	..	763,400	136,890	315,700	1,215,990
	Total	611,920	472,280	656,200	473,510	1,830	2,215,740	344,200	315,700	2,875,640
Sept.	Lorraine	103,670	227,850	584,600	212,140	1,090	1,129,350	14,500	..	1,143,850
	Luxembourg	52,000	56,540	5,320	212,560	40	326,460	205,140	..	531,600
	Meurthe-et-Moselle	329,590	203,490	136,830	53,920	100	723,930	98,430	343,720	1,166,080
	Total	485,260	487,880	726,750	478,620	1,230	2,179,740	318,070	343,720	2,841,530
Oct.	Lorraine	124,830	230,580	625,310	236,590	1,960	1,219,270	14,650	..	1,233,920
	Luxembourg	87,110	62,890	4,360	204,740	200	359,300	206,710	..	566,010
	Meurthe-et-Moselle	303,010	152,870	131,150	27,960	..	614,990	10,340	453,840	1,079,170
	Total	514,950	446,340	760,820	469,290	2,160	2,193,560	231,700	453,840	2,879,100
Nov.	Lorraine	78,850	217,741	519,355	239,946	1,476	1,057,368	14,738	..	1,072,106
	Luxembourg	122,622	81,581	17,920	154,659	..	376,782	185,503	..	562,285
	Meurthe-et-Moselle	188,573	159,516	132,957	51,800	..	532,846	61,739	396,108	990,693
	Total	390,045	458,838	670,232	446,405	1,476	1,966,996	261,980	396,108	2,625,084
Dec.	Lorraine	128,930	218,380	556,520	247,580	870	1,152,280	20,030	..	1,172,310
	Luxembourg	86,970	76,850	12,640	173,180	..	349,640	173,700	..	523,340
	Meurthe-et-Moselle	122,720	156,760	166,630	68,240	..	514,350	63,770	395,060	973,180
	Total	338,620	451,990	735,790	489,000	870	2,016,270	257,500	395,060	2,668,830
Jan. to Dec. 1942 totals	Lorraine	900,698	2,501,418	5,994,958	2,559,455	16,603	11,983,132	172,925	2,980	12,159,037
	Luxembourg	583,241	651,835	59,960	2,107,483	560	4,403,079	1,971,279	..	5,374,358
	Meurthe-et-Moselle	2,276,513	2,426,586	1,361,737	397,810	100	6,462,746	1,082,371	3,969,088	11,514,205
	Total	3,760,452	5,579,839	7,416,655	5,074,748	17,263	21,848,957	3,226,575	3,972,068	29,047,600
July to Dec. 1940 totals	Lorraine	70,500	669,900	1,158,000	475,600	..	2,374,000	16,800	..	2,390,800
	Luxembourg	..	706,700	..	1,210,600	..	1,917,300	767,100	36,500	2,720,900
	Meurthe-et-Moselle	109,100	166,900	121,900	400	..	398,300	99,600	505,400	1,003,300
	Total	179,600	1,543,500	1,279,900	1,686,600	..	4,689,600	883,500	541,900	6,115,000

* FD 4711/45, Bezirksgruppe Südwest der Wirtschaftsgruppe Eisenschaffende Industrie, 'Minetteversand Januar–Dezember 1942'; ibid, 'Minetteversand Juli–Dezember 1940'.

'German' Lorraine, 20·6 per cent to the steel industry of the Saarland, 16·6 per cent to steelworks in Belgium and northern France, and only 11·5 per cent to steelworks in 'French' Lorraine.[1] Complete records of the distribution of minette ore, specifying the precise geographical origin of the ore, seem, however, only to have survived for 1940 and 1942. Since the detailed figures for 1940 are of limited value they are given in Table 40 in summary form only, those for 1942 are given in full.

Only 1 per cent of the ore mined in 'German' Lorraine was exported either to Belgium or France in 1942. The area which Germany annexed was used absolutely for her own supply. Since the iron ores of western France were also used almost entirely for German purposes France was left dependent on the iron ore of the department of Meurthe-et-Moselle. In 1942 57 per cent of this supply was also exported to Germany. In addition 9·5 per cent was exported to Belgium, some part of which must have been for purely Belgian use. In 1940 46 per cent of the ore of the department of Meurthe-et-Moselle were exported to Germany and 11·5 per cent. to Belgium.

If the amount of ore exported from the department of Meurthe-et-Moselle to 'German' Lorraine and to Luxembourg is added to the volume of exports to Germany in 1942 the correct total for these exports is much higher than in Table 39. It is 7,230,697 tons, or 56·5 per cent (rather than 43 per cent). In North Africa total production in 1942 was 262,000 tons; 239,000 tons were exported to Germany.[2] If North Africa is included, therefore, Germany took 57 per cent of French-iron ore output in that year. If the department of Moselle is included in the calculation the proportion taken increases to 76 per cent and the total quantity of iron ore which Germany was able to obtain in that year by virtue of her victory in the war was 19,213,829 tons. By iron content imports of ore from Sweden decreased from 5,395,000 tons in 1938 to 4,197,000 tons in 1942; in the same period imports from France and North Africa rose from 1,893,000 tons to 2,497,000 tons.[3] German supply from France in 1942 was three times the level of her imports from France in 1936, the highest year for such imports before the war.

It is unjustified to assume that the quantity of iron ore exported from the department of Meurthe-et-Moselle remained as high in 1943 as in previous years. Such exports averaged 113,478 tons a month in 1942. Transport plans made one month in advance in 1943 for this traffic show that only between September and November of that year was provision made for the transport of over 100,000 tons of ore monthly.[4] In 1944 the monthly transport allocation

[1] FD 4711/45, Bezirksgruppe Südwest der Wirtschaftsgruppe Eisenschaffende Industrie, 'Erzbergbau. Minetteversand unterteilt in Liefergebiete im Jahre 1941'.

[2] CCDR., v, M.P. 1.

[3] A. S. Milward, 'Could Sweden have stopped the War?', *Scandinavian Economic History Review*, pp. 130–1.

[4] FD 1842/44, Mbh. in F., Wi.Abt., Awi-Transporte, 'Verkehr aus den besetzten Westgebieten, dem Gebiet Südfrankreich und Spanien nach Deutschland und anderen Ländern'.

was even lower. Since the output of iron ore in Meurthe-et-Moselle was so much higher in 1943 the proportion going to Germany was probably lower than in 1942. If we assume that until May 1943, before the advance transport calculations began, there was no change in the proportion of ore mined in Meurthe-et-Moselle exported to Moselle and Luxembourg, and that after May 1943 the transport plans are reasonably accurate guides to the level of these exports the proportion of French ore exported to Germany (omitting Moselle ores) in 1943 would be 49 per cent. This is almost certainly an overestimate, first because transport problems became increasingly acute after summer 1943, and secondly because the quantities so exported may not have increased between January and May 1943 as much as is here supposed.[1] It is only possible to make the same calculation for 1944 by excluding ores from western France and the Pyrénèes, as there appear to be no figures of exports to Germany from those regions other than those published by the 'Commission Consultative'. Omitting those regions, and still excluding Moselle ores, the proportion of ore exported to Germany in the first seven months of 1944 appears as 50·5 per cent.

In Table 41 the proportion of total French iron-ore output which Germany secured during the war is shown both including the department of Moselle as French territory and excluding it. Where no information exists as to the precise output of iron ore in 'German' Lorraine no assumptions have been made as to what it might have been. The estimates made by the 'Commission Consultative', which are based on such assumptions, are included for comparative purposes. For 1940 the estimates omit western France and the Pyrénèes from the calculations, as the only figures available are those of the 'Commission Consultative'. Since, however, their estimates of output in North Africa, and of exports to Germany, tally with German sources, North Africa has been included in the calculation for that year. For 1941, where no separate figure of exports from 'French' to 'German' Lorraine exists, other than that of the 'Commission Consultative', two assumptions have been made about the distribution of Lorraine ores. The first is that 99 per cent of ore from 'German' Lorraine was retained in the German Reich, as it was in 1940 and 1942. The second is that the same percentage of ore from Meurthe-et-Moselle went to Germany in 1941 as in 1942.

What is to be learned from these tedious arithmetical exercises? The procedure which the 'Commission Consultative' used to estimate the quantity and proportion of French iron ore acquired by Germany disguises the changes in German policy during the war. The inclusion of Moselle ore as part of French supply during the war, although perfectly reasonable when the task of the Commissioners is considered, tends to disguise the changes in the

---

[1] The military administration estimated that 57 per cent of French iron-ore supply was for German use in 1942 and 50 per cent in 1943. FD 301/46, Mbh. in F., 'Der Beitrag usw.', Mbh. in F., Wi.Abt., 'Der Beitrag des französischen Raumes . . .'.

proportion of French ore taken by Germany. It does so because the output of iron ore in 'German' Lorraine in the early stages of the war increased more rapidly than that in 'French' Lorraine, with the result that the Commissioners underestimated output in the department of Moselle. If Moselle ore is counted as part of 'normal' French supply during the war, the proportion of 'normal'

TABLE 41

Estimates of the Quantity and Proportion of French Iron Ore taken by Germany
(including Algerian and Tunisian Ore)

(tons)

			per cent
1940 (last 6 months)	excluding Moselle, western France, and the Pyrenees	398,300	36
	including Moselle, but excluding western France and the Pyrenees	2,772,300	78·5
	estimate of 'Commission Consultative', including Moselle		(32·0)
1941	excluding Moselle	7,022,000*	67
	including Moselle	17,275,272	81·5
	estimate of 'Commission Consultative', including Moselle		(78·0)
1942	excluding Moselle	7,230,697	56·5
	including Moselle	19,213,829	76·0
	estimate of 'Commission Consultative', including Moselle		(76·0)
1943	excluding Moselle	8,249,479	49·0
	estimate of 'Commission Consultative', including Moselle		(72·5)
1944 (first 6 months)	excluding Moselle, western France, and the Pyrenees	4,045,695	50·5
	estimate of 'Commission Consultative', including Moselle		(74·0)

* FD 474/45, Mbh. in F., Wi.Abt. II/a, 'Ausnutzung der französischen Wirtschaft für Deutschland', 3 February 1942.

French supply taken by Germany in 1940 and 1941 should be higher. In 1943 and 1944, however, it should be lower. Instead, therefore, of Germany taking a more or less constant proportion of French iron ore in the years 1941–4 it seems likely that she took a declining proportion in each year.

If the department of Moselle is omitted from 'normal' French supply during the war it is certain that from 1941 to the end of 1943 there was a marked decrease in the proportion of French iron ore taken by Germany. It is reasonable to conclude that this change was accounted for by the policy of placing manufacturing contracts in France in greater quantities, and represents a movement away from booty to more sophisticated policies. Omitting the department of Moselle the proportion of total French supply taken by Germany declined from 67 per cent in 1941 to 49 per cent in 1943.

In this light the Speer–Bichelonne agreements appear as a continuation of previous policies rather than a sharp break with the past. Nevertheless, after July 1943 there was a sharp decline in the monthly quota of iron ore exported from the department of Meurthe-et-Moselle to the Ruhr area.[1] It was this which was mainly responsible for the decline in exports to Germany from the department of Meurthe-et-Moselle. Only in May 1944 did the movement of French ore to the Ruhr return to the level of early 1943.

TABLE 42

Exports of Iron Ore from Western French Iron ore Mines

(tons)

	Average annual exports† 1934–8	1941*
Germany	449,000	774,000
Belgium	446,000	7,000
U.K.	227,000	
Holland	85,000	284,000

* CCDR., v, M.P. 1.
† FD 474/45, Mbh. in F., Wi.Abt. II/a, 'Ausnutzung der französischen Wirtschaft für Deutschland', 3 February 1942.

The failure of Germany to organize a greater output of iron ore in France is not so striking as in the case of French coal-mines, because the problem never developed the same urgency as in the coal-mining industry, although at the outset the German administration attributed greater importance to iron ore. To obtain a sufficient quantity of iron ore to satisfy her demands had to be a matter of top priority for Germany. That demand once satisfied, the matter was less urgent than the supply of coal.

Iron ore is very far from being a uniform commodity, and its lack of uniformity must be taken into account in passing any judgement on the level of output in wartime France. Swedish iron ore remained the basis of German steel production during the war. The only French ore which could be substituted for Swedish ore was the low-phosphorous ore of western France. In May 1942, when Swedish ore deliveries fell short of the required total, there were attempts to increase the deliveries from western France to the Ruhr area from about 75,000 tons per month to 125,000 tons per month.[2] From the

[1] FD 1842/44, Mbh. in F., Wi.Abt., Awi–Transporte, 'Verkehr ausden besetzten Westgebieten . . .'.
[2] FD 257/45, Mbh. in F., Wi.Abt. II/a, 'Lagebericht', 22 May 1942.

beginning of the occupation Germany diverted to her own use the pre-war quantities of iron ore which had been exported to Britain and to Belgium. French use of those ores had been further diminished by the quantities exported to Ymuiden in the Netherlands, for destinations in Luxembourg.

Such were the strategic developments in the war that Germany was not obliged to worry about the volume of iron-ore supply from France until the close of 1943. Calculations made by the Planning Office in November of that year indicated that by a thorough mobilization of German ore resources in the event of a total failure of Swedish supply in 1944 German steel output would fall by only 230,000 tons a quarter.[1] The output of iron ore in Greater Germany in 1943 was 9,100,000 tons iron content.[2] Imports of iron ore were 5,860,000 tons iron content; of these imports Sweden supplied 4,640,000 tons iron content. Of the output of Greater Germany almost one half came from the annexed territories and the Protectorate.

TABLE 43

German Iron-ore Supply*

(thousand tons)

	Domestic production (Greater Germany)	Imports from Sweden	Imports from France
1938	15,021	8,992	5,056
1939	18,500	10,038	..
1940	23,344	8,418	398†
1941	39,190	9,260	7,022
1942	36,368	7,975	7,230
1943	39,114	9,550	8,249

* J.-J. Jäger, op. cit., p. 2. FD 3043/49, Section VII, Sc. 119, Rm.f.R.u.Kp., Planungs-amt, 'Eisenerze'.
† Minette ore only.

If the impact of Germany's changed supply situation on the Ruhr steel industry was relatively small, on the more modern German steel industry created by the Four Year Plan, it was very heavy. The annexation of Moselle threatened the complete disruption of the carefully regulated price structure of the German steel industry. The consumption of low-grade domestic iron ores in Germany had always been resisted by the steel producers, but had been advocated by the government on the grounds of national interest. With the enormous increase in the domestic supply of low-grade ore, the economic position of producers forced to use Dogger and Saltzgitter ores was directly

[1] FD 3353/45, vol. 215, Rm.f.R.u.Kp., 'Die Bedeutung der Zufuhr an schwedischen und norwegischen Eisenerzen für die deutsche Eisenerzeugung', 11 November 1943.
[2] FD 3039/49, Section III, Sc. 98, Rm.f.R.u.Kp., Planungsamt, 'Statistische Schnell-berichte zur Kriegsproduktion'. Greater Germany included the Protectorate of Bohemia and Moravia, as well as Lorraine and Luxembourg.

threatened. The difference in steel prices for comparable products between those producers and the Lorraine manufacturers was too great for any compromise policy to be effective. Steel prices had been fixed in Germany on the assumption that variations in raw material costs to different producers were not too great. After June 1940 a much wider gap opened between the relative prices of pig-iron and scrap. Any solution which could embrace the whole of Greater Germany was difficult to find.[1]

German producers were in favour of drastically reducing the output of domestic iron-ore mines. Their fear was that unless Germany took full advantage of the new supply opportunities her industry would be incapable of competition once the war was over.[2] If the price gap between pig-iron and scrap was to be closed a uniform price for iron ore had to be established.[3] To do this meant, in effect, to admit that a considerable part of the investment under the Four Year Plan had had only very limited short-term aims. Consequently, in December 1940, there were further attempts at compromise by allowing the Hermann Göring Werke, constructed for the express purpose of using the Salzgitter ores, to take financial and administrative control of the more efficient de Wendel plant in Lorraine.[4] At this stage of the war the political and economic implications of the Four Year Plan were regarded by the Ministry of Economics as more important than maximum efficiency in production. The aim of post-war policy would be to make German iron production independent of foreign scrap and to lower production costs by improved methods of using low-grade German ores.

The war years were to reveal the essential shallowness of this view. German steel manufacturers were as conscious of the price problems as of the government's political aims. As far as the German war economy was concerned the Hermann Göring Werke proved a white elephant. In 1942 output of iron ore in the area of pre-1938 Germany decreased. It did so in the first war-time year in which large increases in steel production were recorded. In March 1942 the decision was taken to abandon the Dogger iron-ore mines in Baden.[5]

The continued availability of Swedish ore, the difficulties of accommodating a greater supply of minette ore within the National Socialist economy, and the strategic conceptions of the war which prevailed, meant that German demands on French iron ore were easily satisfied in the early stages of the war. With such a ruthless imposition of German control it was not too difficult to acquire the necessary quota. Plans to increase French output above the prewar level did not exist at first. This attitude initiated a long period of slack

[1] BA., R 13 1/382, Rwm., 'Massnahmen zur Beseitigung des Wertunterschiedes zwischen ausländischen, deutschen Eisenerzen und Schrott', 18 November 1940.

[2] Ibid., Wirtschaftsgruppe Eisenschaffendes Industrie to Rwm., 25 November 1940.

[3] Ibid., Rwm., 'Niederschrift zur Frage des Eisenerzpreisausgleichs', 11 December 1940.

[4] Ibid., Rwm., Aktenvermerk über die am 10. Dezember 1940 mit Herrn Generalleutnant von Hanneken im Reichswirtschaftsministerium geführte Besprechung.

[5] FD 3353/45, Rm.f.B.u.M., 'Führerkonferenz', 19 March 1942.

working and low productivity in the mines lasting well into 1942. When the situation became more urgent these habits proved hard to eradicate.

The system of control imposed on the French iron-ore mines was clumsily divided. It was based, like the 'comités de répartition', on the idea that a fixed percentage of total output would be diverted to Germany. In 1943, when the problems were difficult ones, the system proved an obstacle. Even in 1940 it prevented any satisfactory over-all planning of French iron-ore supply. The appointment of the Commissar-General for the minette area was typical of the *ad hoc* administrative arrangements of the Blitzkrieg stage of the war economy. The purpose of the appointment was described by the Four Year Plan Office on 5 July 1940: 'The task of the office so created would be to adjust the iron-ore mines of Luxembourg and Lorraine to the demands of the direction of the war in Germany, and to do so without paying any heed to contingent vested interests, due to financial relationships or to those of earlier owners.'[1] A similar task was carried out in Anjou and Normandy by mining-assessor Corell, appointed by the Military Command on 30 July.[2]

In July 1940 only seven mines in the minette area were still in production In Anjou about half of the miners had disappeared. In western France there were also severe transport problems caused by the war. The harbours at Caen and Nantes were still unusable in 1940.[3] There was a shortage of railway wagons. Sabotage was rife in the western mines. By December, however, in Lorraine 100 mines were in production and in western France monthly production was showing an upward trend.

Once these early difficulties had been overcome there was little change. Efficiency was not demanded by circumstances. The awkward administrative divisions did not prove awkward until, in November 1942, the programme to increase the output of minette ore began. The production increases required both a larger labour force and a greater volume of capital investment. There was no mechanism by which the controlling organs in Metz could carry out such a programme, as Hermann Röchling complained to the military administration.[4] In essence the Metz Office was a distributive organization. Demands for materials, clothing, shoes, and other things had to be forwarded to the military administration, who incorporated these demands in their over-all allocation of contracts in France. The Commissar-General, infuriated by the delay in fulfilling such contracts, began in autumn 1943 to negotiate contracts directly with the French Ministry of Production. The delay was just as long, of

---

[1] FD 774/45, Mbh. in F., Wi.Abt., 'Kurzer Überblick über die Organisation des General-beauftragten für die Eisenerzgewinnung und -Verteilung für die Gebiete Luxemburg und Lothringen im Hinblick auf seine wirtschaftlichen Funktionen'.

[2] BA., R 7 VIII 207, Mbh. in F. to Rwm., 30 July 1940.

[3] Ibid., Mbh. in F., Wi.Abt. II/a, 'Vorbericht des Bergassessors Corell über die Eisenerz-gruben in der Bretagne und Normandie', 19 August 1940.

[4] FD 256/45, Mbh. in F., Wi.Abt., 'Die Gefährdung der Eisenerzförderung in Meurthe-et-Moselle durch eine unzureichende Grubenversorgung', 17 January 1944.

course, as the Ministry submitted all demands to the 'comité d'organisation' for the iron-ore industry. In this case the 'comité d'organisation' was particularly obstructive, since it was a reconstruction of the pre-war ironmasters' trust, that same vested interest which the Commissar-General had been appointed to override. Their usual tactic, when they received such demands from the Ministry of Production, was to write back to the Commissar-General asking him to specify the exact purpose of each requirement.

In early 1944 Röchling attempted to unify the administration of the French iron-ore mines under his own control. The occasion of his attempt was the situation which had evolved in northern France where Thomas raw iron was having to be fed into Siemens Martin furnaces.[1] He wished to attempt a crash production programme in the Pyrenean mines and to draft labour into min-ette mines to the point where a 30 per cent production increase would become possible there. The Metz office was, however, unable to get sufficient building materials to build barracks for the 6,000 prisoners of war whom Röchling wished to use.[2] The military administration had a much better view of the over-all problems of the economy than the Commissar-General. Merely to take labour from other industries to obtain a greater output of iron ore would defeat its own ends. The shortage of labour in the Pyrenean mines, which the military administration held to be the chief cause of the low output there, was mainly to be blamed on the indiscriminate policies of Sauckel.[3]

Procuring the necessary supplies of clothing, wood, and explosives for the mines was a complicated administrative affair. All demands had to be vetted in Paris before being turned over to the Ministry of Production. The intervention of the administration of the Commissar-General in Metz only introduced one more administrative complexity. Frequently local military commanders refused to release explosive to the mines once the demand had been verified.[4] Their fears that it would pass into the hands of the resistance seem to have been only too often justified. The Commissar-General himself took over the problem of wood supply in spring 1942 so that the mine owners could no longer use it as an excuse. The result was that in four months the *Liefergemeinschaft* delivered only 200 of the necessary 20,000 cubic metres of wood.[5] As a consequence the supply of wood was once again turned over to the 'comité d'organisation'. But, as in the coal-mines, the shortage of wood was not the fault of administrative inefficiency. On 30 June 1943 the military administration had to redraw the priority classifications for wood to cope with the shortage, and, since iron-ore mines could not receive one of the higher

[1] FD 256/45, Mbh. in F., Wi.Abt. II/a, Röchling to Röver, 2 February 1944.
[2] FD 307/45, Mbh. in F., Wi.Abt. II/a, 'Vermerk über die Besprechung mit dem General-beauftragten für die Eisenerzgewinnung und-Verteilung', 10 February 1944.
[3] FD 256/45, Mbh. in F., Wi.Abt. II/a, Röver to Röchling, 26 January 1944.
[4] Ibid., Complaints from the Société française des mines de fer, 10, 14, 26 July 1943, etc.
[5] FD 256/45, Mbh. in F., Comité d'organisation de l'industrie des minerais de fer to Wi.Abt. II/a, 6 August 1943.

priorities, it became almost certain that there would be insufficient supply to them, whoever was in charge of distribution. The mine owners themselves, who had been left much less independence in the running of their own firms than the coal-mine owners, let slip few opportunities for righteous indignation, and because of the clumsiness of the system such opportunities were plentiful.[1]

As in other sectors of French production acute transport difficulties were superimposed on the problems of supply. In February 1943 the increased output of iron ore in western France was not translated into larger deliveries because of the shortage of railway locomotives.[2] By November, Sunday working in the Lorraine mines was no longer regularly enforced because there was insufficient transport capacity.[3] The intensification of Allied bombing of transport installations prevented any relief until 1944. The bad weather of early spring 1944 and the changes in Allied bombing policy afforded some relief. It was only of a temporary nature, and before the invasion of France bombing attacks were switched with even greater intensity to road and railway targets in France.

While it is true that the administrative system made the solution of problems of this kind more difficult, and while it is also true that the Commissar-General's staff did not see eye to eye with the officials in the Hotel Majestic on the principles of German economic policy in France, to blame the relative failure of German policy after 1942 on these administrative quarrels would be short-sighted. The primary cause of the production difficulties, as in the coal-mines, lay deeper in French society. Labour productivity fell sharply at the very time when it was most important to the German administration that it should rise.

It will be seen from Fig. 5 that the productivity of the total labourforce (it is impossible to be more specific) in French iron-ore mines stopped increasing after October 1941. Until May 1941 labour productivity was higher in the annexed areas than in the occupied areas. Thenceforward, until the end of 1942, it was normally slightly higher in the occupied areas. Employment in the whole of the minette basin was rather lower until the end of 1942 than it had been before the war; in western France, where the ore was of greater value to Germany, employment tended to be higher than pre-war levels. The

---

[1] 'A German officer came to the mine to get information about deliveries, saying that, when the wagons were placed at the disposal of the mine, the mine must first deliver to Krupp. This instruction is the complete opposite of what was decided by the administrative services in Paris, who gave priority to deliveries to Ymuiden. The mine would like to know exactly on which authority they depend from the point of view of control. At every moment they receive visits from people in the local administration, who seem in no way empowered to make inspections of this kind.' FD 256/45, Mbh. in F., Wi.Abt. II/a, Chambre syndicale des mines de fer de l'ouest de la France to Wi.Abt. II/a, 10 March 1941. The mine is the Mine de la Brutz.

[2] FD 256/45, Mbh. in F., Wi. Abt. II/a, Letter to Röchling, 20 March 1943.

[3] Ibid., Letter from Röchling, 25 November 1943.

average productivity of the whole of the minette area in 1941 settled, like the level of employment, on a lower level, and there was little change until the end of 1942.

Before the war the Lorraine mines had depended to an extraordinary degree on immigrant labour, mainly from Poland and Italy. In 1938 French workers were in a minority in the iron-ore mines there. The events of the war, when the

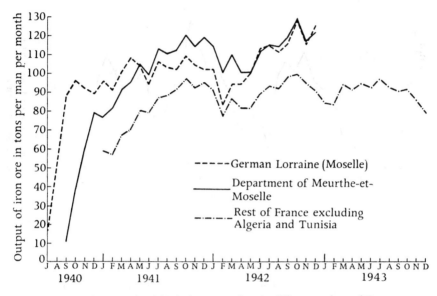

FIG. 5. Labour productivity in iron ore mines in different regions of France.

(FD 282/45, Mbh. in F., Wi. Abt. II/a, Secrétariat Général de l'énergie, Direction des Mines, 'Production de minérai de fer'. FD 4711/45, Bezirksgruppe Südwest der Wirtschaftsgruppe der Eisenschaffende Industrie, 'Erzbergbau, Belegschaftsstand der Erzgruben'.)

mines were in the front line of battle, led to a great exodus of workmen to unoccupied France. Even in December 1940 the labour force was still less than half its pre-war strength. The majority of the workmen taken on between July and December were refugees returning from unoccupied France.[1] This source of supply dried up in 1941. At the end of 1941 the labour force in German Lorraine was 79 per cent of the 1937 total, but over the border in the department of Meurthe-et-Moselle it was only 62 per cent.[1] Wages in Meurthe-et-Moselle had to be set at an artificially low level, consequently they were too low to attract foreign workers into the mines in the same quantities as before the war. Arrangements had been made with the Franco government for a

[1] BA., R. 13 I/1133, Wirtschaftsgruppe Eisenschaffende Industrie, 'Jahresbericht des Generalbeauftragten für die Eisenerzgewinnung und-Verteilung für die Gebiete Luxemburg und Lothringen für das Jahr 1941'.

total of 2,000 Spanish miners to be employed in Moselle, of whom the first 500 began working in December 1941. For Meurthe-et-Moselle the only solution seemed to be to employ prisoners of war. Such a solution was unlikely to raise productivity.

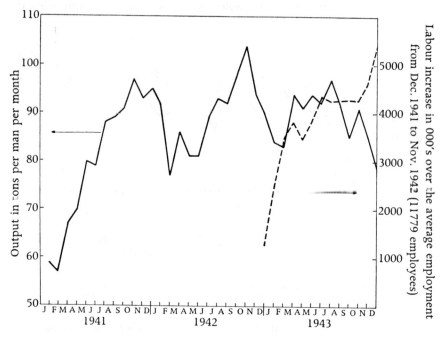

FIG. 6. Output per man in iron-ore mines in France (including North Africa) from January 1941 to December 1943 and increases in employment after November 1942 over the average employment of the preceding twelve months.

When it became essential to increase output in 1943, not only had them been a long period of relatively low output per man but the labour problere had become much harder to solve. The only way was to draft greater quantities of labour into the mines. The labour so drafted was inferior and often hostile. In March 1943 skilled workmen required for work in Germany were requisitioned and replaced by a quota of Jewish workers. Nevertheless, the quality of the original labour force was maintained by the nomination of the mines as 'S-Betriebe'. Only those workmen liable for service under the compulsory service laws were liable to be requisitioned. The problem was more one of desertion by the labour force than of requisitioning for deportation to Germany. On 27 March 1943 legislation had to be passed to block the loophole whereby 'quarry' as opposed to 'mine' workers had been able to break their contract.[1] The great growth of employment in French iron-ore mines after November 1942 coincided with the beginning of a falling trend in labour productivity which was to prove ineradicable in 1943.

In early 1943 the military administration made strenuous efforts to bring about productivity increases, and were temporarily successful. In April, however, the absenteeism rate varied from 18 per cent to 30 per cent from mine to mine.[2] Voluntary holiday working was regarded as a joke by the workers. A policy of paying attendance premiums proved ineffective. Only a very small minority of the work-force responded to such incentives. Nor was harsh discipline effective. Certificates of unfitness were easily obtained from the French doctors, who themselves ignored threats of punishment.[3] In peak periods of seasonal agricultural work the rate of issue of sickness certificates rose sharply, as did absenteeism without any certificate.[4] Attempts to punish slackness by ration restrictions had limited effects, since the ration was already too low for the miners to work properly and they were allowed no extra tobacco ration.

The regime in Lorraine was more draconian than in Anjou and Brittany. The Commissar-General imposed both compulsory Sunday and holiday working. In spite of this, absenteeism was almost as evident as in the western mines. The general level of absenteeism in August 1943 in Lorraine was 16 per cent.[5] The result of the compulsory Sunday working was higher absenteeism rates on Monday. The ferocity with which the administration in Metz tackled these problems, however, did not abate. The Italian prisoners of war drafted into the mines of Meurthe-et-Moselle in October 1943 were subject to regulations of the most terrifying severity. But the attitude taken to the French workers was no less severe. 'Commercial-counsellor Röchling vigorously emphasized that absolute clarity must prevail in the minds of all those Frenchmen engaged in the supervision of transport installations that in the event of any dealings with the enemy they would be punished, without mercy, by death.'[6]

The most rigorous application of such ideas could not compensate for the deteriorating quality of the labour force. In March 1944, output per man-hour rose.[7] In April it fell below the level of February; the fall was attributed

[1] FD 256/45, Mbh. in F., Comité d'organisation de l'industrie de minerai de fer to Wi.Abt. II/a, 12 April 1943.

[2] Ibid., Wi.Abt. II/a, Der Beauftragte für den westfranzösischen Eisenerzbergbau to Röver, 18 May 1943.

[3] Ibid., 'Konferenz', 31 May 1943.

[4] Ibid., Der Beauftragte für den westfranzösischen Eisenerzbergbau, 'Monatsbericht', 16 July 1943.

[5] Ibid., Generalbevollmächtigter für die Eisenerzgewinnung, 'Monatsbericht', August 1943.

[6] Ibid., Mbh. in F., Wi.Abt. II/a, 'Sitzungen mit den Stellv. Kommissaren der Hüttenindustrie in Meurthe-et-Moselle', 11 October 1943.

[7] Ibid., Generalbevollmächtigter für die Eisenerzgewinnung, 'Monatsbericht', March 1944.

to the employment of more prisoners of war.[1] The miners were badly treated, undernourished, overworked, ill-shod, ill-clad, and ill-equipped. It was on such foundations that the edifice of the Speer–Bichelonne agreements had been built.

[1] FD 256/45, Generalbevollmächtigter für die Eisenerzgewinnung, 'Monatsbericht', April 1944.

IX

BAUXITE AND ALUMINIUM

ALMOST the whole of the aluminium manufactured during the war was obtained from one mineral, bauxite, the hydrated oxide of aluminium. Between 1934 and 1938 Germany produced over a quarter of the world's total output of aluminium. Although the greatest producer and consumer of aluminium in the world her domestic output of bauxite was less than 1 per cent of the world's total output.[1] To sustain her enormous increase in aluminium production Germany was therefore almost wholly dependent on the two greatest producers of bauxite in the world over that period, France and Hungary.

The great increase in the manufacture of aluminium in the years before the war was due in no small degree to its value for the armaments industry. In particular the lightness of its alloys caused them to be used more and more for aircraft construction. The expansion of bauxite mining in Hungary, and its recovery from the slump in France, were closely connected with the resurgence of German air power. For France, the second greatest aluminium producer in the world on the eve of the First World War, produced only a quarter as much as Germany on the eve of the Second World War.

The French bauxite deposits were all in southern France. They stretched in an arc from the Spanish frontier to Toulon, but the area most exploited was at Brignoles in the department of Var, an area which passed under Italian occupation. The other major area of mining was in the department of Hérault, but output there in 1938 was less than one-fifth that in the department of Var. Germany could thus only obtain supplies of bauxite at first by bargaining with the Vichy government. Exports of bauxite to Germany had fallen in 1939 to 52,290 tons, owing to an export ban introduced in that year by the French government, but the normal level of German purchases was so high that she was in a very strong bargaining position once the British market had been closed to French exports.

The possibility of securing greater control over a material so vital to German military production was considered immediately after the defeat of France. On 23 July 1940 Göring, as head both of the Four Year Plan Organization and of the Luftwaffe, ordered an inquiry into the way the production potential of aluminium in Germany could be increased by control of the newly conquered territories.[2] The first German negotiator, Dr. Westrick, was managing director of the Vereinigte Aluminiumwerke, the largest German aluminium

---

[1] W. R. Jones, *Minerals in Industry* (London, 1945), p. 32.
[2] FD 288/45, Generalluftzeugmeister, letter to Generaldirektor Koppenberg, 23 July 1940.

TABLE 44

Output of Aluminium in France and Germany*

(tons)

	1913	1929	1937	1938
France	13,500	29,100	34,500	45,300
Germany	1,000	33,300	127,500	165,000

* FD 1808/44, Reichsamt für wehrwirtschaftliche Planung, 'Beiträge zur Wehrwirtschafts-struktur Frankreichs', A. Sauvy *Histoire économique de la France entre les deux guerres.*

TABLE 45

Output of Bauxite in France and Hungary*

(tons)

	France	Exports	Hungary	Exports
1929	666,300	240,400	389,152	100,550
1933	490,500	245,000	72,425	58,779
1934	528,400	282,352	184,991	106,190
1935	512,800	282,200	211,079	227,578
1936	648,000	304,000	329,091	341,649
1937	690,900	301,700	532,652	479,721
1938	683,400	292,240	540,315	362,410
1939	708,510	330,590	500,190	574,090

* FD 288/45, Mbh. in F., Wi. II/a, 'Bauxit, Förderung und Lieferung'. T. I. Berend and G. Ránki, *Magyarország Gyáripara a Második Világháború Elött és a háború Idöszakában (1933–1944)*, (Budapest, 1958), p. 163.

TABLE 46

Direction of French Bauxite Exports*

(tons)

	1929	1934	1935	1936	1937	1938
To Germany	54,300	96,500	78,300	79,400	87,500	84,100
To Britain	67,400	108,900	133,200	150,500	180,100	188,000

* FD 1808/44, Reichsamt für wehrwirtschaftliche Planung, 'Beiträge zur wehrhwirtschafts-struktur Frankreichs'.

manufacturers. His first visit to France preceded Göring's orders by twelve days. When the Committee system was extended into France by Speer, Westrick, as Head of the Special Ring for Light Metals, retained his ultimate responsibility for the placing of demands on France. The change in his formal position reflected the greater complexity of German policy in France. He was at first little more than a private industrialist negotiating for a return to pre-war conditions, and the French industrialists seem to have been more willing than their government to meet his wishes.[1] It was the French government which was mainly responsible for the delay in resuming exports; it did not issue a licence until 19 December 1940.

The first contract for bauxite exports to Germany was for a grand total of 250,000 tons. The second contract stipulated that between July 1942 and June 1943 France would deliver 500,000 tons. Such a quantity was perfectly feasible if French aluminium production were kept at a very low level. In the early stages of the war this was precisely Germany's intention, but by summer 1942 the situation was not so simple. To maintain French aluminium production at the level it had then reached and also to export the higher quantities to Germany would require a monthly average bauxite production of 94,000 tons.[2] The possibility of reducing French aluminium production was small, since 60 per cent of output either went to Germany or was used for German purposes in Switzerland. In fact, for the first six months of 1942 the monthly production of bauxite in France had been substantially below the average level for 1938.

The German response to French objections was to increase their demands to 800,000 tons of bauxite per year. It is clear that this estimate of French capacity was arrived at only in the vaguest way and had little basis in economic calculations. It was a compromise between what the German economic administration in France thought possible and what the German armed forces would have liked to demand. The demands of the latter went as high as 1,500,000 tons a year.[3] On 11 December 1942 France acceded to the new demands. By her agreement she was committed to a monthly production of bauxite of 120,800 tons, twice as high as production in any previous month, if she wished to maintain her aluminium production.

It will be seen that this level was never achieved. Nevertheless, French bauxite production began to increase in the late autumn of 1942, and in 1943 total output rose to 912,000 tons, 222,000 tons higher than the previous highest annual production. In 1943, 484,390 tons were exported to Germany, over twice the quantity of the previous year and over five times the level of exports in 1938. Only in March 1943, however, did the significant increase in exports begin; in February 1943 the volume of exports was less than in September and October 1941.[4]

Superficially Germany was much more successful in her exploitation of French bauxite mines than of coal or iron ore. French output increased by 30

---

[1] See pp. 87–8.
[2] FD 288/45, Comité d'organisation de l'aluminium et du magnésium, letter to Vereinigte Aluminiumwerke A. G., 4 June 1942.
[3] FD 288/45, Mbh. in F., Kriegsverwaltungschef, letter to Chef des Verwaltungstabes, 16 September 1942.
[4] FD 257/45, Mbh. in F., Wi.Abt. II/a, 'Lagebericht', 19 November 1941.

TABLE 47

Output of Bauxite in France and Exports to Germany*

(tons)

	Output	Exports to Germany
1938	683,400	92,000
1940	489,020	
1941	586,267	232,055
1942	644,153†	230,685
1943 Jan.	59,670	23,078
Feb.	56,821	25,722
Mar.	67,352	37,809
Apr.	71,858	43,223
May	79,561	54,022
June	79,398	52,653
July	86,794	48,228
Aug.	91,235	47,579
Sept.	80,537	42,627
Oct.	83,835	33,419
Nov.	80,469	31,304
Dec.	74,555	44,726
Total	912,085	484,390
1944 Jan.		36,059§
Feb.		34,811§
Mar.		48,817§
Apr.	95,000‡	64,241§
May		43,339§
June	86,425	12,955§
Total‖ (first 6 months)		240,222

* FD 288/45, Mbh. in F., Wi.Abt. II/a, 'Bauxit, Förderung und Lieferung'.
† This figure, given both in FD 287/45, Mbh. in F., Wi.Abt. II/a, 'Bauxit Förderung', 27 March 1944, and in FD 288/45, Mbh. in F., Wi.Abt. II/a, 'Bauxit Förderung 1942', 15 March 1944, has been preferred to that of 636,063 as given in the original table.
‡ FD 287/45, Mbh. in F., Wi.Abt. II/a, 'Aufstellung über monatliche Durchschnittsproduktion im Bergbau im Jahre 1938', 6 June 1944.
§ Milch Documents, vol. xlix, Letter from Beauftragte für den Vierjahresplan to Milch, 21 July 1944.
‖ Blanks indicate unknown totals.

per cent above its pre-war levels and her exports to Germany by over 500 per cent. In 1938 Germany had received 12 per cent of total French bauxite production. In 1941, if the bauxite used in France for the manufacture of alumina and aluminium to meet German contracts is added to the total exported as crude bauxite to Germany, Germany received 70 per cent of

French bauxite output in that year.[1] By 1942 the proportion had reached 80 per cent, about equally divided between the quantity exported crude and the quantity refined or manufactured.[2]

Nor, for that matter, was the German control of French bauxite mining particularly harmful to the industry. The quantity of bauxite estimated as the 'normal' demand of the French economy by the Reparations Commission allows for a considerable export surplus. In any case, since the demand for bauxite was so severely influenced by armament construction, the concept of a 'normal' demand is not too apt. The price paid for bauxite and aluminium was sufficient to guarantee some profit to the producer. There was a certain amount of German capital investment in the bauxite industry, especially towards the end of 1943 in an attempt to sustain output at the record level of August of that year.[3] The advantages of this capital investment could scarcely have compensated for the destruction of the mines at Maurienne in the German retreat.

TABLE 48

*Aluminium Production in France**

(tons)

	Production	Quantity taken by Germany
1940 (second 6 months)	30,376	15,374
1941	61,548	34,563
1942	44,285	17,509
1943	46,464	27,285
1944 (first 6 months)	16,765	8,840

* CCDR., v, M.P. 10.

What German policy did do, however, was to confirm an increasing tendency for pre-war France to become an exporter of raw materials. The stagnation of French industrial production in those years had not always been accompanied by a stagnation of raw materials production. Nowhere better than in the case of French bauxite and aluminium production can the curious colonial relationship towards other industrial powers which developed in the 1930s be seen. German wartime policy accentuated this colonial relationship. The corollary of German success in increasing French bauxite production is the decline in French aluminium production after 1941. The gap between the total French and German make which had opened in the 1930s became even

[1] FD 474/45, Mbh. in F., Wi.Abt. II/a, 'Ausnutzung der französischen Wirtschaft für Deutschland', 3 February 1942.

[2] FD 257/45, Mbh. in F., Wi.Abt. II/a, 'Lagebericht', 22 May 1942.

[3] FD 475/45, Ministère de la production industrielle et des communications, letter to Röver 27 December 1943.

wider, but the quantity of aluminium which Germany was able to obtain from France declined after 1941.

It should be said in mitigation of German policy that to increase the production of aluminium in France was peculiarly difficult because of the deficiencies of French capital investment in the previous decade. These deficiencies had already created a bottleneck in French aluminium production, the shortage of alumina-producing plant. There were only five such works in France.[1] This bottleneck persisted throughout the war and its consequence was that Germany was always driven to demand greater quantities of the raw material for herself rather than of the manufactured product.

This relationship ultimately proved almost as dangerous for Germany as for France. The contracts negotiated with the Hungarian government for the supply of bauxite supposed much larger supplies from there than from France, 1,500,000 tons between August 1943 and August 1944, and a greater quantity in the following year. Only in 1943 did Hungarian output rise over 1,000,000 tons for the first time. In December 1943 there were attempts to increase the

TABLE 49

German Imports of Bauxite, 1944*

(tons)

From	Jan.	Feb.	Mar.	Apr.	May	June
France	36,059	34,811	48,817	64,241	43,339	12,955
Hungary	27,501	11,163	40,208	70,532	101,728	109,793
Croatia	9,484	1,972	559	1,940	8,364	11,185

* Milch Documents, vol. xlix, Beauftragte für den Vierjahresplan to Milch, 21 July 1944.

supply of aluminium to the armaments industry by changing the pattern of allocation to consumers, and by developing bauxite mining in Austria.[2] Such remedies might have sufficed for the situation at that time, but in spring 1944, with the creation of the Fighter Staff, began the third of the great drives in German armaments production. In this instance the increase in armaments depended even more on bauxite supply. Bauxite exports from France to Germany reached their peak in April 1944, but in June they fell sharply. In the three months before the Fighter Staff was formed Germany had obtained more bauxite from France than from Hungary. The sharp drop in imports from France coincided with the biggest, and most vital, of all German efforts to increase aircraft production. The 'special actions' taken in Hungary and the Balkans to secure more bauxite were therefore a result of the changed situation in France, a desperate remedy for a desperate disease.

[1] FD 1808/44, Reichsamt für wehrwirtschaftliche Planung, 'Beiträge zur wehrwirtschaftsstruktur Frenkreichs'.
[2] FD 3353/45, Rm.f.B.u.Kp., 'Führerkonferenz', 6/7 December 1943.

The 'special actions' were successful in rapidly changing the main source of German bauxite supply. But dependence on Hungary to this much greater degree could not in fact compensate for the loss of French production. The development of production in Oberdonau in Austria could not realize significant quantities until spring 1945. Germany's available aluminium stocks were exhausted after the end of 1944, and from that time on the total consumption of aluminium depended directly on the stocks and the supply of bauxite. The stocks of bauxite in July 1944 were as high as 1,000,000 tons.[1] In spite of this ample reserve the loss of France would still mean a reduction of 25 per cent in German aircraft production in 1946 supposing Germany still retained Hungary and Croatia.[2]

The apparent success of German policy must therefore be looked at sceptically. Unlike coal and iron ore, bauxite was not vital to the general functioning of the economy; its output must be judged with respect to its importance for the aircraft industry. There can therefore be no meaningful comparison between peace-time and war-time demand. In addition the industry was not without the same problems that beset the coal- and iron-ore mining industries, acute transport difficulties and the hostility of the work-force causing a decline in the productivity of labour.

The transport problems, indeed, were more complicated in one sense than with the more widely consumed raw materials. The distances over which the bauxite had to be moved were very long and the station from which it was mainly moved was under Italian control for some time. In October 1943 the Italian troops tried to prevent German troops from organizing the dispatch of bauxite trains from Brignoles.[3] Basically the transport difficulty was two-fold, the destruction of railway track and equipment by Allied bombing and the confiscation of railway wagons by Germany in the early stages of the war and occupation. But the distance involved in the case of bauxite transports exaggerated these difficulties. Originally the bauxite formed a return cargo for coal trains from Germany to Italy. When this coal traffic disappeared it was difficult to justify the transport of empty wagons from Germany to Provence. The only similar haul in France was that of Pyrenean iron ore to French iron manufacturing centres. The quantities involved in this traffic were smaller than with the bauxite traffic, and in any case it was equally vital and the wagons could not be spared from it for bauxite transport.[4]

The higher output of bauxite which Germany did achieve in France was only obtained by a massive increase of the labour force in the industry. The delivery contract concluded at the end of 1942 stipulated the liberation of

[1] FD 3037/49, Section I, Sc. 72, Rm.f.R.u.Kp., Planungsamt, Letter to Speer, 31 July 1944.
[2] FD 3353/45, Rm.f.R.u.Kp., Letter from Speer to Hitler, 5 September 1944.
[3] FD 475/45, Mbh. in F., Wi.Abt. II/a, 'Bauxittransporte in Südfrankreich', 15 October 1943.
[4] FD 288/45, Mbh. in F., Verbindungsstab, Letter to Armeegruppe Felber, 28 November 1942.

about 900 French prisoners of war in Germany to help in the new production effort. A greater quantity of iron was allocated to the mining companies and the German delegation agreed to pay a bonus of sixteen francs on every ton over three-fifths of the output the French had agreed to provide.[1] On 16 December the French government was already pointing out that the number of prisoners released was not sufficient to solve the problem.[2] This was no mere bargaining point, especially as the demand from the military seems to have been to obtain deliveries of 1,500,000 tons a year from France.[3]

The higher output of 1943, 30 per cent higher than that of the pre-war years, was achieved with a labour force over three times greater than that of

TABLE 50

Rate of Output per Employee per month in French Bauxite Mines*

(tons)

	Average labour force per month	Output per employee
1939	1,337	44·2
1941	1,501	32·6
1942	2,325	23·2
1943 Jan.	2,273	26·2
Feb.	2,254	25·2
Mar.	2,423	27·8
Apr.	2,445	29·4
May	2,817	28·2
June	2,883	27·6
July	2,893	30·0
Aug.	3,078	29·6
Sept.	3,074	26·2
Oct.	3,197	26·2
Nov.	3,329	24·2
Dec.	3,679	20·3

* FD 288/45, Mbh. in F., Wi.Abt. II/a, 'Bauxit, Förderung und Lieferung', 16 September 1942.

the pre-war years. Part of this increase was an influx of Italian workers, and they in particular came to occupy key positions in the mines. At the close of 1943 their withdrawal meant a steadily falling rate of output per man. By July 1943 the rate of output per man had risen well above the low level of 1942, although not approaching by any means pre-war rates. Nevertheless, it looked as though the years of the Blitzkrieg might not have stamped an

[1] FD 288/45, DFCAA., Letter to Hemmen, 11 December 1942.
[2] FD 288/45, Ministère secrétaire d'état à la production industrielle et aux communications to Michel, 16 December 1942.
[3] FD 288/45, Mbh. in F., Kriegsverwaltungschef to Chef des Verwaltungsstabes, 'Produktionsvermehrung', 16 September 1942.

irrevocable pattern on the industry. After July 1943 output per man fell continuously until the end of the year.

Although, therefore, the average level of labour productivity in 1943 was higher than in 1942 this was a temporary achievement only. The continued increase in the labour force in that year was tending, eventually, to reduce the productivity of labour. By the end of the year the level of productivity had again dropped to about half its pre-war level, while the labour force was almost three times as great. Germany thus paid very dearly for her success in increasing French bauxite output, and the payment exacted was of the same kind as in the coal- and iron-ore mining industries.

X

WOLFRAM

WOLFRAM provides a curious example of a commodity, the consumption of which in the world was very small, the output of which in France was extremely small, a commodity scarcely noticeable, either by its weight or its value, in the wartime commerce between France and Germany, a commodity occupying only ten pages in the nine volumes of the report of the French Reparations Commission, and yet of crucial importance to the functioning of the German war economy.

Its great importance stemmed from the fact it was one of the two minerals from which tungsten was chiefly obtained. In Europe it was to all intents and purposes the sole source of tungsten. Tungsten was used as an alloy with steel to produce high-speed cutting tools for shaping armaments steel. Cutting machines using tungsten steel could be run at five times the speed of those using carbon steel and could cut more deeply. Jobs taking hours with carbon steel took minutes with tungsten steel. Tungsten alloy steels were also used in the manufacture of armour-piercing shells and armour plate. Cutting tools with tungsten carbide tips were even more effective than tungsten alloys and their durability greater. Both wolfram and tungsten were therefore of quite singular importance in the war economies of the combatants.

The bulk of the world's supply of tungsten-bearing minerals came from China and Burma. In 1938 they produced between them 24,200 tons of tungsten concentrates out of the total world output of 36,000 tons. Only one supplier of any importance was in Europe, Portugal, who in that year produced 2,800 tons. Almost half the Portuguese production came from one mine, the Panasqueira mine in Beira Baixa. There was a very small output in Spain, and it was on these two sources that Germany had primarily to depend for this raw material of immense strategic importance. It was not found at all within the frontiers of pre-war Germany, and metallurgists were much less successful in producing substitutes for it than they were with nickel or cobalt, both of which were equally rare in Germany.

The scarcity of wolfram in the area controlled by Germany gave rise to one of the chief hopes of the Ministry of Economic Warfare. The production of armaments over any length of time without supplies of tungsten was thought to be impossible. But so small were the quantities of tungsten needed in alloying processes that adequate stockpiles could cover the deficiencies in German supply for several years. The German economy had been organized to deal with this problem by the accumulation of huge stockpiles of non-ferrous metals of strategic importance. In every year of the war until 1944 German consumption of wolfram was higher than supply. Stocks at the outbreak of war were sufficient to cover almost four years' consumption.

TABLE 51

The Consumption and Supply of Wolfram in Germany*

(thousands of tons metal content)†

	1938	1939	1940	1941	1942	1943	1944
Supply	7·9	..	0·9	1·0	1·9	1·8	1·5
Consumption	4·3	..	3·7	3·4	3·0	2·2	1·5
Stocks							
(at end of year)	5·5‡	5·0	3·1	2·7	1·6	1·5	1·3

* USSBS., The Effects of Strategic Bombing on the German War Economy, Appendix 83.

† Tungsten-bearing minerals such as wolfram or scheelite contain, on an average, 60 per cent of tungstic oxide, WO_3.

‡ Stocks in September 1939.

The contribution which France could make to the total German supply of wolfram was a very small one. The mine at Leucamp, in the department of Cantal, had begun production in 1912 and had been established as a producer by the price increases during the First World War.[1] On the eve of the Second World War its production again increased but in 1938 its total output was only twenty-one tons (metal content).[2] The sudden strategic importance of the mineral led the French government to reopen mining activities in 1935 at Puy les Vignes, in the Massif Central near to St. Léonard de Noblat, to try to increase their domestic resources.[3] There was one other mine which was known to contain considerable reserves of wolfram, that of Montbelleux, near to Fougères, in the department of Ille-et-Vilaine, the only adequate source of supply in the occupied zone. Some other small mines from time to time produced tiny quantities of wolfram, usually as a by-product of their principal operations. This was the case, for example, with the mines of Vautry and Cieux in the department of Haute Vienne.[4] The Montmins mine in the department of Allier, near to the town of Vichy, was thought by the Germans to be capable of much greater development; so also were the deposits at

[1] FD 3045/49, Section IX, Sc. 292, Rm.f.R.u.Kp., Planungsamt, 'Überblick über die Wolframvorkommen in Frankreich', 11 June 1944.

[2] FD 1808/44, Reichsamt für wehrwirtschaftliche Planung, 'Beitrage . . .'.

[3] FD 1873/44, Mbh. in F., Wi.Abt. II/a, 'Bericht über die Befahrung der französischen Wolframerzvorkommen im zweiten Drittel des Monats April 1943 durch die Herren Dr. Einecke, Fischer u. Scheibe'.

[4] The position of these mines was curious, in so far as they were part of the combine Huta Bankowa, see above p. 99.

Montdelesse near to Limoges, in the department of Haute Vienne. On the eve of the war the French government itself had begun explorations in Château-Lambert in the Vosges mountains, just on the French side of what was to be the new frontier.

There existed, therefore, an apparently much greater potential supply of wolfram in France than in Germany. But its potentiality was uncertain and the cost of mining the product extremely high. Most of France's own consumption of wolfram before the war was met by imports, although her imports were only one-quarter those of Germany.[1] If the Blitzkrieg were to be successful Germany would not need French wolfram supplies. When it was not successful Germany still did not need French supply, provided supply from Portugal continued to arrive. When the supply from Portugal was endangered French wolfram mines, small concerns scattered in remote areas, ceased to be a matter of indifference to the German administration and became of central importance to the German economy.

The disposal of the annual Portuguese output of wolfram became the subject of constant diplomatic activity to the rival powers, especially as the Allies supposed Germany to be much shorter of wolfram than she actually was. The extent to which either side could exert pressure on Portugal was roughly a reflection of what the Portuguese government thought about the eventual outcome of the war. In the early stages of the war it proved quite easy for Germany to satisfy her needs, but her position in Lisbon deteriorated sharply just at the moment when her domestic stockpiles first approached danger levels. The price which the British government was obliged to pay for the purchase or pre-emption of wolfram in Spain was a sensitive indicator of the course of the war. It rose from £675 a ton in February 1941 to £7,500 a ton half way through 1943; thereafter it fell.[2] Germany, of course, was not affected by the falling prices. Finally, in June 1944, the Portuguese government placed an embargo on the exports of wolfram to Germany.

Consequently in the first phase of the war more interest was shown in the French mines by German steel-manufacturing firms, anxious to integrate vertically with their raw material suppliers, than by the German government. As far as France was concerned this was only part of a much larger operation on a European scale. In 1940 Krupp secured control over the large Knaben molybdenum mine in Norway by an agreement with the Swedish firm which controlled it.[3] They pursued a systematic policy to gain control over the smaller Norwegian wolfram mines and non-ferrous ore mines elsewhere.[4] In

---

[1] CCDR., v. M.P. 1.   [2] W. N. Medlicott, op. cit., ii. 306, 560.

[3] FD 5148/45, File no. 6, Fachabteilung Ferrolegierungen, Stahl- und Leichtmetallveredler der Wirtschaftsgruppe Chemische Industrie, Agreement between Krupp and A. Johnson & Co., 17 September 1940. Seventy-five per cent of the output of the mine was to be delivered to Krupp.

[4] Ibid., Reichskommissar für die besetzten norwegischen Gebiete to Rwm., 17 November 1942.

France their interest seems at first to have settled on the Montmins mine, which, in spite of its tiny output, was thought to have considerable potential. Between November 1941 and January 1942 there was a battle for control of the mine between Krupp and I. G. Farben. I. G. Farben, acting through an intermediary, Bankhaus Worms, finally secured a majority of the shares.[1] Between May and July 1942 I. G. Farben also secured the control of the mine at Château-Lambert.[2]

These activities were quite in keeping with the activities of German firms elsewhere in occupied Europe; they had no impact on the level of wolfram output in France. In any case, since such small quantities of metal were involved, the seizure of stockpiles in occupied territory was more responsible for maintaining German supply than the actual output of ore in those territories. Seizures of stockpiles took place on four occasions in France in 1940 and 1941 and were later covered by payment.[3] On two other occasions there were larger 'requisitions'. The level of wolfram stocks in France reached its peak in June 1942, having been allowed to increase fairly steadily since 1941. Within the space of two months it was reduced from a level almost twenty times that of the monthly output to a level roughly equivalent to one month's output alone.[4]

This large depletion of French stocks marks the beginnings of German anxieties about their own wolfram supply. Once the stocks had been raided so comprehensively it was not long before the first serious attempts were made to increase the output of wolfram in France. On 10 August 1942 Speer reported to the Führer that the Montbelleux wolfram mine had been enlarged.[5] The enlargement of this mine was the beginning of a tentative capital investment programme in the French mines which was to gather momentum as Germany's situation deteriorated, and to rise to a last frenzied effort at exploitation after the Portuguese embargo.

The difficulty in increasing the output of wolfram in France was mainly the geological one, for the production base was very narrow. For Germany it was both a question of reopening mines which had fallen into disuse and attempting to mine deposits previously ignored. For both these policies there was ample economic justification; it was not only in occupied Europe that long-neglected mines of non-ferrous metal ores were reopened during the war.[6] The spiralling prices paid in the Iberian peninsula were bound to have their effect in France, whatever the controls imposed, especially as the main

[1] Ibid., I. G. Farben to Rwm., 14 January 1942.
[2] Ibid., File 2, 'Molybdän Frankreich'.
[3] CCDR., v, M.P. 1.
[4] NA., T.71, Rolls 101, 102, 'Rohstoffübersichten', 603005 ff., 603397 ff., 603686 ff.
[5] FD 3353/45, Rm.f.B.u.M., 'Führerkonferenz', 10–12 August 1942.
[6] See J. Chardonnet, *Les Conséquences économiques de la guerre 1939–1946* (Paris, 1947).

trade route lay through France, and often through the Paris black market.[1] In the German situation of 1943, however, the justification for such a capital investment programme was rather different.

In February 1943 the French government was trying to get miners in non-ferrous metal mines exempted from the labour draft.[2] This was an indication of the increasing interest of the German government. In autumn 1943 all former workers at Puay les Vignes and Château-Lambert were released from captivity in Germany unless they were already employed there as miners.[3] When the explorations at the Montbelleux mine proved successful, 415 hewers, previously at work in the eastern occupied territories, were released from their work there and drafted to Montbelleux.[4] It could be said that these labour increases were probably symptomatic of the labour crisis which was developing throughout France, even in so small an industry German policy was being forced into the same *impasse* as in the larger industries. But the total labour force employed in wolfram mines was very small. At the peak of activity, in April 1944, the number employed at the three mines of Leucamp, Puy les Vignes, and Montbelleux was only 665, 405 of whom were employed at Montbelleux.[5]

An extensive survey of the future mining possibilities in France was carried out in April.[6] Its conclusions were generally optimistic, although they resulted in the abandonment of German pressure on the French government to extend the mines at Vaulry and Cieux, since their production was mainly tin ore. The further explorations at Montbelleux had, however, revealed greater deposits. This mine, and that of Puy les Vignes, were thought capable of bringing about a 150 per cent increase in French wolfram output.[7] These plans, which in the light of subsequent events were not unrealistic, were replaced by the report of a further survey in September. As a result of that survey it was decided to increase French output of tungstic oxide (WO_3) from the level of 6 tons a month which it had then reached to 45 tons a month. There were widespread feelings in the German mining administration that, in spite of their own frequent surveys of French resources, the French government was withholding information from them on the extent of its ore deposits.

---

[1] Although not the only trade route. At one time in 1940 5 tons of wolfram were being carried in some German airline flights from Spain to Italy, W. N. Medlicott, op. cit., ii. 513. Hitler returned to this idea in August 1943. The level of imports from Portugal was about 70 tons a month until that time. Special transport planes would therefore have had to be used. FD 3353/45, Rm.f.B.u.M., 'Führerkonferenz', 5 August 1943. Transport of wolfram had to be carried out by road in 1944 owing to damage to the French railways. FD 3045/49, Section IX, 146, 'Europakreis', Protokoll Nr. 5, 27 June 1944.

[2] FD 287/45, Mbh. in F., Wi.Abt. II/a, Letter from Ministère de la production industrielle et des communications to Röver, 11 February 1943.

[3] FD 258/45, Mbh. in F., Wi.Abt. II/a, Referat Metallerzbergbau-Steine und Erden, 'Lagebericht für das 4. Vierteljahr 1943'.

[4] Ibid., 'Lagebericht für das 1. Vierteljahr 1944'.

[5] FD 287/45, Mbh. in F., Wi.Abt. II/a, 'Übersicht über die Metallerzgruben', April 1944.

[6] FD 1873/44, Mbh. in F., Wi. II/a, 'Bericht über die Befahrung der französischen Wolframerzvorkommen . . .'.   [7] Ibid., Letter to Wi.Abt. VI, 3 June 1943.

In this belief they were encouraged by a variety of informers, varying from industrialists unable to obtain an adequate supply of tungsten, to amateur geologists drawing their attention to nineteenth-century mines.[1]

Even if only the less ambitious of the two plans were to succeed, some increase in the price paid to French wolfram producers was essential. It had fallen by 1943 well below the current level in any market. The official price paid by Germany was approximately four francs a gramme, the black-market price for wolfram carbide in Paris was thirty-six francs a gramme.[1] In these circumstances more and more German purchases had to be made on the black market, which dealt also in ore mislaid on its journey from Spain to Portugal. But the price of wolfram rose so steeply that no increase in the price offered to the French government was likely to close the gap significantly between the official and the black-market prices. German purchases on the black market had to be made with extreme discretion, since they put up the official price of wolfram in Spain and Portugal and reduced the quantity legally on offer in those countries.[2] The policy of buying on the Paris black market had begun in April 1943 on the orders of Göring, and one of the secret black-market purchasing organizations, 'Organisation Otto', had been put in charge. This body's actions were controlled by a special 'Wolfram-Staff' in 1944, but only in order to mop up all available illicit supplies in France. There were even attempts to bribe Spanish customs officials to allow the passage of smuggled wolfram.[3]

The capital investment plan in France could not bring immediate results. It was accompanied by strenuous efforts to increase German imports from Spain and Portugal, and by some capital investment in German mines in Spain.[4] Nevertheless, the output of tungsten in France did increase in 1943. It rose from a monthly average of 23·6 tons in the first quarter of that year to one of 32 tons in the second quarter.[5] But this increase was based on an increase in wolfram production which was very slight, so slight as to be scarcely discernible, and not of long duration.

The transport problems which beset other raw material producing industries did not spare the wolfram mines. 'The transport emergency has meanwhile so deepened that even the supply of relatively limited quantities of explosives to the mines presents difficulties. Often the raw materials which have been produced cannot be carried away while the consumers are at a

[1] Ibid., 'Meldung Nr. 345, Erzeugung von chemisch reinem Wolfram-Metall im unbesetzten Frankreich', 26 August 1942, and many similar letters.
[2] FD 2633/44, Mbh. in F., Wi. II/a, 'Wolframaufkäufe inFrankreich', 1 August 1944.
[3] Ibid., 13 July 1944.
[4] FD 5148/45, File no. 6, Fachabteilung Ferrolegierungen, Stahl- und Leichtmetallveredler der Wi.Gruppe chemische Industrie, Letter from Rwm. to Reichsstelle für Eisen und Metalle, 31 August 1943.
[5] FD 258/45, Mbh. in F., Wi.Abt. II/a, 'Compte-rendu du comité d'organisation des minerais et métaux bruts', July 1943.

TABLE 52

Output of Wolfram in France*

(tons metal content, WO_3)

	Output	
	Wi.Abt. II/a*	Rohstoff-übersichten†
1941 Jan.		..
Feb.		(12)†
Mar.		(10)†
Apr.		(6)†
May		(11)†
June		..
July		..
Aug.		..
Sept.		..
Oct.		..
Nov.		10
Dec.		5
Monthly average	4·8	
1942 Jan.		6
Feb.		6
Mar.		5
Apr.		6
May		5
June		6
July		6
Aug.		5
Sept.		5
Oct.		5
Nov.		8
Dec.		11
Monthly average	4·8	6·2
1943 Jan.	4·5	..
Feb.	4·6	4·2
Mar.	6·7	6·7
Apr.	7·3	7
May	8	..
June	6·3	..
July	7·3	..
Aug.	4·53§	4·4
Sept.	6·80§	6·5
Oct.	8·44§	6·0
Nov.	10·47§	
Dec.	8·17§	
Monthly average	6·9	**

TABLE 52 (*cont.*)

	Output	
	Wi.Abt. II/a*	Rohstoff-übersichten†
1944 Jan.	8·06§	
Feb.	3·8‖	
March	5‖	
April	7·6‖	
May		
June		
Monthly average	10·3‖	

* FD 287/45, Mbh. in F., Wi.Abt. II/a, 'Metallerzbergbau', 5 November 1943.
† NA., T.71, Rolls 101, 102, 603005 ff., 603397 ff., 603686 ff.
‡ Tons of concentrates, metal content not known.
§ FD 287/45, Mbh. in F., Wi.Abt. II/a, 'Übersichten'.
‖ FD 287/45, Mbh. in F., Wi.Abt. II/a, 'Übersicht über die Metallerzgruben.'
** Blanks indicate quantities unknown.

standstill for lack of raw materials.'[1] Once the invasion began the problem was more accute. In July 1944 there was neither fuel nor transport available at Puy les Vignes.[2]

In the case of wolfram mining, however, one difficulty, always present in other industries, was much more acute. So small were the mines and so great their strategic value that they were exposed to the constant danger of attacks from the French resistance movement. In the final stages of the occupation this became the principal reason for German failure to increase output when they were engaged in a hectic last attempt at exploitation.

In November 1943, as Germany's territorial possessions began to diminish and her diplomatic position to deteriorate, the Speer Ministry calculated that at the current rate of consumption Germany now had stocks of wolfram available for only between ten and eleven months.[3] Between February and April 1944 the Spanish government forbade the transport of Portuguese wolfram to Germany across its territory and granted no export permits for its own output.[4] In June Allied pressure forced them to send their available supply to Britain.[5] In that month the Portuguese embargo was declared.

Hitler's response was to order a still greater effort in France.

The Führer has been informed that in the neighbourhood of Vichy in France there are wolfram mines that are partially unexploited because they are not sufficiently

[1] FD 258/45, Mbh. in F., Wi.Abt. II/a, 'Referat Metallerzbergbau-Steine und Erden', 'Lagebericht für das 1. Vierteljahr 1944'.
[2] FD 2633/44, Rm.f.R.u.Kp., Beauftragte für Wolframerzbergwerke Puy les Vignes und Montdelesse to GbA für Wolfram, 29 July 1944.
[3] FD 3353/45, vol. 226, Rm.f.R.u.Kp., 'Die Legierungsmetalle in der Rüstung und die Bedeutung der Chromzufuhren aus dem Balkan und der Türkei', 12 November 1943.
[4] FD 3045/49, Section IX, Sc. 146, 'Europakreis', Protokoll Nr. 3, 5 July 1944.
[5] Ibid., Protokoll Nr. 5, 27 June 1944.

productive. The Führer has therefore ordered that a committee of experts embracing all the relevant internal German departments shall be set up and shall go immediately to France in order to determine on the spot whether individual disused mines should be extended or whether better results would be obtained from the extension of other French wolfram mines. Since wolfram—as we know—is of unprecedented importance for our war economy, the question of the economics of the French wolfram mines should be of no importance whatsoever. Labour would be in any case made available in unrestricted quantity.[1]

This was the origin of the Wolfram Staff, a body of such importance that for a brief spell during the campaign in France it was able to have some slight influence on the military commanders' tactics.

Soldiers were sent to work as miners in order to defend the Puy les Vignes mine against terrorist attacks.[2] The intention was to double the output of the mine at the same time. The mine had suffered two attacks by partisans, on 4 May and 12 May, which had seriously hampered production. Earlier attacks by the resistance movement on the Château-Lambert mine had been less successful, and were in any case less well directed, since until the Montbelleux mine really got into effective production Puy les Vignes remained the chief source of French wolfram.[3] It had been first attacked seriously on 13 March, followed by two more attacks in the space of four days.[4] The attacks had been highly successful, a large part of the equipment having been loaded into two lorries and driven away together with the supply of explosive. The two attacks in May prevented the mine from recouping its lost production. The desperate measure of drafting in soldiers as miners was ineffective. On 14 July the partisans actually took possession of the mine.[5] They were just in time to make use of the new canteen which the Wolfram Staff had installed there. The mine was only able to reopen at the expense of a constantly prepared military task force.

It was too late to achieve much with the smaller mines, although developments were continued strenuously at Montdelesse, and the Wolfram Staff even showed interest in a mine with only seven employees at Chatelus in the department of Haute Vienne.[6] The main hope, given the dangerous position at Puy les Vignes, had to be Montbelleux. In late 1943 that mine first began to produce concentrates in useful quantity.[7] In early 1944 it first replaced Puy les Vignes as the main source of supply. Unfortunately for the Germans it was

---

[1] FD 5148/45, File no. 6, Fachabteilung Ferrolegierungen, Stahl- und Leichtmetallveredler der Wi.Gruppe chemische Industrie, 'Aktennotiz über die Besprechung im Auswärtigen Amt am 5.6.1944 betreffend Wolfram Frankreich', June 1944.

[2] FD 2633/44, Mbh. in F., Wi. II/a, 'Einsatz von 40 Bergleuten als Sonderführer auf der Wolframgrube Puy les Vignes, Frankreich', 19 June 1944.

[3] FD 258/45, Mbh. in F., Wi. II/a, 'Lagerbericht für das 1. Vierteljahr 1944'.

[4] See *Maquis limousin, la dynamite des mines de Saint-Léonard* (Limoges, 1946).

[5] FD 2633/44, Mbh. in F., Wi. II/a, Telegram to Rwm., 24 July 1944.

[6] See the report on the mine, FD 2633/44, Mbh. in F., Wi. II/a, 24 July 1944.

[7] FD 258/45, Mbh. in F., Wi. II/a, 'Lagebericht für das 4. Vierteljahr 1943'.

right in the battlefront when the invasion began. The Wolfram Staff ordered the military commander to keep the mine open whatever the danger. Of so much value had become 4·53 tons of WO_3 a month, the mine's output in April.[1]

By a special decree of the Führer wolfram ore output in France is to be maintained and increased under all circumstances. Therefore the continued exploitation of the Montbelleux mine was ordered by the Commissar-General for French wolfram mines, although the proximity of the front, and the difficulties associated with this, such as failure of the electric current, dive-bombing attacks, and bombardment of the supply roads, make the continued maintenance of the works especially difficult.[2]

On 28 July the Commissar-General repeated his orders to the military commander to keep the mine open at all costs.[3] On 5 August the military commandant at Fougères could defend the mine no longer and ordered its demolition.[4] Since the resistance movement had effectively paralysed the mine at Puy les Vignes French wolfram production for Germany came to an almost complete standstill.

[1] FD 287/45, Mb. in F., Wi. II/a, 'Übersicht über die Metallerzgruben', April 1944.
[2] FD 2633/44, Mb. in F., Wi. II/a, OT to GbA für den Wolframerzbergbau, 20 July 1944.
[3] Ibid., GbA für den Wolframerzbergbau to Befehlshaber Südwestfrankreich, Militär-verwaltung, 18 July 1944.
[4] Ibid., Telegram to Rwm., 5 August 1944.

XI

AGRICULTURE

THE New Order's construction depended on the surplus of foodstuffs in Russia. After the conquest of that country the surplus would be diverted to satisfy the needs of the rest of Europe. Pre-war guesses in Germany of the size of that surplus were optimistically ignorant, estimating the over-all grain surplus in eastern Europe at as high a total as 7,000,000 tons. The *Institut für Konjunkturforschung* calculated it, in 1941, to be about 1,200,000 tons.[1] On the latter calculations Russia could supply neither the bread-grain nor fodder-grain deficits of the rest of Europe. The word surplus, however, had an elasticity of meaning in National Socialist planning. If the export of foodstuffs from European Russia to Siberia were reduced, the deficiencies of supply elsewhere in Europe could be more amply compensated. Were the standard of living of the inhabitants of European Russia to be drastically reduced a still larger surplus would become available.

After the failure of the Blitzkrieg against Russia Germany had to improvise a policy approximating as nearly as possible to these initial ideas. At the height of success in Russia Germany ruled over 65,000,000 inhabitants and an area almost twice as large as that of France, but the area of Russia which could be subjected to systematic exploitation was more nearly akin to that of France and was exploited for a shorter period of time. The size of the German Army in Russia was such that they themselves made considerable inroads into the surplus of food on the spot. The extension of German control in eastern Europe brought several areas with marked grain deficiencies into the New Order. Greece and Croatia both were grain importers, and Finland also needed to be kept supplied. The quantity of food which the German economy itself obtained from Russia was much below expectations.

For this disappointment there were several reasons, many of them relevant to the situation in France also. The circumstances of occupation and the violent changes in the pattern of trade which came with the New Order meant that supplies of fertilizer, of fuel, and, in some cases, of labour and of fodder were much harder to procure. The agricultural sectors of the occupied economies operated under severe restrictions. In these circumstances it was the economies with the more highly developed and productive agricultural sectors that performed the better. The output of food in Denmark increased

---

[1] FD 3045/49, Section IV, Sc. 146, Folder no. 2, Institut für Konjunkturforschung, 'Rohstoffbilanz Kontinentaleuropas'.

during the war. In the Netherlands the food supply was maintained by a successful switch from grain cultivation and sugar-beet cultivation to the cultivation of potatoes.[1] Countries where the level of agricultural productivity before the war had been relatively low, but where it might have been thought a greater reserve of productive capacity existed, saw their levels of productivity sink even further under the weight of the occupation.

The failure of German agricultural policy in Russia was of much more consequence than its success in the Netherlands and Denmark. It threw a mantle of much greater importance over the agricultural sector of the French economy. That sector had retained considerable importance; in 1934 the value of French output of barley and oats was as great as that of motor cars and that of the output of wheat greater.[2] However, the social framework in which agricultural production took place in France meant that its capacity to respond to German demand was very limited. In most areas of France agricultural production took place on small farms. The number of tractors was small compared to other industrial countries, the use of fertilizer restricted, and the yields obtained low. French agriculture entered the period of occupation in a much less healthy state than that of Denmark or the Netherlands.

Yet for all that German policy in France encountered the same difficulties as in Russia, Germany came increasingly to use French agriculture as a substitute for the great agricultural empire in the east of which she had dreamed and on which the New Order depended. During the 1930s Franco-German trade in agricultural products had dwindled to relatively insignificant levels. French agricultural imports from Germany in 1936 attained a value of 3,000,000 Reichsmarks. French agricultural exports to Germany amounted to 5,000,000 Reichsmarks. Grain played no part in French exports, 3,000,000 Reichsmarks being accounted for by fruit and wine and a further 1,000,000 by animal foodstuffs. In all, exports of agricultural produce from France to Germany were responsible for 5·1 per cent of all French exports to Germany by value in 1936.[3] In the nine months before the outbreak of hostilities with France the volume of German imports of primary produce from that country was much lower than in 1936. Imports of wine from France were smaller than from Chile and less than half those from Bulgaria.[4] Italy and Spain became the main sources of supply. French supplies of fruit to Germany became quite insignificant beside those from Italy, Bulgaria, and Yugoslavia.

The occupation of France and the failure of the Blitzkrieg on Russia therefore broke the established pattern of German trade and created a pattern

[1] K. Brandt et al., *Management of Agriculture and Food in the German Occupied and other Areas of Fortress Europe* (Stanford, 1943), p. 410.

[2] M. Weinmann, *Die Landwirtschaft in Frankreich während des zweiten Weltkrieges unter dem Einfluss der deutschen Besatzungsmacht* (Tübingen, 1961), p. 16.

[3] L. Müller-Ohlsen, *Strukturwandlungen und Nachkriegsprobleme der Wirtschaft Frankreichs* (Kiel, 1952), pp. 166–7.

[4] FD 5472/45, Statistisches Reichsamt, 'Sondernachweis der Aussenhandel Deutschlands, Oktober 1939'.

much more akin to that which emerged after the war in western Europe. French agricultural exports to Germany only diminished in the immediate aftermath of the German collapse; by 1950 they were responsible for 41 per cent of all French exports to Germany by value. The pattern of west European trade which laid the basis for the Common Market was partly the result of the failure of Hitler's original strategy.

Some idea of the role of French agriculture in German supply emerges from Table 53. By the late summer of 1943, on the eve of the dissolution of Germany's eastern empire, France had become almost as important a supplier of bread grains and meat as that empire. The strenuous efforts made to increase food production in the harvest year 1942/3 had had as great an impact on France as in the east. Meanwhile the Balkan states had faded from importance as food suppliers; Romania provided Germany with 416,000 tons of bread grains in 1939/40 but with only 8,000 tons in 1941/2.[1]

One of the strangest aspects of German agricultural policy in France was the concentration on animal products, or, to put it another way, the retention of so much grassland at the expense of arable farming. In this respect Germany was unable to reverse the trend of agricultural practice in France in the inter-war period. In the context of a European *Grossraumwirtschaft* this is less surprising than when viewed simply as an aspect of the exploitation of one economy. Nevertheless, the fact that the area of ploughed land in France during the war may have fallen, and certainly did not increase, makes a sharp contrast with other west European countries. It is also reflected in the quantities of agricultural output which Germany obtained during the war.

The estimation of these quantities has been bedevilled by the deficiencies of wartime statistical procedure and by the changing boundaries. The earliest estimates made by Brandt have been revised by Cépède and by Weinmann. These two differ from each other but are certainly preferable to Brandt's pioneer work. Their conclusions may be seen in Table 54.

The amount of foodstuffs, fodder, and animals which Germany obtained from France increased greatly in the year 1942/3, but remained at the same level for the following year. The amount obtained in the year 1941/2 was less than in the first year of the occupation. These quantities were related of course to the size of the harvests of those years, and those harvests in their turn were dependent on the weather. To that extent German policy was face to face with factors beyond its influence. None the less it has been generally considered that German policy in France was not so successful as it might have been in obtaining supplies of food, especially when the drastic reduction imposed on the nutritional standards of the French themselves is taken into account.

In the first place, any radical changes of policy which Germany would have wished to enforce were hampered by the labour shortage. Secondly, the depletion of the capital stock, especially of tractors and horses, and the shortage

[1] H. Kistenmacher, op. cit., appendix 16.

TABLE 53

German Food Imports from Principal Suppliers*

	Bread grains (1,000 tons)				Meat (1,000 tons)				Butter (1,000 tons)			
	1939/40†	1940/1	1941/2	1942/3	1939/40	1940/1	1941/2	1942/3	1939/40	1940/1	1941/2	1942/3
France	..	550·0	485·0	715·0	..	162·0‡	146·0‡	253·0	..	12·2	4·4	15·6
Russia	5·0	325·0	..	..	..	..	264·0	279·0	18·1§	0·8§	23·5§	63·0§
Eastern Gaue‖	177·0	415·0	896·0	711·0	..	69·0	86·0	81·0	..	8·1	16·3	20·5
General-Government	..	15·0	50·0	362·0	15·0	9·0	22·0	49·0	..	..	0·9	0·7
Netherlands	..	1·0	2·0	16·0	163·0	49·0	27·0	27·0	22·7	27·7	3·0	4·4
Denmark	..	..	..	7·0	63·0	190·0	103·0	62·0	86·6	63·6	35·8	37·8
Hungary	310·0	27·0	190·0	57·0	22·0	20·0	15·0	12·0	1·1	..	..	..
Romania	416·0	9·0	8·0	..	..	6·0	8·0	10·0	..	..	..	..

	Margarine raw materials (1,000 tons oil value)				Potatoes (1,000 tons)			
	1939/40	1940/1	1941/2	1942/3	1939/40	1940/1	1941/2	1942/3
France	..	3·0	32·5	5·2	..	..	20·0	296·0
Russia	..	0·4	29·9	127·0	..	..	737·0	1,200·0
Eastern Gaue	..	..	..	..	330·0	540·0	814·0	1,236·0
General-Government	..	..	..	..	..	122·0	139·0	434·0**
Netherlands	6·5	30·0	4·4	..	82·0	56·0	90·0	139·0
Denmark	0·3	0·1	0·3	9·5	..	..	..	15·0
Hungary	..	..	..	..	4·0	..	..	25·0
Romania	..	..	..	..	..	..	..	..

* H. Kistenmacher, op. cit., appendices 16–19.
‡ Includes exports to Alsace-Lorraine.
‖ Danzig–West Prussia, Wartheland, Südostpreussen.

† All the dates refer to the supply year 1 August to 31 July.
§ Includes Baltic States.
** Including potatoes for spirit production.

8214839

S

TABLE 54

Quantities of Agricultural Produce Obtained for German Purposes from France*

Product	Period and quantity							
	1940/1†		1941/2†		1942/3†		1943/4†	
	Cépède	Weinmann	Cépède	Weinmann	Cépède	Weinmann	Cépède	Weinmann
Wheat (tons)	800,000‡	550,000	615,000‡	485,000	790,000‡	714,454	760,000‡	791,801
Milk (hectolitres)§	135,000		425,000		375,000		375,000	
Butter and cheese (tons)§	16,000		19,000		32,000		47,000	
Oats (tons)	637,000	603,420	476,000	458,000	720,000	685,775	521,000	608,240
Barley (tons)	13,000		7,000		29,000		23,000	
Wine (hectolitres)	2,300,000	3,960,400	2,200,000	3,969,580	3,300,000	4,593,985	2,600,000	4,007,080
Potatoes (tons)	42,616‖		58,360‖	20,000	303,100‖	296,000	321,900‖	375,000
Hay (tons)		455,000		326,000		391,000		398,778
Straw (tons)		716,000		243,000		379,007		256,482

	1940		1941		1942		1943		1944	
	Cépède	Weinmann	Cépède	Weinmann	Cépède	Weinmann	Cépède	Weinmann	Cépède	Weinmann
Meat (tons)	97,000		173,000	(161,902)**	212,000	(140,000)**	275,000	(253,461)**	133,000	(211,442)**
Other fats (tons)	2,900		25,000		16,300		2,300		4,700	
Horses and mules	447,000		32,000		121,000		53,000		97,000	

* M. Cépède, Agriculture et alimentation en France durant la IIᵉ guerre mondiale (Paris, 1961), M. Weinmann, op. cit.
† Supply year 1 August to 31 July.
§ Supply year 1 May to 30 April.
** Supply year 1 August to 31 July.
‡ Includes requisitions intended for Belgium.
‖ CCDR, vii, P.A. 9.

of fuel and fertilizers exacerbated by transport difficulties, militated against any radical change. Thirdly, the structure of French rural society was not such as to respond quickly to changed circumstances. The historical heritage of French farming from the eighteenth century and the Revolution was one of peasant farms, low productivity, and rural ignorance. The German administration flattered itself absurdly in supposing that it could change in five years a system that had endured for two hundred, particularly in view of the romantically conservative view of rural France which activated the policy of the Vichy government. Finally, German policy, although in many ways bearing more lightly on the peasant than on any other member of French society, did not succeed in buying his co-operation. The peasant became richer and better fed, but his wish to collaborate with the occupier grew no stronger. The German administration met with passive, undeclared, often unperceived, resistance on the peasant farm just as it did in the coal-mine.

Migratory labour had provided a small part of the French agricultural labour force since the eighteenth century, especially in the northern departments. After the First World War the proportion of migrants increased and many became permanent settlers in France. By 1939 there were approximately 250,000 immigrants engaged in agriculture, of whom about 50,000 were established permanently as cultivators.[1] The transitory migrants were mainly Spaniards, Italians, and Poles, but few Poles were actual cultivators. Many Belgians had settled as peasant farmers and market gardeners in the northern departments. The impact of the German invasion on these foreigners was no less than it was on the labour force of the iron-ore mines. That great body of refugees moving from the path of the invader contained many labourers and cultivators who would not return for the duration of the occupation.

It is not known what proportion of the French prisoners of war retained in Germany were agricultural workers or cultivators. But the original mobilization of the French forces drew very heavily on those sources. Approximately 1,300,000 men from the agricultural sector were called to the colours. Of the prisoners taken, the Ministry of Agriculture estimated that 40 per cent, or 683,000, were formerly employed in agriculture. This enormous labour loss was disguised in summer 1940 by the return of men after the armistice, but by the end of the year it had become apparent that about 13 per cent of the active male agricultural population, and those often the fittest and strongest, were missing.[2]

Such a situation could not be regarded with equanimity by the French government, knowing the kind of demands that the occupiers were likely to make on French food supplies. Not only did practical politics imply some special measures to deal with the problem of agricultural labour, but the whole cast of thought of the Vichy government by itself suggested some such policy. The first Minister of Agriculture in the Vichy government, Pierre

[1] C. Rosier, *La France agricole* (Paris, 1943), p. 361.   [2] M. Cépède, op. cit., p. 210.

Caziot, had long been an ardent defender of the French peasantry. Far from wishing their reduction he hoped for a system of cultivation in which the number of peasant proprietors would be increased. In the peasant he saw the embodiment of all human virtue and the defender of the French tradition.[1] Holding such views his position in the cabinet was strong, for Pétain's own intellectual views were close to his. The so-called Mission of Peasant Restoration proclaimed by the cabinet in August 1940 as part of the National Revolution may seem absurd when judged by its results, but it was not a policy for two years, rather for fifty. It was aimed to secure the long-run transformation of French society.

It was easy for the occupiers to confound Caziot's policy with National Socialist ideas. Their error was soon made clear. The *Reichsnährstand*, in so far as it was an attempt at repairing the strains in German society caused by the rapid economic development of the country, was a revolutionary attempt. The principles on which it was constructed were at least new. The Agricultural Corporation created by Pétain and Caziot was an expression of the purest conservatism. It was unpopular with the peasants, with many members of the government, and above all with the French administration, which saw in it a dangerous, and foolish, rival organization.

Irrespective of government policy there was a 'return to the land' simply because to be there was to be safer and better fed. The rural population was therefore temporarily increased although not always in a useful way. By the decrees of 9 March 1941 and 31 December 1941 farming was declared an activity of particular national interest. Under certain circumstances labour could be drafted to farms. Both laws also placed so high a priority on agricultural labour that the movement of labour out of agricultural jobs could be forbidden. The employment of persons from rural communes in industrial positions, unless they had left the land before 1 September 1938, was illegal.

These remedial measures were eked out in slight degree by German policy. Small numbers of French prisoners were released to help in harvesting. To gather in the 1940 harvest 70,000 were used and of those prisoners returning under the 'relève' about one-fifth had been previously employed in agriculture.[2] These measures could have but little effect. The agricultural survey of spring 1942 recorded a labour force as large as that of the pre-war period. But the circumstances in which the inquiry was carried out make the figures absurd. Householders' returns indicated that everyone living under their roof was employed on the farm. In such a way they could protect their household from the labour draft and at the same time entitle themselves to higher rations. Even were the returns correct, the proportion of women, of the very old, and the very young, in the agricultural labour force would have increased by comparison with the pre-war period.

[1] See his book, *Au service de la paysannerie* (Paris, 1942).
[2] M. Weinmann, op. cit., p. 50.

When every allowance is made for the further slowing down of the exodus from the countryside in France and for the repatriation of prisoners, the number of workers, for the most part drawn from the best age groups, missing from the French agricultural labour force in 1944 by comparison with 1938 could not have been lower than 400,000. In these circumstances the failure to switch from pasture farming to the more labour-intensive types of cultivation such as arable farming or market gardening is still more comprehensible. In agriculture, as in other industries, the New Order was quite unable to solve its labour problems. Indeed, it only created greater problems.

No less an obstacle to German policy than the reduction in the labour force were the shortages of tractors, horses, and fertilizers. The number of tractors in France had always been relatively low in relation to the large area to be farmed. Most of the 35,000 tractors in service at the beginning of the occupation were of foreign origin and in the following five years it was more or less impossible to get spare parts for them. French production had always been very small. In spite of the switching of two substantial firms to tractor production in 1942 and 1943 output diminished during the occupation.[1] Only 348 tractors were turned out in 1944 compared to 2,000 in 1941.[2] By 1944 the stock of tractors in use had declined from 35,000 to 28,000.

This shortage was aggravated by the fuel shortage. Many tractors had to be adapted to function either by means of gas generators or on alcohol. These improvisations were not very satisfactory, although the effort put into the production of gas generators by the German administration was most persistent. Of the possible tractor fuels only alcohol was in sufficient supply and that could scarcely make up for deficiencies elsewhere. Even when top priority was accorded to the needs of agriculture the fuel shortage persisted.

One result of the priority accorded to agriculture in fuel supply was the leakage of fuel to the resistance movement. This fact alone suggests that the fuel crisis bore less heavily on farmers than on industrialists. The shortage of fuel for agricultural purposes was also mitigated by the widespread programme of rural electricity distribution carried out by the Vichy governments. For many farming operations electricity became a more important source of power than oil or coal for the first time in the harvest of 1944.

The number of draught-horses on French farms fell from 2,700,000 in 1938 to 2,110,000 in 1944.[3] The reduction was mainly due to German requisitions for military purposes. It could only be partly remedied by the use of oxen, the number of which increased over the same period by 100,000. In so far as tractors were used by those cultivating the larger units their shortage did not affect the more humble peasant cultivators. They, however, found their activities greatly restricted by the reduction in the number of draught animals.

All cultivators were impeded by the shortage of fertilizers. The gap which

[1] 'La manufacture d'armes de Paris' and 'Les établissements Bernard', CCDR., v, A. 1. 13.
[2] M. Cépède, op. cit., p. 215.   [3] Ibid., p. 213.

had existed before the war between the average yields in France and Germany was widened.[1] In agriculture as in industry the productivity of the occupied fell while that of the occupier rose. This fall in productivity meant that there was no permanent prospect of increasing the total output of food in France. Like the shortage of tractors the shortage of fertilizers was not merely a result of the occupation. Before the war the quantity of fertilizer used in French agriculture varied from region to region. The lack of fertilizer during the occupation only exaggerated the difference between the more advanced and the less advanced agricultural regions in France.

TABLE 55

Effective Consumption of Fuels in France*

(tons)

	1938	1941	Proportionate change by 1941 (per cent)
Benzine	2,685,802	212,547	7·9
Alcohol	100,918	126,314	125·2
Petroleum	132,092	18,130	13·7
Gas-oil	902,544	142,293	15·7
Heating-oil	1,580,386	180,140	11·4
	5,401,492	679,424	12·6

* FD 272/45, Mbh. in F., Wi.Abt. II/a, 'Verbrauchskontingente und Auslieferungen der französischen Wirtschaft 1942 im besetzten und unbesetzten Gebiet (ohne Nord und Pas-de-Calais)', 5 January 1943.

The quantity of nitrogen used by French agriculture decreased by a half between 1939 and 1944, and the quantity of phosphoric fertilizer diminished still further.[2] The loss of North Africa interposed an almost insuperable obstacle to the acquisition of sufficient quantities of phosphoric acid fertilizers, and nitrogen had other equally vital uses in wartime. These deficiencies might have been made up with a greater use of phosphatic fertilizer, the employment of which had shown a steep and continuous rise in the inter-war years. This increase had been based on an increase in the output of phosphates in North Africa more than on an expansion of French domestic production. Since the major source of domestic production was Alsace, the dependence on North Africa became even greater after the armistice.

From Algeria, Morocco, and Tunisia 834,438 tons of phosphates had been shipped to France in 1936 and 972,551 tons in 1937.[3] It was more difficult

[1] E. Woermann, *Die europäische Ernährungswirtschaft in Zahlen* (Berlin, 1944).

[2] M. Cépède, op. cit., p. 236.

[3] FD 281/45, Mbh. in F., Wi.Abt. II/a, letter from Ministère secrétaire d'état à la production industrielle et aux communications, Direction des Mines, 5 April 1943, 'Produktion der Nordafrikanischen Phosphate'.

under wartime conditions in the Mediterranean to move so much, and even
had that not been the case German demands for a stake in this supply would
only have increased. The German administration's efforts to increase the
output of phosphates in France itself, although crowned with some success,
could not compensate for the failure of North African and Alsatian supply.[1]
The largest company, the Compagnie Française des Phosphates, whose main
mine was at Beauval in the department of Somme, had an output of only
4,500 tons a month in 1942. The average monthly output of phosphates in
occupied and unoccupied France in that year was 10,760 tons.[2] Germany
took twice that quantity herself from French North Africa.[3]

In the most favourable conditions the agricultural sector of the French
economy had not shown itself to have much resilience; under wartime conditions no improvement could be looked for. The importance which the Vichy
government attached to agriculture can be deduced from the fact that alone
in the French economy, under the law of 2 December 1940, it received a full
corporate charter. The idea of such a charter had already been mooted at the
beginning of September by the leaders of the most right wing of the agricultural
'syndicats', the Union Nationale des Syndicats Agricoles, who were disturbed
by the growing evidence of independence among the newer peasant associations less dominated by the larger proprietors.[4] The charter imposed a
paternalistic law on the growing strength of these organizations. All existing
associations were forced into the strait jacket of the new corporation,
wherein the regional associations were directed from above by leaders named
by the upper ranks. When joining the corporation the head of a household was
held to have committed the whole of his family too.

In fact, the creation of regional organizations wholly subservient to the
central body was very difficult. The bewildering number of decrees on agricultural organization and their complexity testify to this difficulty. The law of
16 December 1942 tried to enlarge the composition of the regional associations
by forcibly incorporating into them members of the specialized agricultural
services maintained by the government and more under its control, with the
clear intention of reducing the independence of the regional bodies. The
renewal of peasant society in France was to take place on the government's
terms and not on the peasantry's own terms.

The opposition to the government's measures preceded the opposition to
the occupier and the one led naturally to the other. Except where the *Union
nationale* had been strong before the war, in south-eastern France and in
Brittany, the regional organizations refused to be dictated to from above. The
associations that had been crushed by the forced integration into the new

[1] See above, p. 91.
[2] FD 281/45, Mbh in F., Wi.Abt. II/a, 'Gisements de phosphates en exploitation'.
[3] Ibid., 'Bericht über die Phosphat- und Eisenerzlieferungen aus Nordafrika für Deutschland 1941 bis 8.11.1942', 17 November 1942.
[4] See J. Leroy-Ladurie, *Vers une politique paysanne* (Paris, 1937).

corporative body recovered their forces as early as 1941 and began to organize local clandestine meetings. It was in these meetings that the idea of a democratic *Confédération Générale de l'Agriculture* was born.[1] The new body would be as comprehensive as the National Peasant Corporation, but democratic rather than paternalistic. In defiance of the laws governing the corporation the regional groupings secretly carried out free elections for local leaders. At the same time a steady resistance to German demands took place, harder to detect than in industry, but equally present.

The Vichy government not only encouraged the survival of French agriculture in its historic form but also tried to stifle any movement for change originating in agricultural society itself. Exchanges and transfers of land were forbidden other than under the supervision of the prefect. The only changes in the system of landholding tended to greater stability. The laws of 4 September 1943 dealing with tenancies and leasehold effectively extended many leases for the duration of the war.

These policies were not ignored by the German administration, which had been a close observer of the National Socialists' own attempt at rural regeneration in the previous decade. The recognition that ignorance was one of the most persistent problems in such a society led to those prisoners of war who had diplomas in agricultural science being given priority under the various release schemes. Five hundred were so released.[2] Each of the regional field commands in France had agricultural specialists attached to it, and the central German administration also maintained some specialized agricultural services. After the disappointing harvest of 1942 and the weakening of the German position in the east, a greater effort was made to raise the level of productivity in French agriculture by the dissemination of technical information. In April 1943 400 specialists were sent from Germany to give technical help on a local level, the co-called *Landwirtschaftsführer*. By 1944 their number had at least doubled.

Some parts of France were more directly controlled by the occupiers. Along the north-eastern frontier of France a barrier zone had been created into which the deported refugees were not allowed to return. The farms left vacant were administered by a German company, Reichsland Landbewirtschaftungs G.m.b.H., earlier and better known as Ostland G.m.b.H. Its main interests were in the eastern empire and its activities in France were incidental to those greater interests. Farms confiscated from Jews in other areas of France were also taken over by the same organization as well as farms adjudged to have insufficient labour or capital equipment to be efficiently run. The company controlled almost 9,000 separate units of landholding, totalling 170,000 hectares. Although the food produced on its lands did enter into the general total of available food for distribution, it did so to a lesser degree than if the farms had remained French. Some part of the land was used to feed

---

[1] See. G. Wright, *Rural Revolution in France* (Stanford, 1964).
[2] M. Weinmann, op. cit., p. 57.

German cattle which were then re-exported to Germany. There is no evidence
that the direct control of French land by this means was ever used as a means
for demonstrating better methods of farming, the land being merely used
more exclusively in the German interest than if it had remained with its former
owners.

Direct control of the land in this way was certainly a simpler method of
exploitation. But the major part of German agricultural policy was concerned
with devising indirect means by which French agricultural output could be
both increased and changed. The official bread price rose by 19·4 per cent
between 1939 and 1944, but the cost price of production rose five times more.
The gap was bridged by changes in the quality of the loaf and by massive subsidies to the producers, 9, 400,000,000 francs over the course of the occupation.[1]
This subsidy was more in favour with the military administration than with
the government; indeed, the German administration, by frequently refusing
permission to the French to increase the bread price, left the government
little scope for manœuvre. The net result from the German point of view was
to help to sustain purchasing power. Although this helped those families whose
incomes were such that they could not deal on the black market, it enabled
other and wealthier families to use their surplus for black-market dealings,
thus putting up the price of other foods. Nor was the price of bread raised
sufficiently to generate a large enough swing from pasture to arable farming.

The apparent necessity of appeasing the population by keeping the price of
bread relatively low thus hindered a thorough use of the price mechanism to
effect the necessary changes in the composition of total output. The alternative
solution, to sink meat prices to the point where fodder production would
greatly decrease, proved impossible. Without access to imported fodder, meat
prices would have risen even were there no black market to accentuate that
tendency. The official prices offered for meat in fact increased. Between August
1939 and August 1943 the official price of veal rose 40 per cent, of beef 70 per
cent, and of lamb 94 per cent.[2] The increases in milk and egg prices were much
greater.

The area devoted to grain farming in France appears to have decreased at
a rate greater than its rate of decrease in the inter-war period. Unfortunately
the agricultural statistics collected during the occupation are most unreliable.
Under-reporting of the area of land cultivated and of the total product was
the inevitable result of a system of requisitions such as that practised by the
occupier. The farmer gave incorrect information to diminish the tax burden
on himself and to retain a surplus for the black market. For this reason the
apparent decrease of grain farming was probably not so great as it appears
in Table 56.

German price policy had no impact on the long-term trend of French farming. By 1950 the area devoted to grain farming had increased to 8,724,000

[1] H. Kistenmacher, op. cit., p. 86.   [2] M. Weinmann, op. cit., p. 72.

hectares, still well below its pre-war average.[1] Between 1939 and 1941 the reversion to grassland appears to have been at a faster rate than in the inter-war period but thereafter slowed to the same rate. In spite of this the stocks of animals seem to have fallen until the end of 1943, the number of cattle apparently declining from 14,655,100, the average of the years 1935–8, to 13,871,800 in October 1943.[2] This figure may perhaps be discounted as a

TABLE 56

Area Devoted to Grain Farming in France (excluding Alsace-Lorraine, Pas-de-Calais, and Nord)*

(1,000 hectares)

	Average 1935–8	1939	1940	1941	1942	1943
All Grains	9,497	9,127	..	..	8,531	8,131
Wheat	4,820	4,347	4,250	4,540	4,350	4,240
Rye	529	506	510	460	455	455
Barley	690	806	690	740	615	615
Oats	3,008	3,039	2,680	2,590	2,700	2,610
Buckwheat	277	262	..	..	250	250

* M. Weinmann, op. cit., p. 79.

TABLE 57

Approximate Grain Harvests in France, German and French Estimates (not including Alsace-Lorraine, Pas-de-Calais, and Nord)

(1,000 tons)

	Average 1935–8*	1940		1941		1942		1943	
		German*	French†	German*	French†	German*	French†	German*	French†
Wheat	7,076	5,060	5,000	6,370	5,097	5,307	5,082	5,936	5,815
Rye	587	530	..	470	424‡	435	406‡	500	420‡
Barley	979	910	917	1,000	789	830	765	800	715
Oats	4,064	3,230	3,232	3,410	2,700	3,105	2,994	2,900	2,812
Buckwheat	275	..	223	..	181	175	85	175	495

* M. Weinmann, op. cit., p. 79.   † CCDR., vii, P.A. 1, P.A. 2.
‡ K. Brandt, op. cit., pp. 540–1.

result of faulty statistics; in October 1942 the head of cattle was greater than before the war. As German demands became more onerous under-reporting of stocks may have become more frequent. But it is difficult to explain away in the same terms the fall in milk production between 1934–8 and 1943 from 14,290,000 tons a year to 8,114,000 tons. Butter production over the period 1934–8 averaged 202,000 tons, cheese production, 165,000 tons; in 1943 butter production was 149,000 tons, cheese production 47,000 tons.[3] The apparent decline in grain output may be seen in Table 57.

[1] L. Müller-Ohlsen, op. cit., p. 15.   [2] M. Weinmann, op. cit., p. 86.
[3] Ibid., p. 87.

The one success attributable to German price policy and one which wrought a long-term change in the composition of French agricultural output was in the cultivation of oil seeds. Before the war the cultivation of oil seeds had almost died out in France in the face of imports of arachid oils. When the import of these oils was cut off in 1942 much higher prices were offered for domestic vegetable oils. Experiments with a wide variety of plants ensued. The colza bean proved much the most satisfactory. The area planted to oil seeds increased from 19,000 hectares in 1941 to 287,000 hectares in 1944.[1] Although it subsequently decreased it remained at over 200,000 hectares in 1950. In this instance German policy was not so steadfastly trying to reverse a long-term trend as in other areas. The success was a small one, it showed what might have been done with a bolder and more imaginative policy.

In July 1940 the military administration calculated that 1,400,000 hectares of unused land in France could be put to the plough.[2] The ultimate result of German policy was an increase in uncultivated land. In part this was due to the need for the soldiers to have land on which to conduct their military operations. The area of non-agricultural land increased from 3,850,000 hectares in 1939 to 4,570,000 hectares in 1944. So great an increase might be regarded as a normal incident of occupation by so large an army. But the area of agricultural land not cultivated increased from 5,961,000 hectares in 1939 to 6,614,000 hectares in 1944. Far from extending the area of cultivation in France[3] German policy ended by bringing about a net loss of agricultural land.

The very fact of military occupation and the interruption of overseas supply placed severe constraints on German price policy. But what ultimately nullified this policy was the growth of the black market. The resistance of the agricultural community to the occupier was not merely statistical; the black market, however socially unjust, was also an expression of the will to resist the occupier. To eliminate it was impossible, the only way was to come to terms. In July 1942 a large share of the occupation costs was allocated to pre-emptive buying for German purposes on the black market. Between that date and February 1943 93,700 hectolitres of wine and large quantities of food were purchased.[4]

There were many loopholes in the system of control through which food could escape on to the black market. Illegal slaughterings were common; the difference between the official figures for delivery of carcasses and the actual number of beasts slaughtered may have been as high as 350,000 a year. The milk delivery programme, to be enforced properly, needed a system of daily collection of milk. The transport shortage meant that collection frequently took place on every other day. In summer the dairy farmer was more or less driven on to the black market to defend himself.[5] The official butter price rose

[1] M. Cépède, op. cit., p. 302.   [2] M. Weinmann, op. cit., p. 42.
[3] M. Cépède, op. cit., p. 294.   [4] H. Kistenmacher, op. cit., p. 116.
[5] Ibid., p. 59.

from sixty-six francs a kilo in December 1942 to eighty francs a kilo in June 1944; the black-market price rose over the same period from 175 francs to 445 francs. Potato prices on the black market in summer 1944 were roughly double the official price, egg prices were four times the official price, pork prices more than five times the official price.[1]

With so developed a black market country dwellers more and more lived outside the framework of the official economic system. The peasant retained more food for his own consumption, sold on the grey market to his acquaintances at prices above the official level, and on the black market at prices which justified the risk. In the last case he was sometimes selling to agents of the German administration trying to ensure their own supply. Not only did the peasant benefit from the breakdown of controls in terms of his income from sales, the value of his land soared upwards. Peasant farmers were offered prices for their land in 1944 which would have been unimaginable in 1938. The competition on the market between food consumers was accompanied by the same competition for the land itself. Land was a safeguard against inflation and a guarantee of food. In such circumstances, bearing in mind the scarcity of agricultural inputs and the uncertainty of the times, the apparent increase of fallow land is not so surprising.

To the long-run problems of French agriculture, to the shortages occasioned by the war and the occupation, to the depletion of the capital stock, and to the shortage of labour must be added the weaknesses of German policy. All explain the relatively disappointing results which the German agricultural administration obtained in France. The French population as a whole, especially those unable to operate on the black market but able to watch the rise in land values, might well have echoed Adam Smith. 'Whatever keeps down the produce of the land below what it would otherwise rise to, keeps down the revenue of the great body of the people still more than it does that of the proprietors of land.'[2]

---

[1] H. Kistenmacher, op. cit., pp. 98–9.   [2] *The Wealth of Nations*, V, II, i.

XII

CONCLUSION

THE fate of the New Order was settled by military might. In the long battle against overwhelming odds German economic policy in the occupied territories was forced to abandon its earlier concepts. The pressure of economic necessity distorted the New Order until it became that quite different thing, 'the European war economy'. At that moment when the Blitzkrieg in Russia had almost achieved its ends the shape of the National Socialist New Order may be seen. But the moment is a brief one, and once over, official silence falls over the New Order and that New Order itself begins its metamorphosis.

But to return to the starting-point. Could the New Order have survived had the outcome of the military events been different? Had fascism not suffered so resounding a military defeat would not the New Order have collapsed from its own internal weaknesses? The evidence must lead us to the conclusion that the liberal idea of conquest, as a general proposition, was quite unreal.

Economically, the acquisition of France was of great value to Germany. To show it to have been so it is necessary to make a certain number of assumptions, some of them, perhaps, assumptions with which the reader would not agree. My intention in doing so is to put into some proportion, against the resources of her own economy, the resources which Germany was able to derive from France. Such a procedure, although it begs one or two economic questions, has the simple merit of trying to answer a simple question. But if it reduces the liberal argument to the level of the counting-house, I would not wish it to be thought that such is my ultimate intention. I merely wish to show that on that level the advantage to Germany of her conquest is a historical fact and one which gainsays deductions made from the initial premises of liberalism. It will already have become apparent to the reader that the history of labour during the occupation of France provides substantial evidence that the liberal view of conquest was not wholly fanciful, and to these wider issues the argument must ultimately also return

In every year of the war until 1944 the increase in the foreign contribution to Germany's total available product was greater than the increase in the domestic contribution. Until the end of 1942 the greatest single contribution to the increase in government expenditure was the revenue from conquered territories rather than the decline in consumers' expenditures. A report of the Reichs Minister for Finance in April 1944 made provisional calculations of the extent to which the occupation costs paid into the German treasury had contributed to German war finance. For the whole period of the war the income from occupation levies was roughly 40 per cent of the income from taxation. Income from taxation reached its wartime peak in the financial year 1 April 1942 to 31 March 1943. It then declined to the end of the war. 'Special income from abroad', however, reached its highest level in the financial year 1943/4, when it accounted for 38·4 per cent of total treasury income.[1] Forty-two per cent of this 'special income', over the whole duration of the war, came from France. The occupation costs paid by the French government were thus an important source of war finance for Germany in every year in which they were paid. While it is true that the main reason for Germany's lack of recourse to the capital market in the Second World War as compared to the First World War and the consequent 'sounder' appearance of her war finances, was mainly due to the higher levels of personal taxation in 1939–45, the income received from France also played its part in reducing the government's need to borrow.

TABLE 58

*Role of Occupation Costs in German War Finance**
(million Reichsmarks)

Date	Regular receipts	Out of taxation and dues	'Special income from abroad'
1 Sept. 1939 –31 Mar. 1940	18,200	14,600	..
1940/1	39,500	27,200	6,000
1941/2	50,100	32,500	11,000
1942/3	70,600	43,000	19,000
1943/4	73,300	35,000	28,000
1944/5	60,800	31,000	21,000
1 Apr. 1945 –8 May 1945	2,300	1,500	
Total	314,800	184,800	85,000

* F. Federau, *Der zweite Weltkrieg. Seine Finanzierung in Deutschland* (Tübingen, 1962).

The complicated accountancy used for the payment of the French occupation costs hampers any attempt to show their relative usefulness to Germany at different stages of the war. Since the occupation costs in France were never intended merely to pay for the upkeep of the army of occupation, but also to give Germany sufficient purchasing power to exploit the French economy to her own advantage, the movement of the clearing deficit over time could logically be considered as much a part of the actual financial burden on France as the costs themselves. Munz estimates the actual burden of such costs jointly considered on each individual in France as rising from 2,015 francs per head in 1940 to 6,755 francs per head in 1943.[2] The greatest part of the increase

[1] F. Federau, *Der zweite Weltkrieg. Seine Finanzierung in Deutschland* (Tübingen, 1962).
[2] A. Munz, op. cit., p. 51 ff.

is after 1942, the burden on the individual being 40 per cent greater in 1943 than in 1942. Hitler's menacing threats of 3 January 1943 against the French were not empty ones.[1] In Table 59 Munz's estimates of the annual financial burden on France are used to estimate the contribution of these payments to the German economy.

TABLE 59

Occupation Costs and Other Payments from France in Relation to Germany's Gross National Product

Year	G.N.P of Germany (at current Reichs-mark prices)* (million RM)	French occupa-tion costs (cur-rent francs)† (million francs)	Total payments from France incl. clearing deficit (current francs) (million francs)	Occupation costs as a percentage of German G.N.P. at wartime exchange	Total payments as a per-centage of German G.N.P.	
					at wartime exchange	at 1938 exchange‡
1940	145,000	80,000	81,600	2·8	2·8	3·0
1941	156,000	121,500	144,300	3·9	4·6	5·3
1942	162,000	109,000	156,700	3·4	4·8	5·5
1943	170,000	194,000	273,600	5·7	8·0	9·1
1944	175,000	126,900	206,300	3·6	5·9	6·7

* USSBS., Overall Economic Effects Division, *The Gross National Product of Germany 1936 to 1944* (Washington, 1945). B. H. Klein, op. cit., pp. 241–57, has revised these estimates. Part of his revision lies in an amendment of the total income from foreign contributions. G.N.P. as used here is without those foreign contributions. I have used the USSBS. calculations because it was easier to separate their estimates of those contributions from the totals. I have no wish to quarrel with Klein's revision and the reader who prefers his estimates will easily make the small adjustment necessary.
† A. Munz, op. cit., p. 75.
‡ Estimated on the basis of 176 francs to the pound sterling and 10 Reichsmarks to the pound sterling.

France's contribution to the German economy can be seen to have increased from the beginning of 1943. Since France was able to contribute effectively only for the first six months of 1944 her contribution in those six months may be said to have increased proportionately to her contribution in 1943. Between 1941 and 1942, however, there was little change. Some check may be made on these estimates by assuming that the proportion of occupation costs paid by France, 42 per cent, of the total occupation costs received by Germany, is the same as the French proportion in the total foreign contributions estimated by the Wagemann-Institut during the war and the United States Strategic Bombing Survey after the war. The estimates made by the Wagemann-Institut were used to make rough calculations about German National Income during the war and were partly used by the Bombing Survey in preparing its own estimates of Gross National Product.[2] The Bombing Survey's estimates of foreign contributions include the occupation levies paid by France, Holland, Norway, Bohemia, and Poland, the net deficit in Germany's foreign trade balance, the purchases made from foreign countries by invasion currency, and the net product of the annexed areas after the consumption and

[1] See above, p. 117 f.
[2] FD 4422/45, Wagemann-Institut, 'Volkseinkommen, öffentlicher Brutto- und Netto-Aufwand und privater Aufwand'.

capital formation within those areas has been deducted. Within this limited framework these estimates of the total foreign contribution to the German economy are probably too high. It appears that the Bombing Survey did not take sufficiently into account the growing difference between foreign prices, where price control was less effective, and German prices. Whereas the Bombing Survey calculated the total foreign contribution from the beginning of 1940 to the end of 1943 at 104,000,000,000 1939 Reichsmarks, Klein would place it no higher than 85,000,000,000 1939 Reichsmarks.[1]

The assumption that the French share of these total foreign contributions was 42 per cent is not outrageous. The occupation costs themselves were much the largest part of the total, and Germany needed to supply less essential imports to France than to many other occupied areas. On the basis of this assumption the French contribution to German National Income as calculated by the Wagemann-Institut would be 3·4 per cent in 1940–1, 4·0 per cent in 1941–2, and 4·7 per cent in 1942–3. The Wagemann-Institut's calculations of National Income are, however, not very reliable. In computing Gross National Product the Bombing Survey preferred, wherever applicable, the calculations of Dr. Grünig on consumer expenditures, domestic investment, and government expenditures.[2] Using the Bombing Survey's estimates of Gross National Product and their estimates of foreign contributions and making the same assumption about France's share, that share appears as 2·6 per cent of Gross National Product in 1940, 5·4 in 1941, 8·3 in 1942, 8·2 in 1943, and 7·4 in 1944. Such a calculation can do no more than provide additional evidence that the order of magnitude of the French contribution given in Table 59 is roughly correct. The fact that it makes the French contribution in 1942 appear much more important is likely to be a reflection of events in other occupied territories.

What proportion of France's resources did these transfers represent? In every year of the occupation the sum total of payments was greater than French revenue from taxation. In 1940 the disparity was 5,800,000,000 francs, in 1943 it rose to 148,800,000,000 francs. Over the period as a whole France was transferring to Germany a cash sum equivalent to 169 per cent of the whole of her income from taxation.[3] The government's recourse to the Bank of France was inevitable in the circumstances, even though it may be argued that French taxation policy could have been adopted to bring in larger sums. The proportion of these cash transfers to the total expenditure of the French government also rose; they accounted for over 60 per cent of such expenditure in 1943. Over the period 1940 to 1944 as a whole payments to Germany were 49 per cent of total public expenditure. That period is not the same as the

[1] B. H. Klein, op. cit., pp. 252–3.

[2] FD 4422/45, 'Dr. Grünig vor dem Beirat der RWK, Volkswirtschaftliche Bilanz für Deutschland, Grossbritannien und die Vereinigten Staaten von Amerika', 14 December 1944.

[3] A. Munz, op. cit., p. 76.

actual period of the occupation. Were it possible to be more precise the proportion would of course be greater. Approximately one-third of these transfers were covered by taxation, the rest were covered by currency creation and
by borrowing. Germany thus had interest free access to an active capital
market as well as a system of bilateral trading completely in her favour.

There are no estimates of French National Income for the wartime period
except for those guesses made by the Economic Section of the German Armistice Delegation. They estimated French National Income at between
450,000,000,000 and 500,000,000,000 francs in 1942. French guesses placed
it rather lower. The estimates of total available product made for the year
1938 are more exact. Using them rather than the wartime guesses we may say
that the total payments from France to Germany in 1940 were equivalent to
9·3 per cent of France's total available product in 1938. In 1943 they amounted
to almost one-third of France's 1938 product. The wartime movement of the
value of the franc was such that these estimates are probably more inaccurate
at the beginning and end of the period of occupation than for the middle. If
the German and French guesses at French National Income during the war
were used the proportion secured by Germany would appear as high as a
third in 1942 and almost a half in 1943.

TABLE 60

Payments to Germany from France*

	As a percentage of French National Income in 1938 at 1938 prices†	As a percentage of total available product in 1938 at 1938 prices‡
1940	10·9	9·3
1941	19·3	16·5
1942	20·9	17·7
1943	36·6	31·3
1944	27·6	23·6

* Current francs converted to 1938 francs at 1/2·2.
† A. Sauvy, op. cit., ii. 428–44, 575–6.
‡ For the size of total available product, Ministère des finances, *Statistiques et études
financières*, supplément, *Finances françaises*, no. 20, 1953.

The fluctuating prices and the arbitrariness of the Franco-German exchange
rate mean that these calculations can be nothing but vague approximations.
They are doubly so because of the vagueness of the calculations of the Gross
National Product of both countries. Were these calculations, however, uner-
ringly precise, the information they convey would still be of doubtful value.
These are narrowly financial estimates of France's value to Germany. The
estimates of 'foreign contributions' made by the Bombing Survey are not even

complete within the bounds of this narrow framework. They do not include the value of goods and services consumed by German troops outside Germany without payment, nor of the value of booty. Nor do they include the contribution of foreign workers in Germany, which is a particularly grave omission where France is concerned. Indeed, the contribution of French workers in Germany is considered as a part of German Gross National Product.

The first two of these omissions do not greatly distort any calculations about France. There was little reason for the Germans not to pay, and booty was soon abandoned as impracticable. But a great deal of military equipment was surrendered under the terms of the Armistice Agreement. It is a sufficiently large item in the accounts not to be dismissed. Much more serious, however, is the omission of the contribution of French workers in Germany. Without knowing the precise level of productivity of Frenchmen working in Germany it is not possible to remedy this defect except by a series of statistical abstractions placing too high a value on the original evidence.

Foreign workers in Germany were less efficient than German workers, but all observers agreed that the French were more efficient than others. Speer believed the French workers to be the best of all foreign labour, rivalled only by Russian women workers.[1] His view was based on a survey by the *Reichswirtschaftskammer* in 1944, which estimated the productivity of Russian women or French men at between 90 and 100 per cent that of German workers, while that of Dutch and Danish workers was between 50 and 70 per cent that of their German counterparts.[2] Speer may have been taking an optimistic view; although apparently easy to control, the foreign labourers in Germany were indifferent to the quality of their work, the French being no exception.[3] But, if the survey conducted for Speer was a good one, it is beyond doubt that French workers were more productive in Germany than in France.

The sums transferred by French workers in Germany back to France seem to have been larger than those transferred from Germany by any other ethnic group. The only similarly large number of workers of the same nationality were the Russians, and since they were women, and less skilled and more discriminated against, their earnings were much lower. In 1943 at least 277,046,200 Reichsmarks were sent back to France. For the first six months of 1944 the total was almost as great.[4]

The French Reparations Commission calculated the loss to France of that part of her work-force going to Germany, together with those workers in France forced to work for German agencies, by estimating the number of hours of work lost to the French economy. The total was approximately

[1] Speer Report no. 29, Intelligence Report no. EF/LN/2.
[2] E. Homze, op. cit., p. 259.
[3] E. A. Shils, 'Social and psychological Aspects of Displacement and Repatriation', in *Journal of Social Issues*, ii, no. 3 (1946).
[4] E. Homze, op. cit., p. 246.

13,000,000,000 hours of work.[1] To evaluate these working hours the average income per hour of work devoted to internal national production in 1938 was taken as a yardstick. On this basis France could be said to have also lost during the war one-third of the working hours of one pre-war year's production. But because of the difference which existed between the productivity of a Frenchman in Germany and a Frenchman in France the cash value of these hours of work was reduced by estimating seventy-two hours wartime work in Germany at the value of forty-eight hours work in France in 1938. By this process the loss to France was calculated at 71,000,000,000 1938 francs. The coefficient used does not seem to overestimate the total in view of the other evidence about the productivity of French workers in Germany. The productivity of labour in German industry rose by more than 10 per cent during the war in spite of the large number of foreign workers employed.[2] With all respect paid to the patriotism of German workers, and the ingenuity of incentive schemes of payment, this increase of productivity is most likely to have resulted from the greater capital-intensivity of German industry in wartime. It is a frequently observed phenomenon in war economies that the demand for labour produces rapid mechanization of the production process. That mechanization would have affected French and German alike. Since the opposite process took place in the French economy, however, the value of those hours of work to France may well have been less in wartime than in 1938.

To enter by these high-walled arithmetical alleyways is to miss the many receding vistas of France's economic value to Germany. Ultimately it was not the financial value of her conquest which was important to Germany. Nations pursuing modern fiscal policies did not find it hard to finance their part in the Second World War while avoiding disastrous effects on their economies. The war was pre-eminently a war of production, from the outset for Germany's opponents and from the end of 1941 for Germany. These enormous sums transferred from France had their real value in goods, and the ultimate value of any good to a war economy is not measurable by any merely financial yardstick. Nevertheless, the degree to which Germany's financial gains could be exchanged for goods must be considered. For does not the question arise, whether Germany would not have been wiser from an economic point of view to have incorporated the French economy more directly into her own from an earlier stage rather than proceed by the tortuous route of an occupation levy?

By no means all the goods and services obtained from France were paid

---

[1] CCDR., i, ch. 7. See the calculations by A. Piatier, 'La vie économique de la France sous l'occupation', in *La France sous l'occupation*, He estimates the loss at 9,700,000 worker years, 4,500,000 attributable to the loss of prisoners of war, and 5,200,000, attributable to non prisoners of war. Supposing a thirty-six hour week still to have been in force this would mean a total of more than 16,000,000,000 hours of work lost.

[2] USSBS., Overall Economic Effects Division, Special Paper No. 8, *Industrial Sales, Output and Productivity, Prewar Area of Germany 1939–1944* (Washington, 1946).

for, whether in occupation currency or through the clearing mechanism. The French Reparations Commission attempted a comprehensive listing of goods and services according to the method of payment, but in many instances the type of payment remains obscure. There must also remain considerable obscurity around the total sum of goods and services provided. It will be seen that where specific industries have been considered in this book the volume of deliveries to Germany differs somewhat from the estimates of the Commissioners. This was also the case in agricultural production where the quantity

TABLE 61

Value of Goods and Services obtained by Germany from France, 1940–4*

(million francs)

Category	Current francs	1938 francs
Advance deductions of agricultural products	131,818·1	64,720·7
Requisition or utilization of agricultural equipment	12,367·7	5,621·7
Advance deductions of raw materials	106,237·0	57,191·0
Production of manufacturing industry	185,740·7	86,983·8
Seizure of industrial equipment	19,261·8	8,755·4
Advance deductions from transport and communications system and use of that system	265,186·1	120,265·0
War material and military buildings	115,181·0	52,355·0
Quarters for personnel	100,103·9	44,896·5
Specie, precious objects, art objects	26,770·0	12,168·0
Goods and services obtained from the annexed areas	170,590·2	77,541·0
Goods and services obtained from Corsica, Tunisia, Morocco, Algeria	2,905·9	1,320·9
Other charges, services and deductions in advance	14,894·0	6,770·0
Total	1,151,056·4	538,589·0

* CCDR., i, pp. 407–8.

of deliveries to Germany has not been universally agreed. To insist on these differences would not be pedantic, as the Reparations Commissioners certainly had every incentive to exaggerate their claims, although the present evidence does not impugn their honesty. Their task was enormous. For the purpose of a global view their figures may be used with the same reservations as should accompany the National Income calculations for the two countries.

The value of the services consumed, both by the large administration and the army, is striking, although it should be noted that in the case of the largest item, the French transport and communications network, a large part of the total sum covers the confiscation of railway locomotives and trucks, often for use in Germany. The value of the manufactured goods acquired from France, throughout the war, excepting the military equipment seized under the terms of the armistice, appears as 5·5 per cent of the German Gross National Product in 1943, if calculated on the basis of the wartime exchange rate. This is less than the contribution made by the occupation costs in that one year alone. The value of the agricultural products obtained throughout the war is 3·9 per cent of German Gross National Product measured in 1943 and that of raw materials 3·1 per cent. Or, to put it another way, the combined total of these three categories was about one-fifth of the value of private production in Germany during any one war year.

The exploitation of French industry and agriculture by Germany may thus be seen in a perspective where the German effort looks much less successful. It was far easier, after the crushing military victory, to ask for money than to organize the French economy as a part of the German war economy. Nevertheless, the immense presence of Germany, and the manifold ways in which she was able to bring pressure on the French government, meant that the total value of goods and services which, on this reckoning, Germany obtained was roughly equal to one-quarter of her own Gross National Product on the eve of the war.

The gradual change which came over German policy, culminating in Speer's attempt to use French industry as the basis of German consumer goods production, was tantamount to an admission that Germany's need for goods was an overriding one. These changes of policy mean that the type of goods making up the total annual quantity obtained by Germany changed over the period of the occupation. Production for German purposes of certain branches of French manufacturing industry increased after 1941.[1] In autumn 1943 the value of German orders to French consumer goods industries increased sharply.[2]

Until 1941 the volume of French production which was diverted to Germany, and the German orders placed with French manufacturing industry, were established without any over-all knowledge of the precise proportion of French production they represented. In 1941 the *Office Central de Répartition des Produits Industriels* was ordered to collect statistics which would establish how large a part of France's total productive capacity Germany was in fact utilizing.[3] It transpired that in the occupied zone, with the exception of the construction industry, the aircraft industry, and food-producing industries, the general level of deliveries for Germany was between 30 and 40 per cent of total output. If the three industries which were excepted were included the proportion rose to over one half, because the construction industry and the aircraft industry worked almost entirely for German purposes. On the other hand, if the unoccupied zone were included the proportion would have remained at about 30 per cent. The economic section of the

---

[1] See Table 15 above.   [2] See Table 20 above.
[3] FD 3039/49, Section II, Sc. 383, Rm.f.R.u.Kp., Planungsamt.

military administration would not accept this result. They held it to be based on unsatisfactory statistical methods and insufficient statistical evidence; their own opinion was that French production was being exploited for Germany at a level of between 60 and 75 per cent.

The two reports of the Central Contracts Office, of 22 December 1943 and 12 January 1944, gave a long-term view over the value of contracts placed in France. From this it could be seen that between 15 September 1940 and 30 September 1943 the average monthly value of deliveries under contract was 238,500,000 Reichsmarks. Of this total 114,700,000 Reichsmarks a month went to the construction industry, leaving a monthly average of 123,800,000 Reichsmarks to all others.[1] If the monthly average value of contracts to the aircraft industry is also deducted, since neither this nor the construction industry came under the aegis of the *Office Central*, the monthly average value of contracts seems to have remained not far distant from what it had been in 1942. In general, armaments industries and some branches of the engineering industry were producing over the average of 30–40 per cent of their output for Germany, while consumer goods industries were producing at less than the average. In early 1944 contracts to consumer goods producers in France were arranged more frequently and for greater quantities of goods, but from Germany's point of view the success of this policy was not very impressive. In October 1943 the proportion of French production in the former unoccupied zone utilized for German purposes was much smaller than in the former occupied zone.

It will be clear that the quantity of goods obtained by Germany was not the same as the quantity paid for. Nevertheless, the growing demands on the French construction industry were almost certainly responsible for inflating the apparent total of French deliveries to Germany. The quarterly average of these deliveries, according to the military administration, more than doubled by the end of 1943. The building of the Atlantic Wall was an industrial enterprise of vast scope, much the biggest new constructional undertaking in wartime France. When the building of airfields and other defensive installations is taken into account, Table 62, which shows the increasing value of French output for Germany, is perhaps seen in truer perspective. Nor is the increase in total output for German purposes as great as it there appears. The suppressed inflation in France still had its effect in forcing Germany to pay more than the official prices for essential goods, and sometimes even to seek them on the black market. Some allowance for inflation should therefore be made. This allowance would, however, almost certainly be cancelled out by the inclusion in the table of all the hours worked by French workers in Germany and of all the booty taken to Germany. Only that part of the French labour force working for Germany whose labour was paid for out of the occupation levies or the clearing deficit is included.

[1] FD 301/46, Mbh. in F., 'Der Beitrag des französischen Raumes . . .'.

If the statistics of the military administration are accepted, it appears that 1942 was the first year in which Germany bestowed the same importance on the goods and services obtained from France as it had done on the cash. The apparently inexhaustible supply of money diminished rapidly in 1942. At a meeting of the Commercial Policy Committee in the German Foreign Office in November it was decided to press for greater occupation costs.[1]

TABLE 62

*French Output for Germany**

(million Reichsmarks)

Time	Paid from occupation levy	Balance of clearing account	Total
1940 3rd quarter	249		249
4th quarter	1,510	43	1,553
Annual total	1,759	43	1,802
1941 1st quarter	1,208	76	1,284
2nd quarter	1,295	146	1,441
3rd quarter	1,331	262	1,593
4th quarter	1,253	327	1,580
Annual total	5,087	811	5,898
1942 1st quarter	1,657	409	2,066
2nd quarter	1,812	336	2,148
3rd quarter	2,209	408	2,689
4th quarter	2,194	555	2,749
Annual total	7,872	1,780	9,652
1943 1st quarter	2,645	769	3,414
2nd quarter	2,240	908	3,148
3rd quarter	2,418	845	3,263
4th quarter	2,495	793	3,288
Annual total	9,798	3,315	13,113
1940–3 Total	24,516	5,949	30,465

* FD 301/46, Mbh. in F., 'Der Beitrag des französischen Raumes . . .'.

French deliveries of foodstuffs and agricultural produce to Germany were much heavier in the harvest year 1942/3 than in the previous year.[2] The harvest year 1943/4 saw relatively little change. There was no significant category of agricultural produce where the proportion of French production made available to Germany, and also the actual quantity, did not increase in the harvest year 1942/3, so that by the close of that year Germany was taking over 15 per cent of French agricultural output for her own purposes. Of the imports of bread grains into Germany in that year 46 per cent came from France, which had become the most important of Germany's suppliers. The

[1] Hemmen Papers, NG. 4526, 'Sitzung des Handelspolitisches Ausschusses vom 26 November 1942'.   [2] See above, pp. 257–8.

bread ration in Germany depended on the French harvest. If the hopes of
a great German agricultural dependency in eastern Europe had been dashed,
German policy turned France into a replacement.

The contribution which France made to the supply of raw materials in
Germany increased in size and increased much more in relative importance.
As the territorial area over which Germany had command shrank, and as the
German economy began to exploit much more fully its productive capacity
for war purposes, the relative utility of French supply increased. The extraordinary importance which Germany was obliged to attach at the last to the
quite insignificant supplies of wolfram from France bear witness to this.

It was not in fact only in those areas where France was particularly well
endowed with raw materials that she was useful to Germany. In such areas
German control was unrelenting. Including the annexed areas of France
Germany took for her own purposes three-quarters of France's iron-ore
supply, excluding those areas she took about one half.[1] If Alsace and Lorraine
are counted as German territory for the duration of the war Germany was
not as dependent on French iron-ore supply as these figures might suggest.
The supply from all occupied territories to Germany remained lower in 1943
and 1944 than imports into Germany from neutral areas.[2] In both those years
German iron-ore imports from Sweden, measured by iron content, were
larger on a monthly average than her supply from occupied territories. The
quantities of bauxite obtained from France were probably of more absolute
importance to the German war economy. In 1942 Germany took 36 per cent
of total French bauxite production, in 1943 53 per cent, a total of half a
million tons in the latter year, or over four times her annual level of bauxite
imports from France before the war.[3] The coal-mining areas of France which
Germany annexed had their supply diverted entirely to German purposes. In
spite of the constant coal shortage in France she thus lost 15 per cent of her
total output to Germany for the duration of the war.

French output of other non-ferrous metal ores and metals was generally
small. Since such materials were all relatively scarce in Germany, however,
France was made to contribute heavily to total German supply. The contribution came particularly from captured stockpiles which formed a substantial
part of German booty. The relative importance of booty and the quantities of
such materials obtained by Germany can be seen in Table 63.

The total value of the raw materials obtained by Germany was a lot less
than the total value of manufactured goods obtained and lower than the total
value of foodstuffs. If booty alone is considered the total value of manufactured goods would still be higher as the value of military equipment passing

[1] See above, Table 41.
[2] FD 3039/49, Section III, Sc. 98, Rm.f.R.u.Kp., 'Statistische Schnellberichte zur Kriegsproduktion, Jahresheft 1938/44'.
[3] See above, Table 47.

to Germany was as great as the total value of raw materials whether purchased or taken as booty.

From a financial aspect Germany's greatest advantage was the use of the French communications network. By the end of 1943, owing to the deterioration of the capital equipment, to Allied bombing, and to the surrender of 4,300 locomotives to Germany, French railways had only half the stock of locomotives they had had at the beginning of the war. The stock of wagons was

TABLE 63

Non-ferrous Metals and Metal Ores Obtained by Germany from France to the End of 1943*

	As purchases and contracts		As booty and recuperations		Total	Total to 31 July 1942†
	tons	%	tons	%	tons	tons
Copper	125,800	51	121,800	49	247,600	233,724
Lead	36,000	66	18,500	34	54,500	51,786
Tin	7,100	56	5,500	44	12,600	9,753
Nickel	2,100	34	4,000	66	6,100	5,843
Zinc	33,600	42	46,000	58	79,600	..
Alumina	114,200	100	..	..	114,200	..
Aluminium	69,200	92	5,600	8	74,800	(93,550)‡
Magnesium	5,000	93	400	7	5,400	4,193
Scrap	186,000	21	687,000	79	873,000	..

* FD 301/46, Mbh. in F., 'Der Beitrag des französischen Raumes . . .'.
† FD 301/45, Mbh. in F., 'Leistungen der französischen Wirtschaft, usw., . . .'.
‡ Alumina + aluminium on an aluminium basis.

scarcely greater than one half the pre-war stock for the same reasons. The transport of military personnel, and of goods with top-priority classification, goods, that is to say, destined for Germany, took an increasing share of the total train movements in France. The share rose from 66 per cent in December 1941 to 85 per cent in January 1944. France was allowed a greater share in the use of her own internal waterway system, although even here the needs of German construction undertakings intervened to the extent that in 1943 half the weight of traffic carried on the internal waterways was also for German purposes.

Frenchmen formed the biggest section of the male foreign labour force in Germany. Over 630,000 left for Germany between June 1942 and April 1944.[1] Their number was exceeded by the French prisoners of war in Germany, who could also be classed as working for Germany. At the same time a substantial part of the French labour force in France was also working for Germany. The military administration estimated that, of the male French labour force aged between 18 and 50, 2,578,000, or 37 per cent of the total, were directly working

[1] See above, pp. 123 ff.

for Germany either in Germany or in France. Of this number 1,378,000 were employed in France. A further 1,387,000 in France were indirectly employed for German purposes.[1]

Finally must be considered the extent to which Germany was able to turn France into a trading satellite, and the advantage which this accrued to her. No normal state of trade exists, and to that extent there could be no deviation from that state for France. Nevertheless, French imports were reduced by

TABLE 64

Weekly Transport Capacity on French Railways According to Priority Groupings*

(1,000 tons lading)

	December 1941		July 1942		December 1942		July 1943		January 1944	
		%		%		%		%		%
Armed forces	320	16	460	21	510	25	590	29	560	33
'A' priority goods	1,040	50	1,080	49	1,160	58	780	39	880	52
Capacity for the most part being used for German purposes	1,360	66	1,540	70	1,670	83	1,370	68	1,440	85
Capacity for the most part being used for French purposes	710	34	680	30	330	17	650	32	250	15
Total	2,070		2,220		2,000		2,020		1,690	

* FD 301/46, 'Der Beitrag des französischen Raumes . . .'.

two-thirds in value during the war while her exports increased slightly. From supplying 3·7 per cent of German imports by value in 1938 France rose to supplying 18·3 per cent in 1944.[2] Germany had imported foodstuffs from France in 1938 to the value of 29,200,000 Reichsmarks; in 1943 the value of such imports was 537,200,000 Reichsmarks. In 1938 German imports of manufactured and semi-manufactured products from France had been worth 36,400,000 Reichsmarks; in 1943 their value was 732,800,000 Reichsmarks.[3]

With no other European power was Germany able to run an import surplus of such a size. France thus played a vital role in Germany's wartime trading system. With three allies, Romania, Italy, and Finland, Germany maintained a substantial export surplus, the cost of keeping them in the war. Even to some of the occupied territories Germany exported goods to a greater value than those she received in return. Such was the case with Norway, Croatia, and Slovakia. France, Belgium, and the Netherlands contributed massively to Germany's supply, and on the most favourable possible terms for Germany. Germany's own trading position was therefore also changed by the occupation of France.

[1] See above p. 123 ff.   [2] See Table 65.   [3] A. Munz, op. cit., p. 72.

The pre-war trend in which the countries of south-eastern Europe had become the most important source of German supply was broken, and their place was taken by France, with Belgium and the Netherlands in a subordinate role. In 1943 France became the most important supplier of raw materials, foodstuffs, and manufactured goods to the German economy.

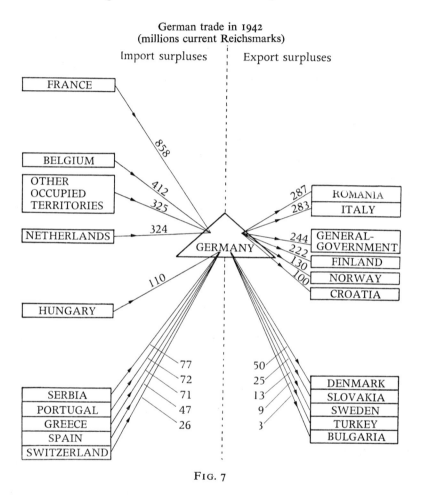

German trade in 1942
(millions current Reichsmarks)

FIG. 7

The German military success in 1940 brought about a change as far-reaching and more sudden than that induced by Schacht's 'New Policy' in the 1930s. After the German occupation of France the pattern of west European trade as it now exists began to emerge. The eastern and south-eastern European countries, which had played an increasing role in Germany's economy in the 1930s quickly declined in importance.

Enough has been written. Whatever the failures of German policy in France, and whatever the degree to which Germany failed to exploit the French economy to the maximum possible limit, her physical gain from the possession of so large and so rich a territory was manifest. But what did the conquest cost Germany?

TABLE 65

German–French Trade as a Proportion of Total German Trade＊

(million Reichsmarks)

Year	Total imports	Imports from France	%	Total exports	Exports to France	%	Import surplus from France
1938	5,449·3	203·5	3·7	5,256·9	237·8	4·5	−34·3
1939	4,796·5	123·4	2·6	5,222·2	145·4	2·8	−22·0
1940	5,012·1	229·6	4·6	4,867·8	13·3	0·3	216·3
1941 1st quarter	1,469·0	124·0	8·4	1,566·0	36·0	2·3	88·0
2nd quarter	1,821·0	186·0	10·2	1,767·0	66·0	3·7	120·0
3rd quarter	1,796·0	204·0	11·4	1,714·0	89·0	5·2	115·0
4th quarter	1,839·0	238·0	12·9	1,795·0	124·0	6·9	114·0
Total	6,925·0	771·3	11·1	6,840·5	317·0	4·6	454·3
1942 1st quarter	1,461·0	204·0	14·0	1,382·0	97·0	7·0	107·0
2nd quarter	2,122·0	325·0	15·3	1.953·0	150·0	7·7	175·0
3rd quarter	2,267·0	382·0	16·9	2,100·0	157·0	7·5	225·0
4th quarter	2,842·0	493·0	17·3	2,125·0	142·0	6·7	351·0
Total	8,691·5	1,441·3	16·6	7,559·6	552·3	7·3	889·0
1943 1st quarter	2,180·0	365·0	16·7	2,080·0	159·0	7·6	206·0
2nd quarter	2,505·0	390·0	15·6	2,496·0	152·0	6·1	248·0
3rd quarter 4th quarter	1,772·0	330·0	18·6	2,019·0	127·0	6·3	203·0
Total	8,258·4	1,416·1	17·1	8,588·0	559·9	6·5	856·2
Jan.–July 1944	4,931·9	903·8	18·3	4,487·8	251·2	5·6	652·6

＊ FD 301/46, Mbh. in F., 'Der Beitrag des französischen Raumes . . .', A. Munz, op. cit., p. 71. The quarterly totals are uncorrected figures and therefore do not exactly correspond with the annual totals which are corrected. They are included to show the persistence of the trend revealed by the annual figures.

To measure the amount of rearmament expenditure which went to the conquest of France is obviously impossible. If the whole of German military expenditure from 1934, when rearmament first made any serious financial impact on the German economy, until the conquest of France had been achieved be considered as a cost of Germany's plans for conquest, and the abortive plans for an invasion of Britain are taken into account, but the conquests of Austria and Luxembourg are omitted as being relatively inexpensive,

German expenditure for the conquest of Czechoslovakia, parts of Poland, France, Belgium, the Netherlands, Denmark, Norway, and for the briefly attempted conquest of Britain, averaged 13,300,000,000 Reichsmarks for each territory.[1] That is less than the payments received by Germany from France in 1943, including the balance on the clearing.

In fact this estimate of the cost of conquest, leaving on one side for the moment the cost of maintaining that conquest, is much too high. Only a part of the armed forces were actually used in the conquest of France. But that objection is a pettifogging one. Calculations of military expenditure in this way are not very meaningful because of the widely differing purposes to which 'normal' budgetary expenditure is applied. These differences may be brought out by a glance at the proportion of 'war expenditure' as a proportion of the total budget for other combatants in the war. In 1943 such expenditure accounted for 84 per cent of the British budget, but only for 59 per cent of the Russian budget.[2] From such a comparison all that is learnt is that the 'normal' British and Russian budgets were used for very different purposes. How much of civilian expenditure might go into the cost of conquest?

But there is a more serious objection yet. In the circumstances of the German and international economies in the pre-war years can any of the German rearmament expenditure be regarded as a cost? Was it not rather a gain? The opportunity cost of such a rearmament programme might be compared with that of other employment-creating projects. In fact the major part in increasing the level of employment in Germany in the first years of the National Socialist regime was played by a traditional public works programme, the building of a modern system of roads. But the economic doctrine of German fascism demanded a rearmament programme. Within the limitations of that doctrine it is impossible to argue that the rearmament programme was a cost to the economy; outside those limitations it may also not have been a cost.

It was a useful adjunct to the programme of economic reinvigoration, to the stimulation of industrial production, and to the creation of employment. The extent to which after 1938 the much higher production of armaments diverted the economy from the production of consumer goods may also be discounted. If consumer goods were sacrificed they were sacrificed to the increase in

[1] There has always been great difficulty in deciding the exact quantity of German government expenditure which could be defined as 'military expenditure'. This is not so much due to deliberate obfuscation of the statistics by the German government as to their refusal to make the arbitrary distinctions made in the budgets of their neighbours between expenditure for civil and military purposes. See K. D. Bracher, W. Sauer, and G. Schultz, *Die national-sozialistische Machtergreifung* (Köln, 1960), pp. 661 ff.; R. Erbe, *Die nationalsozialistische Wirtschaftspolitik 1933–39 im Lichte der modernen Theorie* (Zurich, 1958), p. 34 and passim; and B. H. Klein, op. cit., pp. 4–27. The estimates for expenditure used here are those of B. A. Carroll, *Design for Total War, Arms and Economics in the Third Reich* (The Hague, 1968). They are the most recent, and for one year they are confirmed by documentary evidence.

[2] W. K. Hancock and M. M. Gowing, *The British War Economy* (London, 1949), p. 347; S. N. Procopovicz, *Histoire économique de l'U.R.S.S.* (Paris, 1942), p. 613.

Germany's productive capacity in certain basic industries such as steel, rubber, and oil. Given Hitler's strategic plan, expenditure on those industries was as much military expenditure as expenditure on battle cruisers. Preparation for war was almost entirely beneficial to the German economy in the 1930s.

There remains, however, the loss of men and equipment in effecting the conquest. It will be clear already that the loss of equipment was annulled by the massive gains of French equipment. But what of the men? Can any financial value be placed on their heads? This grisly accountancy was particularly popular in the United States after the First World War, since in that country no worth while claims for destruction of property could be made on the Germans. Clark considered the financial loss to America of her dead service-men to be equal to the capitalization of their future incomes less that part which would have been devoted to consumption. The difference is what the survivors now had to bear because of the death of the others.[1] What a wealth of economic prejudice speaks from such assumptions! Bogart attributed an average social value to soldiers of different nationality, since at different stages of economic development the level of productivity is different. A dead Russian was less than half as big a loss as a dead American.[2]

Verri held the profitability of conquest to be largely determined by the relationship of labour and resources which resulted once the conquest had been achieved.[3] The usual outcome of conquest was an insufficient supply of labour and a consequent diminution of production. However dogged the paths of Verri's predecessors by the fear of over-population, doubts were always present in their minds as to the value of exporting population. The theory of *Lebensraum* ought not to be attributed to seventeenth-century writers. Nor did any express the view that conquest was valuable because it absolutely reduced the amount of labour through loss of life. But, in a decade of heavy unemployment, are dead soldiers a financial loss to the economy? Is not the death of a soldier the cause of a decrease in the national product only if there is full employment and if conditions of labour for the rest of what would have been his working life do not change?

Had the loss of German lives in the campaign in France not been made up by the much greater quantity of workmen Germany was able to draft into her domestic labour force, that loss should still not be counted as a cost to the economy. The impact of war on the rates of labour productivity is so strong that the loss of life should properly be considered as a part of that wider problem. In the event German casualties in France were very small by the side of the number of workers Germany got in return.

There remains only the cost of running the conquered territory. The actual cost of the army of occupation is not known. It was not even known to the

[1] J. M. Clark, *The Cost of the World War to the American People* (New Haven, 1931).
[2] E. L. Bogart, *Direct and Indirect Costs of the Great War* (New York, 1920).
[3] P. Verri, op. cit.

Commercial Policy Committee of the Foreign Ministry nor to the Economic Delegation to the Armistice Commission. Hemmen was simply presented with a total sum established by the Wehrmacht without any breakdown of what that expenditure actually covered. On at least one occasion Wiehl, the Chief of the Commercial Policy Committee, tried to get the High Command of the Armed Forces to give details about the enormous sums which they demanded, but he was unsuccessful.[1] Perhaps they remembered the cautionary lesson of the Italian Armistice Delegation who found themselves without sufficient French funds to pay the costs of their administrative offices in France.

The average cost of maintaining a member of the French Army in the field for one day during the war was twenty-two francs.[2] The limit at which the occupation costs were first fixed therefore would have paid for an army of 18,000,000 men on active service. Hemmen could find no better explanation for the sum than that it was less than the French war budget would have been had the countries still been at war.[3] The troops necessary for the continuation of the war against Britain and all the military expenses directly or distantly connected with that purpose were amply covered. But the occupation costs were used for still wider purposes than that. Black-market activities in France and elsewhere in Europe depended for their financing on the French payments. Indeed, the sum was considered under two heads, 'pure occupation costs', which included the maintenance of the fighting men in North Africa and the fortification of the French shores, and 'expenditure alien to the occupation costs', which could be the larger part of the expenditure.[4]

In autumn 1942 expenditure was beginning to outrun receipts of occupation payments. But of the general monthly expenditure of 700,000,000 Reichsmarks only 150,000,000 Reichsmarks were classified as 'pure occupation costs'.[5] This sum covered aspects of military expenditure far wider than the mere upkeep of the army of occupation and the German administration. The true cost of their upkeep was probably no higher than 75,000,000 Reichsmarks a month. At that time Germany was receiving 456,250,000 Reichsmarks a month in occupation levies.

The profit obtained from France, crudely expressed by the occupation costs, was intended to be reinvested in the prosecution of the next, and more important, stage of the war. German policy was therefore short-term in its intentions as far as France was concerned. In the short-run the liberal idea of conquest was proved quite wrong and its enemies vindicated. But the problem was also a long-run problem and in its wider aspects the liberal theorists would have found some justification.

[1] Hemmen Papers, NG–4198, 'Vermerk über die HPA-Sitzung im A A vom 7. November. 1942'.
[2] DFCAA., i. 160.   [3] Ibid., p. 166.
[4] 'Besatzungskostenfremden Ausgaben'.
[5] Hemmen Papers, NG–4526, 'Sitzung des Handelspolitischen Ausschusses vom 26. November 1942'.

The study of individual industries and the relative failure of German policies of exploitation suggests that that failure was due not only to the contradictions of German policy but also to the falling rates of labour productivity in the French economy. It is the behaviour of the French labour force during the war, and, indeed, the whole history of the French resistance movement, which assert that the economics of conquest cannot wholly be calculated in terms of cash.

The average daily output at the coal face in French coal-mines fell by 39 per cent between 1938 and 1944. Longer hours of work and a bigger labour force kept the output of coal in France slightly above the pre-war level for the same territorial area, but by 1943 these remedies were failing as productivity fell further. In that year also it became clear that the same fundamental problem was at the bottom of Germany's failure to increase the output of the iron-ore mines. In bauxite mines the output per employee at the close of 1943 was roughly half the level of 1939. There was far more absenteeism than in pre-war years. Occasionally acts of deliberate sabotage were committed, but a constant unwillingness, which constituted a form of passive sabotage more effective than more overt acts, prevailed. This state of affairs was not confined to the extractive industries. In June 1942 it took four times as many working hours to manufacture a Fieseler–Storch aeroplane in the Morane Saulnier works as it would have done to manufacture the same aeroplane in Germany.[1] The first Arado aircraft to be manufactured at Saint-Nazaire was sabotaged on 29 May 1942.[1] It would be impossible to prove that the higher accident rates recorded in mines were due to the resistance of the labour force. In part they were caused by the deterioration of the equipment and the influx of less skilled labour. But these higher accident rates were also recorded on the railway system, and so were the higher rates of absenteeism.[2]

Passive resistance of this sort to the occupier cannot be measured. There were many good reasons why productivity should decrease whatever the mood of the labour force. Deterioration both of fixed capital and of the level of skill of the workers had their effect. The chronic shortage of raw materials and fuel meant constant interruptions to the production process. Coal-mining operations, for example, were frequently suspended for lack of pit-props. The workers in many industries had to submit to much longer hours and the work force itself was growing older, especially in mining industries. Finally, there was undernourishment.

The reduction in food consumption in France during the war was more drastic than in other western occupied territories. The consumption of every main category of foodstuffs was reduced by more than one-third. In the Netherlands where the reductions were also very severe the ration remained

[1] FD 671/46, Mbh. in F., Rü–I'A', 'Lagebericht', June 1942.
[2] P. Durand, 'La politique de l'emploi à la SNCF pendant la deuxième guerre mondiale', in *Revue d'histoire de la deuxième guerre mondiale*, lvii (1965).

higher. The reductions in France began, of course, before the occupation, and the French population suffered a longer spell of low rations than the population of either Belgium or the Netherlands. There were the further difficulties that the ration was not always obtainable and that much food had to be bought at very high prices on the black market. The working population was less well fed even than the official rations suggest.

TABLE 66

Food Rations in France and Percentage Drop By Comparison with Average Pre-war Consumption*

(grammes per week)

Commodity	4th quarter 1941	4th quarter 1942	4th quarter 1943
Bread	1,925	1,925	2,100
Meat	250†	180–125	190–120
Fat	125	100 to 70	70–55
Cheese	70	50	50
Sugar‡	500	500	500
Potatoes	..	4–6 kgs	4–6 kgs.

	Drop in French ration in 1940 by comparison with pre-war (percentage)	Further drop 1940–3/4 in comparison with pre-war (percentage)	Ration in 1943/4 in comparison with pre-war (percentage)
Bread	19	11	70
Meat	48	34	18
Fat	56	13	31

* H. Kistenmacher, op. cit., pp. 21–9.
† 180–125 grammes in places with less than 8,000 inhabitants.
‡ Grammes per month.

The effect of these lowered rations on the population was very variable. Since the black market was so prevalent that was inevitable. Nor did German agricultural policy persuade the peasants and smaller farmers to part with so large a part of their surplus as they had sold before the war. The over-all crude death rate in France increased from 15·3 per thousand in 1939 to 19·1 in 1944.[1] The infant mortality rate also increased. But because agricultural producers retained greater supplies for their own consumption and, even more, because access to black-market food supplies was easier and required less cash in the countryside, a marked difference emerged in the vital statistics of the rural and urban populations. While in general the rural death rate increased the general

[1] HNSEE., *Mouvement économique etc.*, op. cit., p. 73.

mortality rate in some of the more remote rural areas improved in the period 1941–3 by comparison with 1936–8. In the department of Indre, for example, it fell by 11 per cent, and in the departments of Mayenne and Orne the fall was almost as great.[1] In the heavily populated urban areas, where most of the working population lived, the general mortality rate rose steeply in those years, so that in the departments of Seine and Seine-et-Oise it was 24 per cent and 23 per cent higher respectively than over the period 1936–8. In Bouches-du-Rhône the increase was 57 per cent.

When allowance is made for all, there still remains the impression that the workers were not prepared to produce for a cause with which they disagreed. Certainly the German administration had no illusions on that matter. They complained that the French work-force was hostile to the attacks on the liberal framework in which they worked.[2] The workers did not like the work-book with which they were issued.[3] Nor did they like being studied to provide statistical information. They had even tried to boycott a concert given at the Gnôme et Rhône works by the Berlin Philharmonic Orchestra. Reprisals against such behaviour only led to a further fall in output.

German policy itself contributed in the early stages of the occupation to this state of affairs. So limited were German aims in respect of the French economy in 1940 that so long as the Vichy government provided the cash and did not impede German actions in those sectors of the economy where Germany had a vital interest it had a certain freedom of action in its own labour policy, especially if that labour policy was designed to further the cause of law and order. Accordingly in autumn 1940 the French government was allowed to follow a policy of mopping-up unemployment by whatever means it could devise. The result was a period of slack working and low productivity. By 1942, when this was not at all in German interests, there was nothing the administration could do to break the habits of slack working, reinforced as they now were by the steady hostility of the population as a whole.

The labour force was violently affected by the invasion. The advance of the German troops was accompanied by an enormous dispersion of the population attempting to avoid the enemy.[4] This disturbance took place at the same time as the collapse of production in those industries which had been particularly involved in the French war effort. In certain areas of France and also in certain sectors of industry there was a dramatic fall in the number of employed persons, while in other areas of the country, particularly in the south-west and in the unoccupied zone, there was an equally dramatic increase in the numbers of those seeking employment. The invasion came with the effect of a

[1] M. Cépède, op. cit., p. 406.

[2] FD 671/46, Mbh. in F., Wehrwirtschafts- und Rüstungsstab Frankreich, 'Lagebericht Mai 1942', 2 June 1942.

[3] Very similar to the 'livret' against the imposition of which their predecessors had struggled in the nineteenth century.

[4] J. Vidalenc, L'Exode de mai–juin 1940 (Paris, 1957).

bomb exploded in relatively placid waters. In September 1940 when the
occupiers attempted a partial labour census the ripples were not yet stilled.

The census applied to industrial firms with more than 100 employees and
to firms in the service sector of the economy with more than 50. It did not

TABLE 67

*Results of the Partial Census of Employment in the Occupied Area of France,
September 1940**

Sector	Number of firms incl. in sample	Total employed in first 6 months of 1939 (monthly average)	Total employed in August 1940	August 1940 employment as percentage of first 6 months of 1939
Mining	83	158,456	134,486	85
Iron and steel	576	353,179	123,675	35
Non-ferrous metals	305	107,415	44,296	41
Chemicals	216	67,107	31,952	48
Textiles and clothing	603	210,804	135,398	64
Hides and skins	115	29,876	20,578	68
Rubber	61	25,570	9,093	36
Paper and cellulose	210	58,628	29,419	50
Stone and earth	158	45,262	20,674	46
Construction	164	48,520	24,429	50
Wood	113	22,886	12,186	53
Foodstuffs	312	87,704	60,376	69
Other industries	7	2,909	1,109	38
Gas and electricity supply	542	35,275	30,229	86
Public transport	112	46,507	22,439	48
Commercial undertakings	523	109,275	64,787	59
Banking and Insurance	199	49,459	35,185	71
Average				55

* NA., T.71, Roll 101, 602972, Mbh. in F., Wi. I/5, 'Ergebnisse der Erhebung von
September 1940 für das besetzte Gebiet Frankreichs'.

apply to the two northern departments nor to the annexed areas. Even in the
occupied zone, however, there was one department, Landes, where the labour
force had increased since 1939. In several departments in eastern and northern
France the number employed was less than half the monthly average of the
first half of 1939. There were also wide variations in the level of employment
in different industries. In metallurgical and chemical industries the volume of
employment was less than half its immediate pre-war level.

In the light of these statistics the policy of the Vichy government and the German administration seems an attempt to get back to some image of normality at whatever cost. The return of the refugees, encouraged by the Germans, could not be accomplished without the creation of a large number of jobs. In August the number of unemployed continued to increase especially in Paris and the other big towns.[1] Prefects were empowered to order a shorter

TABLE 68

Estimated Proportion of Employed Persons in August 1940 by Comparison with Monthly Averages of First Six Months of 1939 by Department*

(percentage)

Landes	115	Charente	76	Seine-Inférieure	52
Vendée	98	Indre-et-Loire	74	Oise	47
Basses-Pyrénées	91	Vosges	72	Doubs	46
Deux-Sèvres	87	Sarthe	67	Seine	46
Saône-et-Loire	86	Yonne	63	Cher	45
Gironde	84	Eure-et-Loir	62	Côtes-du-Nord	45
Vienne	84	Nièvre	61	Loiret	44
Ille-et-Vilaine	83	Côte-d'Or	60	Calvados	42
Maine-et-Loire	81	Aube	59	Meuse	40
Orne	80	Charente-		Marne	39
Morbihan	79	Inférieure	59	Seine-et-Oise	37
Finistère	78	Manche	57	Haute-Marne	32
Mayenne	78	Haute-Saône	57	Aisne	31
Loire-Inférieure	78	Seine-et-Marne	56	Meurthe-et-	
Allier	77	Loir-et-Cher	55	Moselle	27
Jura	76	Eure	54	Somme	27

* N.A., T.71, Roll 101, 602973/4.

working day and the Secretary of State for Finance was empowered to provide funds for public-works projects. According to Bouthillier the government spent 50,000,000,000 francs on financing public works.[2] It was in these circumstances, as the situation deteriorated and there seemed as yet little hope of German policy bringing about an industrial recovery, that the Commissariat for the Struggle against Unemployment was formed under François Lehideux. Its programme of action was outlined in the law of 11 October, published on 29 October in the *Journal Officiel*. It would undertake a modernization of French transport and harbour installations, including some railway electrification. There would be a special programme for Paris, embracing an extension of the underground railway and improvements in the sanitation of the older quarters. Powers for this last plan were taken in the decree published on 22 November.

The realization was less grand than the plan. The work of the Commissariat seems to have consisted largely of forcing compulsory short-time working on

[1] BA., R 7 VIII 207, Mbh. in F., Wi.Abt., 'Wirtschaftsbericht für August 1940', 4 September 1940.
[2] Y. Bouthillier, op. cit., ii. 231.

to employers, no exceptions being allowed until after the winter, when the number of unemployed had fallen to 350,000.[1] The speed with which this heavy unemployment was absorbed can only have been due to the growth of widespread underemployment. In many cases this must have represented a patriotic gesture on the part of entrepreneurs who, encouraged by the government, were prepared to conspire with their employees against the common enemy. Once the unemployment crisis was over production in France settled down at a level more than 25 per cent below that of pre-war. Already a labour shortage rather than an unemployment problem was on the horizon.

But the pattern of events is of greater significance than as an unexplored problem of French history. For it is only too likely that it is a universal pattern rather than merely an aspect of French patriotism. After the invasion of Belgium there were over 500,000 unemployed not counting the refugees. By December 1940 only 219,000 were unemployed. By spring 1941 Belgium was already feeling the nip of a labour shortage.[2] The level of production, however, was lower than in 1939.

Falling productivity is almost certainly endemic to an occupied economy and one of its causes is the reluctance of the workers to work. Increasing productivity is endemic to a war economy. The economies of the occupier and the occupied thus move in diametrically opposite directions. The one becomes more capital-intensive as the demand for labour increase, the other more labour-intensive as the human spirit displays its capacity for resistance.

In spite of reduced food supply, of housing shortages, of longer hours of work, of increases in accidents as the work is speeded up, of capital depreciation, and of lower-grade substituted materials, the general long-run effect of war economies has been to increase the productivity of labour. A programme to manufacture armaments represents the same kind of stimulation to the economy as a public-works programme, but the one is almost inevitably accompanied by a labour shortage, while the other is the result of excess labour. The accelerated rate of mechanization of American agriculture in the Civil War and in the First World War was the result of an increase in the rates of pay of farm labour due to recruitment and higher rates of pay in industry.[3] Improvements in productivity in Britain in the First World War were closely associated with similar large movements of labour.[4] In Germany during the Second World War, in spite of the use of foreign labour, the productivity of labour in industry rose throughout the war. The United States Strategic Bombing Survey estimated the rise at about 12 per cent; Wagenführ's own

[1] Ibid., p. 363. K. Ringel, op. cit., p. 50 ff.

[2] F. Baudhuin, op. cit., p. 299.

[3] E. Altschuhl and F. Strauss, *Technical Progress and Agricultural Depression*, National Bureau of Economic Research, Bulletin no. 672 (New York, 1937); A. Tilden, *The Legislation of the Civil War Period Considered as a Basis of the Agricultural Revolution in the United States* (Los Angeles, 1937).

[4] A. L. Bowley, *Some Economic Consequences of the Great War* (London, 1930), p. 171.

estimates made during the war suggest the increase might have been even greater.[1]

In Germany, as in the economies of the other important combatants during the war, the sectors of industry where employment and output rose were the more capital-intensive sectors. Labour moved both voluntarily and under compulsion from the more labour-intensive sectors of the economy into air-craft manufacture, motor vehicle construction, armaments manufacture, the manufacture of electrical equipment, and similar industries. In all these industries, under the pressure of desperate urgency, continual improvements in the manufacturing process were introduced. There were, of course, limita-tions on this process. In older industries, such as coal-mining, continuing increases in productivity were not possible, while the need for greater produc-tion was always present. Nevertheless, the general movement of labour out of agriculture, building work, service industries, and older industries where improvements in productivity were now very small, such as textiles, was very marked. Similar movements of labour can be observed in both Britain and the United States in the First and Second World Wars.

France suffered from the contrary tendency. The departure of labour from the agricultural sector of the French economy had been slowed down by the unstable industrial situation after 1933.[2] This tendency was only reinforced by the war. To remain on the land was to be safer, better fed, and probably better remunerated. The number of people employed in the central admini-stration grew, not only because of the new conceptions of central government brought by the conquerors but also as part of the government's employment policies. The machinery of price control and commodity control required a great increase in the number of permanent and temporary civil servants. There were also the 'chantiers de jeunesse' to be provided for.[3] The influence of the occupation on French industries was very haphazard and much depended on the source of supply of the basic raw materials. Electrical industries in France suffered particularly, as they were large consumers of non-ferrous metals. In the metal-working industries, where the growth of productivity is particularly marked in the economies of the combatants, productivity in France fell. By 1944 the labour force, 150,000 strong in 1939, had diminished by about 15 per cent; output, however, was in general only 74 per cent of pre-war, although in some branches higher.[4] In the wood-working industries, where Germany made several efforts to bring about a measure of industrial concentration in order to free labour, only 0·5 per cent of the firms were actu-ally closed, and perfume manufacturers managed to avoid the worst conse-

[1] USSBS., Special Papers No. 8, Report 134a; Deutsches Institut für Wirtschaftsforschung, *Die deutsche Industrie im Kriege 1939–1945* (Berlin, 1954), pp. 79 ff.

[2] J. Fourastié, 'La population active française pendant la seconde guerre mondiale', in *Revue d'histoire de la deuxieme guerre mondiale*, lviii (1965).

[3] Y. Bouthillier, op. cit., ii. 370.

[4] CCDR., iii, A. 1. 19.

quences of almost all German actions threatening them with closure.[1] Most astonishing of all, the number of jewellers and makers of small luxury articles increased. The shortage of precious metals effectively closed down the most costly branches of their trade, more effectively no doubt than German administrative action, but the prevalent fear of inflation and distaste for currency ensured that the number of firms was still able to increase by 1944.[2]

Whereas for most of the participants in the war, and even many neutrals, the productive effort necessary meant an escape from the unemployment of the previous decade and a period of dynamic growth of at least some sectors of their economy, for France it meant a continuation of the same disheartening trend of the 1930s. Such may well be the inescapable fate of any occupied economy.

The falling rate of productivity involved conqueror as well as conquered. It was the background to that inflation which was kept at bay only to strike with redoubled effect once the occupation had ended. It is the declining level of productivity, rooted as it undoubtedly was in the resistance of French society to the conquerors, that exposes the flimsy superficiality both of the Vichy government's proud boast that it saved the franc and of the attempts by Speer and Bichelonne to create a 'rational' New Order. The history of German dealings in the international wolfram market is sufficient evidence of the inflationary tendencies that threatened her isolated economic system. The precarious balance of that system was no less threatened by the results of occupation. Where the French worker contrived to keep a reasonable standard of living during the war he did so at the expense of productivity, and in so doing he struck a hard, if indirect, blow for liberal theory against the New Economic Order.

But the vindication of the liberal idea does not necessarily follow from these facts. The disputes about German economic policy, the uncertainties and the mistakes, have to be seen in relation to the historical context of that policy. That conquest, in the long run is not profitable, is too satisfyingly moral a lesson to draw. Each conqueror has his philosophy of conquest and can only act within the bounds of that philosophy. Seen in historical perspective the National Socialist conquests were an attempt to solve the political and economic problems of Germany by solving those of Europe on the same principles. The New Economic Order was ultimately essential if National Socialist Germany was not always to face overwhelming economic problems in a hostile world. The economic developments in Germany after the National Socialist revolution were meaningless in the long run if confined to one country; conquest was inherent in them. But the weaknesses in that philosophy of conquest, the weaknesses responsible for its confusions and failures, were not universal weaknesses; rather they were unique to the development of the National Socialist philosophy.

[1] Ibid., A. 1, 21, A. 1. 25.   [2] Ibid., iv, A. 1. 28.

The National Socialist revolution, like the economic system to which it gave birth, was itself the creation of a distinctive economic and historical process in Germany. Outside the frontiers of Germany that revolution awoke chords of sympathy in very few breasts. Those who were attracted by the idea of the New Order deserve serious study by historians instead of the contemptuous scorn they have received. All were at loggerheads with their own society and most were soon to be at loggerheads with their German conquerors. Thus, Victor Leemans, Secretary-General of the Ministry of Economic Affairs in Belgium and advocate of the economic integration of Belgium and Germany, came into frequent dispute with the German administration in his country. So too Bichelonne, who after constant disagreement with German policy in France, could still believe in September 1943 that a practical solution to the New Order had been found.

The uniqueness of the historical and economic development which created the revolution in Germany meant that it could only be imposed on Europe by force. Hitler was realist enough always to accept that position. Because of that, neither the short-run profitability of the National Socialist theory of conquest nor its long-run difficulties should be taken as anything but unique historical facts. Rather should they lead us to reject the liberal idea of conquest for its unreasoning universality than to justify it.

The instrument by which the New Order was to be created was the Blitzkrieg. Like every plan for war it had, in Clausewitz's words, 'the circumscribing nature of a synthesis'.[1] Its existence as a strategic plan placed severe restrictions on the development of economic policy in the occupied territories. While the Blitzkrieg was at the height of its success the French economy was required only to provide the cash to help finance other campaigns, and some of the raw materials and equipment with which they were fought. For the rest France was left in almost total ignorance of her future role. Many of the developments in the French economy which effectively hampered its exploitation by Germany had already taken place by the time Germany became interested in the wider economic value of her conquest.

Once the Blitzkrieg had failed Germany was brought face to face with the problem that there existed a fundamental opposition between the revolution and the practical means of achieving it. That opposition had always been present, for the revolution made little appeal to other European societies where it was not rooted in their own development. But it had been of little importance to Germany, thanks to the success of Hitler's strategy. However, after the collapse of that strategy the New Order could only be built by mobilizing the occupied economies, in particular that of France, in such a way as to change the shape of the New Order itself. The practical need of fighting the war now came into conflict with the fascist movement and the National Socialist revolution, not only in Germany but in the occupied territories also. Was it

[1] C. von Clausewitz, *Vom Kriege*, trans. J. J. Graham (London, 1962), p. 97.

worth building a New Order which would contain many of the most hated features of the old order?

The war, and the measures necessary to win it, thus became a threat to the purity of the revolution and to the new Europe it had been on the verge of creating. In these circumstances the divided aims of the National Socialist revolution itself became very apparent. The disputes about economic policy in France and Russia were also disputes about the ultimate aims of the revolution in Germany. These divisions were smoked into the open by war's burning brand. It is not surprising that Sauckel should have come to play so dominant a role in German occupation policy. The weakest point of the fascist idea of conquest was bound to be its relations with labour. The French workers struck at the insecure foundations of the whole edifice; they could not be compelled to work more productively. Labour problems had eventually to dominate all other aspects of the economic existence of the occupied powers.

Had there been general agreement on the aims of the revolution, policy in France might still have been coherent once the Blitzkrieg had failed. But the collapse of Hitler's strategy posed again the question (and now with more serious intent): 'What kind of new Europe?' And to that question the National Socialist Party had not one but several answers. Hitler's answer remained the same. The little regard he showed for Laval or Quisling, for Degrelle or Sima, stemmed from his perfectly realistic appraisal of the historical differences between his own society and France, Norway, Belgium, or Romania. His high regard for Mussolini was no mere idiosyncracy, he correctly saw in the Duce a representation of many of the historical forces which had also brought a fascist movement to power in Germany. The less realistic party members supposed their own revolution to be more imminent in other European societies. Such delusions produced Rosenberg's plans for Russia, in Hitler's opinion impracticable dreams. It is this capacity to realize accurately the enormity of the situation that faced him in 1942 that shows Hitler the supreme realist; his life, and his death, show him the supreme fascist revolutionary.

A NOTE ON SOURCES

Unpublished

THE National Archives of the United States contain a great deal of valuable material for the economic history of the Second World War. Their catalogues are so familiar to other historians that I will not bore them with a list of the actual materials used in this book. Suffice it to say that I have referred to them in the conventional way giving the reference to collection, reel of microfilm, and the number of the specific film. As the original documentary collections looted from Germany at the end of the war are returned to the Bundesarchiv so does that archive become one of the most important of the relevant documentary collections, and rightly so. Where I have used materials in the Bundesarchiv I have referred to them by their key signature in the *Findbücher*. Since one of the major parts of the Bundesarchiv's collection is the so-called 'Speer Collection', and since some parts of that 'collection' exist both in the Foreign Documents Centre of the Imperial War Museum in London and also in Washington, it may not come amiss to make some general remarks about the nature of that collection, as far as its history is yet known.

Many of the working papers of the Speer Ministry, including the Minister's own correspondence, were destroyed in the air raid on Berlin on the night of 22/3 November 1943. From that date onwards duplicate copies were kept of the most important papers and this fact is to some extent responsible for the confusion that has since been caused by these papers. When Speer himself surrendered at Flensburg in May 1945 he handed over to his captors a 'bulging briefcase' of documents. These are the statistical papers originally referred to by Chester Wilmot.[1] At the same time he revealed the hiding-places of other documents belonging to his Ministry. These caches contained a set of the minutes of his conferences with Hitler, minutes of the meetings of *Zentrale Planung*, and other important miscellaneous papers.

Many of the papers were filmed by the United States Strategic Bombing Survey. There are sets of these photostats in the Imperial War Museum which are complete, and incomplete sets in the National Archives. The National Archives, however, has a complete set of translations and also has deposited with it the papers of the United States Strategic Bombing Survey itself. Those documents not used by the United States Strategic Bombing Survey seem to have been scattered. In Britain many made their way to Whaddon Hall, where the captured *Auswärtiges Amt* archives were being microfilmed, and were microfilmed there. These are available in the Public Record Office and in the National Archives. The United States and British governments have long carried out a programme of microfilming the captured archives and returning the originals to Germany. Many of the captured collections in Britain were transferred to the keeping of the Air Historical Branch of the Air Ministry from where they have been moved to the Foreign Documents Centre of the Imperial War Museum.

The collections in the Foreign Documents Centre, of course, contain much more than original or filmed Speer Ministry papers. But it is in respect of those papers that most confusion has arisen. The original memoranda of Speer's conferences with

---

[1] C. Wilmot, *The Struggle for Europe* (London, 1952), p. 720.

Hitler are now in the Bundesarchiv. The Foreign Documents Centre has sets of photostats made from those originals. The Bundesarchiv seems to have original copies of most of Speer's reports to Hitler and the Foreign Documents Centre to have photostats. But some of these photostats in the Foreign Documents Centre are of documents which seem to have been handed over at Flensburg by Speer, the originals of which are apparently not in the Bundesarchiv. There appear to be a number of original documents of the same origin in the Foreign Documents Centre which have never been filmed. The Bundesarchiv has most of the Minister's surviving correspondence, which was not microfilmed after the war, but some is in the Foreign Documents Centre. In addition, the Foreign Documents Centre has some files of decrees and reports and the Ministerial chronicle for 1943. The chronicle for other years has not yet been found. A substantial series of the original minutes of *Zentrale Planung* also exists in the Foreign Documents Centre.

Equally useful for this book, however, were the other captured records in the Foreign Documents Centre. I might single out the files of *Wirtschaftsabteilung II/a* of the German High Command in Paris, which seem to have been roughly divided between Washington and London. Those in Washington are available on microfilm. There are also in the Foreign Documents Centre records of the *Reichswirtschaftsministerium*, the *Reichsluftfahrtministerium*, the *Reichsgruppe Industrie*, the *Reichskommissar für die besetzten Norwegischen Gebiete*, the *Rüstungsstab Dänemark*, and various other German agencies together with many private industrial papers. The collection is still growing and now includes some valuable sets of war-crime trial documents and the seventy volumes of the *Handakten* of Generalfeldmarschall Milch.

I have referred to materials in the Foreign Documents Centre by the 'FD' (Foreign Document) numbers originally allocated to them. These numbers refer only to the file itself. I have therefore given in every case the description and date of the document. I cannot pretend that this makes it easy for subsequent scholars to find that document, but I can think of no method which could make it easier. At least they may console themselves that it is easier for them than it was for me. The 'FD' numbers are listed in the original catalogue prepared by Air Historical Branch 6 of the Air Ministry.

Where I have used trial documents I have referred to them by their original Nürnberg reference. With all its disadvantages that at least means that the published excerpts in the official record of the trials can be related to the original document. The documents in the library of the Hoover Institution on War, Revolution and Peace are referred to by a full description of the document.

Published

Immediately after the liberation of France the French government undertook the publication of the documents relating to the discussions of the Franco-German Armistice Commission at Wiesbaden. These are published, in five volumes, as *La Délégation Française auprès de la Commission Allemande d'Armistice*, Recueil de documents publié par le gouvernement français (Paris, A. Costes éditeur, Imprimerie Nationale, 1947–). While it is true that the Armistice Commission declined in importance, the documents published remain of great interest. Of inestimable value for the economic history of the war, lacking only that final authority of actual documents, are the nine volumes of Présidence du Conseil, Commission Consultative des Dommages et des Réparations, *Dommages subis par la France et l'Union Française du fait de la guerre et de l'occupation ennemie (1939-1945)*, Part imputable à *l'Allemagne* (Paris, Imprimerie Nationale, 1947–51). Of a certain interest are the three volumes, *France During the German Occupation 1940–1944* (*La Vie de la France sous l'occupation* (*1940–1944*)), *A collection of 292 statements on the government of Maréchal Pétain and Pierre Laval* (Stanford, The Hoover Institution on War, Revolution and Peace, 1957). Their quality does not measure up to their size. The three volumes contain mainly misleading, self-justificatory statements.

Of more general application, but still containing relevant material, are the *Documents on German Foreign Policy 1918–1945*, Series D (1937–1945) (London, H.M.S.O., 1949–64). The same is true for International Military Tribunal, Nürnberg, *Trial of the Major War Criminals before the International Military Tribunal, Documents in Evidence* (Nürnberg, 1947–9). Two manuscripts written during the war and containing much original material have since been published as books by later editors, G. Thomas, *Grundlagen für eine Geschichte der deutschen Wehr- und Rüstungswirtschaft*, Schriften des Bundesarchivs, 14, ed. W. Birkenfeld (Boppard am Rhein, 1966) and Deutsches Institut für Wirtschaftsforschung, *Die deutsche Industrie im Kriege 1939–1945* (Berlin, 1954). The second book is really the work of Dr. Rolf Wagenführ. Other collections of statistical and economic information deserve singling out. The Institut National de la Statistique et des Études Économiques published some wartime statistical information in *Le Mouvement économique en France de 1938 à 1948* (Paris, 1950). The 208 reports of the Office of Strategic Services, United States Strategic Bombing Survey contain some economic information on almost every aspect of the war. Those who write the history of modern times must sometimes be embarrassed by the amount of published source-material. The appended list has no pretensions to completeness and merely serves as a supplement to sources cited in the footnotes to the book.

Centre belge d'études et de documentation, Commission charbonnière, *La Question charbonnière* (n.d.).

Goebbels, J., *Tagebücher. Aus den Jahren 1942–1943 mit anderen Dokumenten*, ed. L. P. Lochner (Zürich, 1948). (*The Goebbels Diaries*, ed. L. P. Lochner (New York, 1948).)

Halder, F., *Kriegstagebuch. Tägliche Aufzeichnungen des Chefs des Generalstaabes des Heeres 1939–1942*, 3 vols. (Stuttgart, 1962–4).

Hitlers Lagebesprechungen, ed. H. Heiber (Stuttgart, 1962).

Hitler, A., *Reden und Proklamationen 1932–1945*, Kommentiert von einem deutschen Zeitgenossen, Max Domarus, 2 vols. (Würzburg, 1962–3).

Hitler's Table Talk 1941–44 (London, 1953).

Hitler's Secret Conversations (New York, 1961).

Picker, H., *Hitlers Tischgespräche im Führerhauptquartier 1941–1942*, ed. P. E. Schramm (Stuttgart, 1963).

Hitlers Weisungen für die Kriegführung 1939–45, Dokumente des Oberkommandos der Wehrmacht, ed. W. Hubatsch (Frankfurt am Main, 1962). (*Hitler's War Directives 1939–1945*, ed. H. R. Trevor-Roper (London, 1964).)

Kriegstagebuch des Oberkommandos der Wehrmacht (*Wehrmachtführungsstab*) *1940–45*, ed. P. E. Schramm, 4 vols. in 7 vols. (Frankfurt am Main 1961–5).

Statistisches Reichsamt, *Statistische Jahrbücher für das Deutsche Reich*.

BIBLIOGRAPHY

*A bibliography of those secondary works cited in the text and
certain others of immediate relevance*

ABETZ, O., *Das offene Problem. Ein Rückblick auf zwei Jahrzehnte deutscher Frankreichpolitik* (Cologne, 1951).

ALLEN, W. S., *The Nazi seizure of power: the experience of a single German town 1930/35* (Chicago, 1965).

ALTSCHUHL, E., and STRAUSS, F., *Technical progress and agricultural depression*, National Bureau of Economic Research, Bulletin no. 672 (New York, 1937).

AMOUROUX, H., *La Vie des Français sous l'occupation* (Paris, 1961).

ANDRÉ, R., *L'Occupation de la France par les Alliés en 1915* (Paris, 1924).

ANGELL, Sir N., *The great illusion* (London, 1910, 1933).

Annales des Mines, 'Enquête sur les conditions économiques et financières d'exploitation des mines de combustible françaises' (1937).

ANSBACHER, H. L., 'Testing, management and reactions of foreign workers in Germany during World War II', *American Psychologist*, v (1950).

ARMESON, R. B., *Total warfare and compulsory labour* (The Hague, 1965).

ARNOULT, P., *Les Finances de la France et l'occupation allemande (1940/44)* (Paris, 1951).

—— 'Comment, pour acheter notre économie, les Allemands prirent nos finances', *Cahiers d'histoire de la guerre*, iv (1950).

—— *et al.*, *La France sous l'occupation* (Paris, 1959).

ARON, R., *Histoire de Vichy 1940–1944* (Paris, 1954).

BACKE, H., *Um die Nährungsfreiheit Europas* (Leipzig, 1942).

(La) Banque nationale de Belgique sous l'occupation allemande 1914–18. Rapport au roi (Brussels, Imprimerie Nationale, 1918).

BAUDEAU, N., *Première Introduction à la philosophie économique ou analyse des États policés* (Paris, 1767).

—— *Principes économiques de Louis XII, de Henri IV et du duc de Sully* (Paris, 1785).

BAUDHUIN, F., *Le Financement des guerres* (Louvain, 1944).

—— *L'Économie belge sous l'occupation 1940–44* (Brussels, 1945).

—— *Les Finances de 1939 à 1949*. III. *La Belgique et la Hollande*, Collection d'histoire financière, no. 3 (Paris, 1951).

BAUDIN, L., 'Le troc dans notre économie actuelle', *Économie contemporaine* (November 1943).

—— 'An outline of economic conditions in France under the German occupation', *Economic Journal*, lv (December 1945).

—— *Esquisse de l'économie française sous l'occupation allemande* (Paris, 1945).

BAUDOT, M., *L'Opinion publique sous l'occupation, l'exemple d'un département français 1939–1945* (Paris, 1960).

BENTHAM, J., *Principles of international law*, in J. Bowring ed., *The works of J. Bentham* (Edinburgh, 1843).

BEREND, T. I., and RÁNKI, G., *Magyarország Gyáripara a Második Világháború Elött és a Háború Idöszakában (1933–1944)* (Budapest, 1958).

BILLIG, J., 'Le rôle des prisonniers de guerre dans l'économie du IIIᵉ Reich', *Revue d'histoire de la deuxième guerre mondiale*, xxxvii (1960).

BIRKENFELD, W., *Der synthetische Treibstoff 1933–1945. Ein Beitrag zur national-sozialistischen Wirtschafts- und Rüstungspolitik*, Studien und Dokumente zur Geschichte des zweiten Weltkrieges, 8 (Göttingen, 1964).

BLAUG, M., *Economic theory in retrospect* (New York, 1962).

BLEICHER, A., *Elsaß und Lothringen wirtschaftlich gesehen* (Potsdam, 1942).

BLOCH, H. S., and HOSELITZ, B. F., *Economics of military occupation* (Chicago, 1944).

BLOCH, J. (de) (I. S. BLIOKH), *La Guerre*. Traduction de l'ouvrage russe: La guerre future aux points de vue technique, économique et politique, 6 vols. (Paris, 1898); German translation, *Der Krieg*, 6 vols. (Berlin, 1899).

—— *Is war now impossible?* Being an abridgement of *War in the future in its technical, economic and political relations* with a prefatory conversation with the author by W. T. Stead, etc. (London, 1899).

—— *Impossibilités techniques et économiques d'une guerre entre grandes puissances* (Paris, 1899).

BOCCARDO, G., *Dizionario universale di economia politica e commercio*, 3rd edn. (Milan, 1881).

BODIN, J., *Les Six Livres de la république*, 3rd edn. (Paris, 1578), trans. R. Knolles, *Of the lawes and customes of a common-wealth* (London, 1606). (Facsimile edn. of Knollys, ed. McRae, c. 1962.)

BOGART, E. L., *Direct and indirect costs of the Great World War* (New York, 1920).

BÖHME, H., *Der deutsch-französische Waffenstillstand im zweiten Weltkrieg, Entstehung und Grundlagen des Waffenstillstands von 1940*, Veröffentlichungen des Instituts für Zeitgeschichte, Quellen und Darstellungen zur Zeitgeschichte, 12 (Stuttgart, 1966).

BOPP, M.-J., *L'Alsace sous l'occupation allemande* (Le Puy, 1945).

—— 'L'enrôlement de force des Alsaciens dans la Wehrmacht et la S. S.', *Revue d'histoire de la deuxième guerre mondiale*, xx (1955).

BOTERO, G., *Della ragion di Stato* (ed. Venice, 1601), trans. P. J. and D. P. Waley, *The reason of state* (London, 1956).

BOÜARD, M. de, 'La répression allemande en France de 1940 à 1944', *Revue d'histoire de la deuxième guerre mondiale*, liv (1964).

BOUDOT, F., 'Aspects économiques de l'occupation allemande en France', *Revue d'histoire de la deuxième guerre mondiale*, liii (1964).

BOUTHILLIER, Y., *Le drame de Vichy*, 2 vols. (Paris, 1950–1).

BOWLEY, A. L., *Some economic consequences of the Great War* (London, 1930).

BRACHER, K. D., SAUER, W., and SCHULTZ, G., *Die nationalsozialistische Macht-ergreifung. Studien zur Errichtung des totalitären Herrschaftssystems in Deutschland 1933/34* (Cologne, 1962).

BRANDT, K., *et al. The management of agriculture and food in the German-occupied and other areas of Fortress Europe* (Stanford, 1953).

BROSZAT, M., *Nationalsozialistische Polenpolitik 1939–1945*, Schriftenreihe der Vierteljahrshefte für Zeitgeschichte, 2 (Stuttgart, 1961).

Cahiers d'histoire de la guerre, 'L'économie française sous l'occupation', *Cahiers d'histoire de la guerre*, iv (1950).

—— 'Notes sur le procès H. Roechling', ibid. iv (1950).

—— 'Göring et la "collaboration": un beau document', ibid.

CARROLL, B. A., *Design for total war. Arms and economics in the Third Reich* (The Hague, 1968).

CATHALA, P., *Face aux réalités* (Paris, 1948).

CATOIRE, M., *La Direction des Services de l'Armistice à Vichy* (Paris, 1955).

CAZIOT, P., *Au service de la paysannerie* (Paris, 1942).

CÉPÈDE, M., *Agriculture et alimentation en France durant la IIe guerre mondiale* (Paris, 1961).

CHANTRIOT, E., *L'Administration des départements envahis en 1870–71* (Nancy, 1916).

—— *La Lorraine sous l'occupation allemande, mars 1871–septembre 1873* (Nancy, 1922).

CHARDONNET, J., *Les Conséquences économiques de la guerre 1939–1946* (Paris, 1947).

CLARK, J. M., *The costs of the World War to the American people* (New Haven, 1931).

CLAUSEWITZ, C. von, *Vom Kriege*, trans. J. J. Graham, *On war* (London, 1962).

CLÉMENT, G.-R., *Avec l'Alsace en guerre (1940–44)* (Paris, 1945).

COLLATTI, E., *L'amministrazione tedesca dell'Italia occupata, 1943–1945* (Milan, 1963).

—— (ed.), *L'occupazione nazista in Europa* (Rome, 1964).

COURT, W. H. B., *Coal* (London, 1951).

CROUZET, F., *L'Économie britannique et le blocus continental, 1806–13*, 2 vols. (Paris, 1958).

—— 'Wars, blockade and economic change in Europe 1792–1815', *Journal of Economic History*, xxiv (1964).

DAITZ, W., *Der Weg zur völkischen Wirtschaft und zur europäischen Großraumwirtschaft* (Dresden, 1938), re-issued as *Der Weg zur Volkswirtschaft, Großraumwirtschaft und Großraumpolitik* (Dresden, 1943).

DALLIN, A., *German rule in Russia, 1941–45* (London and New York, 1957).

DELVINCOURT, H., 'Problèmes relatifs à l'emploi dans les P. T. T.', *Revue d'histoire de la deuxième guerre mondiale*, lvii (1965).

DENZEL, R., *Die chemische Industrie Frankreichs unter der deutschen Besetzung im zweiten Weltkrieg*, Studien des Instituts für Besatzungsfragen, 18 (Tübingen, 1959).

DIETERLEN, P., and RIST, C., *The monetary problem of France* (New York, 1948).

DORGÈRES, H., *Révolution paysanne* (Paris, 1943).

DURAND, P., 'La politique de l'emploi à la S. N. C. F.', *Revue d'histoire de la deuxième guerre mondiale*, lvii (1965).

EDGE, W. E., *A Jerseyman's journal* (Princeton, 1948).

EINZIG, P., *Hitler's New Order in Europe* (London, 1941).

—— 'Hitler's "New Order" in theory and practice', *Economic Journal*, li (1941).

EMMENDÖRFER, A., *Geld- und Kreditaufsicht in den von Deutschland während des zweiten Weltkrieges besetzten Gebieten*, Studien des Instituts für Besatzungsfragen, 12 (Düsseldorf, 1957).

ERBE, R., *Die nationalsozialistische Wirtschaftspolitik 1933–39 im Lichte der modernen Theorie* (Zurich, 1958).

ERNST, R., *Rechenschaftsbericht eines Elsässers* (Berlin, 1954).

ERNST-WEIS, A., *So war es in Lothringen* (Frankfurt am Main, 1957).

'Esprit de la résistance', in P. Arnoult *et al.*, *La France sous l'occupation* (Paris, 1959).

FARNSWORTH, H. C., *Livestock in continental Europe during World War Two*, Stanford Food Research Institute Papers, 6. [n.d.]

FAWCETT, H., *Manual of political economy*, 7th edn. (London, 1888).

FEDER, G., *Das Manifest zur Brechung der Zinsknechtschaft des Geldes* (Munich, 1919).

FÉDÉRATION DES ASSOCIATIONS CHARBONNIÈRES DE BELGIQUE, *La Belgique devant le problème charbonnier* (Brussels, 1945).

FEDERAU, F., *Der zweite Weltkrieg. Seine Finanzierung in Deutschland* (Tübingen, 1962).

FEILCHENFELD, E. H., *The international economic law of belligerent occupation* (Washington, 1942).

FISCHER, F., *Griff nach der Weltmacht. Die Kriegszielpolitik des kaiserlichen Deutschland 1914–18* (Düsseldorf, 1961), trans. *Germany's aims in the First World War* (London, 1967).

FOURASTIÉ, J., 'La population active française', *Revue d'histoire de la deuxième guerre mondiale*, lvii (1965).

FRIED, J. H. E., *The exploitation of foreign labour by Germany* (Montreal, 1945).

FRIEDENSBURG, F., *Die Rohstoffe und Energiequellen im neuen Europa* (Oldenburg, 1943).

GANZER, K. R., *Das Reich als europäische Ordnungsmacht* (Hamburg, 1941).

GERBER, B., *Staatliche Wirtschaftslenkung in den besetzten und annektierten Ostgebieten während des zweiten Weltkrieges unter besonderer Berücksichtigung der treuhänderischen Verwaltung von Unternehmungen und der Ostgesellschaften*, Studien des Instituts für Besatzungsfragen, 17 (Tübingen, 1959).

GESCHKE, G., *Die deutsche Frankreichpolitik 1940 von Compiègne bis Montoire. Das Problem einer deutsch-französischen Annäherung nach dem Frankreichfeldzug*, Beiheft 12/13 der Wehrwissenschaftlichen Rundschau (Berlin, 1960).

GIES, H., 'NSDAP und Agrarverbände vor 1933', *Vierteljahrshefte für Zeitgeschichte*, xv (1967).

GLAHN, G. VON, *The occupation of enemy territory* (Minneapolis, 1957).

GOUTARD, A., 'Pourquoi et comment l'armistice a-t-il été "accordé" par Hitler?', *La Revue de Paris*, lxvii (1960).

GRAND-JEAN, P., *Guerres, fluctuations et croissance* (Paris, 1967).

GROMAIRE, G., *L'Occupation allemande en France, 1914–18* (Paris, 1925).

GROTKOPP, W., 'Das Werden und die Struktur der französischen Wirtschaft', *Revue économique franco-allemande*, i (1943).

GRUCHMANN, L., *Nationalsozialistische Großraumordnung*, Schriftenreihe der Vierteljahrshefte für Zeitgeschichte, 4 (Stuttgart, 1962).

GUILLEBAUD, C. W., 'Hitler's new economic order for Europe', *Economic Journal*, I (1940).

GUYOT, Y., *La Jalousie commerciale et les relations internationales* (Paris, 1911).

HANCOCK, W. K., and GOWING, M. M., *The British war economy* (London, 1949).

HAUSHOFER, K., 'Die geopolitische Betrachtung grenzdeutscher Probleme' in K. C. von Loesch and A. H. Ziegfeld (eds.), *Volk und Völkern* (Breslau, 1925).

—— *Grenzen in ihrer geographischen und politischen Bedeutung* (Berlin, 1927).

—— *et al.*, *Bausteine zur Geopolitik* (Berlin, 1928).

—— *Wehr-Geopolitik. Geographische Grundlagen einer Wehrkunde* (Berlin, 1932).

—— and VOGEL, W. (eds.), *Weltwirtschaftsdämmerung*. Festschrift zum zehnjährigen Bestehen des Weltwirtschafts-Instituts der Handels-Hochschule, Leipzig (Stuttgart, 1934).

—— *Weltpolitik von Leute* (Berlin, 1934).

HEBERLE, R., *Landbevölkerung und Nationalsozialismus: eine soziologische Untersuchung der politischen Willensbildung in Schleswig-Holstein 1918 bis 1932* (Stuttgart, 1963). Trans. (incomplete), *From democracy to Nazism: a regional case study on political parties in Germany* (Baton Rouge, 1945).

HECKSHER, E. F., *The continental system. An economic interpretation* (Oxford, 1922).

HEIDEN, K., *Der Führer* (London, 1945).

HEILBRONNER, A., 'Le ravitaillement en France', *Revue d'économie politique*, lvii (1947).

HERDEG, W., *Grundzüge der deutschen Besatzungsverwaltung in den west- und nordeuropäischen Ländern während des zweiten Weltkrieges*, Studien des Instituts für Besatzungsfragen, 1 (Tübingen, 1953).

HERRENSCHWAND, J., *De l'économie politique et morale de l'espèce humaine* (London, 1796).

HERVET, R., *Les Chantiers de la jeunesse* (Paris, 1962).

HIRSCHFELD, A., 'Le mouvement coopératif agricole sous l'occupation', *Revue d'histoire de la deuxième guerre mondiale*, lvii (1965).

HITLER, A., *Mein Kampf* (Munich, 1925, 1928, 1939).

—— *Zweites Buch* (Stuttgart, 1961).

HOBBES, T., *Leviathan* (London, 1651).

HOMZE, E. L., *Foreign labour in Nazi Germany* (Princeton, 1967).

HORY, L., and BROSZAT, M., *Der kroatische Ustascha-Staat 1941–1945* (Stuttgart, 1964).

INTERNATIONAL LABOUR OFFICE, *Studies and reports, series B, no. 31, The world coal-mining industry* (Geneva, 1938).

JÄCKEL, E., *Frankreich in Hitlers Europa*, Veröffentlichungen des Instituts für Zeitgeschichte, Quellen und Darstellungen zur Zeitgeschichte, 14 (Stuttgart, 1966).

JACQUEMYNS, G., *La Société belge sous l'occupation allemande 1940–4* (Brussels, 1950).

—— 'Réactions des travailleurs belges sous l'occupation', *Revue d'histoire de la deuxième guerre mondiale*, xxxi (1958).

JÄGER, J.-J., 'Sweden's iron ore exports to Germany, 1933–1944', *Scandinavian Economic History Review*, xv, 1 and 2 (1967).

JANSSEN, G., *Das Ministerium Speer. Deutschlands Rüstung im Krieg* (Frankfurt am Main, 1968).

JONES, W. R., *Minerals in industry* (London, 1945).

JUSTI, J. H. G. von, *Der Grundriß einer guten Regierung* (Frankfurt am Main, 1759).

KARLBOM, R., 'Sweden's iron ore exports to Germany, 1933–1944', *Scandinavian Economic History Review*, xiii, 1 (1965).

KASTEN, H., *Die Neuordnung der Währung in den besetzten Gebieten und die Tätigkeit der RKK während des Krieges 1939/1940* (Berlin, 1941).

KERNAN, T., *France on Berlin time* (Philadelphia, 1941).

KISCH, H., 'Growth deterrents of a medieval heritage: the Aachen-area woollen trades before 1790', *Journal of Economic History*, xxiv (1964).

KISTENMACHER, H., *Die Auswirkungen der deutschen Besetzung auf die Ernährungs-wirtschaft Frankreichs während des zweiten Weltkrieges*, Studien des Instituts für Besatzungsfragen, 16 (Tübingen, 1959).

KLEIN, B. H., *Germany's economic preparations for war*, Harvard Economic Studies, cix (Cambridge, Mass., 1959).

KLUKE, P., 'Nationalsozialistische Europaideologie', *Vierteljahrshefte für Zeitge-schichte*, iii (1955).

—— 'Nationalsozialistische Volkstumspolitik in Elsaß-Lothringen 1940–45', *Fest-schrift für Hans Herzfeld* (Berlin, 1958).

KNIES, K., *Die politische Ökonomie vom Standpunkte der geschichtlichen Methode* (Braunschweig, 1853).

KOEHL, R. L., *RKFDV: German resettlement and population policy 1939–1945* (Cambridge, Mass., 1957).

KÖHLER, L. von, *Die Staatsverwaltung der besetzten Gebiete*, vol. 1, *Belgien* (Stutt-gart, 1927).

KORDT, E., *Nicht aus den Akten. Die Wilhelmstraße in Frieden und Krieg. Erlebnisse, Begegnungen und Eindrücke 1928–1945* (Stuttgart, 1950).

KUCZYNSKI, J., *Die Geschichte der Lage der Arbeiter unter dem Kapitalismus*, Studien zur Geschichte des staatsmonopolitischen Kapitalismus in Deutschland 1918 bis 1945, 16 (Berlin, 1963).

—— and WITT, M., *The economics of barbarism, Hitler's new economic order in Europe* (London, 1942).

LAUFENBURGER, H., 'La vie économique au seuil de l'année 1943', *Revue de l'écono-mie contemporaine* (February 1943).'

—— 'L'économie française au seuil de l'année 1944', *Revue de l'économie contem-poraine* (January 1944).

—— *Crédit public et finances de guerre, 1914–44; Allemagne, France, Grande-Bretagne* (Paris, 1944).

LAVAL, P., *Laval parle. Notes et mémoires rédigés par Pierre Laval dans sa cellule* (Geneva, 1947).

LEBRUN, P., *L'Industrie de la laine à Verviers pendant le dix-huitième siècle et le début du dix-neuvième* (Liège, 1948).

LEROY-LADURIE, J., *Vers une politique paysanne* (Paris, 1937).

LIST, G. F., *Das nationale System der politischen Ökonomie* (Stuttgart, 1841). Trans., *National system of political economy* (Philadelphia, 1856).

LOOCK, H.-D., 'Zur "Großgermanischen Politik" des Dritten Reiches', *Vierteljahrs-hefte für Zeitgeschichte*, viii (1960).

Maquis limousin, la dynamite des mines de Saint-Léonard (Limoges, 1946).

MEDLICOTT, W. N., *The economic blockade*, 2 vols. (London, 1952–8).

MELON, J.-F., *Essai politique sur le commerce* (Paris, 1734).

MÉRIGOT, J.-G., *Le Franc 1938–50* (Paris, 1950).

—— and COULBOIS, P., *Essai sur les comités d'organisation professionnelle* (Paris, 1943).

MICHEL, H., *Histoire de la résistance* (1940–4) (Paris, 1950, 1958).

—— *Bibliographie critique de la résistance* (Paris, 1964).

—— *Vichy: année 40* (Paris, 1966).

MILL, J., *Commerce defended* (London, 1808).

MILWARD, A. S., *The German economy at war* (London, 1965).

—— 'German economic policy towards France 1942–1944' in K. Bourne and D. C. Watts (eds.), *Studies in international history* (London, 1967).

—— 'Could Sweden have stopped the Second World War?', *Scandinavian Economic History Review*, xv, 1 and 2 (1967).

MINISTÈRE DES FINANCES, *Statistiques et études financières*, no. 20 (1953).

MITZAKIS, M., *Principaux Aspects de l'évolution financière de la France 1936–44* (Paris, 1944).

MOLINARI, M. G. de, *L'Évolution économique du dix-neuvième siècle. Théorie du progrès* (Paris, 1880).

—— *Conversations sur le commerce des grains et la protection de l'agriculture* (Paris, 1886).

—— *Les Lois naturelles de l'économie politique* (Paris, 1887).

—— *Comment se résoudra la question sociale?* (Paris, 1896).

—— *Grandeur et décadence de la guerre* (Paris, 1895).

—— *Esquisse de l'organisation politique et économique de la société future* (Paris, 1899).

MONTCHRÉTIEN, A. de, *Traicté de l'œconomie politique* (Paris, 1615), ed. T. Funck-Brentano (Paris, 1889).

MOREAU-NÉRET, O., *Le Contrôle des prix en France* (Paris, 1941).

MORET, C., *L'Allemagne et la réorganisation de l'Europe* (Neuchâtel, 1944).

MORITZ, G., *Die deutsche Besatzungsgerichtsbarkeit während des zweiten Weltkrieges*, Studien des Instituts für Besatzungsfragen (Tübingen, 1954).

—— *Die Gerichtsbarkeit in den besetzten Gebieten. Historische Entwicklung und völkerrechtliche Würdigung* (Tübingen, 1959).

MOSLEY, O., *Tomorrow we live* (London, 1939).

MOUCHOTTE, D.-J., *Problèmes français de crédit et de financement* (Paris, 1942).

MÜLLER-OHLSEN, L., *Strukturwandlungen und Nachkriegsprobleme der Wirtschaft Frankreichs*, Kieler Studien, 22 (Kiel, 1952).

MUNZ, A., *Die Auswirkungen der deutschen Besetzung auf Währung und Finanzen Frankreichs*, Studien des Instituts für Besatzungsfragen, 9 (Tübingen, 1957).

NEUMANN, F. L., *Behemoth: the structure and practice of National Socialism* (2nd edn., New York, 1944).

NOYELLE, H., *La Monnaie et le crédit au service de l'économie française* (Paris, 1941).

PETTY, Sir W., *A treatise of taxes and contributions* (London, 1662).

PETZINA, H. D., *Autarkiepolitik im Dritten Reich. Der nationalsozialistische Vierjahresplan*, Schriftenreihe der Vierteljahreshefte für Zeitgeschichte, 16 (Stuttgart, 1968).

PIRENNE, H., *La Belgique et la guerre mondiale* (Paris, 1928).

PIROU, G., *Le Crédit* (Paris, 1943).

—— *Économie libérale et économie dirigée* (Paris, 1946).

PLUMYÈNE, J., and LASIERRA, R., *Les Fascismes français 1923–1963* (Paris, 1963).

PRATO, G., *La teoria della pace perpetua* (Turin, 1897).

—— *L'Occupation militaire dans le passé et dans le présent* (Paris, 1916).

PROCOPOVICZ, S. N., *Histoire économique de l'U. R. S. S.* (Paris, 1952).

QUESNAY, F., 'Grains', article publié dans l'*Encyclopédie*, 1756, in *Œuvres économiques et philosophiques de Quesnay*, ed. H. Oncken (Frankfurt am Main, 1888).

REDLICH, F., *De praeda militari*, Beiheft zur Vierteljahrschrift für Sozial- und Wirtschaftsgeschichte, vol. xxxix (Wiesbaden, 1956).

—— *The German military enterpriser and his work force*, Beihefte zur Vierteljahrschrift für Sozial- und Wirtschaftsgeschichte, xlvii and xlviii (Wiesbaden, 1964–5).

REITHINGER, A., *et al.*, *Probleme des europäischen Großwirtschaftsraums* (Berlin, 1942).

RENTROP, W., and KAYSER, H., *Europäische Preispolitik* (Munich, 1941).

Revue d'économie politique, 'La France économique de 1939 à 1946', numéros spéciaux, 2 vols. (1947).

Revue d'histoire de la deuxième guerre mondiale, 'Aspects de l'économie française', lvii (January, 1965).

RINGEL, K., *Frankreichs Wirtschaft im Umbruch* (Leipzig, 1942).

ROBBINS, L., *The economic causes of war* (London, 1939).

ROBIN, R., *Des occupations militaires en dehors des occupations de guerre: étude d'histoire diplomatique et de droit international* (Paris, 1913).

ROOS, M. J., *Quinze ans d'aéronautique française, 1932–1947* (Paris, 1949).

ROSCHER, W., *Betrachtungen über die Währungsfrage der deutschen Münzreform* (Berlin, 1872).

ROSIER, C., *La France agricole* (Paris, 1943).

ROUSSY DE SALES, R. de, *My New Order* (New York, 1941).

ROVANI, J., *L'Industrie textile française à l'épreuve de la guerre* (Paris, 1946).

SAUER, W., 'Das Problem des deutschen Nationalstaates', in H.-U. Wehler (ed.), *Moderne deutsche Sozialgeschichte* (Cologne, 1966).

—— 'National Socialism: totalitarianism or fascism?', *American Historical Review*, lxxiii (1967).

SAUVY, A., *Histoire économique de la France entre les deux guerres*, 2 vols. (Paris, 1965–7).

—— 'Heurs et malheurs de la statistique', *Revue d'histoire de la deuxième guerre mondiale*, lvii (1965).

SAY, J.-B., *Cours complet d'économie politique pratique* (Paris, 1829).

SCHAEFFER, I., *L'Alsace et la Lorraine 1940–1945* (Paris, 1953).

SCHÄFFLE, A. E. K., *Abriß der Soziologie* (Tübingen, 1906).

SCHECHTMAN, J. B., *European population transfers 1939–1945* (New York, 1946).

SCHMIDT, P., *Statist auf diplomatischer Bühne 1923–1945. Erlebnisse eines Chefdolmetschers im Auswärtigen Amt mit den Staatsmännern Europas* (Bonn, 1949).

SCHOENBAUM, D., *Hitler's social revolution: class and status in Nazi Germany 1933–39* (New York, 1966).

SCHUMANN, W., 'Das Kriegsprogramm des Zeiss-Konzerns'. *Zeitschrift für Geschichtswissenschaft*, xi (1963).

SCHUMANN, W., and LOZEK, G., 'Die faschistische Okkupationspolitik im Spiegel der Historiographie der beiden deutschen Staaten', *Zeitschrift für Geschichtswissenschaft*, xii (1964).

SCHUMPETER, J. A., 'Zur Soziologie der Imperialismen', *Archiv für Sozialwissenschaft und Politik*, xlvi (1918–19).

SCHWEITZER, A., 'The role of foreign trade in the Nazi war economy', in *Journal of Political Economy*, li (1943).

—— *Big business in the Third Reich* (Bloomington, 1964).

SÉDILLOT, R., *Le Franc enchaîné* (Paris, 1945).

SILBERNER, E., *La Guerre dans la pensée économique du seizième au dix-huitième siècle* (Paris, 1939).

—— *The problem of war in nineteenth-century economic thought* (Princeton, 1946).

SMITH, A., *An inquiry into the nature and causes of the wealth of nations* (London, 1776).

SÖLTER, A., *Das Großraumkartell* (Dresden, 1941).

Statist, 'The value of the Reichsmark' (10 May 1941).

STRENG, H. von, *Die Landwirtschaft im Generalgouvernement*, Studien des Instituts für Besatzungsfragen, 6 (Tübingen, 1955).

THUILLIER, G., 'Pour une histoire de l'économie rhénane de 1800 à 1830: les houillères de la Ruhr', *Annales*, xv (1960).

—— 'La métallurgie rhénane de 1800 à 1830', ibid. xvi (1961).

TILDEN, A. *The legislation of the Civil War period considered as a basis of the agricultural revolution in the United States* (Los Angeles, 1937).

ULSHÖFER, O., *Einflußnahme auf Wirtschaftsunternehmungen in den besetzten nord-, west- und südosteuropäischen Ländern während des zweiten Weltkrieges insbesondere der Erwerb von Beteiligungen (Verflechtung)*, Studien des Instituts für Besatzungsfragen, 15 (Tübingen, 1958).

UNITED NATIONS, *Survey of world iron ore resources, occurrence, appraisal and use*, Department of Economic and Social Affairs (New York, 1955).

VANDERLINT, J., *Money answers all things, or an essay . . . shewing the absurdity of going to war about trade, . . .* (London, 1734).

VERNOUX, M., *Wiesbaden 1940–4* (Paris, 1954).

VERRI, P., *Meditazioni sulla economia politica* (Genoa, 1771).

VIDALENC, J., *L'Exode de mai–juin 1940* (Paris, 1957).

VOLTAIRE, J. F. M. AROUET DE, *Observations sur Mm. Law, Melon et Dutot* (Paris, 1738).

WARLIMONT, W., *Im Hauptquartier der deutschen Wehrmacht 1939–45* (Frankfurt am Main, 1962).

WARMBRUNN, W., *The Dutch under German occupation 1940/45* (Stanford, 1963).

WARNER, G., *Pierre Laval and the eclipse of France* (London, 1968).

WEBER, E., *Varieties of fascism* (Princeton, 1964).

WEINMANN, M., *Die Landwirtschaft in Frankreich während des zweiten Weltkrieges unter dem Einfluß der deutschen Besatzungsmacht*, Studien des Instituts für Besatzungsfragen, 20 (Tübingen, 1961).

WHEATLEY, R., *Operation Sea-Lion* (Oxford, 1958).

WINCH, D., *Classical political economy and colonies* (London, 1965).

WITSCH, J., *Deutschland im Kampf für ein neues Europa* (Jena, 1940).

WOERMANN, E., *Die europäische Ernährungswirtschaft in Zahlen* (Berlin, 1944).

WRIGHT, G., 'Reflections on the French Resistance 1940/44', *Political Science Quarterly*, lxxvii (1962).

—— *Rural revolution in France* (Stanford, 1964).

'X' 'Le marché noir allemand en France', *Cahiers d'histoire de la guerre*, iv (1950).

INDEX